SCHOOL PERSONNEL ADMINISTRATION

Contributors

MARK COSTANTINO   Attorney at Law
LEWIS A. CREW   Director of Educational Personnel, Pontiac, Michigan
BERNARD ESRIG
            Assistant Director of In-service Education, New York City
R. OLIVER GIBSON
            Professor of Education, State University of New York at Buffalo
BERNARD W. KAYE
            Associate Superintendent of Personnel, Minneapolis, Minnesota
CARROLL L. LANG   Director of Personnel, Simi, California
WALTER A. MACCUBBIN
            Assistant Superintendent of Personnel, Baltimore, Maryland
ALVIN J. SCHUMACHER
            Administrator of Personnel Services, Kenosha, Wisconsin
DONALD R. WHEELER
            Associate Superintendent of Schools, Redlands, California

SCHOOL PERSONNEL ADMINISTRATION

JAY E. GREENE

Chairman, Board of Examiners
New York City Public Schools
Past President
American Association of
School Personnel Administrators

CHILTON BOOK COMPANY
Philadelphia   New York   London

Copyright © 1971 by Jay E. Greene
First Edition   *All rights reserved*
Published in Philadelphia by Chilton Book Company
and simultaneously in Ontario, Canada,
by Thomas Nelson & Sons, Ltd.
ISBN 0–8019–5451–7 Trade Edition
Library of Congress Catalog Card Number 77–147252
Designed by William E. Lickfield
Manufactured in the United States of America

ACKNOWLEDGMENTS

In the preparation of this book, the author was fortunate in having the advice and assistance of many persons in addition to the contributors whose names are listed on the title page. The author wishes to express his appreciation to the following individuals who reviewed portions of the manuscript and made helpful suggestions: Paul W. Hailey, Director, Teacher Education and Certification of the State Education Department of Ohio; Frederick Kennedy, Assistant Superintendent of Schools of Compton, California; Dr. Lavern L. Krantz, Professor of Education at Ohio University; Dr. Albert F. Schultz, Director of Personnel of the Milwaukee Public Schools; G. Gary Sousa, Law Secretary of the Board of Education of New York City; and to Dr. Carroll L. Lang, Director of Personnel, Simi, California, who made contributions in several parts of the book.

Numerous members of the American Association of School Personnel Administrators have been helpful directly and indirectly by sharing their knowledge and ideas in many discussions through the years. Among these persons, the author must give particular recognition to the officers of the Association, whom he has known as colleagues and friends for many years, and especially to Charles S. Robinson, Executive Secretary-Treasurer of the Association and former head of personnel in the Kansas City, Kansas, public school system; to Darian H. Smith, Assistant Superintendent for Personnel in the Cleveland public schools, and his staff whose workshop program at the 1969 convention was a source of many stimulating ideas; to Mrs. Ruth H. Satterfield, recording secretary of the Association, whose detailed minutes of "proceedings" of two conventions were a source of useful information; and to many other members of this Association and of the New York State Association of School Personnel Administrators who have shared their thoughts with the author.

Many of the author's colleagues in the New York City school system and on the Board of Examiners have also been helpful through many discussions in which ideas took shape.

The author is deeply indebted to the Research Division of the National Education Association for ideas and statistics and for their permission to use them in various parts of this book; to the Research Division of the American Federation of Teachers for permission to use excerpts from their published works; to Educational Testing Service in Princeton for permission to use excerpts from its copyrighted *National Teacher Examinations Bulletin of Information for Candidates;* to Prentice-Hall, Inc., for permission to reprint pages 54–56 of their book, *Teacher Recruitment—Problems, Promises and Proven Methods,* by Carroll L. Lang; and to many individual authors and their publishers whose words are quoted in this book.

Materials from many school districts were reproduced in this book as illustrations of good practices. They have been appropriately identified, and the author expresses his gratitude for the use of them.

As a participant in several Summer School Personnel Clinic Conferences conducted by Dr. Oliver Gibson at the State University of New York at Buffalo, the author received the benefit of discussions of personnel problems by personnel administrators from various parts of the country.

In performing the extensive research that was needed, the author depended on the help of many patient librarians. Mrs. Joan Luisette, a teacher of library science, was helpful in locating and obtaining many useful references.

Members of the author's own family, whose backgrounds include teaching, psychology and data processing, were also very helpful during the two years in which the manuscript was produced: Natalie, Robert, Anne, Howard, Elaine, Marjorie and Elizabeth.

CONTENTS

SCHOOL PERSONNEL ADMINISTRATION

1 FUNCTIONS OF THE SCHOOL PERSONNEL ADMINISTRATOR

GENERAL STATEMENT

Since the profession of school personnel administration is a relatively new one that has developed to meet the varying needs of different school districts, no specific duties have been uniformly prescribed for the person who fills the position. There is a growing consensus about the functions and status of the school personnel administrator, but there are considerable variations, depending on the size of the school system, the wishes of the school superintendent and the board of education, and the traditions of the district. Although the profession is still in the incipient stage, it may be helpful to point out the administrator's most frequent functions, and the reasons for them.

The functions of the school personnel administrator may be grouped under four headings. First is the process of staffing the schools. It may include recruitment, selection, assignment, promotion, service termination and retirement. The second function is the process of developing personnel policy. Normally, it involves working with employee groups within policies set by the board of education and the school superintendent to develop those conditions of employment in which an optimum teaching environment and attitude can be developed. The third function is that of stimulating and developing staff morale. It involves skill in human relations, giving recognition for service performed with high quality, and releasing the creative capacity of all staff members. Fourth is the process of providing services for staff. It is closely related to staff morale and involves personal counseling, insurance and retirement considerations, and in-service education.

The intent of this chapter is to show how the position of school personnel administrator came to be established, to provide a survey of the functions of the position as delineated in various job descriptions, to discuss some of the intangible or less known responsibilities of the position, to cite some of the uncommon problems which the school personnel administrator should be prepared to meet and some of the developing roles and responsibilities for the school personnel administrator as the position becomes better established and practitioners better trained, and to provide a philosophical orientation to the duties of the position. Changes will evolve as the needs and demands of employees and society change. Other chapters are devoted to the typical responsibilities assigned to the personnel function—the necessary, the expedient and the visible functions such as staff recruitment and selection, record keeping, and negotiations.

HISTORICAL DEVELOPMENT OF THE POSITION

The personnel specialist or administrator is a comparatively new addition to the central office staff of school systems. The factors leading to the establishment of the position include (1) the growth of school districts, including consolidation or unification into larger units, (2) the shortage of teachers in the years following World War II, which created the need for special efforts to recruit and retain staff, (3) the mobility of the population in recent years, which has required growing districts to recruit more aggressively and more widely, and (4) the example of industry, in which personnel specialists have become more common. In recent time a new factor has been added; namely, the necessity for working with employee groups in the negotiating process, which requires special knowledge and skill.

The term "personnel administration" came into general usage during World War I, when a large number of workers had to be recruited, trained and administered in the war effort. Paralleling that situation was the rapid growth in federal and state civil service. At the same time, consumer business and industry were expanding, employing large numbers of people and experiencing problems in recruiting, training and compensating their employees.

The survey movement in school systems, which began in the 1940s, also had an impact on the establishment of the position. Members of educational survey teams frequently had received orientation in business, and by the 1940s business had a sizable number of personnel specialists. During that time, however, paid personnel administration was usually the part-time assignment of an assistant superintendent or some other school official, in most school districts. Indeed, during the 1950s there were probably not more than 50 full-time school personnel administrators in the United States.

Harold E. Moore comments on the development of the position:

> "The first recorded public school personnel administrator was an assistant superintendent in Dallas, Texas, in 1919. Detroit, Michigan, was also one of the early cities to establish a personnel administrative position. Now the position is generally found in medium to large school districts.

"No exact count of the number of such positions is available, but it can be safely estimated that there are about 250 such positions in public school systems. [*Editor's note: since 1966, the number has more than tripled.*] The three most common titles assigned to the positions are director of personnel, assistant superintendent for personnel, and administrative assistant for personnel. These officers are usually responsible to the superintendent of schools, or in very large systems, to a deputy superintendent." [1]

Several states now have their own state and regional associations of school personnel administrators, and in metropolitan areas there are local or county personnel organizations. The general purpose of all these associations is to share better personnel practices, discuss methods of handling personnel problems, exchange information about personnel policies, interpret new laws affecting employees, and consider other practical problems of school personnel administration.

PHILOSOPHICAL CONCERNS OF THE POSITION

Implied above are rather pragmatic causes of the development of the position: it became expedient, because of increasing personnel problems in the 1960s, to assign one or more persons to deal with the concerns of school employees. It is unfortunate that some governing boards and even superintendents have not gone beyond the immediate pinch of necessity, as is evidenced by the limited amount of time and the small staff often assigned to carry out personnel functions, the absence of appropriate responsibilities assigned through the job description, and the placement of the position in an ineffectual place on the organizational chart.

Fortunately, many boards and superintendents are not content with the merely expedient, having greater understanding of the values of a comprehensive and unified personnel program, with the result that more basic and comprehensive responsibilities are assigned to the position. Such broad responsibilities as staff development, staff relationships, and staff evaluations might be included. Conversely, the personnel administrator who lacks insight into the complexities of human behavior or the nature of the educational process, or who lacks an understanding of the comprehensive nature of the personnel program, cannot perform adequately. Since the position of school personnel administrator is relatively new, specific training for the responsibilities of office is available only in a few institutions. More commonly than not, the typical school personnel administrator has had no specific training for the position other than that which he received as a principal or a supervisor. Lacking special preparation, lacking a specific body of research, lacking a commonly accepted definition, the position is indeed in its infancy.

The foregoing paragraph implies that two distinct and parallel courses

3

of action are desirable for the development of this position. The first course is that colleges and universities should establish a specialized program of preparation for school personnel administrators. It is likely that fewer institutions will be needed to give specialized training in this area than for the training of principals and supervisors. Those institutions which do offer such training should offer it in depth. That implies content which provides for a considerable exposure to the dynamics of human behavior and human relationships, some knowledge of sociology, psychology, measurement and testing; an acquaintance with the problems of industrial management and labor relations; a thorough knowledge of the educational enterprise, including educational philosophy, curriculum, methods of instructional technology, school finance, teacher certification, and school law; and, lastly, knowledge of office procedures, supervision of staff members, data processing and staff negotiations. Another way of approaching an understanding of the functions of the school personnel administrator is to consider broader aspects of his work. Thus Castetter has set forth five "major functions" of the personnel administrator [2] :

Planning
Allocating
Coordinating
Influencing
Appraising

To these might be added the concepts of *initiating* and *carrying out*. The training and preparation of the personnel specialist are discussed more thoroughly in Chapter 2.

The second course of action is that governing boards should develop job descriptions which will encourage the best practices, the highest morale among employees, the finest policies and the optimum efficiency of the operation. To achieve these virtues is not necessarily to develop one job description and apply it to all districts, for one that is completely adequate in one situation may not be adequate in another. Factors of size, district philosophy and community characteristics all affect the role of the school personnel administrator, both in the duties assigned to him and in the manner in which he is permitted to function.

THE JOB DESCRIPTION FOR THE CHIEF SCHOOL PERSONNEL ADMINISTRATOR

The responsibilities listed below were developed for a district with approximately 18,000 students.

1. Direct and conduct the program of recruitment, selection, and assignment of certificated and classified personnel.
2. Develop and maintain essential personnel records for all employees.

3. Administer all employee requests for transfer, promotion, leave of absence, health leave, and termination of or retirement from service.
4. Assist the superintendent in the development of district personnel policies.
5. Administer and implement all adopted board personnel policies.
6. Administer the program of providing substitute workers for all employees, both certificated and classified.
7. Direct and conduct research for the improvement of personnel policies.
8. Direct job-analysis studies for the purpose of determining proper job classification for classified employees.
9. Assist with the in-service training program for both certificated and classified employees.
10. Administer the district personnel appraisal program.
11. Supervise the classified employees in the personnel department.

The job description above probably served well the organization of the school district and the community for which it was designed. Nevertheless, as one reviews the description, the following questions come to mind.

What responsibility does the personnel office have for budget preparation and administration? How is the salary appropriation of the district budget administered?

What is the responsibility of the personnel administrator in working with employee groups?

Who performs the function of employee counseling?

Who handles grievances and is generally concerned with employee morale?

Is there a responsibility to work with the colleges in the teacher-preparation program?

Answers to these questions may be incorporated in other job descriptions in the organization. The description itself is inadequate to give a satisfactory picture of the responsibilities of the total school-personnel function.

Given below is a rather complete description of the duties of a personnel department. This description was designed for a medium sized school district which was growing rapidly.

OFFICE OF THE DIRECTOR OF PERSONNEL
1. Administers the personnel programs of the district. Plans and coordinates the functions of the division of certificated personnel, the division of classified personnel, the division of salary administration and records, and the division of payroll.
2. Coordinates the functions of the department of personnel with other departments of the school system and provides technical advice and assistance in personnel matters to all management levels and other personnel.
3. Develops, applies, interprets, and implements personnel regulations.
4. Recruits personnel for administrative, supervisory, teaching, professional, specialist, and classified positions.

5

5. Prepares an annual statistical report on employees for the superintendent and board of education.
6. Maintains liaison with local, state, and national agencies.
7. Supervises the following divisions:

A. *Division of salary administration and records*

1. Administers the salary schedule for all professional personnel. Assists in the development of salary policy and structure. Keeps up to date on local and national salary schedules; prepares studies and reports for the superintendent of schools and board of education which provide the information necessary to maintain a level of compensation competitive with other fields; interprets the salary schedule for personnel.
2. Coordinates and interprets the evaluation program for teachers and other professional personnel. Assists in the development of regulations for the just administration of the professional advancement program for administrative and supervisory personnel, in accordance with the regulations.
3. Maintains position control for all administrative and supervisory positions and maintains an up-to-date application file for prospective candidates for administrative and supervisory positions.
4. Assists in the development of personnel regulations.
5. Develops and maintains a system for personnel records for all professional personnel of the district in order to provide a comprehensive, efficient, accurate, and current personnel record-keeping system; processes the necessary personnel actions for employment, transfer, tenure, retirement, leave, promotion, etc. Maintains the official personnel folder for all professional personnel.
6. Prepares and maintains statistical information on all personnel and submits the necessary statistical reports to the state department of education and the local board of education.
7. Maintains an up-to-date teachers' handbook.
8. Advises professional personnel on retirement procedures.

B. *Division of certificated personnel*

1. Maintains close contact with all departments and schools in planning and anticipating professional personnel needs of the school program.
2. Plans, directs, coordinates and participates in the recruitment of teachers for the elementary, secondary, adult education and summer school programs.
3. Screens and processes applications of candidates; interviews and recommends to the superintendent applicants for appointment and for presentation to the board of education, and assigns teachers.
4. Receives, reviews and processes requests for transfer in accordance with transfer regulations and the needs of the school system.
5. Screens and selects qualified substitute teachers and maintains a register of substitutes.
6. Counsels employees to resolve complaints, difficulties, and other matters related to personnel management and works with other administrators on difficult personnel matters.

7. Processes recommendations for termination of personnel employment. Assembles substantiating information for dismissal of employees and arranges any necessary conferences and hearings.
8. Assists in the development of personnel regulations.
9. Works with the department of staff development in the identification of needs for in-service educational programs and services for professional personnel.

C. *Division of classified personnel*

1. Administers a personnel-management program for all employees assigned to classified services positions, including the clerical, technical, maintenance, custodial, transportation, cafeteria, and special staff personnel of the schools and the central office.
2. Develops programs for recruitment and testing, and is responsible for recruitment, testing, selection and placement of all classified personnel.
3. Develops programs for evaluating personnel performance and makes recommendations for promoting policy and procedures.
4. Receives, reviews, and processes requests for transfer in accordance with the regulations and needs of the school system and with the desires of employees.
5. Develops and maintains an effective, equitable, and current position-classification and pay plan; prepares and revises class specifications; updates the classifications program by periodically reviewing positions and recommending revisions when needed. Maintains close liaison with the county personnel department in order to be consistent, where possible, in job and salary classification.
6. Develops and recommends salary policy and structure for classified personnel, and administers the program. Keeps current on local and federal government salary scales; prepares studies and reports for the superintendent of schools and the board of education to provide the information necessary to maintain a level of compensation competitive with similar jobs in the surrounding area.
7. Develops and maintains a comprehensive personnel-records system for classified personnel in order to provide efficient, accurate, and current personnel data; processes the necessary personnel actions for employment, transfer, permanent status, retirement, leave, etc.
8. Counsels employees to resolve complaints, grievances, credit complaints from merchants, and other matters related to personnel management for classified personnel.
9. Cooperates with the department of staff development and the directors of the various categories of classified services employees in the development of in-service training programs for classified services employees.

D. *Division of certification*

1. Administers, interprets, and evaluates the state laws and county regulations relating to certification; evaluates and approves programs for advanced study; assists in the administration of the personnel program; assists in and advises on the development of personnel regulations.

2. Assists in obtaining appropriate certification for all eligible personnel and advises certificated personnel on maintaining or advancing their certification status.
3. Evaluates the training and experience of employees and determines certification status in accordance with state and county requirements.
4. Advises the division of salary administration and records of changes in the professional status and certification of certificated personnel that require changes in their placement on the salary schedule.
5. Maintains close liaison with, and handles all certification matters through, the state department of education.
6. Posts all necessary certification information on personnel records and keeps such information current.

E. *Division of payroll*
1. Computes earnings for all employees for specific pay periods.
2. Prepares payrolls and delivers pay checks to all employees on scheduled dates.
3. Maintains annual records of all employee sabbaticals and personal and sick leaves.
4. Administers a payroll accounting deduction plan for all employees for such deductions as federal withholding taxes, Social Security, retirement, professional dues, credit union allotments, group hospitalization and insurance, U.S. Savings Bonds, and custodial uniforms.
5. Charges salary expenditures to appropriate budget accounts.
6. Assists in the preparation and distribution of withholding statements to employees and to federal and state agencies. Maintains storage of earnings records, attendance records, and state retirement contribution records.
7. Assists with verification and preparation of the quarterly Social Security report.

The absence of adequate in-service educational responsibilities should be noted in the preceding description. This function is provided under the office of the assistant superintendent of instruction. It is interesting to note that the department of instruction has the responsibility for in-service education for both certified and classified personnel. That may be a reasonable assignment of function, but many personnel administrators favor an organization in which the in-service educational function is placed in the personnel department, for the reason that the personnel administrator is closer to the needs of the district and may be in a better position to assess persons for positions.

It is worthy of note that the payroll function is assigned to the personnel office. It is not common practice, but it is a functional place for the responsibility. With leaves of absence, visiting days, sudden staff additions and unexpected terminations affecting payroll, administration of the payroll becomes as much a matter of policy interpretation as it is a matter of computing salaries. As an arrangement for small to medium sized districts, it reduces duplication of record keeping significantly. And with the payroll in the personnel office there is the related responsibility of budget development with respect to staff needs. In the preceding job description, the personnel administrator has the responsibility for budget development and administration in all those classifications of the budget that involve salaries.

The role of the school personnel administrator has not been indicated in the important matter of staff negotiations. Opinions and practice vary. There is general agreement that the personnel administrator should participate fully in an advisory capacity, but there is disagreement on whether or not he should be the principal representative of the superintendent in the negotiating process. Those who oppose such a role believe that placing the school personnel administrator directly in opposition to the staff may vitiate his usefulness as a guide, counselor, and middle man between staff and management. They also believe that staff negotiations require an expertise, a specialization, which the personnel man may not have.

The Dayton, Ohio, public school system (population, 243,000) has outlined the duties and responsibilities of the personnel department in the concise outline shown here:

DUTIES AND RESPONSIBILITIES OF THE PERSONNEL DEPARTMENT

Dayton Public Schools
education, clerical, medical, dental, and nursing personnel

Personnel Tasks to Be Done
General Responsibilities

A. Coordinating personnel activities with operations in other administrative departments and offices and in schools.
B. Representing the personnel office in meetings of other administrative and supervisory officials in the consideration of general problems of concern to the school system.
C. Representing the school system at general meetings within and outside the school system.
D. Fulfilling administrative assignments having slight or even no relevance to personnel administration.
E. Carrying out divided responsibilities (e.g., administration and personnel).

Personnel Functions

A. Staffing schools and offices:
   1. Determining staff needs.
   2. Conducting short- and long-range recruitment and career nights in high schools plus college and university recruitment.
   3. Screening applicants.
   4. Interviewing candidates.
   5. Consulting with supervisors and directors about staff needs.
   6. Selecting and appointing applicants.
B. Placing teachers and other staff members:
   1. Analyzing staff strengths and weaknesses.
   2. Consulting with principals and supervisors.
   3. Upgrading staff quality.

4. Balancing staffs according to age, sex, race, etc.
5. Handling transfers (teacher-initiated and administratively required).
6. Personalizing placement according to employee preference and the requirements of the school system.

C. Administering and supervising the personnel office:
1. Records: *pre-* and *post*-employment.
2. Personnel folders.
3. Correspondence.
4. Work flow.
5. Files and records.
6. Clerical staff administration and supervision.

D. Administering board and administrative policies and regulations; making recommendations to the superintendent for:
1. Appointments.
2. Health examinations.
3. Certification.
4. Temporary appointments.
5. Qualifications for administrative and supervisory positions and administration of promotional examinations.
6. Assignment and transfer of employees.
7. Promotion and demotion.
8. Appraisal.
9. Probationary period.
10. Dismissals and terminations.
11. Placement of salaries on schedule—send all salary information to payroll department.
12. Absences and leaves.
13. Grievances.

E. Staff utilization:
1. Appraisal: summaries of principal evaluations.
2. Leadership development (selection, training, records); recommendations for graduate study, fellowships, and foundation grants.
3. In-service growth through graduate education.

F. Substitute service:
1. Employment.
2. Placement.
3. Salary.
4. Records.
5. Evaluation.
6. Termination.

G. Adjustment counseling:
1. Working with principals and supervisors in resolving adjustment problems.
2. Counseling teachers and other staff members.
3. Obtaining medical and professional help as required and as available.
4. Information on retirement by age and service, or by disability.

H. Reports:
1. Collecting personnel data and statistics.
2. Preparing status and other special reports.

I. Evaluation:
   1. Analyzing the status of procedures and practices in personnel administration.
   2. Upgrading procedures and the personnel program.
J. Liaison responsibilities to:
   1. Teacher-education institutions.
   2. State department of education.
   3. Local, state, and national personnel organizations.
   4. Community organizations interested in personnel administration.
   5. Professional teacher and leadership organizations.

Employee Relations

A. Lead in the administration of board policies concerning:
   1. Salary.
   2. Working conditions.
   3. Changes in rules and regulations.
   4. Fringe benefits.
B. Representing the superintendent in preliminary discussions on matters of:
   1. Working conditions.
   2. Changes in rules and regulations.
   3. Fringe benefits.

Personnel Policies and Procedures

A. Principles of policy and procedural development and execution:
   1. Put in writing and easily accessible.
   2. Clearly and concisely stated.
   3. Cooperative involvement of staff.
   4. Decision by consensus.
   5. Differentiation between board policies and procedures and personnel policies and procedures.
   6. Provision for implementation.
   7. Plan for systematic interpretation.
   8. Part of orientation program.
   9. Lines of responsibility and authority clearly defined.
   10. Provision for review and revision.

Communications

A. Relationships with staff:
   1. Integrity, consistency in treatment, forthrightness.
   2. Staff members should feel welcome to come to personnel office.
   3. Respect for feelings and attitudes of staff members.
   4. Good human relations.
   5. Written and oral communications with schools.
   6. Visits to schools.
   7. Liaison with professional teacher organizations.
B. Community Relationships:
   1. Awareness of and sensitivity to the importance of good public relations.
   2. Much of the image of the school system may be formed by the way the personnel office treats the public (on the telephone and in person).

3. All members of the personnel staff should treat callers in a courteous, considerate, and businesslike manner.
4. Effort should be made to create a community awareness of the aims and purposes of the personnel organization.
5. Close working relationships with all communications media in the community.

THE PERSONNEL ADMINISTRATOR ON THE ORGANIZATIONAL CHART

Shown below are several patterns of organizations appropriate for various sizes of school districts. They may be construed as showing how the position of the school personnel administrator may change on the organizational chart as a district increases in size. Although personnel administration may be only the part-time function of a school administrator in a smaller school district, it is much too important a function to be performed in any haphazard, unplanned way. As Castetter informs us:

"One of the more serious [fallacies] is that personnel planning is unique to, and only necessary in, large school districts. It is clearly evident, however, that regardless of the size of the operation, the effectiveness of an organization and of the individuals in it demand systematic attention." [3]

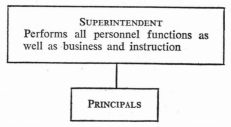

A. For a district up to approximately 2,000 enrollment.

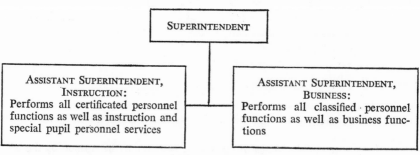

B. For a district of approximately 5,000 enrollment.

STATUS OF THE SCHOOL PERSONNEL ADMINISTRATOR

Titles and salaries of school personnel administrators vary considerably. In part, they vary because in contemporary American culture status is generally determined by the kind of decisions one makes, one's position on an organizational chart, by tradition and by one's personal contacts and abilities. Since the responsibilities and duties of the position have varied greatly in different communities, status titles and salaries have varied similarly.

The school personnel administrator is in a position to make some significant decisions which affect people and their careers, and to that extent they are important and require a considerable amount of judgment. The personnel administrator may recommend employment of an individual or refusal of employment, and sometimes he builds a case for dismissal. Sometimes his decisions have political, as opposed to professional, implications. It is almost wishful thinking to believe that every decision can be based on sound professional judgment. Testing programs, as commonly utilized in large cities, reduce the opportunities for other than professional decisions.

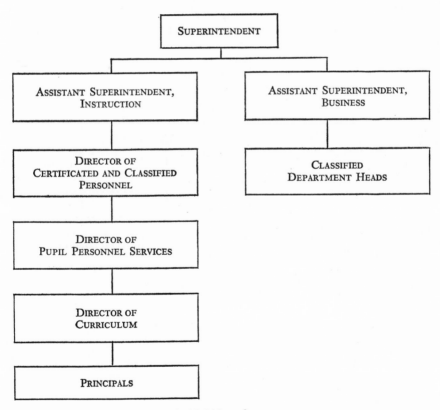

C. For a district of approximately 10,000 students.

The attitudes of staff, consultants and public are also determined by the status of the personnel administrator. If the personnel administrator is to be most effective as a leader of the staff-selection team, his position must be such as to command confidence. Because his is such a vital responsibility, he should report directly to the superintendent. He also needs the protection of the superintendent if he is to withstand pressures to get jobs through favoritism.

As mentioned earlier, the concept of a personnel specialist in school districts is a comparatively new one, and data on the extent and nature of his duties have not been widely disseminated to practitioners. Since people have typically come to this position by routes other than that of specific training for the position, it implies that the personnel specialist has not yet come into his own, that the position has not yet achieved the status which it ultimately may achieve, and that there is insufficient appreciation of the special abilities required to fill the position.

The employment interview, which the personnel administrator must conduct, may be used as one example of the specialized knowledge and skill that are required for the position. The typical administrative training program is not likely to give any training in depth for the employment interview. Since school administrators, in general, are articulate and sensitive to people's needs, and since they possess a general knowledge of the position

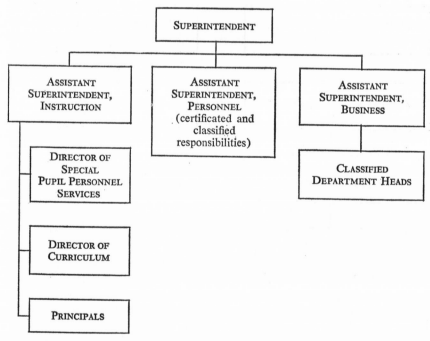

D. For a district of approximately 15,000 students.
14

for which they might be interviewing, they may believe that they are entirely able to conduct an employment interview without further training. A concomitant factor which has diminished the importance of the employment interview is that, in time of few applicants, or even a scarcity, in some fields, a principal or another administrator is grateful indeed just to be able to fill the position. However, the personnel administrator must have specialized knowledge of the procedures, limitations, and values of the interview as a means of staff selection if he is to fulfill his special function. A few such areas of knowledge are the following:

1. The administrator should have some knowledge of the preprofessional experiences that are more closely related to later professional success.
2. He should be aware of different types of interview procedures: i.e., structured and unstructured interviews, utilization of appropriate rating sheets, proper utilization of questions.
3. He should know which characteristics of an applicant can be inferred with reasonable reliability from an interview and which characteristics can not be reliably appraised from an interview.

The other functions of the school personnel administrator similarly require specialized skills and training. And, while general principles of personnel administration can be rather easily identified, optimum application of these principles to specific situations in the matrix of social, political, and professional relationships becomes in some ways an art and in some ways a science. As the training of school personnel to perform specialized functions becomes more common, as research on staff selection and administration is more widely disseminated, and as the gap between research and practice is narrowed, the status of the school personnel administrator will improve.

Typically, the personnel administrator is directly responsible to the superintendent. In the judgment of most school personnel administrators, this is entirely proper. It is not uncommon, however, in a small district to have the assistant superintendent of instruction responsible for the certificated personnel function, as was demonstrated on an organizational chart earlier in this chapter. When the size of the district increases, the assistant superintendent is likely to seek an assistant rather than to establish the position on an equal level. Moreover, when such a position is established, it is often assumed that those classified personnel functions which to this point have been performed by the assistant superintendent for business should be assigned to the personnel office. It may require such an additional responsibility to justify the full-time position of a school personnel administrator. Thus, a personnel administrator's position of lower status is developed on the basis of a comprehensive analysis of a school personnel program.

The personnel administrator must have broad professional contacts.

15

It is most helpful to have contacts in placement offices, college faculties, professional organizations, other school districts, community organizations, the state department of education, the United States Office of Education, and also with personnel men in business and industry. He needs these contacts not only as a source of applicants and to develop answers to problems which inevitably develop but also to ascertain trends in the supply and demand of applicants, personnel policies, and fringe benefits of other institutions and to establish community support and rapport. Schools are in competition with other schools and with industry for employees. As the personnel administrator makes such contacts, he improves both his status and his service to the district.

DEVELOPING PERSONNEL POLICIES

A basic practice of American democracy is to have people participate in the development of policies that affect them. This concept was not inherent in early American education nor has it been true in the labor market generally. The recent developments of the negotiating process and the writing of contracts for school employees are evidence of the fact that employees, both certificated and classified, are now deeply engaged in the development of policies that affect them. The concern, then, is to identify appropriate communication channels for the initiation, development, and appraisal of personnel policies.

One function of management is the establishment, administration and continuous appraisal of personnel policies. Management should take the leadership in this process and one way of accomplishing it is to open a regular communication channel through which employee groups or individuals can meet with the personnel administrator to share in personnel policy development and in appraisal of policies. The alternative is to let policies develop entirely through the formal negotiating process, in which there may be a tendency to develop policies more as a result of a power confrontation, through concessions in the give-and-take process, rather than through sound personnel principles.

It may be appropriate to use both methods in policy development. It should be a function of a representative committee of staff and management to prepare a sound policy on sabbatical leave, for example. The aspect of policy making that might have to be transferred to the negotiating table is determining what percentage of the staff should be granted leave in any one year and the amount of salary to be paid to them during the leave.

Among all the challenges of the personnel administrator, often the greatest test of his leadership is working with his fellow administrators, the board of education, and even the public in policy development and application. In developing and applying personnel policies, he stands between the staff and management, in the form of the school board, the public, and in some situations his superintendent and fellow administrators. It is within

16

this framework of frequently conflicting views that he must work in seeking to develop, apply, and appraise personnel policies that are based upon consensus and upon participation in decision making.

Harold E. Moore says:

> "At no place in the galaxy of duties of the personnel administrator are his qualities as a leader more tested than when working with the staff, his fellow administrators, the board of education, and even the public, than in policy department. Policy gives both direction and security to the personnel process and, if developed through staff participation, provides an avenue for communication in the total organization. The responsibility for the development of personnel policy is one of the principal functions of the school personnel administrator." [4]

RELATIONSHIP TO OTHER ADMINISTRATORS

It was suggested previously that the personnel administrator might report directly to the superintendent and that he should hold a relatively high place in the educational hierarchy. By the very nature of his work, however, the personnel administrator has many close relationships with other administrators. Other administrators may help him significantly in recruiting, selecting, and promoting staff to more advanced positions. They can help him keep up to date in curriculum developments. They can give him counsel in dealing with certain kinds of personnel problems.

Accepting and understanding the role of the personnel administrator on the part of the total staff is the key to good working relationships. The role relationship is related to the job description as well as to the personality and the abilities of the personnel administrator. It is perhaps incumbent upon the superintendent, working with the personnel administrator, to define the role of the latter in order that the role perception may be thoroughly understood throughout the organization. Administrative difficulties are likely to emerge when there are differences in role perception and when there is a lack of clarity about duties and lines of authority.

STIMULATING AND DEVELOPING STAFF MORALE

Webster defines "morale" as a "moral or mental condition with respect to courage, discipline, confidence, willingness to endure hardship, etc." "Employee morale" refers to the manner in which employees react to their leadership, their conditions of employment, and the personal satisfaction they receive from their employment. Good morale tends to be associated with:

1. Receiving recognition for doing a job well.
2. Having opportunities for participation in decision making.

3. Being able to provide a service or a skill which is appreciated by others.
4. Enjoying the job one has to perform.
5. Appreciating the leadership under which one works.
6. Feeling secure in knowing where one stands with his peers.
7. Being able to predict or to understand administrative decisions rather than being surprised by them or resentful of them.
8. Experiencing straightforwardness and friendliness from administrators.

Morale is not a single characteristic. High salaries alone cannot buy good morale nor can extensive fringe benefits. Good morale is more subtly related to the inner needs of man, his ego, his need and desire to be a participating part of a group, his drive to be something unique. In the absence of ego-rewarding experiences, industry has used monetary rewards, including fringe benefits, with the hope that such rewards will be sufficient motivation to improve productivity on the job. The further implications are that money and fringe benefits permit one to enjoy or purchase ego satisfactions after work.

Good salaries and tangible benefits in school organizations certainly contribute to good morale, and it is incumbent upon every school administrator to strive to obtain those benefits for the staff and to ascertain whether or not his schools are keeping abreast of other districts and industries; yet good morale is much more. Every person in the school organization is in some way a contributor to the morale of the organization, but perhaps no person is in a more strategic position to influence morale than the personnel administrator. He can influence to a great extent such morale factors as the following:

1. Assigning people where they can achieve their personal objectives.
2. Counseling people to help them achieve new insights into their abilities or counseling them to take them out of areas where their potential is limited.
3. Providing adequate recognition for services well performed. One of the problems of an industrial society is providing ego-rewarding experiences on the job so that an individual's personal aspirations may parallel the purpose of the organization for which he is working.
4. Adopting policies which are typical of good personnel practices.
5. Providing a means for staff participation in decision making.
6. Exercising common courtesies and fair treatment, which inspire people to develop the best within themselves.

To involve people in decision making and policy development, to provide counseling, to provide news-recognition stories or awards programs—all require a considerable amount of time. The need of the amount in any given district may determine the emphasis that the district desires to place on these points of personnel administration. At a time when employee organizations are testing their new strength and rebelling against autocratic methods of school administration, these qualities of school administration are likely to be highly significant.

The morale of an organization can be changed; it can be improved and, conversely, it can deteriorate sometimes with the slightest provocation. By his status, his catalytic position in the organization, his training and experience, and his knowledge of the decision-making process, the personnel administrator should have a positive contribution to make to the improvement of staff morale.

PREPARING FOR UNUSUAL RESPONSIBILITIES

Problems outside of the routine functions of the school personnel administrator occasionally present themselves. Anticipating unusual problems and developing policies and procedures to meet them is therefore a part of the personnel administrator's function. Only a few illustrations will be given.

Tuberculosis An annual or biannual tuberculin test is a requirement for all school employees in many districts. Such a test can be administered at a reasonably low cost. If an employee is found to have active tuberculosis, it may be appropriate to give a special tuberculin test to all students and adults with whom the employee has come in contact. Such a test usually identifies the disease early in its development, thus making a quick recovery more probable.

A recommended practice is to require the district to keep a record of all school medical tests. When a positive test is reported for an employee, the earlier reports may be helpful in ascertaining the extent and history of the infection.

In case of emergency On one occasion a personnel administrator employed a woman from a distant part of the country, the mother of a three-year-old child. Within a week after her arrival in town she was killed in an accident. It was about two weeks before the personnel administrator, whose records were incomplete, could locate anyone who would claim the body and care for the child.

Accidents can occur at school, too. To prepare for such an emergency, the personnel administrator should have on file the name of a related person. This information should be updated annually at the beginning of each school year.

Identification Some states require that all employees must be fingerprinted at the time of their employment. Fingerprinting reports can be sent to the state department of education which can then determine by policy and/or judgment whether or not the person should be permitted in light of his previous record, to work with children. For other classifications of em-

19

ployees, the fingerprinting report or "rap sheet" may be sent directly to the district. It then becomes the duty of the personnel administrator to determine whether or not the record of the employee is satisfactory for employment.

Mental illness Problems of mental illness are not uncommon in any population of employees, but they are usually difficult to handle. In fact, the severe cases are frequently easier to deal with than the borderline cases. One helpful technique is to provide for psychiatric help in a major medical insurance plan for district employees. The premium for such coverage is modest, and it would take just one tough case to justify the procedure. An alternative, or even a supplement, to insurance is to employ a skilled counselor who is capable of coping with the situation. Such a person should serve in a staff rather than in a line relationship in the administrative organization.

There are no simple ways of handling these kinds of problems. Some cautions may be helpful. First, any statement should be avoided which would accuse an individual of being psychotic or of having a mental problem. It is not the responsibility of school administrators to make medical evaluations. Such statements could even lead to a charge of slander. It would be appropriate to suggest to the individual that he seek professional help. Instituting a policy which provides a generous leave of absence can also be helpful. On occasion, a change of environment or a change of assignment can mitigate the problem.

FUTURE CONCERNS OF THE SCHOOL PERSONNEL ADMINISTRATOR

Implied throughout this chapter is the fact that the position of the school personnel administrator is an emerging one, subject to changes in society, the enactment of laws, the pressures of special interest groups, the findings of research and the development of instructional technology. A brief review of some of these trends may be helpful in understanding the directions of change.

The knowledge explosion One need not stretch his imagination to foresee the increased number of course offerings, particularly in the secondary school. The personnel administrator will need to keep up to date so that he can interview teachers in specialized fields. He will need to know the kinds of equipment and teaching aids available for specialized courses. The knowledge explosion has also taken place in our understanding of human behavior as it is related to motivation, to growth and development, and to group dynamics, including an understanding of the power structure of groups.

Professional training While the contemporary personnel administrator typically has arrived at his position by way of training for and then being a principal, it is only a short time before such training will be inadequate for the complex functions which will be assigned to the position. Specialized

20

training is needed now for future personnel administrators and in-service education will be needed for incumbents.

Instructional technology Instructional technology is in its infancy; its potential is beyond imagination. Television instruction offers some exciting problems. When a teacher prepares a series of televised lessons, who is to determine when such lessons become obsolete? What time should be allotted for a teacher to prepare for a thirty-minute lesson by television? What supporting personnel will be required to "keep the show on the road"? What compensation shall the supporting personnel receive? What tenure rights will television teachers have? How are television teachers to be evaluated? These are all significant questions for the personnel administrator to wrestle within the years immediately ahead.

An even more exciting potential is the field of computerized instruction. It is quite possible that factual material can be presented more efficiently and more accurately by a computer than by a teacher. It is almost axiomatic that the computer can provide infinitely better individual instruction than a live and charming teacher. Because the computer can react instantaneously to a wrong answer, wrong answers may never have to linger in the mind of the student. What are the implications for learning when re-learning or "unlearning" will be a diminishing process? Is it not possible that the whole role of the teacher may change with the advent of teaching by computer? Factual computer learning may take place in the home, in carrells housed in spacious rooms, or even by direct dial radio or telephone.

The problem for the school personnel administrator will be finding persons to program the computer and evaluating those persons to arrange appropriate compensation for them and perhaps establishing the in-service education courses which will help them do their jobs. Another task will be to provide in-service instruction for those teachers whose roles will change because the computer will do some parts of their jobs better than they can.

CHANGING CONDITIONS OF EMPLOYMENT

To keep pace with the knowledge explosion, provision will have to be made for teachers and administrators to return to school, to attend conferences, and to visit other organizations. While the sabbatical leave is currently approaching a luxury in fringe benefits, it may ultimately become a mandatory responsibility. It is rare indeed for a business to survive in today's economy which invests as little in research as does education. Obsolescence in content and methodology is sometimes tolerated and even encouraged in education both by its practitioners and by the public. If one doubts that, he has merely to review the objectives and equipment of many shop classes, with the demands of the labor market in mind; or he can consider the law that mandates foreign language study by virtually all students for such a short period of time that their second language seldom becomes functional.

The use of large numbers of paraprofessionals such as teachers' aides and assistant teachers in the schools has already had a marked influence on the role of the teacher as the leader of an instructional team. This new role of the teacher requires change in the personnel practices of the school district. The personnel administrator should consider in-service education to facilitate the changeover of teachers to a new role; there may be implications for recruitment and staff selection, for staff compensation, and for staff organization. Thus, changing times bring changes to the functions of the school personnel administrator.

One must also consider the future impact of the negotiating process and of district-wide or state-wide contracts. While their future impact has been viewed by some with trepidation, in fact many educationally fine policies and procedures have emerged from the negotiating process, and it is reasonable to expect a trend of constructive negotiations. Ultimately, there may be an impasse. It may come when the recommendations and the pressures of the employee groups, however laudable, proper and philosophically sound, go beyond the willingness of society to support them. The personnel administrator of the future may have a key role in directing the value system of the employee groups and the society that supports the schools, so that instead of an impasse there will be constantly improving relationships, understanding, and sharing of plans as well as goals of education. To achieve that, he will have to perform his myriad functions well.

2 PROFESSIONAL PREPARATION FOR THE SCHOOL PERSONNEL ADMINISTRATOR

GENERAL STATEMENT

Entry into and successful performance in a career as demanding as school personnel administration needs to be backed up by suitable professional preparation. In this chapter a formulation will be developed concerning the nature of professional preparation for the position and role of school personnel administrator. The needs that created the position are still in a state of flux and the expectations have not become clarified or generally accepted. Consequently, the role attached to this emerging position leaves considerable unclarity about the types of professional performance that will be expected in the years ahead. The ways in which functions are attached to the position vary widely, demanding varied competence.

While it is true that role definition is still in process, the general shape of the personnel function has emerged with some clarity, and a number of tasks that require rather distinct performance capability have been identified. Capacity to undertake performance in this role has typically been judged on the basis of general educational preparation together with evidence that the person can work with people and has had success in administering a school as principal or assistant principal. Within the last few years, more systematic attention has been given by universities and by the profession to preparation both before entry into the career (pre-service) and during the career (in-service).

One may think of professional preparation as a form of socialization into a somewhat institutionalized professional role to which are attached expectations requiring a rather complex performance and for which conscious preparation can be made. Given the accelerating rate of social change, roles can be expected to shift in a variety of ways that often cannot be clearly or even vaguely anticipated. Consequently, it is reasonable to expect that the extent and quality of preparation for career performance, and

23

continued in-service preparation will expand and change in the years ahead.

Factors in the emergence of the position of school personnel administrator and apparent current trends will be utilized as a basis for postulating the sorts of performance, both current and anticipated, that can be expected. The analysis will lead to areas of course content, skill development and instructional strategies geared to performance outcomes. Of particular relevance will be requisite knowledge, modes of intellectual analysis which create a base of understanding for performance, and use of degrees of reality (e.g., cases, simulation, and internships) which can serve as a whetstone for intellect and action. The joint roles of universities and professions in preparation for intellectually based performance will be examined. Examples of programs at pre-service and in-service stages will be reported. Finally, some questions and anticipations about the future will be advanced.

NATURE OF PROFESSIONAL PREPARATION

Before advancing to the details of content and method in preparatory programs, it seems desirable to identify and consider briefly the ideas and assumptions that underlie such preparation. The position for which preparation is undertaken may be thought of as social location, in this case the location of the position of school personnel administrator, within the society of the school. Persons performing in surrounding positions, both within the immediate school and in the larger society, will have expectations about his role performance. Those groups—board members and superintendents, teachers, other members of the personnel profession, parents, etc.— are at times referred to as "reference" groups. Who are relevant definers of the role of the personnel administrator? It is probably a mixture that takes its form through a variety of social processes with the professional association seeking to formulate a responsible and responsive role in the face of conflicting expectations. Consequently, socialization into a role involves a *need for understanding analysis of the social forces at work in the environmental school system and larger society.*

A responsible profession has to do more than simply respond to a complex of environmental reference groups; it needs to take some initiative in formulating its social responsibility, normally through its association. If we define a profession in part as "a vocation in which a professed knowledge of some department of learning is used in its application to the affairs of others" (*Oxford English Dictionary*), it would seem that preparation would need to take into account the appropriate intellectual base and some skill in its application to personnel affairs. The "mix of the martini" (intellect and application) often triggers argument about the dry rot of excessive intellectual emphasis and the myopia of excessive emphasis on application. Actually, it seems more useful to think of them as complementary, so that theory enlightens practice and practice tests theory in a symbiotic improve-

24

ment of both. If we assume that the university, consistent with its role, should put its primary effort into intellectual analysis and that the profession should seek to promote skillful application, then *professional preparation should involve a symbiotic liaison between universities and professional associations.* Following this line of reasoning, both professors and practitioners of school personnel administration would be involved in the preparation activities involved in socialization into school personnel administration.

Dual involvement in preparation is important, particularly in connection with what may be called "ideal-real gap." It has been pretty well established that in some fields of professional preparation the university advances an ideal conception of the profession that is so far removed from the reality of the position that both the beginner and the seasoned practitioner are disenchanted. Similarly, the profession may be so concerned with customary practices that practitioners can have difficulty recognizing the need for new ways, thus making useless the fresh insight of the newcomer to the profession.

It seems likely that university-profession activities will increase in frequency and depth in the years ahead. It is already evident that the body of knowledge from the behavioral sciences is growing rapidly in content and relevance; new insights are being gained into the practices of education. This knowledge is bound to increase the ideal-real gap at certain points and to increase the *professional responsibility to be prepared to bring practice up to what is known.*

Professional performance involves the use of professional expertise in the best interests of others. In hiring teachers, is the personnel administrator working in the interests of the teachers? Of the children? Of the parents? Of the school administration? Clearly, all are involved; but what ethical and political problems are involved when parents, teachers and children do not agree on educational ends, and challenge the profession about its means? These differences have increased in the last two decades and it is reasonable to expect their extension into the future. If we accept this line of reasoning, we are led to *the need for preparation in the analysis of public policy issues and formulation of relevant alternative courses of action on personnel matters.*

THE POSITION AND PROFESSIONAL EXPECTATIONS

Specialized positions for attention to the personnel functions began to emerge in industry at about the turn of the century. Tead reports that by 1912 there were at least a dozen corporations with a position to which the personnel function was attached.[1] Its clear institutionalization was signaled by the publication in 1920 of *Personnel Administration* by Ordway Tead and Henry C. Metcalf.

The first personnel position in the public schools of which we have record was created fifty years ago in Dallas, Texas. The intervening half

25

century breaks rather naturally into the two periods before and after the end of the Second World War. During the first period, the position was being introduced slowly, hindered both by its novelty and by the times. A renewed teacher shortage after the end of the last war gave new impetus to the development of the position, especially in terms of recruitment. More recently, a growing emphasis upon personnel relationships—e.g., grievance procedures and collective negotiations—has given further impetus to its development. It is probably fair to say that the position is still in the developmental stage, leaving the possibility of emergence of new dimensions of the position to the future.

We say that the position of school personnel administrator exists in order to attend to the personnel function in schools. What do we mean by the "personnel function"? Some writers have found it useful to list the several tasks that have normally been attended to by the position's occupants. Such lists usually include such tasks as staff recruitment, selection, development and evaluation. However, there is the overarching need for a conceptualization of the role that will help to bring about coherence and unity in the function. It appears to be increasingly useful to think of the personnel function as that of the functional relationship between performance in a position and the school as a social organization. Thus defined in terms of social behavior, the personnel function may be viewed as a form of social exchange of services and rewards between people and a school system. Within this perspective, the personnel function becomes basically one of allocations: the allocation of persons to positions and the allocation of rewards in return for their services. The allocating process may be viewed in three stages which are analytically rather clear, namely, entrance into the system (hiring), service in the system (employment), and departure from the system (withdrawal). Normally, all three phases involve the duties attached to a school personnel position, although for a number of reasons the mixture may vary considerably from system to system. In the early development of the position, the hiring phase received a clear priority, while in recent years the emphasis upon the service or employment phase has increased greatly and will probably become the future functional focus of the position.

When we deal with the rights and duties of people, we are touching directly upon their roles, their aspirations and their identities. Consequently, the personnel function is a socially sensitive location. Also, since the persons involved have different roles, they view the allocating process in different ways (what is a duty for one is a reward for another), making for potential conflict. Thus an essential ingredient of an allocative exchange function is the creation of mediating devices in the process in order to assure reasonable social justice in the process. This task opens up a largely new area. The major point to be made here, however, is that the position of personnel administrator is located within a school system, where there are likely to be differing expectations for performance, creating a degree of role ambiguity

26

and conflict. Some of the more important reference groups with potentially conflicting expectations are the school board, superintendent, parents, teachers and pupils. Because of the variety in expectation, both in place and in time, the activities involved in role performance may vary considerably. Recent issues in the selection and performance of teachers and administrators, dividing parents, community leaders, school-board members, teacher organizations and even pupils, illustrate those differences.

Other factors also cause the role performance to differ from place to place. An important matter is "role boundaries." Where do personnel duties leave off and where, for example, do those of curriculum and business begin? The role definitions are often made in terms of many factors, including local custom, professional standards, personal interests and administrative adaptations. We have already noted that the changing times are changing the role. These differences result in a variety of combinations of performance skills.

What does the foregoing discussion mean for preparation for role performance in the position of school personnel administrator? Does it mean so much diversity exists that there is not much point in specifying content for a preparatory program? Or may it be that one of the administrator's major tasks is simply that of coping with diversity? The answer is probably more the latter than the former. If we make this assumption, as it seems reasonable to do, we are led to the importance of the ability to formulate social situations in one's mind, to undertake social analyses in behavioral terms, and to propose productive courses of action. Such tasks demand broad conceptual competence and intellectual honesty and stamina. Not all of that ability is developed in preparatory programs; the persons must have it within them. We are not clear about the extent of each. But it does seem that the candidate who has strong intellectual-conceptual powers, together with a feeling for social process, stands a good chance for successful role performance.

As implied just above, selective admission to preparatory programs is desirable, even though our limited knowledge about the human competence necessary for successful performance is not very useful. The traits approach, by which certain characteristics of the person are assessed, has been considerably discredited. Rather, the emphasis has tended to shift toward human interaction. Given the above assumptions, it seems reasonable in selection to utilize measures of conceptual power, operational evidence of capacity for social performance, and interest in the type of responsibility that personnel presents. Universities are likely to give priority to the conceptual criterion, while school systems tend to place greater weight on the criterion of social performance. Since the majority of appointments to personnel positions in the past have been made initially from within school systems, it seems reasonable to expect that conceptual powers have not been highly stressed in those selections. Both would seem to be important as a base for effective preparatory program performance.

PREPARATION FOR PERSONNEL ROLE PERFORMANCE:
PRE-SERVICE

Performance is all one piece of cloth—ideas, feelings and actions all together. For analytic purposes, learning is often classified as cognitive, affective and conative, or acquiring understanding, feeling and skill. If we think of preparation as partly in the classroom, emphasizing understanding or cognitive outcomes, and partly in school systems, emphasizing skill in practice, then we may think of a rough division of labor in preparation along the lines shown in Figure I. It assumes that the universities, together with schools and the profession, share responsibility for the socialization of persons into the profession. It also assumes that each should specialize in what it can do best, the university specializing in generalized understandings or cognitive outcomes and the profession specializing in conative or performance skills. Clearly, the distinctions are only a matter of emphasis, for understanding without a feel for its application is superficial, skill without understanding is thoughtless, and both without affective learning, or sensitivity, can be inhuman. Consequently, professional preparation is seen as a cooperative undertaking between universities and schools in a joint relation of understanding and application. Stated another way, the university is seen in a generalizing function and the school in a particularizing function, with each involved in the transductive process of relating practice and knowledge. This conception, together with illustrative areas of study, is shown in Figure II, adapted from Gibson and Roberts.[2]

Typically, a university program of preparation includes (1) a core program dealing with school administration generally, (2) study directed at understanding organized human behavior, (3) the study of the tasks of school systems, and (4) the study of the specialized tasks of school personnel administration. Bretsch has listed the areas of study as follows [3]:

COMMON LEARNINGS
Education as Institution and Process
Basic Concepts—Behavioral Sciences and Other Disciplines
Administrative Process

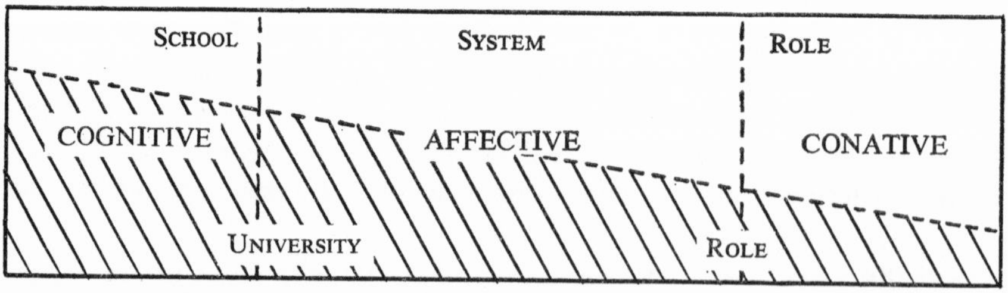

Figure I. *Diagram representing university and school system roles in professional preparation.*

28

Policy Determination
In-service Development
Resolution of Conflict and Guidance
Research

SPECIALIZED LEARNINGS

Understanding Human Behavior
Technical-Managerial
Business-Managerial
Technical Areas

Bretsch goes on to point out that "in the technical areas, considerable preparation is needed in the content areas of the aspects of the task including recruitment, selection of personnel, certification, contract, salary negotiations, fringe benefits, substitute teachers, transfer, orientation and induction, leaves of absence, grievance and dismissal procedures, etc."

Castetter has prepared a list of activities associated with the personnel function [4]:

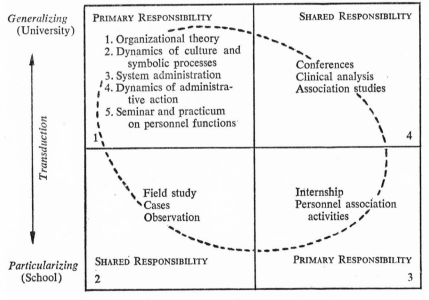

Figure II. *Diagram showing relationships proposed between generalizing and specializing instructional processes and institutional responsibility.*

Note: The oval space is intended to suggest roughly the emphasis that might be placed upon the four areas. It is, however, a very rough approximation that is arbitrary and only suggestive.

29

A. Determining Personnel Need

1. Planning and organizing the personnel function.
2. Relationships of the personnel function.
3. Manpower planning.
4. Data processing and the personnel function.

B. Satisfying Personnel Need

1. Recruitment of personnel.
2. Selection of personnel.
3. Compensation of personnel.
4. Induction of personnel.

C. Maintaining and Improving Personnel Service

1. Appraisal of personnel performance.
2. Development of personnel.
3. Continuity of personnel service.
4. Security of personnel.
5. Personnel associations.
6. Organizational democracy.

For each principal activity, Castetter has also identified goals, sub-activities, and implications for preparation content.[5] His listings illustrate an approach to task analysis and to related instructional activities. Such an analysis is essential to systematic program development, both for the university and for the student.

Specific areas, as indicated in this book, in which competence and knowledge are required by the school personnel administrator are:

1. The educational process
2. Office and business organization
3. Teacher education and certification
4. Personnel recruitment
5. Personnel selection
6. Noncertificated personnel
7. Personnel assignments
8. Salary administration
9. Welfare benefits
10. In-service personnel development
11. Public and human relations
12. Staff negotiations
13. Grievance procedures
14. Legal processes in personnel administration
15. Personnel evaluation and appraisal

In September of 1969, new requirements for administrative positions were adopted by the State Education Department of New York. In accordance with those requirements, a school personnel administrator needs the following preparation in a planned program:

1. Thirty semester hours of graduate study, including eighteen semester hours of graduate study in or related to the fields of educational administration and supervision.
2. An administrative/supervisory internship (or one year of full-time experience in an administrative or supervisory position).
3. Five years of teaching or administrative and/or supervisory experience in the public schools.

In most cases, the school personnel administrator is also required to hold a teaching certificate, although exceptions can be made.

PRE-SERVICE EXPERIENCE REQUIRED

Most persons assigned to the role of school personnel administrator have come up through the ranks of teacher, principal, or other school supervisory positions. Questions have been raised about whether a school-teaching background is essential or not. Can a personnel administrator from industry, or from any other nonschool enterprise, perform successfully as a school personnel administrator? It is contended that such an individual is likely to have a fresh, tradition-challenging approach which may be good for progress. On the other hand, those who advocate the necessity of a school background are mindful of the intrinsic understandings of school life, activities, attitudes and educational goals that may come only from experience and that make it easier for the individual to operate effectively in the social-relationship role of school personnel administrator. Of course there are exceptional individuals who have the capacity to transfer insights and understandings from one situation to another, and who have the ability to rapidly develop new goal understandings and social orientations. There are also individuals with a school background who would be ineffective personnel administrators. It is reasonable to say that people who have broader and more inclusive backgrounds are more likely to have more experiential resources to draw upon for the performance of their duties than are individuals who have limited backgrounds.

UNIVERSITY PRE-SERVICE PROGRAMS

Planned programs of preparation directed toward the role of school personnel administrator have taken shape within the last decade. The design of the program at Ohio University is presented in Figure III. The program at the State University of New York at Buffalo follows the conception presented in Figure II. There, foundations and basic courses in education are followed by two core experiences, Phase I and Phase II. By Phase II, if not before, specialization in personnel is begun. Concomitantly, study is undertaken in the behavioral sciences and the humanities, as well

31

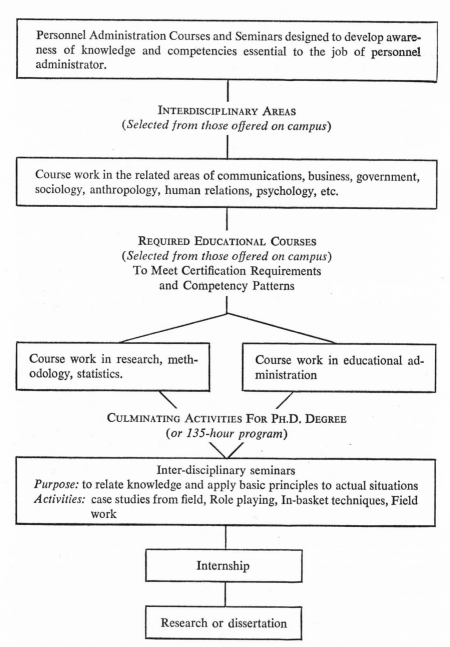

Figure III. *Schematic design for preparatory program for public school personnel administrator at Ohio University in 1968.*

as more advanced work in administration selected on the basis of a personnel program rationale. At about this point, the student may undertake an internship and upon completion of about 60 hours of planned graduate study he may take an oral examination and be recommended for state certification. Selected students go on to further study toward Ed.D. or Ph.D. and completion of a dissertation aimed at a contribution to the understanding of school personnel administration.

PREPARATION FOR PERSONNEL ROLE PERFORMANCE: IN-SERVICE

With the growing body of knowledge, particularly in the behavorial sciences, and with the accelerating rate of change in the nature and complexity of personnel tasks, the need for regular in-service preparatory activities increases. Again it seems both natural and desirable that these activities should be carried on cooperatively between universities and the profession which also represents the schools. In general, three types of mixtures seem likely: (1) activity of the profession with the cooperation of universities, (2) activity of universities with the cooperation of the profession, and (3) joint activities of both. The annual meeting of the American Association of School Personnel Administrators illustrates the first type of cooperation. It is probably accurate to say that many possibilities yet remain to be tried.

Professor La Verne Krantz of Ohio University has stressed the values of the practicum in which students are given opportunities to perform many of the tasks they will be expected to perform on the job, including data-processing experiences.

The second form of cooperation is illustrated by the Clinic Conference for School Personnel Administrators at the State Universiy of New York at Buffalo, begun in 1965 in association with the American Association of School Personnel Administrators. The Conference brochure states in part:

WHAT IS THE CONFERENCE ABOUT?

The Clinic Conference is an in-service education program for school personnel administrators. It is directed at areas of critical concern to the profession. The aim is to help the school personnel man understand his work better.

Often the personnel administrator comes to his position with personnel qualifications but with limited pre-service preparation. Because of rapid expansion of knowledge, the practitioner has to bring his ideas up to date from time to time.

Experience to date shows that the Conference can be particularly useful to:

1. The beginning school personnel administrator who wants to improve his understanding of his work.
2. The experienced school personnel administrator who wants to develop further understanding of his work.

Ideas that can help the personnel administrator come from many sources. The Conference draws upon three main sources:

1. Knowledge from the behavioral sciences.
2. Understandings from experienced practitioners.
3. Insights from other Conference participants.

Joint preparatory activities have not yet taken clear shape. It is reasonable to expect that as the Association and universities gain in experience appropriate preparatory activities will emerge.

CLINICAL INSTRUCTION

It would be a serious omission to close this chapter without reference to the importance of clinical instruction in a program of pre-service and in-service. In its medical origin, clinical instruction referred to that given at the bedside of a sick person. The meaning has been generalized to signify instruction conducted at the site of the events under consideration. Occasionally, the term is extended to include representations of the events through cases and simulation. The effectiveness of the latter has increased in recent years through electronic audiovisual aids such as films, recordings and television.

Direct clinical instruction normally takes place within a school system (cell 3 in Figure II) with a strong professional involvement. The clinical involvement may range from a brief and perhaps intermittent experience through a full year's experience to that of a longer period. The short, less involved type is variously referred to as a "practicum," "participant-observer role," and "clerkship." The full-year clinical experience in close association with decision making in the school is normally known as an "internship." Clinical experience of more than one year takes on some of the marks of "residency."

The practicum or participant-observer clinical study can be very useful in conjunction with university classes to help the student to develop a "feel" for the task and to help him to gain depth of insight. The internship is valuable both in developing further depth of insight through application and in providing opportunities to develop technical skills in contract interpretation, grievance processing, negotiations, legal considerations, interviewing, and many other tasks.

3 THE
PERSONNEL ADMINISTRATOR
AND THE
EDUCATIONAL PROCESS

GENERAL STATEMENT

In our country the public schools were established to meet educational needs of youth in a democratic society. The term "schools" includes not only buildings, facilities, and equipment but also curricula, experiences and activities, and school personnel. Of these elements, it is widely believed that most important in the educational process is the school staff—the teachers, supportive personnel and administrators. The validity of this belief has been illustrated many times in different ways. For example, a subject that a student finds boring during one semester can become a most interesting one the following semester with a different teacher. When graduates of a school get together and discuss their school experiences, they invariably talk about the personalities and the influences of particular teachers. But the schools and the school staff do not have exclusive control over the educational process. There are educative components, such as family, friends, home environment, religious institutions, and the mass media of radio, television, periodicals and newspapers. All have a great influence on the development of the young.

The school personnel administrator, whose job includes the selection of school staff and their in-service development, can have considerable influence on the education of youth. His influence is exercised in many different ways: in the standards and procedures used in the selection of personnel, in the nature and quality of the in-service staff-development program, in the efforts made to terminate the services of unsatisfactory personnel and to retain capable personnel, in his participation as a member of the superintendent's cabinet and in his discussions with other administrators in charge of curriculum, instruction, supplies and building.

In exercising an influence on the educative process, the school personnel administrator is not a free agent. His freedom of action is limited by the policy provisions of the board of education, by the instructions of the superintendent of schools, by the attitudes of other school administrators, and by the traditions and viewpoints of members of the community served by his school district. Available personnel and the training that his personnel have received in college also limit his actions, as do the concerns and opinions of the organized teaching profession and the broad educational movements and trends that may be in vogue.

The administrator cannot serve his school district effectively as a contributor to the educational process unless he has considerable knowledge of current trends in education and in related areas. It is not possible to apply techniques of personnel administration without reference to the educational and sociological climate in which people work.

Of course, it is essential for the school personnel administrator, as a professional educator, to have extensive knowledge of the educational process and to have a background in teaching and in school administration. The essential foundation for all school administrators includes the psychology of learning, principles of education, knowledge of the methodology of teaching, the process of education, methods of testing, and principles and methods of supervision and administration. Such knowledge is essential if he is to serve as a leader of other professionals engaged in the educational process. But such a background would be insufficient if he did not have an extensive orientation to current trends in sociology and in education on the local, state, national and international scenes.

CURRENT EDUCATIONAL AND SOCIAL TRENDS

The past fifteen years have seen many innovations and developments in education and in society. Some of them are considered here.

1. There has been a tremendous increase in the school population and in the numbers of students attending college. In 1940 there were 25,434,000 pupils enrolled in schools below the college level; in 1960 there were some 36,087,000 pupils; in 1966 there were about 43,655,000. The following table shows the changes from 1920 to 1969.[1]

TABLE 1
Public Elementary and Secondary Schools
Pupil Enrollment

1920	21,578,000	1962	36,253,000
1940	25,434,000	1964	41,025,000
1950	25,111,000	1966	42,849,900
1960	33,087,000	1967	43,886,805
		1968	44,961,662
		1969	45,618,578

The college population has also increased greatly since 1940, as evidenced by the figures for full-time attendance at four-year colleges:

36

1,494,000 in 1940; 3,216,000 in 1960; and 6,963,687 in 1967. The following table shows the changes from 1940 to 1967.[2]

TABLE 2
Institutions of Higher Education
Student Enrollment

1940	1,494,000	1964	5,320,294
1950	2,659,000	1966	6,438,477
1960	3,216,000	1967	6,963,687

The greatly increased number of students attending college requires changes in the curricula of public schools to meet different needs. The tremendous increase in students attending public schools below the college level also means adaptation of teaching methods and changes in the scheduling of students to provide for a wider range of interests and abilities.

2. Educational opportunities have been expanded to include pre-kindergarten children, adolescents beyond compulsory-education age, and adults who have special interests. There are more special programs and special courses than ever before. For example, there are special programs for dropouts, for retraining individuals whose skills are no longer required by industry, and for individuals who are seeking either to expand their skills for advancement in industry or to extend their knowledge for entrance into college. There are recreational courses for adults in music, art, photography, literature and a host of other subjects, and there are special courses for mothers and senior citizens. There are procedural questions about whether such programs should be administered by the board of education or by other agencies, and whether such programs should be set up in the public schools or in other neighborhood centers and facilities. For the school personnel administrator there are problems of recruiting, selecting and assigning the special personnel needed and problems of directing the in-service development of such personnel.

3. New curricular subjects have been introduced and significant changes have been made in traditional subjects. Driver education, sex education, motherhood training, and courses in Afro-American history are new courses that have been added to the curriculum of many schools. Substantial changes have been made in the content and in the methods of teaching such traditional subjects as mathematics, foreign languages and English.

4. Changes have taken place in curricular offerings, and in teaching methods, school organization and school plant. The use of paraprofessionals and teacher aides has enabled the professionally trained teacher to devote more time to planning effective group and individual instruction by diagnosing learning difficulties and prescribing individual drill or practice under the supervision of the paraprofessional. Team teaching has been expanded, and differentiated teaching has been introduced. Whereas, in team teaching,

37

all teachers function as equal professionals, the concept of differentiated teaching includes a master teacher or specially trained teacher who performs a vital function in the teaching process while other teachers with different preparation or skills perform other functions. Whenever differentiated teaching has implied different levels of teacher responsibility and performance and different pay scales, teacher organizations and others have had misgivings about the consequences. They are concerned that it could lead to "merit pay" schemes, which have been used to lower salary schedules and which can create animosities among the school staff.

School plants have also been modified to permit more flexible school organization, small group and individual instruction, and special programs. Clusters of schools, sometimes called educational parks, have been built. They often include elementary and secondary schools in the same geographic area. Special skill centers have been established for students seeking special help. Instructional programs have been established and located in storefronts, community houses and churches to meet the special needs of young people, particularly school dropouts in the inner cities.

5. There has been an unprecedented increase in guidance and counseling activities in the schools, accompanying the growth in knowledge of and interest in human behavior. For years there was much talk about individual needs and interests. Now more is being done about them. There is greater understanding of individual students and a greater effort to render individual assistance. Other specialized services have been increased in the movement to deal with students as individuals. These services include medical and dental attention, advisement by school psychologists, school social workers and community counselors, and provision for free lunches, as needed. The personnel needs in these educational and service areas must be met by the school personnel administrators.

6. This is a time of challenge to tradition, a time of innovation in education and social living. The past practices and procedures of the so-called establishment have become suspect merely because they have existed for a long time. Thus the school personnel administrator must examine his practices to see if they are meeting current needs, if they are justified in use or are merely outworn customs that are being repeated because of tradition and inertia.

7. National attention is being focused upon the inadequacy of the education of youth in the inner cities, in ghettos and in other disadvantaged pockets or communities where impoverished minority groups reside. Although there are undoubtedly many sociological and economic causes of the inadequacy of education for the children of the ghettos, one reason that has been cited is the lack of achievement expectation by teachers. The Coleman Report has indicated that pupils perform better when their teachers expect them to do so.[3] When teachers expect substandard performance, their pupils generally work poorly. School personnel administrators would do well to seek teachers who do not look down upon minority groups as hereditary underachievers. Joseph Monserrat has set a better goal, in saying:

"We function from the belief that no one knows the potential of any child until that child is given every opportunity to develop whatever ability he may have. We therefore set out to provide for each child the highest education possible." [4]

Although the schools cannot do the job alone, new ways must be found to solve the educational needs and to meet the aspirations of these youthful members of society. Dr. Harry N. Rivlin reports that "Many colleges and school systems now recognize the importance of preparing urban teachers more adequately for their responsibilities. According to the results of a survey conducted recently by the American Association of Colleges of Teacher Education, more than 200 institutions are either presently conducting programs specifically designed to prepare teachers for urban schools or are planning to introduce such programs." [5]

In an article entitled "Relevance and Pluralism in Curriculum Development," Edmund W. Gordon declares:

> "Much of the school's failure to open itself to changing values and freedom for individuality may be due to its failure to adequately recognize other aspects of the student's life which strongly affect his outlook and his own values." [6]

He goes on to point out the necessity of making instruction relevant to the real world in which every young person lives—or, as he puts it, to "break down the walls between the school and the rest of the community and invite the influences of the home, the neighborhood, the religious and ethnic groups, and even the wider world of politics, into the classroom." [7]

In the same article, Professor Gordon urges a pluralistic approach in education, rather than inclusive education. The latter may have token references to minority groups, or may even lead to reverse racism or chauvinism by dwelling in excessively compensatory fashion upon a hitherto neglected minority. Pluralistic education, on the other hand, "tries to give the student every broadening benefit of living in a society composed of individuals and groups from widely differing backgrounds and cultures." [8] By relating the needs of children of the inner cities to the teacher-training institutions and colleges and by establishing criteria for the selection and training of personnel to serve as teachers and principals in the inner cities, school personnel administrators can make a great contribution in this field.

8. This is a time of social revolution, a time of the surge of minority groups and of youth to seek a greater voice in determining their future in government, society, commerce and industry, in the labor movement, and in the school system. Youth is no longer content to play a passive role in the schools. Provision must be made for meaningful consultation in decision making by administrators and teachers on all levels of performance and administration, including personnel policies. The school personnel administrator must take cognizance of this social revolution in the development and application of his personnel practices.

9. As part of the social revolution of our times, there is the drive to

break down social barriers that separate groups and that limit the opportunities for any one group when compared to the opportunities afforded to other groups. The drive has revealed itself in the demands for greater integration of housing patterns and schools. In the schools, it has called for integration of both children and staff. A special task force put the matter this way: "Careful consideration of the evidence supports the conclusion reached by courts and educators more than ten years ago—that fully integrated education best prepared both minority and non-minority children for full participation in a society of opportunity and diversity." [9]

Another, seemingly opposite, manifestation of this drive to break down social barriers has been the demand for local control of education, or separatism, on the part of some representatives of the black minority. The movement often includes the demand that black teachers and black principals must be appointed to schools in which the student population consists mainly of black children. The school personnel administrator stands between the militant elements of society, who demand extensive and immediate reforms, and the most conservative elements of society, who resist any change. In this framework, the personnel administrator must move forward. But he can move forward only if he has full understanding of the varying sides and underlying motives. In an incisive address,[10] Mayor Richard G. Hatcher of Gary, Indiana, the first black mayor of a major city, describes the frustrated needs and aspirations of the black minority which led to the coining of the phrase "black power," which led to boycotts and to socially organized masses on the march, which led to demands for black separatism in independent "black towns" and which led to organized campaigns to assert political power. He asserts that he supports all forms of black power "which will help America to define itself, to recapture its heritage, to assert its ability, to realize its most immediate demands." He ends with a plea for an age of new humanity to arise in which no man, no matter what his religion, color or creed, may feel a stranger in our land.

Robert Bendiner, who devoted two years to studying various aspects of the decentralization or community-control movement, declared that although administrative decentralization might be desirable for a school district as large as New York City,

> "the extreme decentralization proposed for New York City's school districts would not only intensify segregation but remove from the city's central authority for education any lingering power to reduce such segregation in the foreseeable future. In that sense the movement toward smaller districts is a movement that would weaken the institution of the school board, perhaps fatally, in its role as the guarantor of equal educational opoprtunity." [11]

That, he indicates, is contrary to the national trend in which the total number of school boards has decreased from 106,000 in 1949 to 21,000 in 1969.

40

10. Technological advances have had a considerable impact on the schools. All kinds of audiovisual aids are available to teachers. There is programed instruction utilizing tapes and memory banks. Talking typewriters, language laboratories and special viewers are available. Computers and other data-processing machines are available for personnel activity and for student records. The modern school personnel administrator must be aware of these technological changes and resources and must capitalize upon them in personnel work for the advancement of the educational process.

11. Special funds have been made available by the federal government, by state governments, and by various foundations for special programs for the training of teachers and administrators. These opportunities should be taken by the school personnel administrator.

12. Recent years have seen tremendous growth in the strength and activities of teacher organizations. In the past, many teachers regarded themselves as individual practitioners making individual arrangements for their services. Almost all teachers now recognize the necessity of belonging to organizations on the state, and local level. The organized teaching profession has demanded and won considerable authority not only in matters affecting teacher welfare but in matters of school administration and policy as well. If the school personnel administrator is to effect the educational process, he must know how to work with, and direct the efforts of, the organized profession.

13. Our times have seen a tremendous expansion in the mass media of communication. Millions of inexpensive paperback books are published each year. Newspapers, movies, radio and television are within the easy reach of every person. The mass media are part of the educative process. Their impact must be understood and, to the extent feasible, should be utilized by the school personnel administrator.

14. Certification standards for teachers and school administrators have moved upward through the years. College graduation is a minimum requirement today in almost every state, and there are additional professional requirements for certification. A fifth year of college preparation for teachers is being required in an increasing number of states. There is a strong movement to require six years of preparation for administrative positions in the schools. The content and nature of the preparation for teaching and school administration are constantly being reviewed by state authorities and by colleges and universities. The school personnel administrator should be expected to have an influence on these changes

CURRENT ECONOMIC, TECHNOLOGICAL AND POLITICAL TRENDS

In addition to the foregoing educational and social trends, there are economic, technological and political movements on the national and world scene that have an impact on education and that, therefore, should be recognized and understood by the school personnel administrator if he is to have a proper influence on the educational process. We can mention some of the trends here.

1. Our federal government has become more directly concerned with the welfare of individual citizens. Its concern has been manifested by the expanded social security benefits of medical aid, hospitalization, and care of of the aged, and by the provision of extensive funds for special educational programs and for the training of school staff. The following table shows the increase in allotments of federal funds to education in recent years.[12]

TABLE 3

Federal Funds for Education and Related Activities: 1960–1969

1960	$3,802,000,000	1965	$ 7,674,300,000
1962	4,657,500,000	1966	10,583,500,000
1963	5,232,400,000	1967	12,198,200,000
1964	5,831,400,000	1969	11,265,300,000

2. The trend toward industrialization in our society has continued and the movement of our population from agricultural areas to urban areas has continued, along with an acceleration of the movement of black agricultural workers from the South to northern industrial cities. New machinery has replaced workers who now find that they are not only unemployed but also unemployable unless they receive further training.

3. Specialization of all types has increased, including the specialization of individuals in science, mechanics, law, dentistry, medicine, labor, and business.

4. The scientific revolution has continued at a rapid pace in all branches of science. Man's understanding and achievements have increased in biology, chemistry, physics and medicine. The life span of mankind has been extended; productivity has increased; knowledge has increased; the ability of mankind to combat pestilence, famine and other life hazards has increased.

5. The revolution in communication and travel has been accelerated; the barrier of distance has been broken. Huge aircraft and ships are constantly establishing new records in speed, comfort and safety. Man's knowledge of space and his ability to explore it are part of this revolution. Communication is almost instantaneous around the world.

6. Newly organized or liberated nations have joined the community of the world as sovereign states. These new nations provide new horizons for trade, for education, for human interaction and for human progress.

7. There has been steady growth in prosperity and economic opportunity within this country. The past few years have shown an impressive growth in the productivity and earning power of our people. Prosperity and economic growth have also been achieved widely in other countries of

42

the world. The following tables show the growth in gross national (United States) product from 1950 to 1969 and the growth in personal income in the same years.[13]

TABLE 4

Gross National Product and Personal Income
(In millions of dollars)

	1950	1955	1960	1965	1969
Gross National Product	284,769	397,960	503,734	684,884	931,403
Personal Income	227,619	310,889	400,953	538,893	748,874

8. Prosperity has brought with it inflationary trends which governments have sought to control but which pose a constant national and international problem.

9. There has been a continued growth in population in this country and throughout the world. National and international efforts have been made to control the population growth. A controversial subject with religious overtones, the attempt at control is part of the current scene. The following table shows the population increase in the United States since 1890.

TABLE 5

United States Population (Official Census)

1890	62,947,719	1940	131,669,275
1900	75,994,575	1950	150,697,361
1910	91,972,266	1960	179,323,175
1920	105,710,620	1970	204,766,770
1930	122,775,046		

10. Through the United Nations and other organizations of states, efforts have been made to improve the economic and social conditions of people in disadvantaged areas of the world.

11. Along with the trend toward international cooperation has come a resurgence of nationalism, as evidenced by the establishment of many newly independent countries in Africa and Asia and by the demonstrated determination of such European countries as Yugoslavia and Czechoslovakia to maintain national independence.

THE IMPACT OF CURRENT TRENDS UPON THE EDUCATIONAL PROCESS

William Van Till examines the evolution of the United States and sees an acceleration of the following trends: development of science and technology, urbanization, civil rights revolution, growth of the economy and leisure time, pockets of poverty amidst plenty, flourishing of bureaucracies.[14] Van Till further observes that the great danger of these trends is that they

43

will develop a "powerless man in a powerful society," one who will lose his ability at independent rational thinking to become a cog in a machine.

Considering the National Education Association's *Education in a Changing Society,* Richard I. Miller describes "seven tasks facing public education—tasks rooted in educational values and social forces and trends" [15]:

1. Coping with the knowledge explosion.
2. Developing rational thinking.
3. Teaching controversial issues.
4. Developing social responsibility.
5. Building international competence.
6. Focusing on the individual.
7. Maintaining integrity and courage.

Van Till also suggests four questions in a self-evaluative effort: [16]

1. Does the school program now make a significant contribution to the development of such democratic values as reflective thinking, the worth of the individual and the common welfare?
2. Does the school program now make a significant contribution to illuminating the social realities which characterize our times?
3. Does the school program now represent the best we know of how people learn?
4. Does the school program make a significant contribution to meeting the personal and social needs of American children and youth?

He concludes by remarking that educators face the choice of merely "accepting and reflecting" trends and forces or analyzing them and exercising leadership in pointing out constructive paths.

Ole Sand, writing about bases for decisions in education, summarizes his views: ". . . for questions concerning 'what to teach,' one looks to values, objectives, social forces and trends. . . . For questions concerning 'how' and 'when,' one turns to psychology. . . . The organized fields of knowledge serve as the key sources of data for the 'how' and 'when' dimensions." [17]

A joint committee of the American Association of School Administrators and the Association for Supervision and Curriculum Development described the needs of the teaching staff in a changing society as follows:

> The assumption that underlies this whole report is that classroom teachers and all staff members in a school system of whatever size need support and stimulation, their growth and competency and vision need nourishment and their awareness of responsibility for change needs sharpening.[18]

HOW THE SCHOOL PERSONNEL ADMINISTRATOR
CAN INFLUENCE THE EDUCATIONAL PROCESS

1. *Selection of school personnel.* The standards that the school personnel director utilizes and his procedures in recruiting and selecting teachers, administrators and supporting personnel have a prime influence on the educational process. If his goal is to select personnel whose horizons are limited, who avoid innovations or innovative thinking, who regard schools as insulated from society and not as dynamic parts of it, and who are not likely to be responsive to the indicated needs of youth in today's society, then his influence will not show an awareness of the needs of the times.

2. *Relationship to teacher-education institutions.* The school personnel administrator is in a position to describe to the authorities of the teacher-education institutions the personnel needs of his school system in terms of the training, background and attitudes required of the teachers and principals he seeks to employ. He is also in a position to make specific suggestions about curricula in teacher education. His suggestions must be made in a framework of knowledge both of the principles of good teaching and of the educational needs of today's society

3. *Relationship with organizations of teachers.* A school personnel administrator who is not aware of current trends in education and in society will find himself in a position of merely resisting the efforts and aspirations of teacher organizations. On the other hand, the administrator who has an understanding of current trends will be in a better position to utilize the energies and resources of teacher organizations and to help make them constructive forces in the school district.

4. *As a member of the cabinet of the superintendent of schools.* In many school districts, the superintendent holds regular meetings with his cabinet and the personnel administrator is usually a member of such a cabinet. At cabinet meetings, there is discussion of personnel policies, curricula, school facilities, relationships with the community, and a host of other problems. The school personnel administrator who is aware of current trends is in a better position, as a member of the cabinet, to exercise a constructive influence on school personnel and in related areas.

5. *Relationship with other school administrators.* The personnel administrator on many occasions meets with other school administrators in situations other than as a member of the superintendent's cabinet. He may meet with the administrator in charge of industrial affairs to discuss the personnel needs of a new program. He may meet with the administrator of school supplies and equipment to discuss a plan for in-service training of staff in the use of new equipment.

6. *Relationship with teachers in the field.* The school personnel administrator frequently meets with individual teachers, with committees of

45

teachers, with individual principals and with committees of field administrators. There may be consultations over such matters as grievance procedures, transfer procedures, leaves of absence, needs for special time allowances, and staff-development programs. The school personnel administrator's decisions and advice will be much wiser if based upon an understanding of current movements in education.

4 THE PERSONNEL ADMINISTRATOR'S OFFICE AND STAFF

GENERAL STATEMENT

The school personnel administrator should organize and operate his office in a manner that will reflect efficiency and show concern for the persons being served. The personnel policies of the board of education and the superintendent of schools must be administered in a manner that will earn the confidence and respect of the staff and community for the personnel office. This goes far beyond and is more difficult to accomplish than the development of an organization that is simply efficient.

The very fact that the job responsibility of the personnel administrator is multifaceted calls for an office organization that is capable of handling a variety of assignments well. To form such an organization, the administrator must first consider a number of questions:

1. What responsibilities have been assigned to the personnel office?
2. What organizational plan should be developed to care for those responsibilities?
3. What should be the function of each area and position in the organizational plan?
4. What kind of people should be employed to work in the office?
5. How should the paper work flow through the office?
6. What office forms are needed?
7. How should intra-office communication and exterior information be handled?
8. What facilities and space should be provided?
9. What special equipment would be useful?
10. To what extent can automated data processing be used?

Answers to the foregoing questions form the basis for organizing the office of the school personnel administrator. It is hoped that the following

47

presentation may also serve to challenge the personnel administrator to take a good look at his present organization. He certainly needs:

1. To determine whether or not the design of his present operational plan effectively handles the responsibilities assigned to his office.
2. To reexamine the flow of work through the office with the thought of improving the system.
3. To stimulate the staff to reexamine existing facilities and to suggest desirable improvements.
4. To be conscious of the need for maintaining friendly contacts with applicants and staff members.
5. To maintain cooperative working relationships with other organizations.
6. To have a great concern for the adequacy and safety of the personnel records.
7. To determine whether he, as a school personnel administrator, is setting a proper tone of efficiency and good personal relationships; for the example he sets by his actions may be more persuasive than words.

DUTIES AND RESPONSIBILITIES

There appears to be no fixed table of responsibilities that should be assigned to every school personnel office. Each office must be organized on an individual basis to perform the activities assigned to it. The size of the school system to be served, the relation of the school department to other municipal or governmental agencies and departments, the place that the personnel office holds in relation to other departments in the school system, and the amount of authority that is delegated to the personnel office all have marked influence on the number and types of responsibilities assigned to the personnel office. Thus the first step in setting up or in appraising the effectiveness of the personnel office is establishing its duties and responsibilities.

1. Recruiting, selecting, transferring and assigning staff members.
2. Maintaining a screening procedure for the formulation of employment and promotional lists.
3. Determining the certification status of instructional staff members.
4. Determining the placement of each staff member in his appropriate position on the applicable salary schedule.
5. Maintaining adequate and accurate personal records of all staff members.
6. Processing payrolls for all staff members as well as certifying overtime pay and pay for sundry services.
7. Issuing checks on dates set on a prearranged schedule.
8. Maintaining accurate records of absence, sickness, vacation, and other leaves for payroll application.

9. Supplying financial and employment information to other municipal agencies—auditing division, budget director, retirement system.
10. Administering a program of physical examination for staff members.
11. Assisting in the organization of staff-improvement programs for both certified and non-certified personnel.
12. Forwarding statistical information to the data center for its use in meeting requests for such information.
13. Maintaining a counseling service for individuals with special problems.
14. Cooperating closely with professional organizations through consultant and committee service and through participation in conferences and discussion groups.
15. Conducting an orientation program for new teachers.
16. Maintaining a service designed to supply substitute teachers when needed.
17. Assisting in teacher-negotiation conferences and in implementing agreements, such as grievance procedures, after they have been accepted.
18. Developing job descriptions for positions.
19. Maintaining a position-control system in order to stay within budgetary limits.
20. Participating in staff promotional procedures.
21. Providing for the evaluation of staff performance.
22. Conducting terminal interviews.
23. Administering "fringe benefit" programs.

It is doubtful that all of the above activities would be assigned to one personnel office, but it is a possibility. Most of them, and perhaps one or two unmentioned items, are assigned to all personnel offices. The two variables are the number and variety of duties and the volume of work. Volume is more directly related to the size of the school system than are duties and responsibilities, and it can often be cared for by an increase of staff. It is important to design an office organization which can efficiently care for the responsibilities assigned to it and at the same time be structured so as to allow for expansion.

DETERMINING THE ORGANIZATION OF THE OFFICE

The next step, after the duties and responsibilities have been listed, is to determine which ones should be grouped together for assignment to a single unit or person and what skills are needed by the person or unit performing the duties. For example, staff-improvement activities include a number of related duties, such as staff orientation, in-service training and special workshops. Staff recruitment, selection and assignment might also

49

be a natural grouping of duties to be performed by a single unit or person. It might be desirable to separate the administration of certificated personnel from that of noncertificated or classified personnel, if the problems are substantially different. A determination must also be made about the knowledge and skills required of the person or unit charged with performing the combined duties. For example, the abilities of the staff recruitment and selection person would be different from those of the individual responsible for arranging staff in-service activities or from those of the individual responsible for maintaining payroll records.

The intricacy and size of the office organization must, of course, depend upon the number and kinds of responsibilities assigned to it as well as the size and complexity of the school system it is to serve. The following general principles should be observed regardless of size.

1. The organization must be such that routine matters flow smoothly through the necessary processing procedure.
2. The organization must be flexible enough to care for peak loads and exceptional requests.
3. Each member of the organization should be assigned a specific responsibility, but at the same time he should have knowledge of duties and responsibilities assigned to at least one other staff member so that he can assist in emergencies.
4. Each individual should be assigned to the work station which would make the best use of his talents.
5. An organizational chart should be developed to indicate lines of authority and functions of various sections of the organization.
6. Each member of the organization should have sufficient knowledge of the duties and responsibilities of other staff members so as to be able to ask intelligent questions of the proper person. A work-flow chart should be made available.

The scope of the personnel office's activities is so varied and is basically so involved in the success of other divisions of the school system that its administration seems to demand a high-ranking official who reports directly to the superintendent of the school district. So important is personnel direction, and so essential is it for the superintendent to be in close and direct touch with staff personnel problems and attitudes, that there should be no intermediary between the head of the division of staff personnel and the superintendent.

The organizational chart in Table 1 depicts a proposed plan for a large personnel office which is charged with conducting written teacher examinations, scoring interviews and preparing graded lists of persons eligible for assignment. The chart indicates areas of operation under two coordinators and one director. The organization suggested can readily be revised to allow for any expansion or contraction that may be desired, depending upon the size of the system, the volume of work and the variety of duties of the personnel office.

50

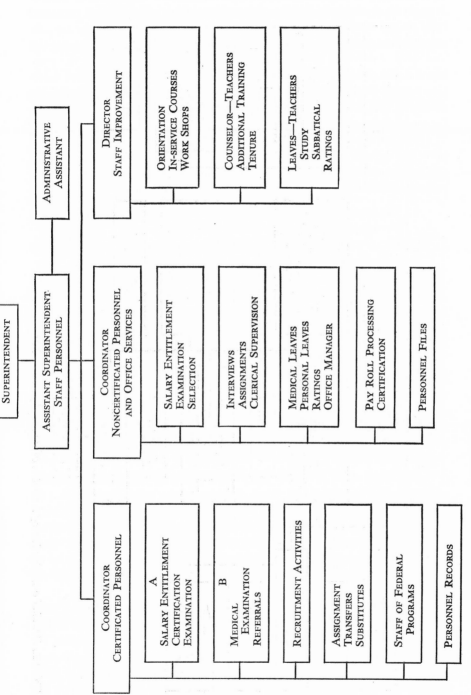

Table 1. *Organization of a school personnel office.*

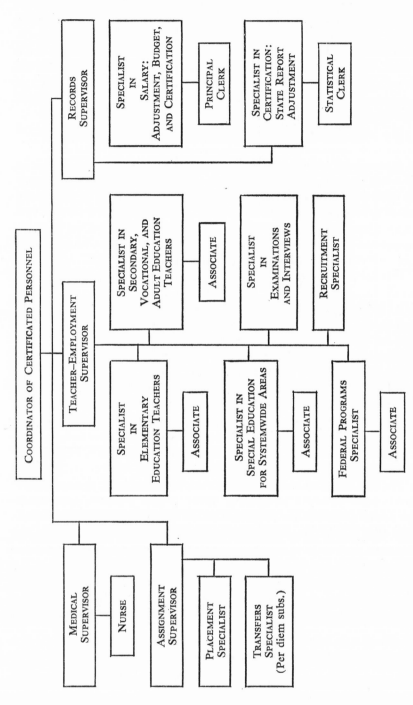

Table 2. *Detailed organization of a section of a school personnel office.*

The chart obviously does not indicate how many people are required to staff such an organization comfortably, and it would be incorrect to assume that the responsibilities assigned to each block should be cared for by identical classifications of staff members. For example, in referring to the organizational chart, one can assume that area B can be adequately cared for by a small number of professional staff members who have clerical assistance. That is not true of block A, because it involves examination of applications for teaching positions—evaluation of reference and previous experience and of scholastic preparation.

In a large system, a number of specialists would be needed to care for applicants for specific teaching areas, and each of these specialists might need professional assistants. The size of staff, of course, would vary with the services required, but as the functions of school personnel offices become more uniform in school districts of similar size, there should be established some acceptable ratio of personnel staff to employees. At the present time there are great variations. An informal inquiry revealed situations in which there was one clerk for 1,400 employees in one school district, while another school district had one clerk for every 450 employees.

It is helpful to examine in detail a possible organizational plan (Table 2) for the section supervised by the coordinator of certified personnel (which includes block A of Table 1).

It should be noted that the detailed chart suggests titles (which may be varied) to be used for various positions. In most large offices, there are more than one grade of supervisor and various grades of other titles which provides some flexibility for assigning salary grades and responsibilities to the indicated positions.

An associate in the city to which the chart refers is a professional staff member assigned, on a full year basis, to assist a specialist to carry the work load of his area. On the chart, associates have not been assigned where it is assumed that competent secretarial-clerical staff members might be of sufficient assistance. The associate could be a teacher assigned to this position. For staff recruitment, all specialists might be involved, as well as professional staff members from other areas of the school system. Such supplemental assistants are not shown on the chart. A sufficient secretarial-clerical staff should also be available, assigned either as secretaries to the professional staff or as members of a secretarial pool administered by the office manager.

Detailed patterns of organization and duties must, of course, be developed for each area of operation; when that has been completed, the whole proposed structure must then be reviewed, with the following questions in mind:

1. Have proper titles been assigned to the positions?
2. Do positions with comparable responsibilities have the same title or pay scale?

53

3. Does the leader of each work area have sufficient assistance to carry the work load involved?

The determination of relative degrees of responsibility can be made only after a study of the job descriptions, which should be prepared for each position in the personnel office. Every staff member should have, in writing, an outline of what is expected of him, even though it is a simple desk routine.

A sample job description for a specialist in elementary school personnel work follows.

TABLE 3

Job Description for Specialist in
Elementary School Personnel

I. *Function*

Under the direction of the supervisor of teacher employment, the administrator is to be responsible for the personnel services for the elementary school staff and to serve as a resource person in giving personnel information.

II. *Duties*

1. Assists in recruiting and interviewing candidates for positions in the school system.
2. Reviews applications and transcripts for the purpose of determining the eligibility of candidates for admission to the written examination.
3. Assists in the administration of the written examination and the personal interview.
4. Verifies references and evaluates the educational records and previous experience of candidates for the purpose of determining placement on the salary scale.
5. Serves as a counselor to educational employees having specific problems.
6. Carries out such other duties as may be assigned.

An illustration of a desk-responsibility outline follows.

TABLE 4

Desk-Responsibility Outline for
Application Clerk

A. Receive all requests for applications.
   1. All requests must be stamped with date of receipt.
   2. Send acknowledgment letter, application, brochure and salary schedule.
   3. Retain request letter, filing alphabetically. When application is received, request letter and acknowledgment should be filed with the application. If specific information is requested send letter to specialist concerned.
B. Receive all completed applications.
   1. Date receipt of application.
   2. Send acknowledgment letter.
   3. Complete log card, showing where application has been routed (elementary, secondary, special). If transcript is enclosed, it should be kept with the application and logged on card.
C. Receive all transcripts.

54

1. Stamp date of receipt on transcript—all transcripts must be stamped before any further action is taken.
2. Log receipt of transcripts, using same card as that used for application.
3. File transcript with application if it is available.
4. Trace application and route transcript accordingly (elementary, secondary or special).
5. If there is no record of an application, the transcript should be filed in the transcript file pending receipt of more information.

    There should be *one* file in alphabetical order for all transcripts that are not placed with applications.

    If the application has been forwarded to the subject area for review, and the transcript is received in the meantime, the specialist's desk must be sure that the transcript is promptly filed with the application. Return the transcript to the central transcript file if the application is not available.

The above procedure should facilitate prompt response to all inquiries about action taken on applications and transcripts.

FUNCTIONS OF EACH AREA AND POSITION SHOWN ON THE SAMPLE ORGANIZATIONAL CHART

Assistant superintendent: overall direction and long-range planning of the personnel program. Serves as liaison in personnel matters within the system as well as with outside agencies, as required.

Administrative assistant: assists the assistant superintendent in caring for many items of a non-routine nature that are referred to personnel.

Coordinator of certificated personnel: coordinates and supervises the work of all areas assigned to him, including:
1. Recruitment, selection, assignment and transfer of teachers;
2. Keeping of adequate records involving personal items as well as training and experience;
3. Supervision of medical services;
4. Provision for counseling staff members who have personal problems, when needed or requested;
5. Salary and certification status of professional staff members.

Coordinator of noncertificated personnel and office services: coordinates and supervises the work of all areas assigned to him, including:
1. Recruiting, selecting and assigning noncertificated staff members;
2. Providing counseling for members of the staff, when needed or requested;
3. Approving all leaves of absence caused by illness or personal business;
4. Periodically obtaining efficiency ratings of employees;
5. Supervising the office staff of the personnel division;
6. Supervising the secretarial-clerical staff in the schools;
7. Supervising the payroll operation;

55

8. Maintaining adequate records of attendance and personal files for all employees.

Director of staff improvement: assumes the responsibility for the coordination and supervision of all programs tending to improve staff performance. Shows leadership in creating and developing such programs. Confers with persons requesting study or sabbatical leaves and with those who need specific courses to complete certification or to obtain tenure. Works closely and cooperatively with the instructional and business divisions in designing and conducting activities to meet evident needs of both educational and classified personnel. Periodically obtains performance ratings of staff members and counsels those who need improvement.

Supervisor of teacher employment: reviews the work of the specialists who interview and process the applicants for teaching positions. Considers appeals on salary placement or examination scores.

Specialist: examines each application in detail for training and experience and determines the certification status of the applicant as well as his placement on the existing salary schedule. The specialist also assists in recruitment and in conducting structured interviews (formal interviews for which questions are prepared in advance and at which formal rating scales are used). One specialist is charged with conducting teacher examinations and interviews. Using the score obtained from these two sources, he prepares graded lists of the persons who are eligible for appointment. The appointing officer then selects someone from the appropriate list to fill a vacancy. The specialist also conducts examinations and interviews and prepares graded lists for promotional purposes. The appointing officer acts within policy in selecting a person from a list. In many systems, the selection for any vacancy is limited to one of the first three or five names.

Associate: assists a specialist; paid at the teacher-salary level. The area of responsibility matches that of the specialist to whom he is assigned. His salary should be adjusted for service beyond the teaching year since many staff members assigned to the personnel office have a busy summer.

Medical supervisor: approves the physical conditions of applicants for employment. In many systems, each employee must pass a physical examination, usually administered in one of two ways, before employment. Either the applicant goes to the doctor of his choice and submits his doctor's report to the medical supervisor, or the school system provides examination facilities for those who care to submit to an examination by the medical supervisor. In either case he must approve the applicant for employment. In some places, a tuberculosis test or an X ray is required annually. All such reports are referred to the medical supervisor.

Assignment supervisor: supervises the placement of new teachers, approves and implements transfer requests, and provides per diem substitutes when needed.

The assignment of teachers is an involved procedure and the assigning officer must take many factors into consideration. Among them are the following: the degree to which the educational preparation and experience

56

of the applicant meets the needs of the vacancy, the acceptability of the applicant to the principal of the school, the degree to which the applicant would fit into the school community, and the attitude of the applicant with regard to the location of the school. When the assignment of teachers is made the responsibility of the personnel office, the advice of subject supervisors who have interviewed the applicants is of great assistance. Additional assistance is needed when assignments and transfers are made for the fall semester.

The assistance needed in supplying per diem substitutes depends upon the office plan to handle requests for assistance. Generally, such detail can be handled by a competent clerical staff working under guidance.

The responsibilities of the supervisor of assignments probably justify a high salary classification. In some school districts, the assignment to teaching positions is made by the educational division concerned. Whichever plan is followed—assignment by personnel or by educational division—the procedure for processing employment authorization is not much affected.

Records supervisor: keeps accurate records of all experience and training acquired by employees before employment and while employed. Changes in training and status affect the salary and certification of an employee. The supervisor must see that this information is constantly updated and relayed to the data processing center so that, at budget time, the information obtained from the center is accurate.

The state department must also be kept informed of changes in the certification and salary status of each employee so that the proper amount of state financial aid may be forwarded to all school districts.

Statistical records—such as how many per diem substitutes are used and for what purpose, how much sick leave is used, how many personal business leave days are used, and the extent to which sabbatical leave is used—are compiled for easy reference.

SELECTION OF STAFF FOR THE PERSONNEL OFFICE

Persons selected must not only meet the necessary physical and educational requirements but also possess designated technical ability and a high degree of emotional stability.

Job descriptions should be prepared for all positions in the office of the personnel administrator. Descriptions should indicate the over-all function of the position, the supervising officer, an outline of the duties, and the training and experience required.

A number of persons will be found to meet the specifications outlined, but the real task of selection then begins; for the qualities necessary to provide the proper atmosphere in the personnel office go beyond the written job description. To function in a personnel office successfully, the staff must be able to work cooperatively with each other, to absorb criticism—justified as well as unjustified—by disgruntled persons without losing poise, and to be adaptive in assisting persons with problems; key members of the staff must be willing to make themselves available to serve beyond normal hours.

A sympathetic personality, ethical responsibility, good judgment, and a high sense of integrity to maintain principles in the face of outside pressures are also required.

A personnel office which is able to form a staff of people who are honest in their dealings with other staff members, helpful in conferences, firm but just in their interpretations of rules and policies, sympathetic in listening to the problems brought to them, and truly concerned with the feelings of staff members toward the school system and the personnel office will be able to inspire a feeling of trust and respect for the office on the part of employees and the public. A personnel office must earn this attitude.

The creation of such an attitude involves the entire office staff. Frequently, the clerks determine the reputation of the personnel office because they receive the brunt of complaints or demands. These office workers need the full support of every member of the office staff and should be congratulated when they handle difficult calls with propriety, courtesy and good judgment.

THE FLOW OF PAPER WORK THROUGH THE OFFICE

The efficient operation of a plan for handling paper work in an office requires that the staff know the reasons for each step to be taken. If an employee knows the reason for the activity assigned to his desk, his sense of responsibility for the accurate performance of his task is likely to be increased, which certainly tends to promote efficiency in the office.

Flow charts can be prepared that diagram, for each staff member involved, the place of his responsibility in relation to other members working closely with him. The sample chart shown in Table 5 depicts in graphic form the path an application for a teaching position follows until it reaches the permanent file of folders prepared for each professional staff member.

It has been found that the act of constructing such a chart is extremely helpful to the person charged with the design of office procedure. The very act of setting up a proposed procedure in diagrammatic form brings clearly to the attention of the designer any small items that could impede the process. The foresight thus provided and acted upon can save hours of confusion and correction later on.

The flow chart presented here does not represent an actual situation, but it may be used to point out some important operations in a large personnel office.

1. It is important to acknowledge the receipt of an application and to set up a card file to indicate that it has been received.
2. The specialist, after studying the application and the submitted transcript, determines the certification status of the candidate. Applications of fully certified persons are then sent to the examination section for further processing.

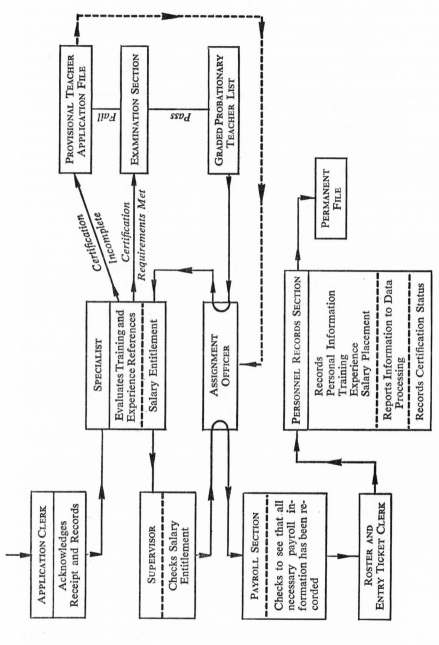

Table 5. *Flow chart of teacher applications and employment-record processing.*

3. Responsibilities assigned to the examination section vary according to the requirements of the school system, but some of them are:
   a. Conducting a written examination, if it is desired;
   b. Conducting a structured interview;
   c. Preparing lists of teachers who are eligible for probationary assignment.
4. The assignment officer then selects a name from the probationary teacher list prepared by the examination section and refers the proposed assignment to the appropriate specialist for salary entitlement. After it is checked by the supervisor, the application is sent back to the assignment officer, who then makes a firm offer of salary and school placement to the applicant. (There may be times when the specialist, in conference with the applicant, sets the salary before the assignment officer makes his decision, which shortens the procedure somewhat.) The dotted line in Figure 5 indicates that the assignment officer may take names from the provisional file if no appropriate graded probationary teacher list exists.
5. The remainder of the procedure follows a similar pattern in many personnel offices. If additional functions are assigned to the personnel office, they can be added to the flow chart.

No flow chart can possibly show all the small items that make up the entire office operation, and certainly none can give a person complete knowledge of the amount of paper work demanded of the personnel office.

OFFICE FORMS NEEDED

For recruitment:
1. Application form. Sample forms used by various school systems may be obtained from them upon request. From these samples, one may be designed to fit a particular situation. Some personnel administrators have suggested the development of a standard application form, and it would facilitate processing by placement offices and applicants would find it easy to use when applying to different districts.
2. Salary schedule. A brief outline of the prevailing salary program should accompany the application form.
3. Recruitment posters for use on bulletin boards.
4. A pamphlet giving desired information about the local school system and its community.
5. Form letters for responding to inquiries about positions. A personal note is preferable.

For employment:
1. A reference request (to be sent to persons whose names have been submitted by the applicant).
2. A contract (to accompany the letter offering a position).

3. A form authorizing employment (to be submitted by the assignment officer). This important document can be used for providing an original record of the date, level and nature of the assignment and for providing essential data for transfer to data processing. An entry authorization (Figure 6), discussed later in this chapter, is used as the authority to employ educational staff members.
4. An entry ticket (containing name, address, marital status, sex, school to which assigned, social security number, salary).
5. Withholding certificates for income tax deduction.
6. If appointments are made by the assignment officer in the personnel office, a form indicating the kinds and number of vacancies to be filled must be prepared for office use by the area of the school system to be served. This form should contain all information needed by the assignment officer and should be forwarded to him for appropriate action.
7. A detailed information blank (to be completed by the applicant and forwarded to the state department of education for certification).
8. A physical examination form (to be completed and forwarded to the supervisor of medical services).

For active file records:
1. Forms on which to record attendance and leaves.
2. Forms on which to record personal information (educational training, previous experience, degree and certification status, salary placement, courses taken after employment, etc.) It is suggested that this form be kept in duplicate. The original should never be allowed to leave the personnel office. The duplicate may be loaned if a tracer card is substituted for it.
3. Forms on which to record progress reports on probationary teachers.
4. Forms on which periodically to record the ratings of employees. The forms should be designed to provide for comments on areas of competence and weakness so that employees may be counseled. When a rating sheet is sent to the personnel office, it should bear the initials of the person being rated in order to indicate that he has seen the document, which prevents unpleasant situations from arising when an individual disclaims knowledge of his rating.
5. Forms on which to record the results of structured interviews.
6. Forms to be filled out by principal and supervisor when teachers resign. They may show the ratings each of these persons has given to the teacher and should include the question, Would you reemploy this teacher? Similar forms should be developed for noncertificated staff.
7. A number of cards to be used for recording receipt of an application and where filed, for maintaining an alphabetical list of all employees, and for recording the service record of per diem substitutes.

8. Forms to be used by staff members applying for leaves of absence, salary increments, etc.

For updating records:

1. Any change in the personal information or professional status of a staff member must be reported to all local and state offices concerned. That can be accomplished through the use of tickets prepared in packs with carbon inserted, the number of tickets in each pack to be determined by the number of duplicate copies needed. In addition to the staff member and his immediate superior, copies should be sent to the payroll bureau, the pension system office, the city auditor, the research division, and the head of the division to which the person is assigned. A copy should also be placed in the office record file of the person concerned.

Four types of tickets should be prepared:

Entry ticket;

Change ticket: to be used for changes in status, salary, name, address, etc.;

Transfer ticket: to be used when a staff member is moved from one school or office to another, which might involve a change in payroll number whereas a change ticket would not;

Cutoff ticket: to be used when a person is to be removed from the payroll. It should show the reason for leaving: retirement, death, discharge, resignation. If resignation, some reason should be given.

2. A form should be provided to acquaint the state office of education and the research division with changes that occur in educational status. Advanced degrees and changes in certification should be reported on a regular basis.

Conveyance of Information and Responses to Inquiries

The procedure for handling statistical information has been mentioned previously. The accurate compilation and transmission of such information is a vital part of the personnel operation. The establishment of good rapport commences when a person requests information about a school district. If the request comes by mail, the office should not be content simply to mail an application form and recruitment information. A letter expressing interest in the individual's request and thanking him for his inquiry should accompany the material sent.

If an interview is held on a college campus or away from the office, a letter should be sent to the interviewed person expressing pleasure in his interest and offering any further service that might be desired. The receipt of an application should be acknowledged by a personal letter informing the applicant of further processing information that might be required. A warm-toned letter should be sent to an applicant who is about to be employed. It should accompany the contract and should provide information regarding the person's assignment. During the school year, letters of inquiry from staff members should be answered as promptly and completely as possible. It is also good policy to invite further questions or to suggest an interview if the matter has not been fully cleared.

It is of prime importance that items which affect the entire staff, such as those which follow, should receive special attention in order to insure thorough staff coverage.

1. The general personnel policies of the board of school commissioners should be incorporated in their book of rules and made easily available to all staff members.
2. The personnel office should prepare a handbook, for the use of its office staff, on how the rules should be interpreted and implemented.
3. If a rule requires interpretation or its implementation needs description, such information should be made available to the entire staff.
4. Changes in rules or their interpretation should be made known to the staff as soon as the changes occur.

FACILITIES AND SPATIAL REQUIREMENTS OF THE PERSONNEL OFFICE

Location of the personnel office. The office should be located in the general administrative office of the school district. That section of the office which interviews applicants for positions must be easily accessible to those applicants (both professional and nonprofessional). The section which cares for the personnel records should be easily accessible to the personnel staff and the staff of other educational divisions which have need of such records. If personnel offices are decentralized for various administrative purposes, records must nevertheless be maintained in accordance with criteria set down.

Design of the personnel office. The office should be of such area and design as to allow for the following:

1. Reception areas for applicants and persons who have appointments with personnel officers
2. Individual offices for personnel officers who may be called upon to talk privately with persons who came to see them. Such offices should be so designed to prevent private conversations from being heard by persons outside the office.
3. If a private secretary is assigned to an officer, a work-space in close proximity should be provided.
4. A fireproof room with bank-vault type doors, to be closed each night. The room should be large enough to house all personnel records and should allow space for the desks of the head file clerk and assistants. It would afford needed protection of records from fire and vandalism.
5. A room for the assembling of materials for distribution and the housing of special office equipment.

6. A medical suite with provision for examination of applicants and a reclining area for employees who may become ill during the day.
7. A room containing lockers for the use of staff members.
8. Offices should be made attractive and should convey a feeling of courtesy, since much of the office personnel's time is devoted to personal interviews with members of the staff and general public.
9. Ample lighting, ventilation and air conditioning.
10. Adequate facilities for lunch.
11. Drinking water and adequate lavatories, conveniently located.
12. Ample elevator service.

SPECIAL EQUIPMENT NEEDED

1. Microfilming equipment to microfilm all inactive personnel records over three years old. Filing space becomes a real problem when staff turnover and acquisition are large each year.
2. A microfilm reader. It is necessary that a file of the microfilmed records be kept in the personnel office and that a combination microfilm reader and printer be provided for the use of the staff.
3. A machine to reproduce letters or other documents saves much of a secretary's time and eliminates possible transcription errors.
4. A machine to stamp the date and time of receipt of all correspondence coming into the office is of great value in preventing unpleasant situations.
5. If per diem substitutes are to be assigned daily by the personnel office, a recording tape system should be used. Calls for the assignment of substitutes could be made during the evening hours and dealt with early next morning from the tape recording. Dial-a-card or other automatic dialing should be a part of the telephone equipment.
6. The installation of a modern method of filing is desirable.
7. Automatic typewriters may be worthwhile in some personnel offices.
8. An alert office manager should be aware of recent developments in this field. He should be in frequent contact with vendors of office equipment and developers of electronic equipment in order to obtain ideas that might improve the operation of his office.

USE OF DATA-PROCESSING MACHINES IN SCHOOL PERSONNEL ADMINISTRATION

Each personnel office should have available the services of an automated data-processing unit for the purpose of recapturing information quickly and accurately. Usually a data center is established to be of service to the entire school system. The several departments and divisions call upon its services as needed.

Types of useful information recoverable:
1. Printed payrolls (biweekly or as needed).
2. An up-to-date card index of all staff members.

3. An alphabetical listing of all staff members showing their school location.
4. A matrix showing the location of staff members on the salary schedule by service step and training category.
5. Computed estimated cost of proposed salary schedules.
6. A matrix showing the academic preparation and length of experience of staff members.
7. A record of the sick leave and vacation entitlement of each staff member.
8. Tabulated certification statuses.
9. Information for state and federal reports and data for questionnaires.
10. Information for studies involving race, sex, marital status, age, etc.
11. A position control for budget analysis.
12. Information for an annual recruitment report on source of entry, teaching level, extent of training, experience, age, and so forth.
13. Teacher "cutoffs" tabulated by reasons given.

Transmission of information. Of course information must be fed to the data center either by use of the tickets already mentioned or by use of specially prepared forms. Such a form is used to authorize teacher employment as well as to supply information for data processing.

In Baltimore, as in most other cities, the personnel division assigns teachers. With the advice of subject supervisors, a director may recommend an assignment to an assistant superintendent, which indicates the reason for having the signatures of both administrators on the form.

These are some of the features of the form to which attention should be directed:

1. The tabulations at the top of both sides of the form are for the use of various persons who process the form as it flows through the personnel office.
2. The second section of the form is a duplicate of the entry ticket. It is designed so that any typist can copy the information onto the entry ticket with little instruction.
3. All items in the left-hand column of the form and some items in the blocks above are preceded by letters. They are column-heading codes used in data processing and indicate the proper placement of the information in each item.

Electronic Data Processing for Personnel in Memphis. The school system of the City of Memphis (pop. 537,000) has used I.B.M. data processing in personnel administration. A report published by I.B.M. describes their program as follows: [1]

APPLICANT PROCESSING

The applicant's procedure is designed to make more manageable the paperwork involved in employing more than 500 college graduates each year. An applicant fills out an application form. The information on the application form is typed onto a transmittal form, which is sent to the computer center. The interview ratings are shown on this transmittal form, and the information from the transmittal form is punched into an applicant's card. There is one card for each applicant in the applicant file. Periodically, the entire applicant card file is printed to help the personnel division locate the file folders of qualified applicants in order to set up job offer interviews and to be sure that none are overlooked.

The applicant's procedure is set up to enable the personnel division to requisition a partial listing from the computer center of applicants qualified for a certain position, determined by specified parameters.

An amendment form allows the division to change, update, or delete cards in the master applicant file.

PERSONNEL REPORTS AND STUDIES

Employee books showing a printout of certain more frequently used information about each person are printed periodically, as are other statistical and summary type reports. The personnel and payroll master, for example, is used to print a list of those employees becoming eligible for service award pins and to identify those teachers who will be eligible for retirement.

In the area of expense analysis and budgetary control, the expense codes are generated based on the subject a teacher is teaching and the number of times the teacher teaches that subject each day. This information is used to develop a function code plus an object code that shows how expense is distributed against the budget control.

An average annual salary report, by school, and a qualification of high school personnel report are printed for the personnel office. Similar reports are sent to each school supplying the information needed to complete reports to the Southern Association of Colleges and Secondary Schools.

MONTHLY PAYROLL

The exception method of reporting is used in the monthly payroll. Once an employee is made active on this payroll by the personnel division, a full month's compensation is paid for each full month worked, unless makeup time or absences are reported. The personnel division determines rates of pay and notifies the payroll office of beginning and ending dates of employment. The monthly absence report shows the names and numbers of all teachers in alphabetic order. Space is provided on it for reporting three sets of absences on one line. Additional lines on other pages may be used for writing in additional absences.

The number of days absent, the code indicating the amount of deduction, and the beginning and ending date of each period of absence are shown on the form. A code explaining the reason for the absence is necessary in addition to the code for the amount of the deduction.

The completed monthly absence and makeup report is forwarded to the personnel division on the date specified in the pay schedule, which is published separately.

REPORTING AND SCHEDULING

The master schedule builder and student scheduling programs are used not only to schedule students in the schools but also to do essentially the same job of scheduling elementary teachers into their fall in-service training program. (See example.)

A mark-sense card is used to collect information about the subject a teacher is teaching each period, the number of pupils enrolled in each section being taught, and the days the classes meet. Certificate information on each teacher is obtained in punched cards from the State Department of Education in Nashville. The information about each teacher from both the mark-sense cards and the punched cards is then recorded on the payroll personnel master file. A preliminary report is printed and used by administrators to make sure that each teacher is teaching within his area of certification and is not carrying an excessive pupil load. The report is corrected, reprinted, and forwarded to the State Department of Education.

MACHINERY NEEDED

The type and amount of machinery needed in a data center vary with the size of the system and the amount of detailed information supplied to the center for processing. Small systems—those with a staff of 1,000 to 1,500—

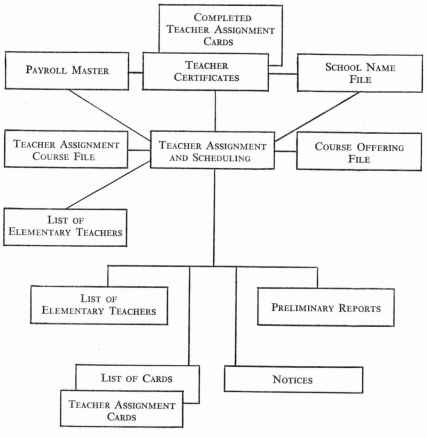

assignment and scheduling processing.

could operate with a key-punch machine, a sorter and a tabulator. A system having 1,500 to 2,500 teachers would need auxiliary equipment such as a verifier, an interpreter, a collator and a reproducer. Systems which are still larger would need to install optical scanning equipment and computers. It is also recommended that large systems store the information sent to them on disks which lend themselves to the quick recovery of information. School districts that call substitute teachers centrally may place their home telephone numbers on punched cards which automatically dial the number when inserted in a special telephone. It is a great time saver.

THE FUTURE

When we "look into the future far as eye of man can see," the development of electronic communications has fantastic possibilities. Even now it is possible for a personnel office to be linked to a data center with teleprocessing equipment operated in such a way that much paper work can be eliminated. For example: assume that such equipment has been installed and that information has been stored on disks and coded by the use of social security numbers. The following is then possible.

1. The personnel office requests, by special telephone, certain data from the data center. Within a few seconds, the requested information automatically appears on a screen in the personnel office, where it can be easily read. At the same time, the requested data may be automatically typed on a receiving typewriter in the personnel office.
2. A change is made in the information relating to an individual. By special telephone, the personnel office gives the person's social security number directly to the computer and then transmits the correction that is to be made. The receiving equipment locates the proper disk position of the number called and automatically corrects the stored data, thus eliminating the use of paper transmission.

CAUTIONS

It is important that all information transmitted to the data center is accurate, and that requires careful scrutiny at the source—the personnel office. The availability of data processing does not mean that the staff of the school system can be reduced. Positions needed in the data center will balance those that were needed when statistical information had to be compiled by hand; such persons may even be entitled to higher salaries.

Because of the demands upon the data center, it is necessary to establish a policy to determine the priority for servicing requests. And, in setting up a data center, a question will arise about the nature and amount of data to be stored. The decision in this case must depend upon whether or not the information will be used after storage. There should be a useful purpose behind each decision to store information on the disks. In some large communities, the fiscal office of the community and the fiscal office of the school system each has a data-processing center. In such a situation, both centers should be coordinated so that their data can be interchangeable.

5 TEACHER EDUCATION AND CERTIFICATION

GENERAL STATEMENT

Since the founding of the first normal school for the training of teachers in Massachusetts in 1839, there have been frequent discussions and appraisals of the content of and procedures in teacher education. These discussions have reached national proportions at various times in the history of teacher education. For example, at the turn of the century, when normal schools began to transform themselves into degree-granting teachers' colleges, their offerings came under national scrutiny. The advent of vocational education after World War I drew national attention to the need for teacher training in that area. In the 1950s, the adequacy of teacher education came under public scrutiny when the Russians seemed to demonstrate technological superiority by orbiting the first earth satellite, which they called Sputnik. In the mid 1960s, teacher education again came under national scrutiny as a result of the social revolution involving minority groups and the widely expressed dissatisfaction with education. As new needs were recognized and as criticism mounted, national conventions were called, formal studies were made by individuals and groups, books were written and changes were initiated. Teacher education today is substantially different from what it was even ten or twenty years ago, and it is likely to change even more drastically in the future.

HISTORICAL BACKGROUND OF TEACHER EDUCATION

The idea that special training was necessary to teach children was not widely recognized in early education. In the early church-controlled schools, clergymen taught as they remembered being taught when they were children. When secular schools were established, they remained religiously oriented, and there were no special requirements for a teaching post other than the candidate's moral and religious acceptability to the authorities. Instruction in the higher schools of learning was controlled by the universities, whose concern was with the training of specialists whose depth of learning was certified through the universities' examinations. Indeed, the public schools of Massachusetts had been established for about two centuries before the first normal school for teachers was created in 1839. After that, normal schools were established in other states as well. Entrance requirements to a normal school varied in the different states, but it was not uncommon for graduates of elementary school to be accepted for the one- or two-year training period in the normal school. Knight informs us that "As late as 1900 the typical normal school provided only two years of work beyond the high school." [1]

As long as the normal schools concentrated on preparing teachers for the elementary schools, little attention was paid to them by the universities and colleges. However, at the turn of the 20th century, when normal schools began to transform themselves into teachers' colleges and they began to institute the training of secondary school teachers, not only in methods and other education courses but in content courses as well, the universities began to take hostile notice of the upstarts. There was criticism of both the standards of instruction and the standards of scholarship in the teachers' colleges. It is undoubtedly true that the early courses in pedagogy were not well organized, or scholarly, or profound in content. Knight tells us:

> "Organized materials for pedagogical instruction were scarce until after 1900, and the practical experience of the early professors of pedagogy formed the large part of the material of their courses. The standards of their work, which was limited to a few fields, were not always high and their claim to scientific character could not always be supported. . . . These and other conditions caused courses in pedagogy early to fall under the heavy prejudice of other departments. They still suffer from this affliction." [2]

In the 1900s, when special departments were established in universities and colleges to provide instruction for future secondary school teachers, their courses and the professors of education who were appointed to them were relegated to a second-class position in the university. This attitude has persisted through the years.

Criticism of teacher education and the conflict between professors of education and professors of liberal arts and sciences reached a crescendo in the 1950s after the Russians succeeded in orbiting Sputnik, apparently demonstrating technological superiority over the United States. Criticism was to the effect that teachers were spending too much time learning how to teach, and not enough time learning what to teach. Education courses had long been criticized by students and even by practicing teachers as being repetitive, thin in content and impractical. College professors of liberal arts and science, newspaper editors and prominent nonprofessional leaders took up the chorus of criticism. John Keats, the prominent author who wrote

71

a book entitled *Schools Without Scholars,* also wrote a critical article entitled "How well are our teachers being taught? Never worse!" in *Better Homes and Gardens* in May of 1958. All those people, and even some school administrators, hard-pressed to obtain teachers in a time of teacher shortage, seemed to concur in the view that it was not necessary to know how to teach, but only to know the subject. Although the middle position eventually was adopted—that it is necessary to know both *how* and *what* to teach—substantial changes and improvements were made in programs of teacher education as a result of the controversy. One outcome of the controversy was a movement, in many collegiate institutions, toward a total university involvement in teacher education in which the responsibility for the preparation of teachers was shared by the liberal arts and science faculty with the pedagogic faculty. Courses for future teachers were taught by the same professors who taught all the undergraduate students, and curricular innovations in teacher education were discussed by representatives of the total institution.

The mid 1960s represented another period of soul searching by teacher-education faculties and criticism by individuals concerned with public education. The cause of the criticism was the dissatisfaction expressed by leaders of minority groups with the lack of success and the lack of relevance of the educational program for Negro children and other minority groups in urban areas, and particularly in the economically poorer inner city. The critics maintained education was anachronistic, that it had been designed for the suburban middle class, that it had more of an agricultural orientation than urban orientation. It was claimed that the graduates of teacher-education institutions were either poorly prepared or not at all prepared for teaching inner city children. Complaints were directed not only toward inadequacies in methods of teaching but also toward both young and experienced teachers' lack of understanding of the background and needs of inner city children.

PURPOSES OF TEACHER EDUCATION

The basic purpose of teacher education has not changed through the years. It is still to prepare teachers to meet the educational needs of children in school. While the purpose of teacher education seems simply expressed, concomitant questions have made it a complex and controversial subject.

Teacher education becomes controversial as the responsibilities of the teacher change to meet new needs. For example, there is the question of whether the teacher is to teach for the world as it exists or as it will be. If the teacher is to meet the needs of the present, then his procedures must be of one type, but if he is to be concerned with the needs of the future, if he is to exercise social leadership, then his procedures must be of another type. Concepts of the proper scope and responsibilities of teachers have differed in various times and places. Controversy has also arisen over changes in methodology to meet new needs. Thus, emphasis on conformity and disci-

72

pline was followed by the child-centered concept of the classroom, by permissiveness, progressivism, and group planning. There has been controversy over the methodology employed in particular subjects as well. Methods of teaching reading have been challenged, as have methods of teaching spelling, arithmetic, history, foreign languages, sciences, and almost all other subjects. Because of disagreement over methodology and because there is no single authority that orders a particular approach, teacher education has been far more flexible than most people realize, while seeking to "meet the educational needs of children" in a constantly changing society.

SELECTION OF STUDENTS FOR TEACHER EDUCATION

A general misconception is that anyone can teach. Unfortunately, that notion has been lent credence by the general laxity of standards for accepting students in teacher-education programs in college. During the recent years of the teacher shortage, few students who applied for admission to teacher-education programs were turned away. Indeed, there has been a belief among college students that, if you failed admission to any of the other professions, you could always turn to teaching. The lack of selectivity was also the fault of the large number of institutions that offered teacher-education programs. In 1959, according to Hodenfield and Stinnett,[3] there were 1,147 collegiate institutions preparing teachers, compared to some seventy-two approved medical schools (according to *World Almanac*). Another reason for the lack of selectivity has been financial. Teacher-education courses can be made to yield a surplus to a college, since laboratory space need not be utilized and since large groups of students can be taught by part-time staff members. According to a 1969 Education Professions Development Act report, the cost of preparing physicians or dentists varies from $5,000 to $12,000 per year, whereas the cost of training teachers is about $1,000 a year. There is also a constant demand for teacher-education courses in all collegiate institutions. It was for those reasons that some colleges introduced teacher-education courses. It has also been possible for some students to avoid selective standards by picking up enough courses at various institutions on a part-time basis to qualify for state certification; yet many excellent teachers have entered the profession in this way. Reports have shown that students entering teaching careers have, on the average, scored lower on various tests of mental ability and achievement than students entering other professions, such as medicine and engineering.[4]

The generalization about inadequate selection standards does not include all collegiate institutions. Many are seeking to enforce reasonable standards of selection, and their number will grow as the teacher shortage is eased. Different bases and criteria are used by different institutions in selecting students to enter the teaching curriculum. Some institutions use scores obtained on a standardized college entrance test. Others require an interview and a review of the student's academic record. A few are interested in personality factors: the relationship of the individual to his peers and to children. Some institutions offer a course called "orientation to teaching" during the freshman year. Performance in the course is part of the selection process. There is, of course, the question of whether criteria such as mental achievement, success in an interview, and academic grades correlate sufficiently with success in teaching to warrant using them for teacher selection. One may similarly question the use of such criteria for entrance into other professions. So far there has been no definitive evidence for accepting or rejecting such criteria, but there are enough practical reasons for warranting careful selection. Since selection for one of the other major professional programs generally comes after three of four years in college, whereas selection for a teacher-education program may begin as early as the sophomore year, it is doubtful that the same types of criteria or standards can or should be applied

CURRICULUM OF THE TEACHER-EDUCATION PROGRAM

The Portion of an Individual's Program Devoted to Pedagogy

During the 1950s, it was common to hear the complaint that too much of an education student's time was devoted to education courses. Since that was not generally true, it is probable that critics had in mind extreme instances. Certification requirements vary among the states and undoubtedly the requirements of education departments of colleges vary, but in the vast majority of situations the requirement of courses in pedagogy for teaching in secondary schools ranges from 12 to 18 semester hours, plus a student-teaching experience which may count up to 10 credits. Since the average baccalaureate program requires approximately 120 credits, or semester hours, spread over eight semesters, it may be said that one semester out of eight is devoted to pedagogy. To teach in elementary schools, requirements vary from 24 to 36 semester hours, which might represent approximately two out of eight semesters, or one year in a four-year college program. The program of the normal schools that formerly prepared teachers for elementary school included many courses beyond the required 36 credits in social studies, English, arithmetic, and other basic studies. Some of the teachers' colleges have continued such a program. Hodenfield and Stinnett [5] have given the example of one college that prepares elementary-school teachers and requires 61 credits in pedagogy, as follows:

Courses	Semester Hours
Professional Orientation	3
Audio-Visual Education	2
General Psychology	3
Educational Psychology & Evaluative Techniques	3

74

Courses	Semester Hours
Student Teaching & Direction of Student Activities	12
Professional Practicum including School Law	2
Music for Elementary Grades	2
Teaching Music in Elementary Grades	3
Science for the Elementary Grades	3
Teaching Elementary Science	3
Art for Elementary Grades	2
Teaching Art in the Elementary Grades	3
Teaching of Language	3
Teaching of Social Studies and Geography	3
Teaching of Health	2
Children's Literature	3
Teaching of Arithmetic	3
Child Development	3
Teaching of Reading	3
Total	61

Requiring 61 credits of pedagogy is an extreme situation. Most school administrators and teachers do not believe that one or two semesters out of eight is too much to devote to pedagogy. Paul Woodring, in a speech to the American Society of Newspaper Editors in Washington in April, 1958, as cited by Hodenfield and Stinnett, expressed the following thought:

"to see the need for these skills, ask yourself what you would do if you were placed in front of a class of third graders tomorrow. What would you teach? What books would you use? How would you organize a day? What methods would you use in teaching reading and arithmetic? Perhaps you know the answers to all these questions, but many beginning teachers do not—and this includes many teachers with an excellent liberal arts background." [6]

Those who wish to teach a particular subject in secondary schools are required to take from 34 to 40 semester hours in the subject they wish to teach. Since there has been a movement in many states to require five years of preparation for teaching on a permanent certificate, without increasing the number of courses in pedagogy, it would seem that prospective teachers have sufficient opportunity in their collegiate programs for extensive study of the liberal arts and sciences.

James Conant, in a comprehensive study of the education of American teachers, found that most teacher-preparation programs require one or two years of the total undergraduate collegiate program. He states that ". . . four years of college [are] adequate for teaching in elementary schools, assuming that two of the four college years are devoted to a general education . . ." [7] He states further: "If one insists on more free electives, then a five-year

continuous program will result. I am convinced, however, that such a pro-
longation before the teacher takes his first job is unnecessary and unwise." [8]

For secondary school teaching, Conant recommends the "all-university"
approach in which the academic major is taught by the faculties of the
liberal arts and sciences and the pedagogy by the faculty of education. He
opposes preparation to teach more than one academic subject because he
does not believe that it is possible to prepare adequately in more than one
specialized area. Following that assumption, Conant cites typical programs
for the preparation of secondary school teachers of different subjects.

As a program of study for a teacher of social studies, he offers the
following outline: [9]

Courses	Semester Hours
General education, including 9 hours of history, 3 hours of sociology or anthropology, 3 hours of political science, 3 hours of economics, 3 hours of general psychology	60
Educational psychology	3
Philosophy of history or sociology of education	3
Further history	39
Further political science or geography	3
Further economics	3
Practice teaching and special methods	9
Total	120

His proposal for the education of a secondary school teacher of mathematics is the following:

Courses	Semester Hours
General education, including 6 hours of mathematics, 12 hours of science, 3 hours of general psychology	60
Educational psychology	3
Philosophy or history or sociology of education	3
Physics or chemistry	6
Field of concentration (mathematics)	39
Practice teaching and special methods	9
Total	120

Conant's reasons for including physics or chemistry in the preparation of
teachers of mathematics are to offer wider opportunities for a fifth year of
study and to make provisions for the occasional use of the teacher of mathematics as a science teacher.

It is desirable to have a fifth year of preparation for permanent teacher
certification. Many educators believe that the fifth year of preparation
should follow one's appointment as a teacher because it would enable the
young teacher to utilize his new experiences in teaching, his needs and
desires for new skills, and additional background to determine the nature of

his fifth year of academic activities. For some it might include additional courses in pedagogy; for others it might include additional courses in the subject he is teaching; for others it might include a combination of courses, including courses that are related in some way to his academic life.

REAPPRAISAL OF CURRICULAR NEEDS OF THE TEACHER-EDUCATION PROGRAM

In 1960, a group of distinguished educators convened to make a critical appraisal of the professional aspects of teacher education. A report on their deliberations was issued in 1962. After defining the functions and commitments of a teacher, they envisioned five areas of teacher preparation: [10]

1. Liberal education.
2. Specialized knowledge of the subject to be taught.
3. Professional knowledge, which includes understanding of the role of the school, the contributions of the behavorial sciences, and an appreciation of interrelated components of the education of process.
4. Practice teaching under adequate supervision.
5. Unified theory.

The report further identified seven distinct needs in teacher education: [11]

1. Need to screen students entering the teaching profession for quality and to involve superior students.
2. Need for greater cooperation between subject-matter departments and education departments of colleges.
3. Need for more liberal education and more general education.
4. Need to reappraise the relation of general education to professional education with a view to eliminating what is not essential.
5. Need to bridge the gap between colleges and lower schools in fashioning and improving curricula in the latter.
6. Need to develop a unifying theory of teacher education able to rest on clearly stated assumptions and organized into a logical pattern.
7. Need to make teaching more professional through changes in the role and function of the teacher.

NEW APPROACHES IN TEACHER EDUCATION

The 1960s saw many innovations in teacher education. In 1961, a task force representing the National Commission on Teacher Education and Professional Standards and the National Education Association issued a report entitled *New Horizons for the Teaching Profession* (Margaret Lindsey, editor). In a lengthy section entitled "Preparation of Professional Personnel," the report views the teacher both as a person and as a professional educator and seeks to relate his or her preparation to knowledge, ability, and skills in both categories. The report divides the preparation into three categories, all of which must be unified:

"General education basic to continuing growth as a person, specialization providing scholarly knowledge of the subjects or areas to be taught, professional education leading to understanding and skill in professional performance—each part must continue to be integral in both pre- and in-service programs of all professional educators. But their interrelation must be recognized and a program of professional preparation must be designed to erase the unnatural and unnecessary dividing line." [12]

Also highlighted in the report is the need to increase the direct experiences of prospective teachers during their preparatory period. Great value is attributed to an internship in teaching which would follow student teaching. Nor is teacher education regarded as complete when an individual has been graduated and has obtained certification as a teacher. In-service education is as important as pre-service education. The all-university approach to teacher education—the cooperation of the colleges of liberal arts and sciences with the department of education—is favored here.

In 1963, the National Teacher Education and Professional Standards Commission brought hundreds of educators and other interested people together to discuss innovations in teacher education. The results of that conference were published in 1964 under the title, *Changes in Teacher Education—an Appraisal*. Among the changes that were reported in teacher education were the following,[13] which are here summarized:

1. *Use of Television*. Television has been used for student teachers to view their own performance and for student teachers to view the performances of others. Television is also useful in giving teacher-education students an opportunity to know groups of children in different working and playing situations. Through television, teacher-education students can view pupils being interviewed by psychologists or guidance counselors, pupils working in groups to produce a school newspaper or a play and students in any other aspect of school life. Their actions can form a realistic basis for discussion in student-teaching classes. In-service education programs have also utilized television. For example, a new program of teaching reading, arithmetic and fine arts was introduced in the New York City public schools through a series of television seminar programs which were telecast after school hours. Teachers were organized into groups under a discussion leader to view and discuss the programs that were televised to them.

2. *Use of Audiovisual Aids other than Television*. Other types of audiovisual aids, such as recordings, sound films and film strips, have been used to give students in teacher-education programs a realistic background in the group activities, conversations and self-expression of children in inner cities. Interviews with parents, social workers and community leaders have been recorded for playback and discussion in teacher-education programs.

3. *College Faculty Changes*. Changes have varied from the total reorganization of a faculty to the introduction of new faculty members who

have specialized backgrounds. In one instance, an entire school of education was reorganized to reduce the number of separately compartmentalized programs into fewer, broader and interrelated programs in which there was a greater intermingling of students and in which new services were provided. In other situations, there were descriptions of greater cooperation among members of the faculty in liberal arts, sciences and education. Of great importance was the employment of instructors in student teaching who themselves had extensive experience in teaching on the public school levels. A frequent criticism of the student-teaching experience has been related to the faculty members who conducted it. It has been contended either that those faculty members never taught in the public schools or that their teaching occurred so long ago as to make their advice impractical. It was reported that outstanding teachers are being obtained from the public schools and added to college faculties to conduct and administer the student-teacher experience. In other situations, faculty members participated in a special exchange program with public school teachers so that each group could learn the problems and procedures of the other for their mutual benefit.

4. *Co-operative Education.* Dr. Ralph Tyler, Director of the Center for Advanced Study in the Behavioral Sciences at Stanford University, suggested a work-study arrangement that would be available to prospective teachers in their undergraduate years. Such plans have been made available to students in other fields in a few other colleges.

5. *Curriculum Study Center for Teacher Education.* This type of center, set up jointly by colleges and boards of education, was intended to improve the in-service education of teachers and to make available to students in teacher-education programs the combined resources of sociologists, psychologists, curriculum experts and practical school men whose investigations would be of value to teachers and prospective teachers.

6. *Internship Programs.* Various types of internship programs have been tried. In some districts, the internship experience is a fifth year experience, with a student employed in the school district for a half a day or half a week and taking courses during the other half day or the remainder of the week. The length of the internship varies from one semester to a year. In some situations, it is served during the end of the fourth year. The main purpose of the internship is to give the students practical experience, which becomes the basis for discussion of educational practices and theory.

7. *The Teaching Corps.* Pilot projects were initiated in the early 1960s and became federally financed projects in the later 1960s. In these projects, liberal arts graduates were recruited for special training in order to serve in the schools of the inner cities. Their service was preceded by intensive teacher training in selected institutions. They were then assigned, in groups, to schools in various cities to serve in poverty areas of city school districts. Master teachers with special backgrounds and training in teaching such children were assigned as guides to the Teaching Corps.

8. *Cadet Teachers.* "Cadet teachers" was a term applied to under-graduate students who had an interest in becoming teachers and who were permitted to serve on a part-time basis as assistants to teachers in public schools. For their services they were paid a nominal per hour stipend. These experiences, it was hoped, would help to motivate young people to enter teaching and to increase their background of experience in the field.

9. *Earlier Experiences with Children in the Teacher-Education Program.* Whereas most student teaching in the past occurred in the senior year of college, a great many teacher-education institutions determined to provide working experiences with children at an earlier opportunity. Thus individuals who expressed an interest in teacher education were urged to work with children as early as their sophomore or freshman year. This experience took place in settlement houses, in community playgrounds, in child-care centers, in hospitals, in orphanages, in after school play centers, in summer camp programs and in other situations where children were gathered in groups for care, instruction or play.

10. *Varied Student-Teaching Experiences.* In the past, student teaching experience was concentrated in a single school because it was convenient to do so. Usually, the school was near the college or was located in a relatively well-to-do, comfortable neighborhood. More recently, changes were made so that student teaching is required in more than one school and includes, wherever possible, experiences in inner city school districts. Whereas, in the past, student teaching involved occasional visits to schools and occasional teaching practice, changes were made to require a more sustained experience in which the student teacher spends full days and, indeed, full weeks in the school to sample the wide variety of experiences that a teacher faces in a typical day, including escorting classes to their rooms and rating papers after school.

THE IMPACT OF THE SOCIAL REVOLUTION OF THE 1960S ON TEACHER EDUCATION

The social revolution of the latter half of the 1960s has had an extensive impact on teacher education. Civil rights leaders pointed out that the benefits of education and other advantages are not being properly shared by minority groups, including the twenty-two million Negroes in the United States. The shortcomings of education in the inner cities were graphically revealed in the high dropout rates of students; low achievement in reading, arithmetic and other fundamentals; the high rate of staff turnover; and low expectation by teachers. National leaders also pointed to the disadvantages of education in rural poverty belts in the United States. Movements arose to decentralize educational administration so that communities might more effectively control or be involved in their school systems. There were demands for greater teacher accountability to the community and there was often acrimonious discussion of the extent to which laymen might properly

80

evaluate teachers. Although professional educators believed that critics were demanding too much of the schools and were omitting from proper consideration political, social, and economic factors that cause deprivation and unequal opportunity in education and life, nevertheless the criticism had sufficient validity and impact to destroy complacency and to bring about substantial changes in education and in teacher education. Unprecedented sums of money were made available by federal, state and city governments and by private foundations for special programs of teacher education; pre-service and in-service programs were implemented to develop better intergroup relationships and understandings. There was a critical examination of all traditional practices and theories: for example, in some communities the use of IQ scores was discontinued because many teachers regarded an IQ score as a permanent ceiling on a child's achievement and were therefore low in their expectations for children from disadvantaged homes. There was also a reassessment of homogeneous grouping of children and of the multitrack school curriculum because it was recognized that children from disadvantaged homes were generally and often automatically, assigned to low achievement groups. In order to heighten teacher understanding of the problems of inner city children, greater use was made of audiovisual materials in teacher training. The great increase in the use of aids, usually drawn from the surrounding community, has given a new perspective to the role of the teacher as a leader of an instructional team. In addition, the following types of changes were instituted in teacher-education programs as a result of the social revolution of the late 1960s:

1. Active recruitment to enroll more Negroes and other minority-group members in teacher-education courses.
2. Requiring prospective teachers to have courses in Afro-American history and culture or arranging for such courses to be available for those prospective teachers who find it desirable to take them.
3. Emphasis upon courses in human relations and intergroup sensitivity for prospective teachers and for teachers in service. Through such courses it was hoped to establish better intergroup relationships and understandings, with teachers serving in a leadership role in the community. It was also hoped that teachers would develop better understanding of the abilities and aspirations of minority groups.
4. Use of appropriate materials, recordings and other audiovisual aids to give prospective teachers better insight into the problem of living in the inner cities so that those whose background did not include such experiences might vicariously develop a better understanding of the problems and background of the children that they would be teaching.
5. An increase in the study of sociological and anthropological elements in teacher education in order to develop a broader un-

derstanding of group relationships, group characteristics and the interrelationships of groups.

6. Increased responsibilities given to students in developing and evaluating the curriculum and the organization and standards of the teacher-education institution and in formulating faculty-student relationships.

7. An increased exposure to experimental procedures and materials designed to reduce the educational disadvantages of children; for examples, the utilization of various types of computers and teaching machines designed to individualize instruction, such as those developed by I.B.M., R.C.A., and McGraw-Hill; and the reorganization of school programs and staff, as in the M.E.S. (more effective schools) program, which is advocated by the American Federation of Teachers.

8. Establishment of pilot or experimental programs of teacher education in various universities with the support of federal funds. Such programs replace formal education courses with increased field experiences under supervision, intensive work with small groups of children, clinical discussions and weekly seminars under joint professional sponsorship, increased freedom to choose elective courses and the guidance of advisors.

Special efforts were urged to educate teachers to meet the "urban crisis." The N. E. A. Task Force on Urban Education declared in a report that "radical changes are needed in both the content and the organization of present programs," and they urged that college students become more involved in planning their own programs, declaring:

> "A teacher in the schools of the urban crisis cannot be really effective unless he derives from study and from his own experience sufficient knowledge and understanding of urban sociology, anthropology, and behavioral psychology to have some insight into the values and the goals of his children and their families. . . . Preparation programs must give every prospective educator the opportunity to work with children of different races and backgrounds." [14]

The Task Force called for a closer relationship between colleges that prepare teachers and urban school systems in order to ensure the development of good teacher-education programs. They also urged the establishment of a Special Project on Urban Education to develop programs, improve instructional patterns, improve teacher education and render necessary assistance in bringing about changes to meet the urban school crisis.[15]

TEACHER CERTIFICATION

HISTORICAL BACKGROUND

As public education in the middle of the 19th century began to develop into a state function, reforms were demanded in the method of certifying teachers. In previous years, certification of teachers was a local responsibility, sometimes exercised by a local religious leader, sometimes by a political office holder and sometimes by a local school board. The purpose of certification was and is to protect the public interest by establishing appropriate standards of preparation and experience for those who would teach in public schools. As applied in the early years of American public education by thousands of local communities, standards of certification and selection were low and frequently dictated by the whims of one influential individual, by the availability of funds and by temporary pressures and expedience. Local ethnic or religious preferences played a part in certification procedures. In many rural areas the local groups were notably not qualified to select or certify their teachers. In some communities, written and oral examinations were administered for the certification of teachers.

As state departments of education assumed responsibility for the public school system, they also assumed the responsibility for the certification of teachers. Their methods of certification varied, according to Conant, who stated that

> "state departments of education had begun to accept as a basis for certification completion of a course of instruction in one of the normal schools or colleges they controlled. This alternative to examinations simplified their tasks. Thus, by 1850 several states had two certification devices: first, completion of an approved course of studies in a state regulated institution; and second, examination." [16]

By 1900 there was a great expansion of learning in what has been called the scientific revolution, accompanied by more requirements for teacher certification. The normal schools developed a more extensive curriculum for teachers, insofar as subject matter was concerned, but they were reluctant to engage in "vocational education," which was the university scholar's description of courses in pedagogy. Since more and more teachers were coming from the universities to meet the expanding need for teachers, public and normal school administrators who were convinced of the necessity of proper teacher preparation influenced state education departments to include the requirement of courses in pedagogy for certification. According to Conant:

> "Since the state came more and more to depend for its supply of teachers on graduates of the universities and of colleges with traditional academic orientation, those who believed in the desirability of pedagogical courses found it necessary to utilize forces outside the colleges and universities. Their solution was a series of laws establishing requirements for courses in education to be taken by all candidates for certification." [17]

When it developed that universities were unwilling to tailor their preparation to teacher-education graduates, state departments of education

83

also introduced requirements of specific courses in the academic subjects that an individual was preparing to teach. Conant states further: "It is important to note that such certification regulations were in a sense imposed upon the universities and colleges as a result of pressure from the coalition of state department officials and public school people." [18]

Conant offers that explanation as background for the schism between the pedagogic and the academic faculties of universities, which became most acute in the early 1960s. In any case, the pattern was set for state certification requirements that included specific courses of preparation, either at approved institutions (normal schools) or at institutions in which programs were approved, and the passing of state teacher examinations. That was the situation in the early 1900s. Gradually, however, examinations were discontinued as a means of state certification because they delayed the certification process in times of teacher shortage and because the examinations were disapproved of by collegiate institutions as excessively regimenting and restrictive of their curricula. In time, every state discontinued the use of examinations, although a number of large cities continued to use them as a basis for impartial selection of school staff in accordance with civil service procedures. In the 1960s, three or four states reinstituted the use of examinations for teacher certification.

While state certification was in effect in only three states in 1898, teacher certification has been a state function in all of the states since 1951. Massachusetts was last to adopt a statewide teacher-certification law that placed this authority in a state board of education. The change from local to state certification was a most significant step in the professionalization of teachers and in the improvement of their preparation. Local certification was based almost entirely upon "education and good moral character." Certification required four or more years of college or a baccalaureate degree, including specific courses in pedagogy and in academic subjects. In a number of states, a master's degree was required. As the requirements for teacher certification were increased, the number and variety of teaching certificates also increased.

RECENT PROBLEMS IN CERTIFICATION

After the National Education Association established the National Commission on Teacher Education and Professional Standards (NCTEPS) in 1946, greater attention was given to problems of teacher certification on the national level. The subject of teacher certification was discussed at a number of national conventions and was included in a published report of the National TEPS Commission in 1961 entitled *New Horizons for the Teaching Profession*. The report described some of the vexing problems of state certification:

1. Wide variation of state certification requirements among the states.
2. Undesirable features of counting credits and courses as the basis for certification.

3. A questionable relationship between certification requirements and teaching competency
4. Failure to place responsibility for teacher education upon the teacher-education institutions.
5. An excessive number of teaching licenses or certificates.
6. Use of the teaching certificate to perform functions which are inappropriate, such as enforcement of proper teacher assignments. [19]

It was also pointed out that there was not even agreement over the use of terms. In some states the document which authorizes service as a teacher is called a "certificate"; in other states it is called a "license"; in some states it is called a "credential." Such terms as "permanent," "standard," "regular," "provisional," "temporary" and "emergency" are also used to describe certificates in different states. The NCTEPS report also made recommendations, which are here summarized:

1. Existing standards for issuing teaching certificates should be simplified and improved. Standards for certification should be formulated by appropriate representative groups, and the responsibility should be placed more specifically upon the teacher-preparation institutions.
2. The number of teaching certificates issued by a state should be reduced to a minimum.
3. There should be a clarification of who should be required to hold teaching certificates and who should not. For example, there is the question of whether social workers or psychologists should be certified by teacher-certification authorities or by their own national or state associations.
4. The profession and the institutions should play a more important role in the formulation and enforcement of certification standards.

ACCREDITATION OF TEACHER-EDUCATION PROGRAMS

Another move that affected teacher certification was the organization in 1952 of the National Council for Accreditation of Teacher Education (NCATE), which described itself as follows:

"The National Council for Accreditation of Teacher Education representing five constituent organizations is a non-profit, voluntary accrediting body devoted exclusively to the evaluation and accreditation of teacher-education programs. It is recognized by the National Commission on Accrediting as the only national accrediting agency for the field of teacher education, which includes programs for the preparation of teachers for all grades and subjects on the elementary and secondary school levels and programs for the preparation of school service personnel for these levels." [20]

The Council has representatives of the following organizations on its governing board:

American Association of Colleges for Teacher Education
Council of Chief State School Officers
National School Boards Associations
National Commission on Teacher Education and Professional Standards
National Education Association
National Association of State Directors of Teacher Education and Certification
Learned Societies

The evaluating teams of NCATE have been concerned with the following standards when they visit an institution which seeks its accreditation: [21]

1. The objectives of the teacher-education program.
2. The organization and administration of teacher education such as to facilitate the continuous development and improvement of the teacher-education program.
3. Student personnel programs and services for teacher education related to (a) admission and retention in teacher-education curricula, (b) advising and registration, and (c) records and placement.
4. Faculty for professional education—preparation and experience background.
5. Curricula for teacher education specifically planned in terms of common needs of all teachers and the special needs of persons.
6. Professional laboratory experiences for school personnel.

Before the advent of NCATE, accreditation, or recognition of the teacher-education programs in various colleges, had been accorded entirely on investigation by state education departments. Each state education department did so for the institutions within its borders, although there were some regional and national attempts at accreditation prior to the founding of NCATE. There were, of course, regional accreditation associations of colleges which, however, served to accredit the overall collegiate offering and were not directed toward teacher-education programs. The American Association of Colleges for Teacher Education had made a beginning in national accreditation prior to NCATE, but its efforts did not have a wide impact. At the time it was replaced by NCATE, it had accredited the teacher-education programs of 284 institutions.

The 15th annual list of NCATE, effective September 1, 1968, to August 31, 1969, contained the names of 462 colleges and universities and their accreditation status. It must be pointed out that NCATE accreditation is voluntary. State education departments still determine the acceptability of teacher preparation, but more and more state departments have been willing to accept NCATE accreditation without further inquiry. Although only 462 teacher preparatory institutions out of 1200 are NCATE approved, these institutions prepare approximately 75 percent of all graduating teachers.

1. An increase in overall requirements. A bachelor's degree is required for a teaching certificate in all but three or four states, and in a number of states a fifth year is required for a permanent certificate. For supervisory-administrative certificates, many states have moved from a requirement of four years to five years, and some to six years.

2. Greater flexibility has been accorded to teacher-education institutions. The number and nature of specific courses required by a state have been reduced. State certification officers have moved toward accepting the completion of approved programs in colleges without reviewing specific courses presented by each applicant. Many states have moved to accept accreditation by NCATE in lieu of their own investigation and accreditation.

3. The number and variety of teaching certificates have been reduced.

4. Advisory bodies have been set up by law in various states or by practice. Advisory bodies relate to the chief state officer in the matter of teacher certification as representatives of the profession. The tendency here has been to give the profession a greater voice in determining the qualifications of new entrants.

5. Whereas the practice in many states was to issue life certificates or certificates that had only a one-year term, the practice recently has been to issue teaching certificates that are valid for a three-to-five-year period, or to grant life certificates if there is a program of in-service education. The trend is to increase flexibility in granting state certificates. There has been considerable criticism by school administrators, as well as by college authorities, of delays, of the length of time required for state certification of individuals, and of inflexibility in insisting upon specific requirements. In many states, however, steps have been taken to facilitate the process of certification.

6. There has been a tendency to promote the free movement of teachers seeking employment across state lines. To achieve that, many states have discontinued certain specific requirements, such as a course in the history of the particular state, or any other specific which made it difficult for a teacher of another state to cross the state line. In 1942, there were sixteen states with so many specific requirements that they eliminated competition by out-of-state teachers. No more than one or two states have continued such requirements. By 1965, there were twenty-eight states that granted some reciprocity privileges in certification to teachers who were graduates of NCATE-accrediting institutions. In 1967, a reciprocity contract was affirmed by eleven states in the eastern portion of the country, forming the Northeast Compact, in which each of the states agreed to accept as equivalent to its own a certificate in elementary school teaching obtained in any of the states. There is still little reciprocity among other states.

In 1968, the Interstate Certification Project was funded federally under Sect. 505, Title V, ESEA to promote reciprocity of teacher certification among the states. Included with teachers were specialists, guidance counselors, school psychologists, school administrators, school social workers and other school professionals. Under the address of the State Education Department of New York at Albany, literature was prepared that pleaded for such reciprocity, explained its advantages, and suggested the procedures by which it could be accomplished—namely, by state legislation to effectuate an interstate agreement. A steering committee consisting of individuals from various states was formed. They pointed out that previous efforts, based upon understandings among state certification authorities, had not worked and that it was a waste of talent if certified professionals from one state could not begin to teach in another state. In 1968, four states enacted the Interstate Agreement on Qualification of Educational Personnel (Maryland, Massachusetts, New York and California). Subsequently a total of eighteen states enacted the agreement: Maryland, Massachusetts, New York, California, Vermont, South Dakota, Indiana, West Virginia, Minnesota, New Hampshire, Maine, Idaho, Rhode Island, Hawaii, Connecticut, Wisconsin, New Jersey and Washington. A major reason why reciprocity has not expanded further is that certification requirements among states are not equal, and therefore some states do not wish to grant certification to individuals who have met lower requirements in other states.

The 1967 edition of *A Manual on Certification Requirements for School Personnel in the United States* summarizes preparation-certification standards and certification requirements for teachers, supervisors, administrators and special school-service personnel. In the introduction to the manual, the editor declares that varying standards and procedures among the states make for an "inexcusably complex and confusing situation" and describes "areas where it would seem possible for the states to reach substantial agreement":

1. A basic rationale for the free movement of qualified teachers across state lines.
2. A simplification of the number and names of types of certificates.
3. A universally accepted definnition and design for implementation of the "approved program approach."
4. A reasonably uniform approach to state accreditation of teacher-education programs.
5. A reasonably uniform approach to providing democratic participation of the teaching profession in the formulation of certification requirements.
6. The establishment of review boards to examine credentials and backgrounds of applicants to determine whether exceptions to established prescriptions of requirements may be made.
7. Finding antidotes for widely alleged defensiveness about current practices in teacher education and certification.[22]

The manual further indicates that in 1967 there were four states (Nebraska, North Dakota, South Dakota and Wisconsin) and Puerto Rico that did not require a bachelor's degree for beginning elementary school teachers. All states required the baccalaureate for beginning secondary school teachers, and Arizona, California and the District of Columbia required five years of preparation. Eighteen states required completion of a fifth year of preparation for a permanent or an advanced certificate.

Table 1 indicates specific minimum requirements for elementary school teaching certificates.[23]

Table 2 indicates specific minimum requirements for secondary school teaching certificates.[24]

The manual also indicates that requirements for administrators have been increased markedly. In 1967, fifty states required the master's degree for school superintendents and eighteen states required six years of preparation. Only California required a doctor's degree or seven years of preparation.

Table 3 summarizes minimum requirements for administrative certification.[25]

Thought has been given to the certification of paraprofessionals such as teacher aides who serve in instructional programs. Since such positions are still in the process of being defined and since communities have great latitude in selecting personnel to fill them, state certification requirements have not generally been adopted. It is noteworthy, however, that by 1967, according to the N.E.A.'s *Manual on Certification Requirements,* five states (Georgia, Iowa, Michigan, Wisconsin and Florida) indicated certification provisions for paraprofessionals or teacher aides.[26] The requirements in those states did not apply to all teacher aides, nor were they as specifically defined as were those for teachers.

TEACHER EDUCATION AND THE PROFESSION OF TEACHING

If teaching is to be regarded as a profession, then teacher-education programs must include, in addition to the skills and knowledge that are required of practitioners, an orientation to and an induction into the attitudes, ideals and other characteristics of the professional educator. Discussion of whether teaching is or is not a profession is more than an academic exercise in logic. Such a discussion helps to clarify the duties and functions of teachers, including their relationships to the public, to students, to their colleagues and to the administration of the school, and clarifies their responsibilities to themselves and to society in general. Although concepts of the specific attributes of a profession may change from time to time, the basic concepts remain. For example, at one time it was believed that collective bargaining or negotiations was not compatible with professional status, but it is now commonly regarded as acceptable. Although at

89

Table 1

Specific Minimum Requirements for Elementary School Certificates Based on Degrees *

State	Degree or College Years of Preparation Required	General Education Required, Semester Hours	Professional Education Required, Semester Hours	Directed Teaching Required, Semester Hours (Included in Column 4)
1	2	3	4	5
Alabama	B	59	27	6
Alaska	B	—	24	C
Arizona	B	40	24	6
Arkansas	B	48	18	6
California	5[a]	45	20	180CH
Colorado	B	AC	AC	AC
Connecticut	B[b]	75	30	6
Delaware	B	60	30	6
D. of C.	B[c]	NS	15	C
Florida	B	45	20	6
Georgia	B	40	18	6
Hawaii	B	100	18	AC†
Idaho	B	42	20	6
Illinois	B	78[d]	16[d]	5
Indiana	B	73	27	8
Iowa	B	40	20	5
Kansas	B	50	24	5
Kentucky	B[e]	45[f]	24	8[g]
Louisiana	B	46	24	4[h]
Maine	B	64	30	8
Maryland	B	80	26	8
Massachusetts	B[i]	—	18	2
Michigan	B	—	20	5
Minnesota	B	NS	30	6
Mississippi	B	48	36	6
Missouri	B	46	20	5
Montana	B	AC	AC	AC
Nebraska	B	AC	AC	AC
Nevada	B	—	18[j]	4
New Hampshire	B	—	AC	6
New Jersey	B	30	36	6[k]
New Mexico	B	48	24	6
New York	B[l]	75	24	—
North Carolina	B	48	24	6
North Dakota	B	AC	16	3
Ohio	B	60	28	6
Oklahoma	B	50	21[m]	6
Oregon	B	—	20	—[n]
Pennsylvania	B	60	36[o]	6
Puerto Rico	B	16	20	6
Rhode Island	B	—	30	6
South Carolina	B	45	21	6
South Dakota	B	60	20	6
Tennessee	B	40	24	4
Texas	B	60	18	6
Utah	B	AC	26	8
Vermont	B	AC	18	6
Virginia	B	59	18	6
Washington	B[p]	AC	AC	AC
West Virginia	B	40[q]	20	6
Wisconsin	B	40[r]	26	8
Wyoming	B	40	23	C

Table 1 Footnotes

Legend: — means not reported; AC means approved curriculum; B means completion of the bachelor's degree; 5 means the bachelor's degree plus a fifth year of appropriate preparation, not necessarily completion of the master's degree; C means a course; NS means not specified; CH means clock hours.

* Professional requirements listed are the basic requirements for degree or lowest regular certificates. Some variation from the professional requirements as stated in this table may be found in the requirements for specific certificates listed for the respective states in Chapter II.

† Not included in Col. 4.

[a] For the standard certificate; a bachelor's degree for the conditional certificate.

[b] For the provisional certificate; five years for the standard certificate.

[c] For elementary and junior high school.

[d] Bachelor's degree with a total of 120 s.h., including 78 in general education and 16 in professional education; the remaining 26 can be in either.

[e] For the provisional certificate; five years for the standard certificate.

[f] Plus 13 s.h. in general academic subjects (English, social science, mathematics, art, music).

[g] A teacher who has taught successfully for four or more years is required to take only 4 s.h. of practice teaching or a seminar of 4. A teacher who has had two years of successful experience may take a seminar dealing with professional problems instead of the 8 s.h. in practice teaching.

[h] The specified requirement in clock hours of actual teaching and observation is 90, 45 of which must be in actual teaching.

[i] Completion of the bachelor's degree or graduation from a four-year normal school approved by the State Board of Education.

[j] For a three-year certificate; for a five-year certificate, the requirement is 30.

[k] The practice-teaching requirement is 150 clock hours, 90 of which must be in actual classroom teaching.

[l] Five years required for the permanent certificate. A provisional certificate is issued upon completion of the bachelor's degree with 24 s.h. in education *and* 300 clock hours of practice teaching. Credit for practice teaching is optional with the college—maximum for 300 clock hours is 10 s.h. The provisional certificate is valid for five years; nonrenewable; holder must complete requirements for the permanent certificate.

[m] For the standard certificate; for the temporary certificate the requirement is 12.

[n] Required, but there is no specific hours requirement.

[o] Eighteen in professional education and 18 in content subjects for the elementary schools.

[p] For the provisional certificate; five years for the standard certificate.

[q] The state requires 85 s.h. of "nonprofessional" credit.

[r] Recommended.

TABLE 2
Specific Minimum Requirements for Secondary School Certificates
Based on Degrees*

State	Degree or College Years of Preparation Required	General Education Required, Semester Hours	Professional Education Required, Semester Hours	Directed Teaching Required, Semester Hours (Included in Column 4)
1	2	3	4	5
Alabama	B	44	21	6
Alaska	B	—	18	C
Arizona	5^a	40	22	6
Arkansas	B	48	18	6
California	5^b	45	15	120CH
Colorado	B	AC	AC	AC
Connecticut	B^c	45	18	6
Delaware	B	60	18	6
D. of C.	5^d	NS	15	C
Florida	B	45	20	6
Georgia	B	40	18	6
Hawaii	B	100	18	AC†
Idaho	B	—	20	6
Illinois	B	42	16	5
Indiana	B^e	50	18	6
Iowa	B	40	20	5
Kansas	B	50	20	5
Kentucky	B^f	45	17	8^g
Louisiana	B	46	18	4^h
Maine	B	64	18	6
Maryland	B	—	18	6
Massachusetts	B^i	—	12	2
Michigan	B	—	20	5
Minnesota	B	—	18	4
Mississippi	B	48	18	6
Missouri	B	25	20	5
Montana	B	AC	16	AC
Nebraska	B	AC	AC	AC
Nevada	B	—	18	4
New Hampshire	B	—	18	6
New Jersey	B	—	24^j	6^j
New Mexico	B	48	18	6
New York	5^k	60	18	6
North Carolina	B	48	18	6
North Dakota	B	—	16	3
Ohio	B	100	17	6
Oklahoma	B	50	21^l	6
Oregon	B^m	—	14	$—^n$
Pennsylvania	B^o	60	18	6
Puerto Rico	B	—	29	5
Rhode Island	B	—	18	6
South Carolina	B	45	18	6
South Dakota	B	—	20	6
Tennessee	B	40	24	4
Texas	B	60	18	6
Utah	B	AC	21	8
Vermont	B	AC	18	6
Virginia	B	48	15	4-6
Washington	B^p	AC	AC	AC
West Virginia	B	40^q	20	6
Wisconsin	B	$—^r$	18	5
Wyoming	B	40	20	C

Table 2 Footnotes

Legend: — means not reported; AC means approved curriculum; B means completion of the bachelor's degree; 5 means the bachelor's degree plus a fifth year of appropriate preparation, not necessarily completion of the master's degree; C means a course; CH means clock hours; NS means not specified.

* Professional requirements listed are the basic requirements for degree or lowest regular certificates. Some variation from the professional requirements as stated in this table may be found in the requirements for specific certificates listed for the respective states in Chapter II.

† Not included in Col. 4.

[a] Secondary certificate: five years of college preparation. Secondary-temporary: bachelor's degree and completion of an approved program; valid for five years only (grades 7-12).

[b] Between October 1, 1966, and October 1, 1967, California will permit preliminary certification of secondary teachers with a bachelor's degree, completion of student teaching, 6 s.h. of postgraduate work at the upper-division or graduate level, 14 s.h. in the major, and 12 in the minor (minor not required with academic major in subject commonly taught). A master's or higher degree in a subject commonly taught in the public high schools is acceptable in lieu of the student teaching, major, minor, and postgraduate requirements for purposes of meeting requirements for preliminary certification. Secondary preliminary certification is granted only if a statement of intention to employ is submitted by a California public school administrator. Course work requirements for the initial issuance of this credential increase 6 s.h. on October 1 of each year.

[c] For the provisional certificate; five years for the standard certificate.

[d] A master's degree is required for the permanent certificate for senior and vocational high school.

[e] A master's degree is required for the permanent certificate.

[f] For the provisional certificate; five years for the standard certificate.

[g] A teacher who has taught successfully for four or more years is required to take only 4 s.h. of practice teaching or a seminar of 4. A teacher who has had two years of successful experience may take a seminar dealing with professional problems instead of the 8 s.h. in practice teaching.

[h] The specified requirement in clock hours of actual teaching and observation is 90, 45 of which must be in actual teaching.

[i] Completion of the bachelor's degree or graduation from a four-year normal school approved by the State Board of Education.

[j] The practice-teaching requirement is 150 clock hours, 90 of which must be in actual classroom teaching.

[k] A provisional high school certificate is issued for academic fields based upon completion of a bachelor's degree with 18 s.h. in education; 8 are to be in methods and practice teaching. A minimum of 80 class periods of practice teaching is required. The provisional certificate is valid for five years; nonrenewable; holder must complete requirements for permanent certification.

[l] For the standard certificate; for the temporary certificate the requirement is 12.

[m] For the provisional certificate; five years for the standard certificate.

[n] Required, but there is no specific hours requirement.

[o] Twenty-four s.h. of postbaccalaureate work required for permanent certification.

[p] For the provisional certificate; five years for the standard certificate.

[q] The state requires 100 s.h. of "nonprofessional" credit.

[r] Patterns for general education must be approved by the state superintendent and be filed in his office.

TABLE 3

Summary of Minimum Preparation Required by States for
Administrative Certificates (as of January 1, 1967)

Number of College Years of Preparation or Degree Required	Number of States Requiring		
	Elementary School Principal	Secondary School Principal	Superintendent of Schools
1	2	3	4
7 years or doctor's degree	0	0	1
6 years plus, but less than doctor's degree	0	0	1
6 years	3	3	18
Master's degree plus, but less than 6 years	8	8	4
Master's degree	35 [a]	37 [a]	26 [a]
Bachelor's degree plus, but less than 5 years	3	2	0
Bachelor's degree	2	1	0
Less than bachelor's degree	0	0	0
No certificate issued	1	1	2
Totals	52 [b]	52 [b]	52 [b]

[a] Includes Puerto Rico, which does not specify an advanced degree but the bachelor's degree plus 30 s.h. Also includes the District of Columbia and Virginia, which do not issue administrative certificates but do require the master's degree for endorsement on other types of certificates.

[b] Includes D.C. and Puerto Rico.

one time payment for additional work, such as coaching teams, directing plays or guiding school newspapers, was not regarded as compatible with professional status, payment for such activities is also now regarded as acceptable. According to most dictionary definitions and definitions offered in many publications, the essential elements of a profession are (1) a body of knowledge and skill which must be mastered, (2) application of knowledge and skill in performing service for others, (3) self-regulated standards of performance in accordance with high social and ethical purposes, and (4) emphasis upon performance of service rather than upon economic gain. Lieberman has further enumerated the characteristics of a profession: [27]

1. A unique, definite, and essential social service.
2. An emphasis upon intellectual techniques in performing this service.
3. A long period of specialized training.
4. A broad range of autonomy for both the individual practitioners and the occupational group as a whole.
5. An acceptance by practitioners of broad personal responsibility for judgments made and acts performed within the scope of professional autonomy.
6. An emphasis upon the service to be rendered, rather than the economic gain to the practitioners, as a basis for the organization and performance of the social service delegated to the occupational group.

7. A comprehensive self-governing organization of practitioners.
8. A code of ethics that has been clarified and interpreted in its ambiguous and doubtful points by concrete cases.

While some of the characteristics of a professional teacher are given attention in some teacher-education programs, other characteristics may be neglected. Generally speaking, few teacher-education programs pay much attention in organized fashion to the development of professional ideals. There are also practical factors that injure the professional status of teaching. As a result of the shortage of teachers, for example, individuals have been put into teaching positions with little or no professional training, and without having gone through an institutionally approved program. The availability of this type of backdoor entrance to a teaching career may lead students to avoid the long period of specialized training. If standards of admission to a collegiate teacher-education program are either low or non-existent, the status of the teaching profession is lowered. If the teacher-education program itself is deemed impractical, theoretical, repetitive and lacking in substance, the status of the teaching profession suffers. The unfortunate consequence of lowering the status of a profession is that capable individuals will not desire to enter it. That is disadvantageous for education and for society.

Efforts have been made in some collegiate institutions to develop an esprit de corps among education students by having them join a teacher-education club or similar organization while they are still undergraduates. The voluntary activities, discussions and group decisions form an important orientation to the self-directed activities of the professional educator. National organizations of teachers, such as N.E.A. and A.F.T., have offered pre-service memberships to undergraduate education students and have sponsored collegiate organizations of such students in an effort to develop professional attitudes and responsibility. Teacher-education undergraduates should also be habituated to reading professional journals, appropriate periodicals and books, and to attending conferences and conventions. These are normal channels of self-directed improvement that are engaged in by practitioners of all professions.

Other professions have a code of ethics consisting of self-imposed regulations of behavior, and there has been considerable discussion through the years of a code of ethics for teachers. There has been no national agreement on the specifics of such a code, although at different times, the N.E.A. and other associations have formulated such codes. Even if there is no agreement, discussion of a code of ethics among education students is helpful in clarifying the responsibilities, duties and characteristics of professional educators.

There are many ways of developing professional teachers. Personal attitudes, behavior and ideals may be developed directly or indirectly in the cur-

95

riculum in which pedagogic training is given. Voluntary extracurricular activities may be utilized for this purpose, or a separate course may be offered on the nature of the teaching profession. Brochures and articles on the subject may be distributed for reading by education majors. The responsibility for developing a professional attitude must be shared by many individuals and groups, including the collegiate faculty and teacher organizations. School administrators, school board members and the public also have a role to play, for they must treat teachers as professionals who share in educational planning and decision making and who should be paid salaries commensurate with professional duties. Above all, there must be instilled in the education student, beginning at the outset of his preparation, the desire to become a professional in the broadest sense.

THE SCHOOL PERSONNEL ADMINISTRATOR AND TEACHER EDUCATION

In many respects the school personnel administrator occupies an intermediate position between the public school system and the collegiate institution. In his recruitment and selection of teaching staff, he is in a position to point out to the collegiate institution the strengths and weaknesses of their products as revealed in the classroom. To that extent, he can exercise considerable influence on teacher-education programs and curricula. For example, he may have occasion to report to a given university that its graduates are lacking in certain practical elements of classroom management, or are weak in their ability to plan lessons or to use audio-visual materials. Since collegiate institutions are sometimes ahead of school districts in experimenting with new techniques and procedures, the school personnel administrator may be in the position of urging school administrators to go along with, and indeed to encourage, experimentation with which he may be acquainted as a result of his working relationships with collegiate institutions. He may also find himself in the role of interpreting new teaching procedures to the school administration. The school personnel administrator must know the characteristics of the teacher-education programs in various institutions, so that he can locate teachers for special programs. In order that he may fulfill that function satisfactorily, the administrator must meet with college placement officials and with heads of education departments and professors of education, so that he can develop familiarity with the practices of the institutions that he has contact with. He must also attend conferences and conventions at which teacher-education programs are discussed, and his reading of periodicals and books must include those that deal with teacher education. The cooperation of the school personnel administrator may be needed by a college in obtaining full-time or part-time personnel who have public school teaching experience to serve on collegiate faculties for student teaching or for teaching methodology. The personnel administrator may also be involved in setting up exchange programs between pro-
96

fessors of pedagogy and school personnel so that each may be better equipped to fulfill his function in education.

One of the problems that must be solved by the profession itself is a definition of the relationship of teachers to those who perform auxiliary services, such as social workers, psychologists, and guidance counselors, as well as a definition of the relationship between teachers and paraprofessionals. Should such people be considered part of the teaching profession? What should be the nature of their preparation for service? Should their preparation for service include courses in pedagogy? Should they be certificated? What requirements should they meet? What should be their daily working relationships with teachers? Those are some of the questions that must be answered.

6 PERSONNEL RECRUITMENT

GENERAL STATEMENT

Teacher recruitment is a multidimensional, continuous activity involving much more than a hunting expedition. Of course, a good program of teacher recruitment includes visits to sources of teacher supply for the purpose of locating and contracting prospective teachers. That is a necessary short-range activity, but there are concomitant long-range activities that have an important bearing upon the success of a teacher recruiter on the road or at home. In its broadest sense, an effective teacher-recruitment program must be based upon the cooperative efforts of the board of education representing the community, the school superintendent and his administrative officers, the school staff, and the offices of the school personnel administrator.

Recruitment should be considered the most essential phase of the school personnel program. The demand for quality teachers is high, and personnel administrators will find it increasingly difficult to staff classrooms without using systematic plans to locate and attract competent teachers for service in their districts.

SHORT-RANGE ASPECTS OF TEACHER RECRUITMENT

1. *Policy decisions basic to personnel recruitment.* An essential first step in teacher recruitment, one which should involve the board of education and the school superintendent, is the formulation of guidelines for selecting personnel for the school system. Such questions as the following must be answered: What are the responsibilities and powers of the school personnel administrator? What standards of professional and personal qualifications are to be required of prospective teachers? Is the personnel administrator or his representative empowered to offer contracts? If so, on what bases

and with what limitations? What procedures are to be followed from the first contact through induction into service? What authority will the board of education delegate? What authority will they retain? What budget is allowed for staff recruitment? What portions are to be spent for various purposes? A board of education may set general or specific requirements to be sought in prospective staff members. For example, they might endorse a recent statement of the N.E.A. Task Force on Urban Education:

> "Urban schools need educators . . . who demonstrate their belief in the real worth of each child, who respect children of different racial and socio-economic backgrounds, and who know and respect the values and customs of these backgrounds." [1]

Boards of education may also set more specific requirements for training in special fields, courses or experience. Such special requirements are usually set in consultation with the school superintendent and his advisors.

2. *Preparation for the college visit.* Careful preparation is needed for visits to the teacher-placement office of a college. Estimates must be made of vacancies for the ensuing year. Usually, when the recruiter visits a college campus in January, February or March, his school system's budget for the ensuing year will not have been established. He does not know how many positions he will have, or how many teachers will have to be replaced. He must, however, make a working estimate of his probable needs. This procedure has inherent risks of error, but with the approval of the superintendent and the board of education estimates of staff needs must be made. The experiences of previous years, in terms of staff turnover, leaves, retirements and school growth, are the best guides to current needs. Firm offers of jobs should not be made for every estimated vacancy. Experienced school personnel directors have made firm offers for from 50 to 80 percent of estimated needs, allowing latitude for other offers to be made when the budget becomes more definite. The visit to a college placement office should be arranged by mail or telephone well in advance of the date, and a letter of notice or reminder should go out approximately two weeks before the visit is undertaken. The availability of prospective teachers should also be considered. Such information may be obtained from the college itself.

3. *Use of statistical data.* General statistics on the supply of and demand for teachers are also available from the U.S. Office of Education and from the Research Division of the N.E.A. The data provided have relevance for both short-range and long-range aspects of personnel recruitment. For example, it may be useful to know, by comparison with staff size, the national trends in numbers of teacher-education graduates. Table 1 reveals the substantial increases, particularly among secondary school candidates, during the years indicated.[2] It should be borne in mind that only 60 to 80 percent of all education graduates actually enter teaching and that the two other major sources of teachers are former education graduates who re-enter teaching and liberal arts graduates who turn to teaching.

TABLE 1

Estimates of the Total Number of Public School Teachers
and the Number of Teacher-Education Graduates
Ready for Employment Each Year Since 1955–56

Session	Total teachers	Elementary Teacher-education graduates of previous year Number	Percent of total	Total teachers	Secondary Teacher-education graduates of previous year Number	Percent of total
1	2	3	4	5	6	7
1955–56	733,000	37,712	5.1	408,000	49,697	12.2
1956–57	751,000	40,801	5.4	447,000	56,785	12.7
1957–58	786,000	44,029	5.6	473,000	65,062	13.8
1958–59	815,000	45,318	5.3	491,000	69,093	14.1
1959–60	832,000	47,836	5.7	524,000	71,585	13.7
1960–61	858,000	52,630	6.1	550,000	77,573	14.1
1961–62	869,000	51,866	6.0	592,000	77,322	13.1
1962–63	886,000	57,854	6.5	621,000	84,489	13.6
1963–64	908,000	61,979	6.8	669,000	96,378	14.4
1964–65	940,000	72,581	7.7	708,000	101,552	14.3
1965–66	965,000	77,773	8.1	746,000	112,436	15.1
1966–67	1,005,000	77,703 *	7.7	783,000	122,208 *	15.6
1967–68	1,027,000	76,607 †	7.5	816,000	121,554 *†	14.9
1968–69 (est.)	1,039,000	89,941 *†	8.6	853,000	146,511 *†	17.2
1969–70 (est.)	1,061,000	105,551 *	9.9	881,000	174,344	19.8

Source of staff size: U.S. Department of Health, Education, and Welfare, Office of Education. *Projections of Educational Statistics to 1976–77*. Washington, D.C.: Government Printing Office, 1968. Table 23. (Fall staff size includes number of part-time teachers.)

* Persons prepared to teach specific subjects, librarians, and guidance counsel-ors are classified as secondary, consistent with practice in earlier years. Persons prepared to enter employment as school psychologists, school social workers, school nurses, and other ungraded assignments are not included.

† Estimate may be from two to six percent lower than actual numbers, owing to incomplete reports in two states.

An N.E.A. publication provides varying types of national and state statistics on teacher supply and demand.[3] For example, Table 2 compares the supply of beginning teachers with the demand, based upon an N.E.A. formula called the "adjusted trend criterion," which includes the components of (a) new positions created by increased enrollment and (b) replacements for teachers who discontinue service. Of course, local trends may differ from national trends as a result of factors such as major modifications in a school program, major reductions or increases in pupil-teacher ratios, expansion or decreases in federal programs, local building of public housing, local economic conditions, actions of collegiate institutions in the area, changes in military regulations for deferments and changes in certification requirements.

Statistical trends in numbers of education graduates by states are also available in publications, as indicated by the following sample enumerating graduates preparing to teach in elementary schools.[4]

TABLE 2

Summary of Estimated Supply Compared with the Adjusted Trend Criterion
Estimate of Demand for Beginning Teachers in 1968, Elementary School
and Secondary School Subject Areas, by Rank

Assignment	Numerical difference in the estimated supply of beginning teachers and estimated demand based on		Percent of teacher-education graduates entering the profession	Estimated additional supply if 70.0 per cent of graduates entered	Additional demand if estimated re-entry rate is reduced by 10 percent	General condition
	Percent distribution in 1967	National estimate				
1	2	3	4	5	6	7
Mathematics	−2,977	−3,578	69.1	93	−293	Critical shortage
Natural and physical sciences	−2,033	−2,367	63.1	780	−266	Critical shortage
Trade, industrial, vocational, technical	−1,489	−954	44.2	157	−51	Shortage
Special education						
Elementary	−743	+1,855	71.9		−161	Low supply
Secondary	−484	+734	71.9		−46	Low supply
Industrial arts	+789	+801	70.3		−65	Low supply
Elementary, regular instruction	+1,865	+4,438	78.1		−2,945	Low supply
English language arts	+35	−503	65.1	1,294	−498	Low supply
Distributive education	−174		51.6	87	−12	Low supply
Junior high-school subjects	−802		80.7		−41	Possible shortage *
Physical and health education						
Elementary	−1,258	−504	69.8	1	−72	Possible shortage *
Secondary (tot.)	+2,707	+5,033	67.6	349	−206	Ad. supply
Men	+2,329		63.5	583	−95	Ad. supply
Women	+378		74.2		−111	Low supply
Agriculture	+333	+459	57.2	262	−24	Near bal.*
Home economics	+950	+1,491	63.4	447	−97	Near bal.*
Art						
Elementary	−175	+469	67.5	21	−33	Near bal.*
Secondary	+1,329	+2,017	66.2	220	−73	Near bal.
Business education	+1,111	+1,592	63.5	585	−133	Near bal.
Music						
Elementary	−1,042	−68	76.0		−72	Possible shortage *
Secondary	+1,129	+2,363	67.5	166	−97	Ad. supply
Foreign languages						
Elementary	+105	−2	75.6		−7	Near bal.*
Secondary	+1,403	+1,907	64.7	478	−128	Ad. supply
Social studies	+4,995	+5,648	59.0	2,976	−317	Ad. supply

* Information is not sufficiently complete to allow an accurate estimate of the
supply and demand condition.

TABLE 3
College Students Receiving Degrees and Prepared to Teach in the Elementary School, 1967 and 1968, by State

State	Bachelor's Degree						Master's Degree					
	Graduates of 1968			Total, 1967	1967 to 1968		Graduates of 1968			Total, 1967	1967 to 1968	
	Men	Women	Total		Net Change	Percent Change	Men	Women	Total		Net Change	Percent Change
1	2	3	4	5	6	7	8	9	10	11	12	13
Alabama	48	1,162	1,210	1,070	+140	+13.1	8	93	101	105	−4	−3.8
Alaska	4	23	27	21	+6	+28.6						
Arizona	146	790	936	891	+45	+5.1	107	283	390	444	−54	−12.2
Arkansas	69	783	852	713	+139	+19.5	10	72	82	59	+23	+39.0
California	245	1,917	2,162	2,142	+20	+.9	369	2,486	2,835	1,742	+1,115	+63.9
Colorado	94	899	993	871	+122	+14.0	19	92	111	135	−24	−17.8
Connecticut	137	969	1,106	1,069	+37	+3.5	110	253	363	209	+154	+73.7
Delaware	18	149	167	142	+23	+17.6				1	−1	−100.0
D. of C.	2	118	120	250	−130	−52.0						
Florida	236	1,831	2,067	1,712	+355	+20.7	118	183	301	405	−104	−25.7
Georgia	60	1,448	1,508	1,169	+339	+29.0	12	73	85	78	+7	+9.0
Hawaii	5	226	231	233	−2	−.9	1	191	192	173	+19	+11.0
Idaho	34	226	260	401	−141	−35.2	6	1	7	10	−3	−30.0
Illinois	320	2,523	2,843	2,470	+373	+15.1	64	52	116	102	+14	+13.7
Indiana	212	1,829	2,041	2,072	−31	−1.5		9	9	7	+2	+28.6
Iowa	94	1,620	1,714	1,101	+613	+53.7		6	6	3	+3	+100.0
Kansas	117	1,403	1,522	1,321	+201	+15.2	51	126	177	262	−85	−32.4
Kentucky	193	1,606	1,799	1,573	+226	+14.4	6	38	44	33	+11	+33.3
Louisiana	142	1,433	1,575	1,404	+171	+12.2						
Maine	52	291	343	318	+25	+7.9						
Maryland	102	953	1,055	979	+76	+7.8	25	72	97	75	+22	+29.3
Massachusetts	248	1,061	2,109	1,573	+534	+33.9	94	125	219	211	+8	+3.8
Michigan	429	3,752	4,181	3,976	+205	+5.2	93	199	292	296	−4	−1.4
Minnesota	403	1,945	2,048	2,117	+231	+10.9	61	32	93	76	+17	+22.4

102

State												
Mississippi	79	1,101	1,180	1,183	−3	−.3	10	43	53	34	+19	+55.9
Missouri	178	1,747	1,925	1,739	+186	+10.7	3	20	23	9	+14	+155.6
Montana	63	525	588	580	+8	+1.4				15	−15	−100.0
Nebraska	273	1,219	1,492	1,296	+196	+15.1	5	16	21	19	+2	+10.5
Nevada	8	96	104	113	−9	−8.0	5	11	16	5	+11	+220.0
New Hampshire	31	341	372	279	+93	+33.3	1	5	6	10	−4	−40.0
New Jersey	255	2,412	2,667	2,176	+491	+22.6	20	19	39	47	−8	−17.0
New Mexico	30	297	327	312	+15	+4.8	11	33	44	61	−17	−27.9
New York	818	7,463	8,281	6,713	+1,568	+23.4	565	4,544	5,109	1,309	+3,800	+280.3
North Carolina *			1,851	1,643	+208	+12.7			287	276	+11	+4.0
North Dakota †	59	426	485	425	+60	+14.1				1	−1	−100.0
Ohio †	301	4,315	4,616	4,566	+50	+1.1			51	88	−37	−42.0
Oklahoma	195	1,195	1,390	1,390			70	241	311	311		
Oregon	97	922	1,019	1,069	−50	−4.7	1	5	6	22	−16	−72.7
Pennsylvania	617	4,521	5,138	4,560	+578	+12.7	21	55	76	50	+26	+52.0
Rhode Island	65	437	502	433	+69	+15.9	17	26	43	69	−26	−37.7
South Carolina	26	794	820	646	+174	+26.9	1	2	3	6	−3	−50.0
South Dakota	47	591	638	614	+24	+3.9	5	16	21	13	+8	+61.5
Tennessee	124	1,397	1,521	1,272	+249	+19.6						
Texas	494	4,285	4,779	4,464	+315	+7.1	88	271	359	368	−9	−2.4
Utah	135	877	1,012	970	+42	+4.3			2	1	+1	+100.0
Vermont	31	229	260	209	+51	+24.4		2	2	4	−2	−50.0
Virginia	65	1,195	1,260	1,077	+183	+17.0	1	45	46	34	+12	+35.3
Washington	222	1,747	1,969	1,512	+457	+30.2						
West Virginia	68	668	736	503	+153	+26.2						
Wisconsin ‡	214	1,522	2,177	1,981	+196	+9.9	50	93	143	106	+37	+34.9
Wyoming	11	118	129	124	+5	+4.0						
Total	7,916	70,199	80,407	71,519	+8,888	+12.4	2,040	9,859	12,201	7,284	+4,517	+67.5

* All institutions did not report bachelor's and master's degrees data by sex for 1968 and master's degree data by sex for 1967.
† Some institutions did not report master's degree data by sex for 1968.
‡ Some institutions did not report bachelor's degree data by sex for 1968.

4. *Use of materials as recruitment aids.* Attractive pictorial booklets are of some value in teacher recruitment. They should show the buildings, children, staff, community and available facilities of the school system. The essential features of the school system should be indicated attractively and truthfully. No school system can afford to prepare brochures that are not truthful representations of actuality. Not only is it unethical but it does not take long before the true reputation of the district is revealed, and return visits to the college placement office will be less welcome and certainly less successful. Some school systems have prepared pictorial folders, film slides and even sound movies as recruitment aids. It is reported that such elaborate efforts have had diminishing results.

Recruitment brochures or leaflets should include the following information: salary schedules; school enrollment; class sizes; population; geographic location; requirements for certification and other specifics of eligibility; housing and living accommodations; fringe benefits, such as medical insurance, sabbaticals, other leaves of absence; tenure provisions; opportunities for advancement; in-service programs; and educational cultural and recreational opportunities.

5. *The application form.* Either before or after the interview, the prospective teacher should fill out an application form. Some school personnel administrators prefer to have the more detailed application filled out only if the applicant is being seriously considered for employment. However, if the application is filled out before the employment interview, it may become a partial basis for the interview in a discussion of the applicant's background and experience. Whether filled out before or after the interview, it provides necessary information for follow-up investigation and for transcribing to permanent records of the school system. Various types of application forms are used by different school systems. Each application form should be adapted to the needs of the particular school system that is using it. Some of the desirable features of an application form are the following: convenience of size for filing, adequate space for essential information, adequate space for notations by the interviewer and adequate space for subsequent entries during the career of the teacher, inquiries limited to essential information within the limitations of law, items arranged for facility in reading and analyzing, information given concerning responsibility for obtaining transcripts or certificates. Of course, if the school system has machine processing, the information called for should be of such nature and arrangement as to facilitate machine processing.

Most application forms require such information as the following:

> Name, address (permanent and temporary), telephone number.
> Name or names by which the applicant was formerly known.
> Date of birth, citizenship, marital status.
> Teaching subject and level of school service sought.
> Collegiate major and minor subjects.

Degrees conferred and names of institutions conferring them.

High schools and colleges attended and dates of attendance.

Chronological statement of places of employment (both teaching and non-teaching).

Teaching certificates held, if any.

Names and addresses of individuals who may serve as professional and personal references.

Report of medical examination or medical history.

In some school systems, applicants are asked to indicate whether they have ever been discharged from employment and whether they have ever been arrested. They may also be asked to tell succinctly why they are applying to the particular school system.

Legal considerations are involved in the preparation of an application form. For example, in some states it is forbidden to inquire about nationality, religion or loyalty, or to request the submission of a photograph. References and transcripts should be obtained by the personnel administrator directly from the original sources rather than from the applicant

6. *The employment interview.* Representatives of a school system who are recruiting teachers on college campuses or other places away from the offices of the school personnel administrator are usually given the authority to offer or to recommend the offer of a contract to acceptable candidates. Usually, the contract is for a year and subject to renewal if service is satisfactory. In many large cities, the candidate is required, during his year of service, to pass a required examination in order to achieve "regular" status and tenure.

Since the recommendation of the offer of a contract by the recruiter is usually based upon the candidate's collegiate record and an employment interview on the college campus, the teacher recruiter should receive training in conducting employment interviews. His employment interview should not be aimless, or vaguely general, but should be specifically directed toward ascertaining those qualities of an applicant that may be reliably discovered during an interview. The questions he intends to ask should be prepared in advance. He should have a printed form with specified criteria for recording his reactions to the prospective teacher. He should avoid dominating the interview and should allow the applicant to do most of the talking. He should allow ample time for the applicant to ask questions and should encourage questions. The point of the establishment of rapport between the interviewer and the interviewee is to present a fair picture of the interviewee, most of whom are somewhat tense in an employment interview. The experienced interviewer watches for evidence of tension or nervousness reflected in tight knuckles, perspiration, dry lips or even tremors on the part of the prospective teacher. These manifestations may have no bearing on the teaching ability of the applicant. The experienced interviewer therefore begins with some informal questions about the applicant's college,

105

recent experiences, and interests in order to set the applicant at ease and to establish communication.

The teacher recruiter should recognize the limitations of the interview. One school superintendent, who was able to interview all applicants for teaching positions himself, is reported to have claimed that he was able to tell a good teacher by the way the applicant walked to his desk after entering the door. Through an interview, one is able to judge the ability of an individual to discuss various topics and one is able to appraise certain discernible characteristics, such as grooming, mannerisms and poise. One cannot, in the typical interview, reliably discern the dedicated teacher, the excellent disciplinarian, the conscientious performer, and so on. So it is desirable to supplement the interview by using such records as the college can make available concerning the work habits and other performance characteristics of the prospective teacher. Questions asked of a candidate about his relationship with pupils or his method of teaching may reveal the candidate's ability to discuss professional topics, though not necessarily his ability to perform. That is not to belittle the value of a candidate's expressed knowledge of professional practices. It is merely to alert the teacher recruiter to the fact that there is a difference between knowledge and performance. One teacher recruiter, instead of using questions, had large pictures of particular classroom situations which he asked the prospective teacher to discuss. He had a picture of a teacher working with a small committee in one corner of the room while other members of the class were doing other work. He had another picture of a teacher sitting, relaxed at her desk while the class was busy studying. The pictures served as vehicles for discussion of the candidate's knowledge of professional practices.

7. *The recruitment interviewers.* Many school personnel administrators have found it desirable to delegate trips to various individuals selected from the school staff. But practices have varied. Some administrators have preferred to use young teachers who have three to five years of experience as teacher-recruitment interviewers because they may more easily bridge "the generation gap." Others have asked school principals or teachers who have substantial experience to make teacher recruitment trips. Teachers who were graduates of particular colleges have been sent back to those colleges to do the teacher recruitment there. No single pattern has proved definitely more valuable than another because there are so many variable factors. In all cases, however, the recruiters must be briefed adequately, must prepare in advance, and must have appropriate materials and information to give to the prospective teachers on the college campuses.

There are tangential advantages in allowing school personnel other than those in the central personnel office to participate in teacher recruitment. Such personnel will get to know the problems of staff recruitment at first hand and will be more likely to develop a sympathetic understanding of the problems in the rest of the school staff and in members of the community. Sharing the problems of staff recruitment more widely is thus more likely to bring favorable responses to the school personnel administrator's efforts to improve staff recruitment.

A study of recruitment procedures in 320 large public school systems by Gilbert et al. indicates that the individual who most frequently does the recruiting and selecting of teachers outside a radius of twenty-five miles is the director of personnel or one of his staff members (75.9 percent of the 320 school systems). A principal is used as his representative in 41.2 percent of these school systems. The superintendent of schools performs this function in 33.8 percent of the schools. The director of elementary or secondary education does the recruiting for the personnel director in 31.9 percent of these school systems. A classroom teacher is used to perform this function in only 3.4 percent of these large school systems.[5]

8. *Cost of recruitment.* The cost of staff recruitment varies from school district to school district depending upon the district's size, the staff turnover, and locations of colleges and other sources of supply. To a great extent the cost may be hidden because administrators involved in recruitment may be giving their services on a part-time basis while they perform other duties in the school district. Thus the indicated costs usually consist of advertising materials and travel expenses. A publication of the National School Public Relations Association indicates that "the typical industry cost for recruiting an engineer is about $1,000" and one personnel director is quoted as believing that the cost of recruiting a teacher may run from $600 to $1,000 for those who must recruit at long range.[6] It is recognized that staff time is the most expensive part of the operation. Other estimates obained by that publication varied from $100 to $325 per teacher. The 1969 collective bargaining agreement between the United Federation of Teachers and the Board of Education in New York City set up a $500,000 fund for teacher-recruitment activities to be planned jointly by the U.F.T. and the Board, with increased emphasis upon recruiting minority-group teachers.

9. *After the employment interview.* Prospective teachers wish to be told whether or not they have obtained their positions as soon as possible. Some college placement directors prefer that no contract be issued at the time of the placement interview. In a situation where some receive contracts and others who may still be under consideration do not, there may be a lack of privacy as a student is almost compelled to tell his classmates that he did not obtain a contract. Such situations have led to unhappiness and sometimes resentment on the part of prospective young teachers. It is desirable to send a letter of acknowledgement to those interviewed during the week or two following the interview. Common courtesy and proper relationships require that those who are not employed be informed as politely as possible of their status. If it is possible to inform the prospective teacher of the exact nature and place of his assignment, that would be ideal. However,

since the school personnel administrator may not immediately have information about the individual's school and class assignment, specific information should follow the contract or notice of employment as soon as possible.

A study comparing the times of notification of appointment to candidates for September positions in large city school systems and in a number of small districts indicated that May is the most frequent month of notification (about 33 percent of the school systems). About 23 percent of the school systems studied send notifications in April, and about 19 percent do so in June.[7]

10. *Other information about applicants.* The personal interview conducted by the teacher recruiter provides one source of information concerning the prospective teacher, but the interview per se has limitations as an instrument of appraisal. Other information should be sought. Reports about personal habits, abilities, and interests of prospective teachers should be obtained through the placement office from college instructors who have worked with the individual. When standardized test scores, such as those obtained in the National Teacher Examination, are available, they should be included in the appraisal. It may be desirable to have a sample of the applicant's ability to write correctly and clearly. While waiting for the interview, therefore, applicants may be asked to write a brief statement on a suggested topic, such as why they prefer teaching a particular subject, individualized instruction, the importance to teachers of a good background in liberal arts and sciences, or any other suitable topic that provides the interviewer with a sample of the prospective teacher's ability to write. Some cities require that applicants take examinations of their own construction before beginning service or during the first year of teaching. Other cities may require all applicants to be fingerprinted for referral to F.B.I. files. References are useful for those who have previous experience, and reports on college students' part-time work experiences in summer camps or other jobs may be useful to the personnel administrator in making a decision on the selection of prospective teachers.

11. *Off campus teacher recruitment.* Although most teachers are recruited from the ranks of college seniors, many teachers are obtained through other sources. Experienced teachers frequently wish to change from one locality to another for a variety of reasons. One source of such referrals is the college placement office, where personnel enrolled for advanced degrees may leave their names for placement.

Teacher employment agencies make available the names of prospective teachers. Some school personnel administrators have used newspapers to advertise teaching positions. Teachers' organizations, realizing the importance of having a voice in the selection of colleagues, have participated in recruitment. One such organization has referred to its role as "teacher-to-teacher recruitment." State teacher associations have taken part in recruitment by advertising staff needs and trends in their publications, by

108

supporting Future Teacher Clubs, and by cooperating with state education departments. Personnel needs should be made known to the staff through publications issued to the staff.

Teacher recruiters sometimes have set up interviews with applicants in hotel rooms. That may be acceptable where experienced personnel are concerned, but college placement officers have frowned upon the practice as far as college students are concerned.

Teachers' conventions also provide opportunities for recruitment, particularly with respect to experienced teachers interested in changing their positions. Announcements of teaching opportunities, together with the times and places of interviews, are usually displayed. For supervisory and administrative positions, conventions such as that of the American Association of School Administrators, held annually in Atlantic City, are the scenes of extensive recruitment activities.

When inquiries and credentials come to the school personnel administrator by mail, it is desirable to obtain references or some personal appraisal. Sometimes a personal interview can be arranged with a colleague of the school personnel administrator who resides in the city from which the applicant's letter is sent. In all cases, a friendly letter individually typed and welcoming the inquiry should be sent in response. An application form, a statement of requirements, and a pictorial brochure about the school system should be enclosed.

Retired policemen, firemen, military personnel, businessmen, post office workers and other civil service personnel who retire between the ages of 45 and 50 have become successful teachers. Advertisements in civil service publications and in trade union publications have yielded results.

State education departments have rendered valuable assistance to school districts in broad recruitment programs, including these activities:

1. Arranging statewide or regional career conferences on teaching.
2. Providing advice on teacher recruitment to school districts.
3. Preparing, printing and distributing teacher-career pamphlets.
4. Developing special programs for retraining teachers and for training liberal arts graduates as teachers.
5. Providing funds and other incentives to teacher-training programs.
6. Making available teacher supply-and-demand status in the state.
7. Encouraging public schools to provide Future Teacher experiences.

A study of the resources used by 320 large public school systems revealed that placement bureaus are the most frequently used resource. The percentage of the 320 school systems using each resource is indicated in Table 4.

TABLE 4
Resources Used in the Recruitment of Applicants

1. Placement bureaus of teachers' colleges, liberal arts colleges, and universities — 95.6%
2. Voluntary application — 94.4%
3. Direct recruitment on campuses of teachers' colleges and universities — 85.3%
4. Commercial teacher agencies — 37.8%
5. Published announcements of open positions — 37.2%
6. State departments of education — 33.4%
7. State teachers association — 30.3%

LONG-RANGE TEACHER RECRUITMENT

1. *Teacher satisfaction and high morale.* The best all-around stimulus in teacher recruitment is a satisfied staff whose morale is high. The good word somehow spreads to the sources of supply both in the community and beyond, so that applicants are eager to obtain positions. Job satisfaction and high morale result in lower staff turnover and, therefore, fewer vacancies. In simple arithmetic, it is easier to recruit one new teacher who is likely to remain for several years than to recruit several teachers for the same position because none remains very long. Studies have indicated that job satisfaction is the most powerful element in reducing teacher turnover and in attracting new teachers, more powerful than a higher salary schedule. Staff satisfaction and high morale are based upon many factors: good working and social relationships with supervisors and colleagues, good community relationships, opportunities for creative expression, adequate supporting services, fair salaries and fringe benefits. Some of those factors —such as salaries and fringe benefits—the school personnel administrator may not be able to control directly. If he is to discharge his responsibility for obtaining a good school staff, however, he must seek to exert as much influence as he can to improve recruitment. If he is to be successful in exerting influence, he must be informed about salary schedules and working conditions in neighboring communities, and he must keep up with statewide and national trends. Information is available from publications of the U.S. Office of Education, the Research Division of the National Education Association, the American Federation of Teachers and other organizations, and directly from colleagues in school personnel work.

The average annual salaries of instructional staff from 1949–50 are indicated by states in the following table.[9]

Here is a comparison between the earnings of public school personnel and other professionals. It is notable that the average salary of school personnel is still substantially below that of other professional groups and that the gap that existed in 1960 has not diminished.[10]

A long-range personnel recruitment program should include statistical forecasts of needs for, say the next five years. The forecast should include student enrollment, teaching staff, administrative staff, supporting staff and paraprofessionals, and should indicate projected growth or decline in each

110

TABLE 5
Average Annual Salaries of Instructional Staff by State,
Selected School Years, 1949–50 through 1969–70
(in dollars)

State	1959–60	1961–62	1963–64	1965–66	1966–67	1967–68	1968–69	1969–70 *
1	2	3	4	5	6	7	8	9
50 states and D.C.	$5,174	$5,710	$6,203	$6,786	$7,129	$7,709	$ 8,194	$ 8,901
Alabama	4,002	4,070	4,820	5,350	5,800	5,900	6,050	6,954
Alaska	6,859	7,350	8,233	8,598	9,392	9,660	10,887	10,993
Arizona	5,590	6,150	6,610	7,165	7,430	7,840	8,465	8,975
Arkansas	3,295	3,678	4,098	4,755	5,113	5,702	6,291	6,445
California	6,600	7,200	7,700	8,600	9,000	9,450	9,800	10,746
Colorado	4,997	4,502	5,950	6,577	6,824	7,175	7,425	7,900
Connecticut	6,008	6,471	7,021	7,562	7,959	8,450	8,900	9,400
Delaware	5,800	6,242	6,677	7,532	7,804	7,994	8,400	9,300
Florida	5,080	5,549	6,176	6,378	7,085	7,700	8,600	8,600
Georgia	3,904	4,499	4,933	5,550	6,075	6,775	7,200	7,372
Hawaii	5,390	5,625	6,145	7,025	7,910	8,176	8,300	9,600
Idaho	4,216	4,761	5,075	5,856	6,012	6,200	6,400	7,081
Illinois	5,184	6,350	6,707	7,225	7,525	8,800	9,300	9,950
Indiana	5,542	6,081	6,492	7,292	7,663	8,269	8,350	9,574
Iowa	4,030	5,042	5,494	6,067	6,531	7,333	8,167	8,867
Kansas	4,450	5,036	5,448	5,957	6,270	6,723	7,217	7,811
Kentucky	3,327	4,232	4,613	5,200	5,680	6,288	6,750	7,450
Louisiana	4,978	5,246	5,299	5,987	6,598	6,980	7,200	7,220
Maine	3,694	4,619	5,100	5,600	5,950	7,288	7,288	8,059
Maryland	5,557	6,021	6,557	7,105	7,547	8,315	9,269	9,885
Massachusetts	5,545	5,900	6,860	7,350	7,550	7,770	8,350	9,175
Michigan	5,654	6,295	6,703	7,200	7,650	8,475	9,492	10,125
Minnesota	5,275	5,550	6,375	6,800	7,050	7,500	8,000	8,720
Mississippi	3,314	3,623	3,931	4,327	4,707	4,821	5,912	6,012
Missouri	4,536	5,142	5,587	6,027	6,307	6,858	7,372	8,095
Montana	4,425	5,000	5,550	5,900	6,300	6,650	7,050	7,950
Nebraska	3,876	4,400	5,030	5,350	5,800	6,250	6,700	7,855
Nevada	5,693	6,181	6,480	7,322	7,786	8,491	8,739	9,615
New Hampshire	4,455	4,886	5,314	5,843	6,207	6,539	7,276	8,018
New Jersey	5,871	6,300	6,738	7,233	7,647	8,162	8,775	9,500
New Mexico	5,382	5,750	6,222	6,598	6,740	7,300	7,560	8,125
New York	6,537	7,000	7,800	8,400	8,500	9,000	9,400	10,200
North Carolina	4,178	5,087	5,205	5,523	5,869	6,494	7,041	7,744
North Dakota	3,695	4,300	4,915	5,375	5,515	6,085	6,300	6,900
Ohio	5,124	5,700	5,957	6,558	6,782	7,631	8,050	8,594
Oklahoma	4,659	5,069	5,302	5,894	6,103	6,253	6,853	7,139
Oregon	5,535	5,970	6,492	6,953	7,274	7,978	8,385	9,200
Pennsylvania	5,308	5,661	6,143	6,830	7,181	7,528	8,133	9,000
Rhode Island	5,499	5,900	6,300	6,750	6,975	7,620	8,178	8,900
South Carolina	3,450	3,865	4,318	4,847	5,421	5,816	6,025	7,000
South Dakota	3,725	3,900	4,500	4,850	5,000	5,700	6,200	6,700
Tennessee	3,929	4,151	4,770	5,217	5,755	6,146	6,520	7,290
Texas	4,708	5,375	5,539	6,080	6,075	6,774	6,794	7,503
Utah	5,096	5,283	6,106	6,525	6,780	6,935	7,400	7,970
Vermont	4,466	4,780	5,450	5,808	6,200	6,585	7,085	8,225
Virginia	4,312	4,764	5,287	5,898	6,342	6,936	7,550	8,200
Washington	5,643	6,129	6,511	7,185	7,597	8,258	8,640	9,500
West Virginia	3,952	4,432	4,730	5,433	5,917	6,335	6,600	7,850
Wisconsin	4,870	5,603	6,124	6,650	6,954	7,504	8,350	9,150
Wyoming	4,937	5,596	5,840	6,572	6,635	7,163	7,375	8,532

Sources:

Column 2 from: U.S. Department of Health, Education, and Welfare, Office of Education. *Statistics of State School Systems, 1959–60.* Circular No. 691. Washington, D.C.: Government Printing Office, 1963. p. 77–78.

Columns 3, 4, 5, 6, 7, 8 and 9 from: National Education Association, Research Division. *Estimates of School Statistics*, various issues.
* Advance estimates.

TABLE 6

Average Earnings of Public School Personnel and Other Professional Groups

Professional group	Average salary for calendar year									
	1960	1961	1962	1963	1964	1965	1966	1967	1968	
1	2	3	4	5	6	7	8	9	10	
Public school instructional staff	$ 5,266	$ 5,333	$ 5,754	$ 6,015	$ 6,315	$ 6,572	$ 7,015	$ 7,285*	$ 7,871*	
Public school classroom teachers	4,863	5,088	5,355	5,587	6,061	6,292	6,600	7,027*	7,585*	
Accountants and auditors †	7,488	7,812	8,028	8,340	8,616	8,890	9,202	9,706	10,240	
Attorneys †	11,596	12,144	12,696	13,308	13,728	14,499	14,751	15,416	16,057	
Chemists †	8,164	9,300	9,804	10,212	10,608	11,024	11,535	12,399	13,052	
Engineers †	9,100	9,792	10,152	10,680	11,184	11,575	12,022	12,717	13,381	
Scientists employed in research and development work										
Nonsupervisory, without doctorate		9,720	10,104	10,656	11,184	11,652	12,228	12,852	13,620	
Nonsupervisory, with doctor's degree		12,564	13,152	13,788	14,328	14,904	15,660	16,356	17,136	
Supervisory, without doctorate		14,172	14,748	15,504	16,212	16,884	17,472	18,168	19,032	
Supervisory, with doctor's degree		16,272	16,992	17,820	18,444	19,092	20,016	20,736	21,636	

* Partially preliminary.
† Weighted averages of mean annual salaries, computed by the NEA Research Division.

category, taking into consideration retirements and other terminations, leaves of absence, anticipated changes in pupil-staff ratios, and consequent recruitment needs and sources.

2. *Future Teacher Clubs.* Any child who shows an interest in teaching should be encouraged to enter a teaching career. One of the ways of encouraging interest is through Future Teacher Clubs, in which the emphasis should be on activities related to teaching rather than on lectures and exhortation. Some of the student activities in such clubs are the following: assisting teachers in class management, tutoring individuals and small groups of younger pupils, visiting teacher-education institutions, attending selected faculty meetings, assisting in the use of teaching equipment, viewing appropriate films on teaching careers, and discussing student experiences with representatives of Future Teacher Clubs from other schools. Programs may also include listening to invited speakers who have unusual backgrounds in teaching (such as Peace Corps experience), listening to student teachers describe their experiences, analyzing causes of behavioral problems and even discussing basic elements of lesson planning. The faculty adviser of a Future Teacher Club can obtain assistance from national organizations such as T.E.P.S. in Washington, D.C., which publishes a monthly news letter entitled *The Future Teacher*. The choice of a proper faculty adviser for the Future Teacher Club is as important as the program. The adviser must have unusual rapport with young people and must be enthusiastic about teaching. Some school systems have given their high school seniors greater responsibility in performing simple teaching functions under the guidance of professional teachers and have called them the Senior Teacher Cadet Corps. The successful faculty adviser of a Future Teacher Club must be as resourceful in recruiting members and maintaining the prestige of the club as is the successful team coach. The adviser obtains recommendations of good material from faculty, pupils and parents, and finds appropriate opportunities for service to the Parents' Association, the faculty, the administration and the student body. Publicity about teaching careers is also to be made available to the entire student body on bulletin boards and in assemblies and school newspapers. Special effort should also be directed toward recruiting members of minority groups for Future Teacher Clubs.

3. *Maintaining contacts with students after they enter college.* Former members of Future Teacher Clubs and others who enter college and enroll in teacher-preparation programs should be contacted during their junior or senior year by a representative of the school personnel administrator. Effort should be made to maintain a student's interest in the school system from which he graduated. Copies of Future Teacher publications and copies of the school staff bulletin may be sent to education majors. Invitations should be sent to education students to return to visit their alma maters on special occasions.

4. *Relations with teacher-preparation institutions.* The school person-

113

nel administrator's office must maintain good relations with college placement officers and other administrators. More than a once-a-year visit is called for, including reporting to the college how successful its education graduates have been. It is also important to make available up-to-date information on school district staff needs, salary schedules, and so on. If a large school system anticipates an expansion in any of its curricular programs, news of the anticipation should be passed on to education students so that they know about the expected needs. The story is told of one college with half-full industrial arts courses and a nearby school system with a critical shortage of industrial arts teachers. When a college informs its student body about teaching opportunities, it performs a recruitment activity. If a college is not too distant, a school system can cooperate with its students, faculty and administration by accepting student teachers and by encouraging visits by professors and involving them in joint meetings to discuss problems of common interest such as curriculum changes and in-service courses for teachers. In recent years, teacher-preparation institutions have been criticized for their failure to prepare teachers to meet current teaching problems in urban communities. If educational curricula are to meet the many changing needs of schools, there must be continuous communication between schools and colleges, and the school personnel administrator can play a leading role in the process.

5. *Utilizing staff in recruitment.* Teachers and supervisors of the school staff who, during the summer, study at colleges also attended by prospective teachers should be encouraged to regard themselves as teacher-recruitment ambassadors from their home school system. Printed materials should be furnished to staff members, and ideas for teacher recruitment should be solicited from them. The serious concern of teacher organizations with recruitment and selection has been exhibited in contract agreements negotiated with their representatives. The 1968 agreement between the Syracuse Board of Education and the Syracuse Teachers Association (N.E.A.), for example, contains these clauses:

> "Recruitment of teachers shall be continuous, extensive, and intensive. . . . The Association shall cooperate with the Board in measures required for a successful recruitment program. . . . The Association will provide a list of teachers who are willing to make themselves available for interviews and other recruiting purposes."

6. *Retraining of existing staff.* Special needs sometimes may be met by retraining present staff members. If there is a shortage of teachers of any subject, programs can be developed that may induce members of the staff to undertake in-service retraining to prepare themselves to teach in the shortage areas. State and federal funds have been made available for such purposes. Retraining can take place after school or during the summer at colleges or in off-campus programs arranged with the cooperation of colleges. It may be necessary to provide incentives for teachers to engage

114

in retraining. Successful incentives have been the following: the school system has paid tuition costs, an additional weekly stipend has been paid, and salary raises have been arranged for teachers completing a retraining program. It is possible to televise special courses either as "sunrise semesters" or as weekend broadcasts. Some state education departments have financed retraining programs. One such program, called LOIS (locally originated in-service teacher training), was developed as a two-week summer course to retrain elementary school teachers to teach mathematics.

7. *Teacher recruitment utilizing community sources.* In most communities there are individuals who prepared for teaching but who have never taught. Such individuals may be induced to return to teaching if they can be reached and assured that their services are welcomed. In one community, letters were sent home with pupils urging parents who had appropriate training to communicate with the school personnel administrator. Advertisements of teacher needs via radio, television and newspapers have been tried by school personnel administrators. Part-time teaching programs for housewives who once taught and refresher programs for others who want to return to teaching have been arranged.

A second community resource lies in commercial establishments, which frequently bring specialists into a community. Their wives may be qualified teachers interested in serving the schools. Some school personnel administrators, therefore, have developed contacts with the placement offices of large businesses.

Community resources are used widely in obtaining teacher aides, whose use has increased greatly with the assistance of state and federal funds. Of the various types of teacher aides, some have little education and perform routine tasks. Many, however, are high school graduates and some even have several years of college or community college education. In some school systems, principals are authorized to recruit such personnel directly from the local community. In other cities, the school personnel administrator's office does the recruiting with the aid of civic groups. Under either plan, the central office should maintain records of all employees.

SPECIAL PROGRAMS IN TEACHER RECRUITMENT

1. *Liberal arts graduates.* After graduation, for various reasons, a considerable number of students who majored in academic subjects decide that they wish to enter the teaching profession. The school personnel administrator should identify and assist such individuals. He may do so directly when such individuals apply for teaching positions by referring them to special college programs. He may also enlist the aid of institutions by urging them to establish special postgraduate summer courses or late afternoon courses for the professional preparation of liberal arts graduates. It may thus be possible to obtain the teaching services of liberal arts graduates after a special summer program or, on a half-time basis, while they

concurrently undertake a special education program. In many states, an individual can obtain a temporary teaching certificate if he has a baccalaureate degree and enrolls for six credits of professional courses. Many types of programs have been developed for such liberal arts graduates. In New York City, an extensive advertising program in the mass media resulted in thousands of letters of inquiry. A special ten-credit education program was established during the summer in cooperation with some of the colleges in the metropolitan area. The City of New York assumed the payment of the tuition fees for some 1500 students in the program. The credits were usable toward master's degrees. At the end of the summer, those who completed the program were appointed to schools. The results were regarded as satisfactory by the professional staff and the program was repeated in subsequent summers. No formal comparative study has been published of the effectiveness of those teachers compared with graduates of normal teacher-education programs.

2. *National Teacher Corps.* The United States Office of Education established a special program to train individuals interested in serving economically underprivileged areas. A national recruitment effort obtained hundreds of volunteers with baccalaureate degrees who, after basic courses and orientation, were assigned to teach in inner city schools under the supervision of experienced teachers. Concurrently, they were required to take further university training in education.

3. *Utilizing and retaining student teachers.* If a city or community has student teachers in its schools, special efforts should be made to retain their services after they graduate. Personal and professional relations between a student teacher and a principal and his staff can be important factors in influencing the student teacher to remain as a staff member. The school personnel administrator can act as intermediary between principals and student teachers.

4. *Recruiting members of minority groups as teachers.* Many school districts are making special efforts, in a variety of ways, to recruit members of minority groups for their staffs. Efforts have been made to reach qualified individuals who reside within the school district or within traveling distance by advertisements in the mass media and by obtaining the aid of placement offices and community leaders. Visits are made to college campuses where there are significant numbers of minority group members; visits are made to colleges where the student body is predominantly black. Some large cities have sent recruiters to colleges on islands off the mainland, such as Puerto Rico. Teacher aides have been recruited from minority groups and have been aided to obtain degrees and professional training that would help them to qualify as teachers. Letters have been sent to college students to persuade them to enter teaching and return to their home district. In the longer range, high school seniors of minority groups may be guided to enter teacher-preparation courses in colleges and may be aided by scholarships.

116

Some school personnel administrators sincerely believe that a factor in their inability to successfully recruit black teachers is the dearth of competent black applicants. Black teachers can be found. Competition for them as prospective staff members is keen because they are being wooed by business, industry, and graduate schools.

The search for qualified personnel should not be restricted to specific kinds of schools or certain geographic areas. The emphasis should be placed upon identifying interested and competent candidates. Minority-group recruiting should not be done only at minority institutions, even though they are the most obvious recruiting source.

A serious problem is that the standards of academic preparation in some institutions have been below the standards of the recruiting school district. However, it should be recognized that motivated adults can overcome earlier schooling deficiencies in relatively short periods of time. Thus in-service staff-development programs can and should meet individual needs for self-improvement in all areas in which it is sought.

Techniques for improving the recruitment climate for minority-group teachers should be oriented toward the candidate rather than centered around the employer. Among the valuable attributes is sincerity. If the recruiter can convince a teaching candidate that he is sincerely interested in him and in the contributions he can make to the school district, the recruiter will have achieved an important step in the interviewing process.

It takes effort to convince minorities that advertised jobs are open to them. Even though much progress in equal opportunity has occurred recently, many of today's teachers who belong to minority groups grew up in an era of inequality. Effort is required to overcome their early impressions and to convince them of increased opportunities. Begin by sharing your interest in recruiting such teachers with your current employees.

The recruitment program should be conceived and carefully planned as a continuous, long-term activity. The search should be to locate and attract qualified personnel of all ethnic groups who have the competence needed to accomplish the educational goals of the community.

SPECIAL PROBLEMS OF RECRUITMENT FOR INNER CITY SCHOOLS

Personnel administrators in large cities have found it difficult to staff schools in the inner city. Staff assigned there frequently sought transfers to schools in more pleasant surroundings. New teachers either did not appear or, after a brief experience, resigned. Several solutions to this problem have been attempted. One was to improve teaching conditions in order to make teaching more attractive. Class size was reduced in such schools. Additional supervisory personnel were assigned and more special remedial teachers, school psychologists, social workers and other supporting personnel. Teachers in such schools were given fewer classes to teach per day. Such steps are

117

part of a program called, by one community, More Effective Schools, which has been endorsed by the American Federation of Teachers.

A second approach to the problem was to require that student teachers spend part of their student-teaching experience in inner city schools. The purpose was to acquaint young teachers with conditions in such schools. It was found that student-teaching experiences in inner city schools dispelled fear of the unknown, so that new teachers came to recognize that teaching in such schools was not hazardous but represented a worthwhile challenge.

In addition to changes in student teaching, efforts have been made to improve preparatory courses so that new teachers are better prepared to cope with the problems of inner city teaching. In many collegiate institutions, preparation for teaching is still oriented exclusively toward middle-class children or even toward a rural society. Changes in courses have included the utilization of audiovisual resources to give prospective teachers a better understanding of children in the inner city. Service in community agencies during the sophomore or junior year has also helped to reorient future teachers. Changes in collegiate textbooks have been made and collegiate faculties have been reoriented.

In some cities, there was discussion of giving extra pay to teachers who serve in the inner cities, a step which was opposed by school personnel as being divisive and an improper incentive. In one large city, this approach was called "combat pay" and the teachers' union opposed it. Compulsory transfer of experienced teachers to schools of the inner city has been suggested by some but opposed by others because it is believed that teachers assigned under compulsion are not likely to give their best efforts and that they will seek transfers as soon as they can.

The quality of supervisory, administrative help available in inner city schools has been a decisive factor in reducing staff turnover in such schools. It was found that two schools in the same section, separated by a few blocks, had widely varying rates of teacher turnover. An informal study indicated that the differentiating factor was the caliber of the school principal and his assistants. The school with the more capable principal and supervisory staff was found to have greater staff stability and staff satisfaction, with fewer resignations or requests for transfer.

USING REFERRAL SERVICES FOR TEACHER RECRUITMENT

1. *N.E.A. search.* In 1967, the National Education Association established a program called "N.E.A. Search," which is intended, through the use of computers and data processing, to provide information to personnel administrators on teaching vacancies and on the availability of teachers. Under the plan, a school personnel administrator or his district is required to pay either a nominal fee for each applicant referral or a somewhat larger fee for each teacher hired. The personnel director describes his vacancy on a form. The prospective teacher describes his qualifications on a form. A com-

puter matches vacancies and applicants, and referrals are made. Among the difficulties that arose in the early use of the plan was an insufficient number of applicants compared to the demand for teachers.

2. *Guide to better teaching opportunities.* A second nationwide effort to make available prospective teachers to school personnel administrators was launched by the publishers of *The Grade Teacher*. Personnel administrators were able to advertise their vacancies in a basic listing that was to appear in one of the issues of the magazine, which would be sent to several hundred thousand teachers and teachers in training and to seniors at teacher-education institutions. The cost of an advertisement in 1968 began at approximately $200.

3. *The "ASCUS File" and "ASCUS Annual."* The Association of School, College and University Staffing developed a plan for teacher placement. In its publication, called the ASCUS Annual, personnel officers placed full-page or quarter-page advertisements for teachers.

4. *Teacher employment agencies.* There are a number of commercial agencies for teacher employment. State employment offices, too, usually have a professional section which includes teachers.

5. *Use of electronic devices.* It is predicted that the computer and other electronic devices will play a large part in teacher recruitment in the future. A publication of the National Public Relations Association gives this picture of the future:

> "From the university computer, the school district will receive electronically reproduced candidate credentials. When the director of personnel spots a set of papers that interest him, he contacts the university to set up an interview. The placement office is now equipped with phonovision and he is able to see Susie Smith as he talks to her on the telephone. It isn't necessary to make the trip to College X to interview Susie; he can do it in the comfort of his office." [11]

Computers can make available information about the courses and experience of applicants, and they can convey detailed information to applicants at college about the school districts that are seeking their services.

RECIPROCITY IN TEACHER CERTIFICATION

A problem that has faced school personnel administrators who are engaged in teacher recruitment outside their own states has been obtaining certification for teachers whose preparation or service was done in other states. In some states, there are specific requirements, such as a course in the state's history, which must be met by those who wish to teach in the state. Some states require more credits in education courses or academic courses than other states. In some states, a baccalaureate degree is required; in others, a master's degree is needed. Efforts are being made to

119

develop reciprocity in certification among states. On the eastern seaboard, for example, a number of states have joined in a regional agreement to accept individuals who are certified as teachers in any other state. In 1968, the federal government funded a project to promote reciprocity among states through state legislative action. By 1969, approximately 28 states had initiated legislation for this purpose. Where there is no arrangement for reciprocity, delays may occur which are troublesome not only to the school personnel administrator but to the teachers as well. Delays in the expansion of reciprocity are caused by substantial differences in requirements among various states, by fears that some states would lose more than they would gain, and by unwillingness of some state educational authorities to give up direct control of teacher certification in their states.

RECRUITMENT OF SCHOOL ADMINISTRATORS

In many communities, school principals and other staff administrators are usually selected from the community's staff, which is a practice that provides an avenue of advancement for teachers. Increasing efforts are being made, however, to diversify the backgrounds of school administrators by attracting capable individuals from other communities. This practice has been conducted through a number of channels:

1. College placement offices have a file of experienced teachers or supervisors who are interested in obtaining positions elsewhere.
2. Letters may be sent by supervisors or experienced teachers in one community to the superintendent of schools in another community requesting consideration for administrative positions.
3. Recommendations may be sought and obtained by school personnel administrators from other personnel administrators serving in other communities.
4. Professional files, such as the ASCUS File, and professional magazine advertisements may be used to locate qualified applicants.

Although considerable funds and efforts are expended in recruiting teaching personnel, there is comparatively little expenditure for the recruitment of school administrators other than superintendents. Studies have indicated that most school administrators other than superintendents are selected informally from the local school staff.

EVALUATION OF THE TEACHER-RECRUITMENT PROGRAM

Periodically, there should be an evaluation of the teacher-recruitment program or an evaluation in cooperation with an outside agency. The objectives of teacher recruitment should be reviewed and the procedures, both short-term and long-term, should be reviewed in the light of the objectives. In this connection, a check list might be used such as the one prepared by the American Association of School Personnel Administrators in their

120

booklet entitled "Standards of School Personnel Administration." An essential part of such an evaluation should be the appraisal of personnel recruited during the period under consideration.

The following check list, in the form of a questionnaire, was devised for self-evaluation in a staff-recruitment program.[12]

INVENTORY OF RECRUITMENT COMPETENCE

Identify the activities in which your district engages which can be construed as contributing to recruitment for the profession.

1. Do you support a Future Teacher Club?
2. Do your counselors have adequate material available for students who may consider teaching?
3. Do local teachers' groups or service clubs or other agencies in your local area have scholarship funds available for worthy students who want to become teachers?
4. Have you presented the problems and opportunities of teaching to your professional staff in order that they will use their professional influence judiciously in advising students about teaching?
5. What changes have you made in classroom organization, teaching assignments or personnel policies and benefits which will make teaching a more attractive profession in your district?
6. In what way have you worked with legislators to enact laws which are appropriate for the improvement of the teaching profession?
7. Have you provided your local newspaper with appropriate copy regarding an objective analysis of the teacher shortage and the rewards of teaching?
8. Have you supported programs in the mass media which have featured the best in teaching?
9. Have you worked with colleges in order to obtain improved counseling for students and improvements in the teacher-education program?

Identify or appraise your activities directed to recruiting for the district.

1. What personnel policies does your district have which are deterrents to recruitment and which could be changed to encourage recruitment to the district?
2. What are the factors in your district which attract teachers?
3. What factors exist in your district that are deterrents to recruitment? How can these be changed?
4. What evidence do you have to show that you are getting your fair share of competent teachers?
5. Have you made reasonable effort to release teachers who are not performing to your satisfaction?
6. Have you planned recruitment trips to colleges so that the colleges will have sufficient lead time to identify applicants to your specifications?
7. Have you provided the placement offices with literature about your district? Is your literature attractive, reasonable in cost and accurate?
8. Do you inform placement offices when you have filled positions?
9. Do you describe your teaching vacancies in sufficient detail so that the positions will merchandise well?
10. Do you advise applicants of the status of their application?

11. In what ways have you encouraged the staff to participate in recruitment?
12. Do you and others who participate in the employment interview have the training, experience and insight to conduct depth interviews?
13. Are you making appropriate use of the doors to the labor pool for your district?
    College Placement Offices
    United States Mail
    State Employment Offices
    The Professional Staff
    Large Major Industrial Establishments
    Newspaper Advertisements
    Professional Journals and Subject Matter Organizations
    The ASCUS Service and N.E.A. and Professional Organizations
    American Association of University Women
    Service Clubs
    Former Teachers
    Teachers on Substitute Lists
    Retired Military Personnel
    Returning Peace Corps Personnel
    Exchange Teacher Programs
    County and State Education Offices
    Recommendations from Neighboring Districts
    Radio and Television Programs and Announcements
    Other
14. Do you keep adequate records of teacher turnover, causes of terminations, and how do these figures compare with districts of similar characteristics?
15. What is the attitude of the public toward the recruitment program?
16. What is the attitude of the professional staff toward the recruitment program?
17. Does the cost of the recruitment program appear to be reasonable?
18. Have you assessed the image of your district accurately?
19. Have you developed forms and procedures for recording interview and other pre-employment data and transmitting them to others in the line of privileged communication in an efficient and economical manner?
20. Do you follow up on the applicants you have employed to determine the situation, person or policies which persuaded them to accept employment in your district?
21. Have you made reasonable effort to keep track of former teachers residing in your area with a view toward their eventual return to service?
22. Have you sponsored programs (in addition to student teaching) for college students in your district in order that they may be encouraged to apply for positions?
23. Have you maximized your opportunities for participating in intern training programs for teachers as well as for student teaching?
24. Have you employed college students as teachers' aides?
25. Have you maximized the opportunity for the employment of college

students as noon yard supervisors, cafeteria workers or maintenance workers?

26. Have you developed a working relationship with neighboring school districts which would provide for sharing the services of competent teachers in scarce fields?
27. Have you considered the employment of two part-time teachers for one full-time position?
28. Have you taken advantage of teachers in industry who can be freed from a part of their industrial assignment in order that they can teach a class or two?
29. Does your district have good working relationships among the board, superintendent and the employees?
30. Have you gone the extra mile in providing opportunities for innovations and experimentation which will appeal to certain kinds of teachers?
31. Do you provide hospitality and housing services for new teachers which will make them appreciative of your district immediately upon their arrival?
32. What evidence do you have that you and your district are up to date on the best accepted personnel practices and policies?
33. How do you appraise your orientation program for new teachers?
34. Have you assigned teachers in accordance with the agreement you made with them during the interview?
35. Have teachers been adequately informed of the procedures they must follow to obtain teaching aids, supplies and outside purchases?
36. Does your office have the reputation of being firm and fair?
37. Do you like your job?

7 PERSONNEL SELECTION

GENERAL STATEMENT

One of the most important duties of the school personnel administrator is that of staff selection, including: teachers; supporting personnel such as counselors, social workers, and psychologists; principals, assistant principals, department heads and other administrators; secretaries; noncertificated personnel such as custodians, bus drivers, lunchroom workers and paraprofessionals. Staff selection has dimensions different from those of staff recruitment, although there are overlapping and complementary activities. The prime goals of staff recruitment are to attract available personnel, to interest and encourage prospective teachers and others to apply for work, to increase the available pool of qualified persons, and to effectuate measures that will reduce staff turnover. Staff selection follows or is part of recruitment and it presupposes that a greater number of individuals are applying than are needed and that the school personnel administrator is in the position of making choices among applicants. Since the effectiveness of a school system is determined largely by the effectiveness of its school staff, it is clear that the selection of a proper staff is one of the basic duties of the school administrator.

The personnel administrator can make choices with no guides other than his own subjective judgment, or he can utilize systematic appraisal techniques that will provide him with objective data and comprehensive information about each applicant.

Studies have shown that, in most communities, staff selection is based on an employment interview and a review of available references. In 1952, Otto reported that the majority of school superintendents relied primarily on "the old eagle eyes" to select staff members who would become good principals.[1] In 1965, McIntyre found that a major weakness in school staff

124

selection is an enduring propensity to oversimplify the job and to substitute flashes of intuition for the difficult, analytical task of appraising abilities.[2]

When school personnel administration was the part-time duty of a busy school administrator, the subjective unsystematic approach to staff selection was understandable. But as school personnel administration becomes a recognized profession—as it becomes the full-time specialty of an administrator and his staff—in an ever-increasing number of communities, the selection of school staff will become more professionalized and systematic.

TRAITS AND ABILITIES SOUGHT IN STAFF MEMBERS

The first step in a systematic plan of staff selection is the definition of the qualities and characteristics to be sought in individuals or groups of individuals. This step, in fact, should take place before recruitment begins. It is recognized that there are difficulties in defining as well as in appraising desirable patterns or characteristics of teachers' behavior. There are successful teachers with one set of characteristics and other successful teachers with different combinations of characteristics. David G. Ryans, who has devoted years to the study of teachers' characteristics, came to the conclusion that the behavioral characteristics of effective teachers are almost too complex for generalizations. Nevertheless, the process of selecting members of the school staff goes on from year to year, and attempts must be made by responsible administrators to define general and specific characteristics, knowledge, and abilities which individuals should possess if they are to be selected as teachers. Should a science teacher have a background in chemistry as well as in physics? Should music teachers be able to teach instrumental as well as vocal groups? Should a fine arts teacher be able to paint and sculpt? Should the individual be strong in community orientation, in planning lessons, in developing class discussions, in stimulating the interest of the class? In large school systems, definitions must usually be applied to groups. In small school systems, characteristics desired in a single teacher may be formulated. The formulation of characteristics should be an enterprise shared with representatives of teachers, field supervisors, the school superintendent, and the board of education or other representatives of the community.

OBTAINING APPROPRIATE DATA CONCERNING APPLICANTS

The next step, after defining the characteristics to be sought in applicants, is to decide upon the procedures, activities and instruments to be used in obtaining data. Hall and Vincent, reviewing the literature on teacher-selection methods in 1960, reported that (1) school administrators rely upon the interview as a primary method of selection, (2) examinations are being used more extensively in selection, and (3) letters of recommendation are still widely used as a basis for selection even though they have been shown to be of dubious validity. Hall and Vincent cautiously conclude that a wide variety of techniques and tests have been used to select teachers, but that, "until more is known about predicting effective teaching and the behaviors which characterize effective teachers, little can be done to develop techniques and instruments for selecting teachers." [3]

Arthur L. Benson accepts the view of Hall and Vincent that the criteria of teacher effectiveness have not been fully defined, but declares that "the validity of tests for appraising certain knowledges and abilities of prospective teachers has been repeatedly demonstrated by research." [4] It would thus appear that, as long as certain knowledges and skills are considered desirable in teachers, reliable and valid instruments for their appraisal should be used.

Instead of basing staff selection on subjective, incomplete information, it would seem better to use systematic procedures and the best available instruments in order to make available more reliable information and data for judgment. For example, an applicant's academic background and preparation in the subject he wishes to teach may be ascertained by studying his collegiate transcript, by a written test, or, to some extent, from an interview. An applicant's ability to demonstrate a process in a trade subject may be ascertained from references or by having him perform some typical tasks under observation. A physical examination yields information about an applicant's health. Court records and social security records may be helpful in some cases. Data on an applicant's skill in teaching can be obtained by observing him teach a lesson. Other special tests can be devised to obtain additional data. Test constructionists have offered this advice, that results are likely to be most valid and reliable if the testing situation and the testing elements or challenges closely parallel the real activities that an applicant is expected to perform.

Larger cities have had more formalized procedures of staff selection that include the use of objective examinations. A study made in 1966 compared 62 smaller school systems near New York City having school populations ranging from 320 to 11,694 with 320 large public school systems having school populations above 12,000; the study was concerned with methods employed in staff selection. [5] It was found that only one of the smaller school systems used objective examinations, whereas 12.8 percent of the large school systems used them.

Using examinations for staff selection has been challenged on the following grounds:

1. They do not adequately measure teacher competence.
2. They penalize those who have gone through nonstandard teacher-preparation programs.
3. Studies have not demonstrated their predictive validity.
4. Basic elements of teaching success are not measurable by examinations.

5. They are expensive.
6. They degrade the educational profession.
7. Examinations delay the teacher-selection process.
8. They impose rigidity and unnecessary restraint on teacher-education institutions.

On the other side, some school personnel administrators believe that the data provided by objective examinations constitute a better basis for staff selection than the informal judgment of an interviewer, for the following reasons:

1. The use of formal procedures, including examination scores, enables the personnel administrator to make his choices on merit and fitness alone and to defend his choices against unprofessional pressures and charges of discrimination.
2. Tests do appraise basic knowledge and specific skills that are valuable assets to a beginning teacher.
3. The professional courses taken by prospective teachers do have valuable subject-matter content, the understanding and retention of the basic elements of which are measurable.
4. The use of formal examinations in teacher-selection has not in fact inhibited diversity in teacher-education programs because great diversity does exist.
5. The absence at the present time of nationally accepted accreditation and the existence of wide variations in the quality of teacher-education graduates compels the school personnel administrator to use appropriate instruments to appraise the preparation of the individual applicant.
6. State certification of teachers, unlike state certification of lawyers, dentists, physicians and other professionals, is based almost entirely upon the number of college credits or courses, with no use of state board examinations. Examinations for teaching positions serve to appraise basic competence to the same extent that state board examinations do for other professions.
7. Business and industry, which formally engaged and promoted staff on the basis of subjective judgment, have increasingly turned to the use of tests and other objective instruments of appraisal in their personnel operations and have found them useful.
8. A broader profile of an applicant's knowledge, abilities, understanding and attitudes, including subjective and objective measures, provides a more reliable, comprehensive basis for staff selection than does subjective judgment alone.

WRITTEN TESTS

One source of data concerning applicants for school staff positions is a written test.

A publication of the American Association of Administrators of School Personnel set forth the following functions of written examinations [6]:

1. To eliminate individuals who have not mastered the tools of culture, such as language, writing, elementary mathematical processes, manipulation of symbols, and the like.
2. To secure the generalist and not the specialist alone.
3. To reveal the candidate's functional knowledge of the content which the teacher is expected to teach.
4. To test the individual's depth and breadth of acquaintance with the world around him.
5. To indicate the intellectual promise of the teacher.
6. To test the candidate's ability to attack the problems of his profession in a scientific way.

Written tests used in staff selection may be of short answer or essay type. They may be prepared by outside agencies, such as the National Teacher Examinations (N.T.E.) of Princeton, N.J., or by other organizations that prepare and administer various types of background tests, inventories and aptitude tests; or they may consist of tests prepared locally under the supervision of the school personnel administrator.

Larger cities, such as New York, Chicago, Los Angeles, and Boston, have prepared and administered their own written tests which are similar in purpose and, to some extent, in design to those administered by N.T.E.

The National Teacher Examinations, administered by the Educational Testing Service (E.T.S.), are offered at testing centers throughout the United States. According to N.T.E., these examinations are designed to measure an individual's academic achievement in pre-service preparation for teaching by assessing the knowledge he has acquired in major aspects of his general education, his professional preparation and his teaching specialty. They do not attempt to measure directly his personality, interest in children, or ability to motivate learning. Educators from all parts of the country, representing a wide variety of interests in the teaching profession, advise E.T.S. on governing policies and developmental aspects of the N.T.E. program. Specialists in various teaching fields, nominated by national societies and associations, outline the content of examinations in their fields and write or review the test questions. N.T.E. does not set a passing or failing mark. Their examinations result in scores on the various parts and in a scaled total score which the school personnel administrator may use as he sees fit. The school personnel administrators may set their own minimum score requirements for appointment to their school system. Thus the minimum score required by different cities differs in accordance with their needs and purposes. If a school system requires the submission of an N.T.E. score, the applicant applies directly to N.T.E. and requests N.T.E. to send a copy of his scores to the school system in which he seeks employment. These short answer tests consist of a set of common examinations

128

designed to be generally appropriate for all teachers and a set of Teaching Area Examinations from which the applicant may select the test designed for his particular subject and grade level. The common examinations include questions related to psychological foundations of education, societal foundations, and teaching principles and practices; written English expression, social studies, and literature and fine arts; science and mathematics, sampling both professional education and general background. The Teaching Area Examination includes art education, the sciences, business education, English, mathematics, music, and others. A fee is charged for entering the National Teacher Examinations, which take an entire day. Some sample questions, taken from the National Teacher Examinations Bulletin of Information for Candidates, follow.

Directions: Each of the questions or incomplete statements below is followed by five suggested answers or completions. Select the one which is best in each case and then blacken the corresponding space on the answer sheet.

A. A student begins working on his homework during a class discussion. It would be best for the teacher to
   1. call the student aside after class and explain that when he does homework in class he sets a bad example for the rest of the students
   2. make a general announcement to the effect that homework is not to be done during the class activities
   3. say nothing because students carrying heavy schedules need some classtime for preparing homework
   4. ignore the situation because some students benefit more from individual study than from class discussions
   5. ask the student his opinion on an issue concerning the topic under discussion

B. The most valid argument against using schoolwork as punishment for misbehavior is that
   1. it is not so effective as physical punishment
   2. it may interfere with desirable extracurricular activities
   3. pupils who are disciplinary cases frequently do not need the extra schoolwork
   4. it may make the pupil regard all schoolwork as distasteful
   5. it may take so long to finish that the pupil will not connect it with his misbehavior

Directions: In each of the sentences below four portions are underlined and lettered. Read each sentence and decide whether any of the underlined parts contains a grammatical construction, a word use, or an instance of incorrect or omitted punctuation which would be inappropriate for carefully written English. If so, note the letter printed beneath the italicized portion and blacken the corresponding space on your answer sheet. If you find no errors in any of the italicized portions, blacken the space labeled E. No sentence has more than one error.

3. If Henry enjoys *this* kind of performance, why *don't* he arrange to
                 A   B

   accompany *us* boys *more* frequently?
           C   D

4. Never had the fortunes of England *sank* to a *lower* ebb *than* at the
                                           A   B   C

   moment *when* Elizabeth mounted the throne.
           D

Some school personnel administrators have used essay and short answer questions in the belief that there are some intellectual functions that essay questions measure better than short answer questions. Essay questions may be either in the subject matter of a teaching area or in professional information on the teaching level. Essay questions may also be included in written tests for administrative positions. Some sample questions from a written test for the position of assistant principal in New York City follow.

A.

Assume that the situations described below fall within the administrative and supervisory areas assigned to you as the assistant principal. For each situation described,

    (a) set forth, with justification, the immediate action you should take, if any, and

    (b) set forth, with justification, what further plans you should propose for long-range remedial measures.

1. While walking to school in the morning, one of the students was struck by a snowball. The entire right side of his face is flaming red, and he seems unable to open his right eye. He explains that he was near school and had continued on his way. You are the only supervisor available at that early hour.

2. During your first week of service as an assistant, you observe that traffic on your floor verges on chaos. Few teachers are on duty. Pupils stop to drink at water fountains during passing. Pupils push, run, and shout while traveling from one class to the next. There seem to be no school rules concerning traffic.

3. One new teacher of fine arts, which is not your area of supervision, teaches in a classroom on your floor. She is continuously sending for you to quell the unruliness which prevails in most of her classes. You find the major part of your day is devoted to this matter since she sends an "SOS" to you four or five times a day.

4. You note that the daily substitutes on your floor seem to view themselves as little more than "baby-sitters." In some instances, children are told to do homework. At times, written work which is substantially "busy-work" is assigned. Frequently, no assignment is given pupils and classes are in disorder. You discuss this situation with the other assistants and are told that these conditions are common throughout the school.

5. A teacher on your floor tells you by written message that she had timed

children's reading at the beginning of the period now in progress. She had put her watch down on the desk. A few minutes later the watch was gone. She asks for your help.

B.

Both you and the principal are newly assigned to a junior high school comprising grades 7, 8, and 9 located in a low socioeconomic area of the city. The other three assistant principals have had two or three years of experience in the school.

Early in October, the principal holds a conference to discuss some aspects of the school's discipline problem. Present are the assistant principals, the two guidance counselors and the dean of discipline. At the conference, the principal indicates that he is disturbed over the fact that the school, last year, had 31 full-scale suspensions, each requiring a hearing at the district office. The school's discipline procedures are also described and discussed at the conference. It becomes clear that, although the other assistants are each assigned to a grade, they have little or no formal responsibility for discipline. The school uses a discipline referral card which provides for an account of the offense and the steps taken by the teacher before making the referral. Teachers send these referral cards to the dean, who interviews and deals with the offenders. The dean is a strong and energetic person with a health-education background and 21 years of teaching experience. He obviously prides himself on his ability to handle the disciplinary program of the school. As the conference proceeds, it becomes clear that the characteristic way of dealing with a pupil who presents serious behavior problems is to change his class and hope for the best. When the teachers complain loudly enough, the pupil is transferred again. There is strong pressure from some members of the Parent-Teacher Association to "get rid of" pupils who prevent the others from learning. Many staff members hold the same view. Of late, other members of the Parent-Teacher Association and some community groups have charged that pupils are railroaded into suspension.

The principal says he has just attended the first suspension hearing of the term at the office of the new district superintendent, who did not sustain the suspension because in his opinion the evidence was insufficiently documented. The district superintendent also felt that the school did not appear to have fully exhausted its resources before resorting to suspension.

Before closing the meeting, the principal announces that he is assigning you to overall supervision of the school's pupil-personnel services, including discipline and guidance, and that he is assigning you the responsibility for developing a plan for strengthening and improving the school's program for dealing with disturbed and disruptive pupils. He directs the other staff members present to extend their full cooperation.

1. Evaluate the current program for dealing with disturbed and disruptive pupils, indicating its strengths and weaknesses.
2. Set forth in adequate detail the plan you should present to the principal for improving the school's program for dealing with these pupils, giving reasons for each proposal you make.

WRITTEN PERSONALITY TESTS

School personnel administrators have also experimented with the use of various paper-and-pencil attitude or psychological tests. These have been useful in conjunction with other information available on an applicant but they have not been used widely because they are expensive to administer and because some personnel administrators have questioned their validity for offering or denying a job.

INTERVIEW TESTS

1. *Purposes of the Interview Test* The purposes of the interview test are to appraise the ability to communicate orally, to explore range of interests and attitudes, to appraise the ability to organize and apply knowledge in discussion, and to assess those aspects of voice and personality which may be discerned in an interview situation, including poise, bearing, appearance, and command of language. The interview test is different from a general interview that is intended for a particular purpose, such as learning about the background or special interests of a person. Thus the interview test differs from an interview in determining whether an applicant is better suited for appointment to an academic or a vocational high school or whether he has a suitable background to be made faculty adviser to a school newspaper, for instance. The interview test is used to determine whether an applicant has certain requisite qualities that are desirable in all teachers in the school district; it may result in a rating that will determine his place on a list used for appointment to vacancies.

A study of teacher-selection procedures in some 400 cities indicated that attempts to appraise the following characteristics (listed in descending order of frequency of occurrence in interview check lists) are made during interviews [7]:

1. personal appearance
2. speech
3. attitudes toward his work
4. philosophy of education
5. potentialities for professional growth
6. interest in children or youth
7. logical thinking
8. extensive cultural background
9. ability in subject matter that candidate proposes to teach
10. extensive outside interests
11. extensive democratic outlook
12. knowledge of current affairs
13. extent of community contacts
14. emotional stability
15. ability to establish rapport

One might genuinely question whether the interview, as normally administered, would be an adequate basis for forming judgments on some of the above characteristics, such as *potential for professional growth, emotional stability, interest in children,* and other complex characteristics. During the course of an interview in which a job is at stake, the verbal responses may be far different from behavior in a real situation.

2. *Procedures in Conducting Interviews* Various studies have indicated that some form of interview is the universally accepted method of personnel selection. However, interview procedures differ markedly in different communities throughout the nation. A study made by Gilbert and others in 1966 indicated the following practices in the use of interviews for school staff selection: [8]

a. In 54.6 percent of the large public school systems the interview is conducted by a single person. In 21 percent of the smaller school systems a single person conducts the interview. Where the interview is conducted by more than one person or by a committee, the composition of the interviewing committee in the small and large public school systems is the following:

TABLE 1
Individual Serving on Interview Committee

	Small School System	Large School System
1. Principal	83.9%	38.8%
2. Superintendent	72.6%	15.9%
3. Department chairman	48.4%	13.4%
4. Director of personnel or a member of his staff	32.3%	32.2%
5. Director of elementary or secondary education	21.0%	24.7%
6. Supervisor	17.7%	23.1%
7. Assistant principal	16.1%	8.1%
8. Subject-matter specialist other than classroom teacher	9.7%	12.2%
9. Classroom teacher	8.1%	4.1%
10. Member of board of education	1.6%	0.6%

b. The same study pointed out that the time allotted for the interview test is typically 20 to 30 minutes.
c. The study indicated that a checklist, or special form for recording judgments in the interview tests, is utilized in only 27 percent of the large public school systems that give the interviews and in only 11.3 percent of the small school systems.
d. The study also indicated that approximately 36 percent of those doing the interviewing are given little if any training to conduct interviews.

The interview is a universal tool for staff selection, but apparently much more understanding, research and effort are required to make this tool serve more adequately the function which is expected of it. Although the interview is by its very nature less objective than written tests, it has the sanction of public approval as a method of selection and it has withstood legal challenges of its objectivity. In a court decision in 1936, the Court of Appeals of New York ruled as follows:

> "The oral test serves its purpose in a competitive examination. Obviously it may be employed as a test of knowledge. In addition, it may be used to test other qualities. For example, in the selection of teachers it may be necessary to appraise their voices for carrying power, distinctness, etc. . . . The above qualities may be tested objectively, albeit orally. A definite standard may be formulated. . . ." [9]

In some interviews conducted by a committee, the representative of the personnel administrator serves as spokesman for the applicant, briefing the members of committee on the background of the applicant before he appears, introducing him to the committee when he enters and taking leave of the applicant after the interview has been concluded.

When an applicant is interviewed separately by members of a committee, each member is given a separate room and the applicant proceeds from one to the next. Each interviewer may be concerned with the same topics, although the specific questions may vary; or each interviewer may be given a different area for inquiry.

When the interviewers meet together as a committee, they may record their ratings without discussion, with the average or median rating of the committee becoming the official rating of the applicant. In some committee interviews, there is discussion before ratings are given. In other committee interviews, each member of the committee is asked to make a tentative, independent rating of the applicant. This is followed by discussion and then the members of the committee are free to change their tentative ratings or retain them. Independent ratings without discussion have the advantage of providing a more varied profile of rating with less possibility of influence by a dominating member of the panel. On the other hand, ratings that are given after discussion may still have variations of individual judgments but they are based upon an awareness of the strengths and weaknesses of the applicant as noted by different members of the group and pointed out in the discussion.

Interviews may be held during the school day, if the interviewer or members of the committee and the applicant are available. They may also be arranged for holidays, weekends or evenings. Practices concerning test schedules have varied in different cities, but it is generally conceded that interviews should be held at times when both the applicant and the members of the panel are not too fatigued to perform effectively.

Experienced personnel interviewers have suggested that not more than eight applicants for teaching positions be interviewed during a normal day by an interviewing panel and not more than six for administrative positions. If too many applicants are scheduled for interviews during a given day, the interviewers become fatigued, so that applicants coming at a later time may be at an advantage or a disadvantage in comparison to others.

When applicants are interviewed in college placement offices, there are problems that must be considered. Since students may have arranged interviews during their free hours, it is most important that the interview time schedule be adhered to. Comments should not be made about other school districts that may be considering an applicant. An applicant's waiting period may be profitably used by making available pictorial literature about the school district. Students who arrive late should be set at ease before being interviewed. A record should be kept of those interviewed and those who did not appear. All students who appear should be interviewed. College placement officials are unanimous in asking that all who are interviewed receive a response, whether they are selected or not, and placement offices also wish to know the results. Opinions vary about whether a contract is to be offered on the spot or not. Many college placement offices prefer that the offer be made afterwards, by mail, so as to avoid embarrassment for those who do not receive contracts the same day and in order that the interviewer may have an opportunity to consider all who have appointments before decisions are made. It is also recommended that faculty members concerned with teacher education, particularly with student teaching, be visited by the school district's interviewer, if at all possible, in order to share ideas about the needs of the schools, the program of the college, and the success of former graduates.

3. *Problems in Reliability and Validity of Interviews.* School personnel administrators should be aware of some of the problems of reliability and validity associated with the use of interviews. Reliability is concerned with the consistency of measurement of a test. Do repeated applications of tests yield the same results? Validity is concerned with the extent to which the test measures that which it is intended to measure. One of the earliest studies of the reliability and validity of the oral interview was made by Barnes and Pressey in 1929.[10] In the study, six committees of four graduate students interviewed candidates and rated them on a seventeen-point scale. In rating the same candidates, some interviewers differed by as much as fourteen points. The coefficient of reliability was approximately .30. Morse & Hawthorne, in 1946, reporting the experience of the Los Angeles Civil Service Commission with oral interviews, found a higher coefficient of reliability.[11] More recent studies of the reliability of interviews have indicated that reliability is increased when the criteria to be rated are objectified and made more specific, when the interviewers are given more training, and when appropriate check lists are provided for recording judgments.

In 1932, Corey studied the validity of the interview for teacher selection by having twelve judges interview and rate eight girls—prospective teachers—for such qualities as neatness, conceit, humor, refinement and beauty. The ratings of the interviewers were compared with the ratings of the same girls by their close friends. The results were so poor that Corey

135

concluded that "Experimental evidence has clearly demonstrated that it is impossible to judge character and personality traits by means of an interview." [12]

In 1934, by defining variables more specifically and by carefully standardizing examining conditions, Trimble obtained a reliability coefficient of .82 and a validity coefficient of .49.[13]

In 1949, David G. Ryans suggested improvements in the interview process in an article entitled "The Interview in Teacher Selection Can Be Improved and Used Effectively." [14] In addition to suggesting clarification of criteria, Ryans proposed the use of several interviewers separately.

Some have wondered whether interview tests measure the same elements measured in a written test. If that were true, then either the written test or the interview might be superfluous. A study published in 1951 reported a correlation of .05 between the oral English test and the written test administered to 117 candidates for elementary school teaching positions.[15] Other unpublished studies made in the 1960s by the Board of Examiners of the New York City school system indicated a similarly low correlation between the interview test and the written test, which signified that the two tests might be measuring different abilities.

4. *Types of Rating Scales*

A. A "check list" is used to indicate whether or not an applicant possesses certain characteristics; for example, resourcefulness, sympathetic interest in children, poise, tact, awareness of recent educational trends.

B. A "numerical scale" indicates the extent to which an applicant possesses a given characteristic. Numerical scales may differ, some scales running from 0 to 100, others from 0 to 10 and others from 0 to 5. When numerical scales are used, the rater may write the number that he himself chooses or he may select a number that has been printed on the rating sheet.

C. A "descriptive scale" allows the rater to write descriptive words which summarize an applicant's traits without quantifying his rating arithmetically. For example, the rater might write the following: sincere, enthusiastic about teaching, extensive interests, wishes to be active in community, understands methodology.

D. A "ranking scale" is one in which individuals are rated for rank with respect to any characteristic and in relation to others in the group.

E. A "man-to-man scale" compares the applicant with known individuals, not necessarily within the group, for specific characteristics.

F. A "graphic scale" sets up characteristics on a line with varying descriptions of the intensity of the characteristics printed below or above the line. The rater is asked to check the point on the line that best describes the applicant with respect to that characteristic. For example, the characteristic may be "effectiveness in community relations." The description of the maximum intensity of this characteristic may be the following: "Applicant is highly respected by all members of the community, shows outstanding community leadership." Along the same line a description of

136

lower intensity of the characteristic may be set forth, such as "He is accepted by some members of the community, occasionally attends community meetings." Along the line there might be four degrees of intensity described, and the rater would indicate the approximate place along the line that he would rate the applicant with respect to the characteristic.

No one of the above scales has proved to be superior to the others, although in recent years greater interest has been shown in the graphic scale.

Study and research on the interview as a means of staff selection have indicated the following: (1) For greater reliability and validity, the variables or characteristics listed on the interview rating sheet should be characteristics that may reasonably be discerned during an interview test. For example, conscientiousness, honesty, leadership and zeal in performing work may require on-the-job observation and may be less reliably ascertained in an oral interview test than may logical presentation of ideas or ability to apply principles to practical situations. (2) The number of variables or characteristics should be relatively few in number, from seven to eleven, rather than a larger number which the rater cannot bear in mind. (3) A better assessment of an individual may be made in an interview if more than one person conducts the interview either in committee or separately. (4) More reliable results are obtained when a rating scale or a written check list is used by the interviewer for recording observations and judgments on the applicant.

Following is a typical sample interview rating sheet. In New York City, a form is used by an interview panel which does not have knowledge of the specific background and training of the individual. The judgment of the panel is based entirely upon the applicant's performance during the interview test. His training and experience are evaluated at another time by a different committee. The same rating form has been used on the teaching and administrative levels.

5. *Problems Related to the Use of Interviewers*

A. *Number of Interviewers.* It is desirable to have more than one interviewer. When only one person conducts the interview to determine whether an individual is to be employed or not, it is often the personality of the interviewer with his special predispositions that determines selection, rather than the personal characteristics of the applicant. At least two or three interviewers of different backgrounds should appraise the applicant, either sitting as a committee or separately. Several studies have indicated that separate interviews in which each interviewer records his findings are more revealing than a committee-conducted interview. Some school personnel administrators arrange for an interview by a committee consisting of a principal, a subject supervisor and a member of the personnel administrator's staff. In some cities, a teacher serves as a member of the interviewing panel. In one city, interviews are recorded on tape so that individuals who are not accepted may be given an explanation that includes a playback of the recorded interview. Although there have been pressures in various

Interview Appraisal of Applicants

Name of Applicant _____

Position Applied for _____ Date of Appraisal _____

	Rating	Comments

PHYSICAL CHARACTERISTICS
  Personal Appearance _____ _____
  Health and Vitality _____ _____

FAMILY HISTORY _____ _____

INTERESTS _____ _____

ABILITY TO COMMUNICATE
  Voice _____ _____
  Oral Language Facility _____ _____
  Ability to Present Ideas _____ _____
  Ability to Accept Ideas _____ _____

PERSONALITY CHARACTERISTICS
  Dependability _____ _____
  Poise _____ _____
  Sense of Humor _____ _____
  Initiative _____ _____
  Creativity _____ _____
  Adaptability _____ _____
  Ability to Work with Others _____ _____
  Commitment to Profession _____ _____
  Empathy _____ _____
  Emotional Stability _____ _____

JUDGMENT AND REASONING _____ _____

MORAL FITNESS _____ _____

COURSE PREPARATION
  Scholarship _____ _____
  Breadth of Knowledge in
    Specialized Areas _____ _____
  Breadth of Specialized
    Knowledge of Education _____ _____
  Breadth of Gen. Knowledge _____ _____

EXPERIENCE _____ _____

GENERAL COMMENTS: _____
_____
_____
_____

Examiner _____ Summary Rating   [   ]
A—Outstanding; B—Above Average; C—Average; D—Below Average; U—Unsatisfactory

parts of the country for greater control of staff selection by the community, it has generally been conceded that the screening of applicants for teaching positions should be done by competent professionals. Boards of education representing the community retain the power of appointment of individuals screened and recommended by the school superintendent, but boards rarely do more than require that the applicant be introduced to them for a courtesy interview. On some occasions, particularly in smaller communities, members of the board of education have participated in the selection interview. Teachers' organizations have recognized the desirability of participating in the selection process. The 1968 contract negotiated by the Board of Education of Syracuse, New York, with the Syracuse Teachers' Association (N.E.A.) contains this provision:

> "To the extent feasible, the Association will be involved in the recruitment and selection process. . . . Whenever a teacher is a member of a selection team, that teacher's views shall carry equal weight with those of another member of the team."

B. *Training and Selection of Interviewers.* There is little doubt that interviewers should receive training and orientation for their tasks. McIntyre stated that "raters should be trained and not just turned loose on the naive assumption that the rating of human behavior is a simple chore that anyone with a pencil can perform." [16] Their training may be achieved (a) by mimeographed or printed leaflets which provide guidance in the purposes and techniques of interviewing, (b) by practice sessions for the interviewers under the leadership of a competent person, and (c) by arranging for group discussion of interviewing techniques.

Untrained interviewers evince weaknesses such as the following: (a) such poorly phrased questions are asked that the applicant does not understand them, (b) purposeless questions are asked which do not yield information about the characteristics of the applicant, (c) the interviewer talks too much, so that the applicant is denied sufficient opportunity for responding to questions, (d) the interviewer reacts emotionally to the applicant, so that a biased judgment is made, (e) the interviewer becomes antagonistic toward the applicant, so that the applicant is inhibited from presenting a typical response, (f) the interviewer fails to follow up revealing leads, (g) questions go beyond the limits of proper interrogation.

Members of interviewing committees should be individuals with good judgment who have had extensive experience in the work for which the applicant is applying, and who have a sympathetic attitude toward other people and a high degree of integrity in performing professional service. In some situations, pressures may be exerted on interviewers to favor one or another job applicant. It is desirable to have members of minority groups on interviewing committees. In order to assure equitable treatment of all applicants, it is desirable that the interviewing committee does not include individuals who are related to or socially involved with any of the applicants.

139

Some interviews have a lead-off man, a staff member who has studied the applicant's record and background and who serves as the applicant's advisor during the interview.

6. *Some Cautions for Interviewers*

A. *Generosity factor.* Some interviewers rate individuals higher than they deserve out of a desire to "give them a break" in getting the job. It has been suggested that interviewers should assume that they are meeting an average applicant and that they should therefore concentrate on noting the characteristics in which the applicant before them is below or above average.

B. *Severity factor.* Some interviewers rate individuals lower than they deserve because of a tendency to compare them with the most capable, experienced personnel they have known.

C. *Central tendency.* Some interviewers tend to give individuals ratings that cluster around the average with respect to all characteristics, neglecting the lower and higher elements of the scale.

D. *Halo effect.* Some interviewers who are impressed by a single characteristic of an individual may rate that individual high in all other characteristics solely as a result of a single impression.

E. *Logical error.* Some interviewers group traits together by rating them all high or low even though there are differentiating aspects of the traits.

F. *Acquaintance error.* Some interviewers rate an individual high or low because of the recollection of his reputation.

G. *Social pressure.* An interviewer may rate an individual high or low because others in the committee have so indicated their judgment.

A study made by Richard A. Siggelkow suggested four criteria for measuring the success of an interviewer [17]:

1. Does an interviewer give the applicant an adequate opportunity to express himself?
2. Does the interviewer conserve time by not discussing matters that are available in other records?
3. Does he give the applicant adequate information about the community in which he is to serve?
4. Does he use key questions to obtain insight into the applicant's philosophy of education?

Other criteria for evaluating an interview are the following:

1. Were the conditions of the interview such as to permit the applicant to present himself well? Was the lighting satisfactory? Was the interview free from interruptions? Were both parties comfortable during the interview?
2. Was the interviewer able to give total attention to the applicant or was he pressed for time, distracted by interruptions?
3. Did the interviewer "oversell" his district, or did he beat down or talk down to the applicant?

4. Will the interviewer be able to fulfill all statements made during the interview?

5. Does the applicant know what will be the next step following the interview?

7. *Materials for Interviews*

A. *Structured, unstructured or semistructured interviews.* In unstructured interviews, the interviewer or the members of the interviewing committee are free to ask any questions that occur to them. In semistructured interviews, the interviewer or committee of interviewers is given a list of questions or topics for use as guides during the interview. Other interviews are more specifically structured, with a passage or questions given to the applicant in advance for his study. The interview then revolves around the passage or the questions studied in advance by the applicant.

B. A summary sheet of information about the preparation, experience and work references of the applicant may be made available to the members of the panel before or after the interview. When the background sheet is not made available until after the interview, the reason given is that it is desired that the interviewing committee form a judgment based merely on performance during the interview, unaffected by knowledge of the individual's background. The following is a structured type of interview test used in an examination in New York City for the position of chairman of a junior high school social studies department.

OBSERVATION OF TEACHING PERFORMANCE

Observing the applicant in a teaching situation is one of the best methods of appraisal. Observation may take place by visiting the applicant while he teaches his own class, if it is possible to do so. Otherwise, the personnel director can arrange to send the applicant to a school to teach an assigned lesson while being observed by the principal or departmental chairman. When this is the procedure, it is desirable for the applicant to familiarize himself with the pupils by sitting in on the class while the regular teacher teaches. The applicant should be given a suitable amount of time and a study room in which to prepare himself to teach the class. The principal or departmental chairman who observes the applicant in action should be asked to prepare a written report for the personnel administrator. Various forms have been developed in different cities for reporting the observation of teaching performance.

In an informal study made by a member of the Board of Examiners of the New York City school system, ratings achieved by individuals on a single teaching test before a rater who had no prior knowledge of them were compared with on-the-job ratings given to them by their principals for a period of years. A high positive correlation was found between their ratings in the so-called teaching test and the ratings given by their own

Examination for License as Chairman of Department in Social Studies in Junior High Schools

DIRECTIONS:

1. You will be allowed one hour in which to study the following selection analytically.
2. You may write notes which you may consult during the interview test, but you may *not read* your notes to the examining committee.
3. You are to leave this sheet and your notes with the examiners at the conclusion of the test.
4. The interview test will be conducted by a committee of three examination assistants.

DURING THE INTERVIEW TEST:

1. You will be allowed a total of 15 minutes in which to answer without interruption the questions that follow the passage appearing below. The allotment of time per question will be left to you.
2. The examining committee will then ask you additional relevant questions pertaining to any of your answers or to the passage under discussion.

* * *

Assume that you have been appointed as chairman of the social studies department of a junior high school. The school draws its pupils exclusively from the neighborhood. The ethnic distribution of the children is 33% Negro, 12% Puerto Rican, 55% others. A large segment of the student body comes from a nearby low-income housing project. Most of the others come from middle class homes. Only a small group of parents are actively involved in school matters.

Your district superintendent requires that school goals be set and implemented so far as possible every school year. The goals for the year just ended which have pertinence for the social studies department are as follows:

1. Continuance of the program to foster sound inter-group relations in all areas of the curriculum.
2. Schoolwide promotion of the use of mass-media to create in students an awareness of the current political and social scene.
3. Schoolwide emphasis on improvement of notebooks and note-taking in all subject areas.

At the conference with your new principal he indicated that an acting assistant principal had supervised social studies in the year just ended, and that little had been done to implement the goals which had been set.

QUESTIONS

Discuss the methods, techniques, and approaches you should introduce and employ in order to achieve the goals outlined above. Include in your statement:

a. Your proposals for the coordination of your plans with those of other supervisors in the school working to achieve these goals, and

b. the procedures you should use to determine the progress made by the social studies department by the end of the first year.

Teaching Test Report Form

1. For an *acceptable* or *better* performance indicate, as your recommended general evaluation, a rating of 60/100 or above (depending on the quality of the teaching).
2. For a *poor* or *very poor* performance indicate, as your recommended evaluation, a rating of 55/100 or less (depending on the quality of the teaching).
3. Your recommended general evaluation should represent your total impression of the applicant's teaching effectiveness in the test.

INSTRUCTIONS: Please check the column (following each item) which, in your judgment, best describes the applicant's quality of performance.

THE LESSON	Very Poor	Poor	Accept-able	Good	Supe-rior
	0–45	50–55	60–65	70–80	85–100
1. The lesson plan (attached hereto)					
2. Motivation					
3. Aim: appropriateness					
4. Extent to which the aim was achieved					
5. Use of previous experience of the pupils					
6. Clearness of presentation					
7. Development of the lesson					
8. Skill in questioning					
9. Skill in dealing with answers					
10. Use of teaching aids					
11. Effectiveness of demonstration (if any)					
12. Ability to maintain interest					
13. Value of content of lesson					
14. Extent of pupil participation					
15. Quality of pupil participation					
16. Social interaction among pupils					
17. Teacher-pupil rapport					
18. Teacher's contribution in the field of knowledge					
19. Application					
20. Summary of the lesson					
21. Class management					

THE TEACHER

	Very Poor	Poor	Accept-able	Good	Supe-rior
22. Personal fitness: appearance, poise, vitality					
23. Teacher's use of oral English: voice quality, enunciation, use of English					

Recommended General Evaluation   /100

principals. This evidence reinforces the belief that, wherever possible, observation of teaching performance should be one of the tests for the selection of teachers.

ABILITY TO DEMONSTRATE

In some teaching areas it is desirable for the teacher to have the ability to give demonstrations requiring manipulative or muscular skill. For example, a teacher of science often finds it desirable to demonstrate the performance of a laboratory experiment to his class. A teacher of health education is often required to demonstrate acceptable form in various physical activities. A teacher of a particular trade subject should be able to demonstrate the use of various tools. School personnel administrators have therefore required prospective teachers of such subjects as have been indicated to demonstrate their skill. Rating sheets such as the following have been devised for the consultant's report on observed skills.

PHYSICAL AND MEDICAL EXAMINATION

Good physical and mental health are required if an individual is to be a successful teacher. In dealing with children, parents and members of the community, teachers and school administrators are subject to many strains and pressures. Continuity of instruction for children requires minimum absences. It is thus important that reasonable standards of physical and mental health be established in the selection of teachers. Some school systems have their own medical examiners to whom applicants are sent. Other school systems refer applicants to approved medical examiners, requiring that an appropriate form be mailed to the personnel administrator. Some school systems permit an applicant's own physician to fill out a medical form. It has been found preferable to require physical and medical examinations given by an approved physician rather than to permit the applicant to submit a testimonial from his own physician. The staff physician is more likely to be objective in his evaluation of the applicant's health and he will know the standards required for service.

REVIEW OF EXPERIENCE AND RECORD

Although previous work experience, both in other jobs and in connection with collegiate classroom work, would seem to be very useful guides to a school personnel administrator in selecting staff, the reliability of such reports and references has left much to be desired. Professional literature abounds in lists of characteristics which teachers should possess, such as sincerity, integrity, creativity, interest in the welfare of children, self-control, flexibility, initiative, and so forth. However, gaining information about the extent to which an applicant possesses any of those traits has proved to be difficult indeed. One reason has been the difficulty of defining the characteristics in such a way that they can be reliably reported by a former super-

Performance Test for License as Teacher of Music in Secondary Schools in New York City

Applicant's Name _____

Sub-Test (a)—PIANO

Selections	Ratings	Comments	Specific Faults (Check)	
Prepared Selection: (Title)	Max. 25		Tempo Phrasing Dynamics Style Tone	Right hand facility Left hand facility Use of pedal Accuracy of notes Accuracy of rhythms Over-all technical fluency
National Anthem	Max. 11		Tempo Phrasing Dynamics Style Tone	Right hand facility Left hand facility Use of pedal Accuracy of notes Accuracy of rhythms Suitability as accompaniment for assembly singing
Sight Reading Selection: (Title)	Max. 14		Tempo Phrasing Dynamics Style Tone	Right hand facility Left hand facility Use of pedal Accuracy of notes Accuracy of rhythms Over-all technical fluency
Total Piano	/50			

visor or college professor. Another difficulty lies in the complexity of human behavior. In the interaction of human beings in one situation, an individual may display one characteristic or set of characteristics, while in another situation he may display different characteristics. A third weakness of reference reports stems from the fact that many individuals are reluctant to give unfavorable references, while some individuals are unduly severe. Although experienced school personnel administrators seek references from places of prior employment and from college authorities, they view such evidence as part of a profile, not as the total basis for a decision. Kenneth McIntyre stated that "Among the most common, and least helpful, devices used in the selection of school principals are letters of recommendation . . . unless the recipient knows the letter writer's writing habits he has no way of identifying the useful letter in a stack of nonsense." [18]

According to a report by Gerhard, Lang and Perry M. Kalick in 1966 on "Teacher Selection, Policies and Procedures," approximately sixteen percent of the large school systems in this country make no follow-up inquiries for references.[19] However, some school personnel administrators report that they have obtained the most reliable information by using telephoned inquiries rather than by formal written reference forms. There has been a move in large cities to reduce the confidentiality of references on the ground that an individual should have an opportunity to refute an adverse reference. In New York State, a bill was introduced in the Legislature to require giving copies of all references to applicants. In New York City, fingerprinting has been required of new applicants and the prints have been referred to appropriate police authorities for reports. It was discovered that approximately four percent of all applicants for teaching positions in New York City had some criminal or police record that was worthy of attention. A sample form used to obtain references on applicants follows.

Personality Tests

Knowledge of the personality or behavioral characteristics of prospective teachers is very important. The most reliable knowledge probably comes from the observation of behavior during an interview test, a teaching test, or an internship, or from observation reports by college faculty who have worked with the applicant.

Pencil-and-paper tests of personality are available and some school personnel administrators have used them to obtain background information about applicants. Among them are the Guilford-Martin Inventories, the Gordon Personal Profile, and the Minnesota Multiphasic Personality Inventory. The Strong Vocational Interest Blank and the Kuder Preference Record yield information on interests. Attitudes and values are revealed in the Allport-Vernon-Lindzey Study of Values and the Minnesota Teacher Attitude Inventory. Predictive value of such tests apparently has not been sufficiently established where competitive job seeking is involved, so that these tests have not been widely used by school personnel administrators.

146

Reference Form

To: _____   Date:_____

_____

_____

_____ has applied to the Austin Public

Schools for a position in the field of _____

Will you please give us your candid opinion of the candidate's personal and professional qualifications as indicated by the items below? This report is confidential and will not be shown to the
candidate. Your cooperation is greatly appreciated. Please return this form to ERNEST W. CABE,
JR., Assistant Superintendent, Austin Public Schools.

Sincerely yours,
IRBY B. CARRUTH
Superintendent of Schools

Please place a check-mark in the appropriate column after each statement. The term *average* should be considered as descriptive of the large middle group in the distribution of persons you have supervised.	Outstanding	Strong	Average	Minimally Acceptable	Weak
General Appearance—grooming, dress, physical features, taste					
Physical Fitness—health, vitality, energy					
Personality—poise, warmth, congeniality					
Character—values, habits, reliability					
Social Qualities—friendliness, cooperation, tact					
Emotional Stability—self-control, consistency of behavior					
Native Ability—intelligence, alertness, judgment					
Voice—pitch, modulation, articulation					
Use of English—grammar, vocabulary, pronunciation					
Preparation—scholarship, knowledge of teaching field					
Management—effectiveness in routines and organization					
Discipline—motivation, control					
Attitude toward Children—understanding, empathy					
Ethics—loyalty, cooperation, professional interest					
Citizenship—loyalty, respect, civic participation					
Teaching Results—pupil growth in scholarship and attitudes					
General Rating					

Would you employ the above applicant as a teacher?   Yes_____   No_____

General Evaluative Statement:

Name_____   Address_____

Position_____   Date_____

147

Teaching internships have been used in some communities as a basis for staff selection. Under such arrangements, prospective young teachers serve a part-time apprenticeship or internship during which their performance is evaluated. Those who show promise of being successful teachers are given regular teaching contracts at the end of their internships. Similarly, in school situations where paraprofessionals may advance to teaching positions by taking additional course work, their service records as teacher aides or assistant teachers are evaluated in determining whether or not to give them teaching contracts.

SUMMARIZING DATA OBTAINED FOR EACH APPLICANT

A task that the personnel administrator will want to perform is the organization and quantification of the data he has assembled in order to make comparisons among applicants. This can be done in profile form with separate scores indicated numerically or graphically or it can be done by a total score consisting of weighted parts. The following two forms suggest some characteristics and weights for the purpose of illustrating the approach. There are, of course, other ways of quantifying such data, other ways of presenting profiles of applicants, and other ways of organizing the assembled data.

THE DECISION TO EMPLOY

The right to employ is usually vested in the board of education, a governing board, or some similar group which is legally charged with responsibility for the school system. Boards of education usually give superintendents of schools the authority to nominate individuals for appointment to the teaching, administrative or classified staff. Screening of applicants is usually done for the superintendent by his personnel administrator, board of examiners, or other appropriate agency or individuals.

Acceptance of the nominations of the superintendent by the board of education varies in different communities. In many places, approval by the board of education is *pro forma,* on the grounds that the superintendent of the school system is the best one to determine the professional competence of applicants and that, since he has the responsibility for an effective educational program, he should be given freedom in selecting his staff. In other communities, members of the board or the president of the board may insist on a more active role in the decision to employ, on the grounds that personal acceptability of the applicant to the lay community is essential. Often, such board members believe that they have considerable insight into the professional know-how required, which leads them to believe that their judgment ought to prevail. Active involvement in the decision to

A

Applicant_____

Characteristic	Superior	Above Average	Average	Below Average	Inferior
Communication Skill		x			
Teaching Skill			x		
Academic Knowledge	x				
Professional Knowledge			x		
Overall College Record		x			
Community Orientation					x
Understanding of Children			x		
Personal Appearance				x	
Health				x	
Attendance Record			x		

B

Applicant_____

Characteristic	Raw Score	Weight	Weighted Score
Communication Skill	80	2	160
Teaching Skill	60	4	240
Academic Knowledge	90	2	180
Professional Knowledge	60	2	120
Overall College Record	80	2	160
Community Orientation	40	2	80
Understanding of Children	60	2	120
Personal Appearance	50	2	100
Health	50	1	50
Attendance Record	60	1	60
		Total Weighted Score	1270
		Average Weighted Score	63.5

employ by board members is more frequent when administrative positions are being filled than when teaching positions are. The role of the board and the administration should be clear on this point, to prevent misunderstandings.

The involvement of board members in staff selection has always been a delicate matter of balancing professional judgment of professional qualifications against the serious concern and deep interest of informed lay members of the policy-making board. At times, frictions have developed between the superintendent and lay board members concerning staff appointments, during which charges of favoritism and excessive meddling have occurred. The staff usually supports the superintendent in such disputes. In recent years, concepts of school decentralization with increased community control, community involvement or community participation have focused greater attention upon this issue of staff selection. It would seem best, under controversial conditions, (a) to have the roles of the board of education, the superintendent and the personnel administrator clearly defined at the outset, (b) to be sure that the representatives of the board of education are consulted about those aspects of staff selection that are generally conceded to lie within the jurisdiction of a lay board (i.e., delineating personnel qualities and characteristics to be sought and general criteria to be applied), (c) to utilize objective data in the selection process and to summarize findings so that the reasons for recommendations are readily apparent, (d) to develop an understanding by the board of education about the procedures followed by the personnel division and to obtain advance approval of such procedures.

SELECTION OF SUPERVISORY AND ADMINISTRATIVE PERSONNEL

In his book entitled *Selection and On-the-Job Training of School Principals,* Kenneth E. McIntyre declares: "The quick, easy foolproof method of selecting professional personnel has never been found. Unfortunately, however, much more is known about selection than most practitioners are using." [20] In 1961, the Research Division of the N.E.A. estimated that only twenty-one percent of the nation's urban school districts followed a definite plan in selecting candidates for promotion. In 1960, a study by C. H. Briner led to his conclusion that there was neither a rational nor a systematic procedure employed in the selection of administrative personnel in most school districts.[21] Castetter declared that "all too frequently an administrative vacancy occurs in a school system, and because of the absence of systematic planning, the choice of a successor may be the result of pressures for a 'favorite son,' political manipulation, lack of time to locate a suitable replacement, and so on. In effect, selection is made in default of planning." [22] Yet in 1968–1969, according to an N.E.A. estimate, there were about 119,515 supervisory and administrative personnel

150

serving in the schools.[23] The principles and procedures of staff selection that have been described so far in this chapter also apply to the selection of school principals, assistant principals, departmental chairmen and other school administrators.

It is easy to assert that we should select as administrative personnel those individuals who possess leadership qualities. However, defining leadership qualities has become all the more difficult as it has been found that leaders possess varying traits and that different circumstances may require different combinations of traits and characteristics of leadership. It is possible, though, to define certain measurable qualities or characteristics that seem to be related to the demands made on the school supervisor or administrator.

In selecting administrative personnel, it is important to encourage all who meet stated requirements to apply for consideration. In many school districts, principals and other administrators are tapped for promotion without formal procedures of selection. In other school districts, only individuals nominated by administrators in service can be considered for promotion. Limiting the number of applicants may ease the process of selection, but there are disadvantages, particularly in larger school districts. In the first place, the superintendent of schools cannot possibly know all the potential leaders well enough to merely handpick the best ones. Open announcement of opportunities for promotion, acceptance of applications from all who are eligible, and genuine use of clearly defined selection procedures (1) often uncover high-caliber individuals who have not been noticed for various reasons, (2) raise staff morale by giving fair opportunities for promotion to all and by showing the staff that their administrators have been chosen by fair and reasonably objective methods, and (3) raise the level of staff competence by increasing the number of individuals who prepare for promotion in the best professional sense.

Some school districts follow a policy of limiting promotional opportunities to individuals who have risen through the ranks within their own school districts. Others almost always bring in outsiders. A balance of the two practices is probably best if the school district is to benefit both from the capabilities of those who have risen within the ranks and who therefore know the local problems and from the various backgrounds of administrators who have developed in other communities.

McIntyre states that "the first step in selecting school principals or any other professional leader is the statement of organizational goals and the prospective leader's responsibilities for the fulfillment of those goals." [24] Thus the duties and requirements of a particular position should largely determine the methods of selection and the materials used in the selection process. For example, the content of a written test for a school administrator's position should be appropriate to a position in the community in which the administrator will serve. Of course, such a written test, if given at all, would be different from any used in the selection of teachers. The interview would similarly differ from that which is conducted for applicants for teaching positions.

The following passage and questions were used in an interview test for the principalship of an elementary school in a large school system. To use a structured interview based upon a real but unidentified situation, it was believed, would give more insight into the applicant's ability to consider and deal with school problems. Secondly, a discussion of real problems would be more revealing than generalizations about principles and practices of supervision remembered from books. Thirdly, using the same material for discussion by all applicants would yield better comparisons.

SPECIALIZED TESTS IN THE SELECTION OF SCHOOL ADMINISTRATORS

1. *Supervision Test.* This test has been used to ascertain whether or not applicants for supervisory and administrative school positions can appraise observed teaching by recognizing good teaching and the elements of inferior teaching and by being able to make suggestions for the improvement of an observed lesson. The test may be conducted in several different ways. A group of applicants may visit a teacher and her class. Chairs are usually provided for the group at the rear of a large room in which the teacher is conducting the lesson. The applicants make notes during the lessons, then they proceed to a different room where they write a critique of the observed lesson. Their critique is then rated on a scale prepared by a committee of experienced supervisors who have observed the same lesson. The rating scale indicates the strengths and weaknesses observed in the lesson. For example, the committee might agree that the lesson had been excessively dominated by the teacher, that the questioning had been poor, that the children had not been sufficiently challenged. They might agree on strengths, too, such as a high degree of interest on the part of the class, creativity in planning, good use of visual material, and so on. In New York City in an extensive examination for the position of principal, it is not possible for the entire group to visit a classroom together, so closed-circuit television is used to televise the lesson from the teacher's classroom to an auditorium where the hundreds of applicants view the lesson on a large screen and make notes on the teacher's performance. The same type of test may be administered individually in a less formal manner by having an individual applicant visit a class and then discuss his observations with the selection committee that accompanied him.

2. *Inspection Test.* In this test, a selection committee visits an applicant in his school for a half day or a full day to appraise his on-the-job competence. In preparation for the visit, the applicant is asked to answer a questionnaire describing his school and setting forth his goals, activities and achievements. The questionnaire is used to structure the inspection test, which may involve reviewing the evidence of the applicant's achievements as apparent in his file, visiting classes with him and discussing his procedures, and observing him in the performance of his duties. An ap-

152

Examination for License as
Principal of a Day Elementary School

INSTRUCTIONS:

1. You will have approximately one hour during which to study the following passage and to prepare for the discussion with the examining panel. You may make outline notes to use as a guide during the interview.
2. Do not place your name or initials on the notes which you prepare during the study period. Identify them *only* by writing thereon the interview number assigned you.
3. In the first 15 minutes of the interview you are to present without interruption the comments you have prepared during the study period. (You may refer to your notes, but you may not read them aloud.)
4. The following half hour or so will be devoted to answering relevant questions put to you by members of the examining panel.
5. Hand this selection and your notes to the examining panel at the end of the test period.

* * *

It is a commonly accepted fact that, in certain aspects, schools differ widely one from the other. The communities in which they are located differ; members of the teaching staff differ in preparation, background, and personality; pupils differ in ability, interests, and needs; parents differ in their attitudes toward the role of the school in the lives of their children as it affects marks, discipline, health, and all-round growth. These divergences pose a problem for educators throughout the country.

Some feel that the situation must be met by organizing schools so that each one is unique, thus enabling it to solve its own special problems most effectively. In such a school, programs would be continuously tailored to meet the specific circumstances involving all the groups referred to above. Furthermore, the school administration would be alert to the need for any additional changes as the situation continues its normal pattern of dynamic development.

On the other hand, some who consider the over-all goals of elementary education of paramount importance call attention to several matters which they think need careful consideration before any widespread adoption of such a flexible program is effected. What would happen, they ask, to the basic core of learning to which every child is entitled. Furthermore, the transfer of pupils from one school to another, they maintain, might involve a difficult adjustment for children and parents; this problem would be particularly important in areas of population mobility in which children are least able to adjust to changes in program.

A. What are your reactions to the ideas expressed in the above passage as it applies to the over-all responsibilities and duties of principals of elementary schools?

B. Amplify your statement of reactions by discussing the specific problems enumerated below which you might well face in administering an elementary school.
   Generously illustrate your treatment of each by citing examples from realistic school situations.
   1. Determining the role of the school, if any, in preserving dynamic equilibrium in a changing community.
   2. The need to develop meaningful standards for evaluating pupil performance.
   3. The need to implement properly the science course of study.

Number assigned to applicant for this interview test:_____

praisal report is prepared by the visiting committee for the school personnel administrator. Some of the topics that have appeared on inspection-test questionnaires are the following:

1. Name and description of present school.
2. The title and nature of your present position; length of time serving this position.
3. Prior positions held during the past ten years.
4. Present teaching, supervisory, administrative and other assignments.
5. In succinct form, background information concerning present assignment that may be of value to the visiting panel in understanding your problems.
6. Membership on committees dealing with pedagogic interests both within and outside of your school.
7. Responsibilities as elected officer in any professional organizations.
8. Courses given by you; articles or books written by you.
9. A statement of the five most important problems that you are trying to solve in the performance of your current duties.

3. *Field Test.* Applicants are asked to visit a school or an educational facility such as a recreation center that is not the one in which they are serving, and they are required to write or to offer orally a report appraising the school or facility they have visited. For example, applicants for the position of supervisor of school libraries might be asked to visit a particular school library and to make an appraisal of the services, resources and facilities of the library. Arrangements for this type of test, as well as for other types of tests, must be carefully made well in advance. Each person who participates in the conduct and administration of the examination must have his role carefully defined if the test is to provide the information that is desired and if it is to be administered fairly to all.

4. *Conference Test.* If the nature of an administrator's duties is such that he would be required to work with groups of individuals, and if success in interpersonal relationships is an important element of the position, a conference test may be arranged. If an applicant is visited to be observed as he carries on his duties, he may be asked to assemble a committee of his staff members for the purpose of conducting a conference. The topic should be of actual importance to him and the group. He should be given time to prepare for the conference. A visiting committee can learn much from his procedures in conducting the conference and from the relationships that are revealed during the conference. If no visit is made to the applicant in his own school environment, he may be called to the central office to conduct a conference with individuals who have been assembled for the purpose. Again, the topic of the conference should be an important one and the individuals assembled should be concerned with the topic.

Rating sheets for the conference test have included the following criteria:

A. Content of conference
   1. Comprehensiveness of treatment of topic
   2. Relevance with respect to topic
   3. Relevance with respect to conferees
B. Conduct of conference
   1. Manner of opening
   2. Contributions of the applicant
   3. Quality of leadership shown
   4. Group participation creditable to applicant
   5. Manner of closing conference
C. Outcomes
   1. Definiteness of outcomes
   2. Adequacy of results achieved
D. Speech
E. Aspects of personality not stated or implied above

A variation of the conference test has been utilized by some personnel-selection specialists. It has been called the "group discussion test," the "group interview," and the "leaderless discussion test." In this variation of the conference test, a group of six or seven individuals, who may all be applicants for the same supervisory position, are brought together for a round table discussion, with an informal chairman appointed by the personnel director merely to keep the discussion moving. The chairman's participation should be neutral since he is not being rated. It is the group of applicants whose performances in the group-discussion situation are being rated for clarity, sensitivity, leadership, rapport, etc. Members of the rating panel view the discussion and make notes on the quality of participation of each applicant, the extent of participation, and relationships with others in the group; they especially note who makes significant contributions, who misleads discussion, who brings it back to the point, who challenges authority, who supports his views with data and logic, who encourages others to participate, who keeps the discussion lively and interesting, who is easily "baited" or angered, who is passive, who uses disproportionate lengths of time, and who is recognized as a leader by the group.

OBTAINING REFERENCES FOR ADMINISTRATIVE PERSONNEL

References sought for prospective administrators should be adapted to the nature of the duties that such personnel are to perform. Although references are useful in many respects, school personnel administrators realize that they are not always accurate, for reasons that have already been set forth. Although it may be desirable to have the evaluations of a teacher's colleagues, of parents in the community who know him, even of students who know him, certain practical considerations make it inadvisable to seek to obtain reports directly from such sources. Comments on such relationships must come from the individuals who have been charged with the responsibility of supervising the applicant. In evaluating the experience of individuals applying for a principalship, it is more worthwhile to consider the background of an individual who has served in an intermediate administrative position than to consider the background of a classroom teacher. Generally speaking, an applicant's experience is most revealing to a personnel administrator when it is closest in nature to that of the position sought.

IN-BASKET PROBLEMS

One of the major studies of school principals was done by Hemphill, Griffiths and Frederiksen in their research on administrative behavior and traits of elementary school principals.[25] While it was not their intention to develop a procedure for the selection of principals, the analysis they performed on the duties and characteristics of elementary school principals and the procedures they utilized for investigating those characteristics form a useful background for a personnel administrator's process of selecting supervisory administrative personnel. They also clarified the decision-making function of the school administrator, revealing its multidimensional aspects. Their "in-basket" technique of presenting the prospective elementary school principal with a succession of realistic problems to which he is expected to react can be utilized further by school personnel administrators during interviews or other tests in order to obtain insights into the administrative behavior of the applicant. Simulations of school conditions by films, recordings and printed material also provide personnel administrators with approaches for appraising applicants.

INTERNSHIPS

A method that is growing in popularity for the selection of supervisory and administrative personnel is the process of internships. With the cooperation of a collegiate institution, selected individuals are assigned to one or more experienced supervisors. The internship is usually concurrent with course work. During their internships, prospective administrators and supervisors are given many duties to perform which give them training and insight into their own behavior as potential administrators. Appraisal of an internship becomes a valuable guide for the school personnel administrator in determining whether or not an individual has the qualities and abilities for assignment to an administrative post. Although internships are still in the formative stage, certain values and deficiencies have been recognized. Among the problems are the following:

1. The number of available internships is limited.
2. The criteria for selecting interns have not been sufficiently established.
3. Once a school system has made the investment of putting an individual through an internship, the college and other parties—includ-

ing the experienced administrator to whom the intern has been assigned— are reluctant to rate the intern adversely.

Favorable reports have been received about several of the administrative internship programs. In 1967, Trump and Karasik reported on a foundation-supported internship participated in by fifty-five "administrative interns," forty-seven schools located in eighteen states, and twenty-four participating major universities, with the cooperation of the National Association of Secondary School Principals.[26] The purpose of that internship program was to serve as a pilot project for the selection and on-the-job training of prospective principals and administrators. The interns were assigned to carefully selected schools characterized by innovative efforts in curriculum, organization and teaching methods. They served full time over a period of two years, and were selected and supervised jointly by the school district and the university. Among the favorable elements reported in this project were the following:

1. The program in both the participating school and the university benefited from the effort and stimulation of the internship. Old ways of doing things were challenged; stronger efforts were made to solve problems.
2. There was a strong emphasis on improving instruction and not on administrative details.
3. Thirty-eight of the fifty-five interns who subsequently became principals and assistant principals reported that the internship had helped them to get ready for instructional leadership.

SELECTION PROCEDURES IN BUSINESS AND INDUSTRY

Nowadays, large business organizations utilize carefully defined methods of staff selection. Paul C. Baker of Standard Oil Company of New Jersey, in a position paper delivered at a conference on teacher-selection methods arranged in 1967 by the Board of Examiners of the New York City school system, described the selection procedures generally applied by the operating affiliates of Standard Oil Company of New Jersey. The responsibility for selection is shared by several staff departments and line management, as defined in manuals of administrative procedure:

1. Announcement of Openings—Employment Department
2. Applicant Screening—Employment Department
3. Pre-employment Testing—Training Department
4. Medical Examination—Medical Department
5. Interview Committee—Employee Relationships Department and Line Management
6. Security Check—Security Department

157

7. Check of Former Employer and Credit Reference—Employment Department
8. Summary Evaluation—Representatives of Line Management and All Concerned Staff Departments

Their testing program includes a number of pencil-and-paper tests intended to supply supplemental information concerning the applicant's mental ability and attitudes. Their battery of tests cover the following areas:

1. *Intelligence.* Can the man learn to do the job? Will he be able to keep up with changes in the job? Will he show sound judgment in crucial situations?
2. *Educational Achievement.* Does the man have the basic education on which to build?
3. *Attitudes.* Does he have the attitude, opinions and personal history that have been shown to be characteristic of successful employees?
4. *Job Knowledge.* Does the man know the principles and theory of his craft? Does he know the standards of practice of his craft?

Each applicant is interviewed by a three-man committee. The declared purpose of the interview is to gather data about the applicant available only in a face-to-face situation. The types of questions for which answers are sought are:

1. How well does he express himself? Listen?
2. Does he show self-control?
3. Is he enthusiastic, highly motivated?
4. How well does he think?
5. Does he have the ability to learn?
6. Will he be able to work well with others?
7. Is he able to integrate his education and experience?
8. Will his personal appearance and manner add to or detract from his ability to work with others?

Their interviews run from 30 to 40 minutes. Each interviewer records his impressions of the applicant on a form especially designed for the purpose. In order to make independent judgments, interviewers record their evaluations without benefit of consultation with fellow interviewers. Applicants are compared with other applicants and are ranked. They are then compared to the best people in the kinds of jobs for which they are being interviewed and are compared to the interviewer's own standards, based on his experience as a supervisor. Using these comparisons, interviewers then determine which people on the rank-order list of applicants are acceptable or meet the standards. Representatives of various departments are consulted and have a voice in the selection of individuals. The employment department, the training department, the medical department and the department in which the opening exists all share in the selection.

According to Douglas W. Bray of the American Telephone and Telegraph Company in a paper on personnel-selection practices in industry

158

presented at the same conference, the Bell System also uses carefully defined and developed selection procedures in selecting its staff. Of particular interest was the description of the Assessment Center of the Bell System, which has been set up to develop procedures to process male and female employees who are candidates for management. The work of the Assessment Center involves (1) definitions of the qualities relevant to job performance, (2) selection or construction of techniques for eliciting behavior representative of these qualities, (3) systematic observation of the resultant behavior by trained observers who are intimately familiar with job demand, leading to (4) judgments on the candidate's strengths in each quality and in overall promise. The major techniques at the Assessment Center are a leaderless group discussion, an individual fact-finding problem, an individual administrative list of problems to be solved known as the in-basket, an interview, and a few paper-and-pencil tests of knowledge and mental ability. Assessees are brought together in groups of twelve for a period of approximately two to five days. The assessment staff consists of seven or eight supervisors who were first-level management themselves and who now supervise first-level jobs. They are given up to three weeks of training before beginning assessment work. Follow-up studies of the assessment process have shown that the method does, in fact, select a higher proportion of better-than-average first-level supervisors and also a considerably higher percentage of those who have potential for still further advancement. In addition, the method has proved to be highly acceptable both to management and to those assessed.

Following are some of the variables on which the candidates are rated:

1. Scholastic aptitude
2. Oral communication
3. Written communication
4. Human relations skills
5. Personal impact
6. Awareness of social environment
7. Self-objectivity
8. Behavior flexibility
9. Need for approval of superiors
10. Inner work standards
11. Need for approval of peers
12. Resistance to stress
13. Tolerance of uncertainty
14. Range of interests
15. Energy
16. Organizing and planning
17. Decision making
18. Analytical ability

SELECTION SOLELY BY MERIT AND FITNESS

The most basic principle of school staff selection is that selection should be made only on the basis of merit and fitness. This principle is so important that it has been made one of the fundamental goals of the constitution of the American Association of School Personnel Administrators. The foundation of a school system is not its buildings, its facilities, or its supplies. It is the teaching staff. Teachers have a pervasive, far-reaching influence on the attitudes of the young and, to that extent, on the future of

159

our country. During the course of his service over a number of years, one teacher may influence thousands of young people. The magnitude of his influence makes it all the more imperative that merit and fitness be the sole determinants for selection of every teacher and every supervisor and administrator. The public must be reminded of the vital importance of this principle because all too many people believe that anyone can teach, that anyone can head up a school, and that specialized professional competence is not necessary for the selection of teachers.

The importance of professional competence in staff selection has been accentuated in recent years as organizations of teachers have grown stronger and as statutory protection has made it increasingly difficult to terminate the services of teachers once they have been appointed. Moreover, the normal human relationship between the supervisory staff and teachers usually makes it unpleasant and difficult to terminate the services of school staff members who may be lacking in competence. Once a teacher or school administrator is put on the job, many forces converge to keep that person on the job; it is therefore imperative to make a wise selection at the beginning. As Kenneth E. McIntyre aptly phrases the thought in his book on the selection of principals, "The best time to solve a personnel problem is before the problem signs a contract." [27]

Among the strongest supporters of the "merit and fitness" principle of teacher selection are members of the teaching profession who realize that the education of children as well as the prestige of the profession are damaged by marginally qualified or unqualified teachers. In recent years, the organized teaching profession has shown its concern by demanding a stronger voice in the training, certification and selection of school staff.

A policy statement of the New York State Teachers Association (N.E.A.) in 1968 included this resolution: "That the New York State Teachers Association maintain its stand that school districts should employ only fully qualified teaching personnel who comply with state teacher certification requirements." A contract negotiated with the Syracuse, New York, Teachers Association (N.E.A) by the board of education included these provisions: "To the extent feasible, the Association will be involved in the recruitment and selection process. Whenever any vacancy in a promotional position occurs between September and June, it will be publicized by the Superintendent by means of a written notice placed in the weekly administrative bulletin." The United Federation of Teachers issued a special bulletin entitled "The Missing Teachers and How to Find Them" in which they urged improvement of teaching conditions and salaries and opposed lowering the standards for selecting teachers.

THE URBAN CRISIS AND STAFF SELECTION

Staff selection has become more controversial and critical in recent years as a result of the recognized urban crisis. Educational aspects of the urban crisis have been reflected in criticism of the attitude and performance of the school staff; dissatisfaction with curriculum, facilities and achievements of schools of the inner city; and demands for decentralization of the schools, a greater voice in staff selection by local communities and the elimination of *de facto* segregation in the inner city schools.

Reports have increasingly focused upon certain characteristics of school personnel that must be given special attention in the selection process. An N.E.A. Task Force declared that

> "Urban schools need educators . . . who demonstrate their belief in the real worth of each child, who respect children of different racial and socioeconomic backgrounds, and who know and respect the values and customs of these backgrounds. . . . The principal and teachers of an urban school must be able to carry on the important process of communication with the total community in which they work." [28]

In an effort to solve the ills of inner city education, some cities have made plans to decentralize school administration and to give the decentralized districts greater power in the selection of school staff. The stated advantages are that (1) the staff will feel closer to the local district and will be more responsive to its needs, (2) the residents of the local district will have a greater interest in their schools because they will have greater control, (3) the special staffing needs of the local community will receive greater attention because it will control staff selection, and (4) the red tape of centralized selection will be avoided. Critics of decentralized staff selection point out the following: (1) it will be expensive because of duplication of staff-selection efforts, (2) it will narrow the choice of staff and staff horizons because local districts are likely to promote their own staff and to choose personnel in tune with local attitudes, thus leading to staff segregation instead of integration, (3) the poorest schools of the inner city are likely to get the poorest teachers because experience has shown that the best teachers are more likely to choose the best sections, and (4) staff-selection standards are likely to be lowered, compared with citywide standards, because local pressures will be greater to employ persons who are less qualified but favored.

The widely expressed dissatisfaction with the methods and results of staffing schools of the inner cities will compel school personnel administrators to give this problem the highest priority. That is not to say that administrators alone, or their methods of selection, can solve the problem. Teacher-education institutions, organizations of school personnel, boards of education and government authorities must face the problem together, but the school personnel administrator must play a leadership role in any such effort.

8 CLASSIFIED OR NONCERTIFICATED PERSONNEL

GENERAL STATEMENT

The term "classified personnel" is used interchangeably with "noncertificated personnel" or "noninstructional personnel." The first term is generally preferred because people do not like to be identified as "non" anything. Further, the term implies that persons serving in this capacity are classified into different kinds of positions with significantly different kinds of preparation and levels of responsibility. To an extent, the same is true with the other principal class of employees—certificated personnel, those required to hold a license to teach, supervise, counsel or administer. The distinction is not entirely consistent, for classified personnel are sometimes required to hold certain licenses denoting professional achievement. A school architect and a certified public accountant are examples, but their licenses have not been developed for specific school use.

Classified personnel comprise about one third of all employees of a typical school district. Their services may be grouped into several broad classifications, including clerical and fiscal, cafeteria, custodial, grounds, plant maintenance, and transportation. Recently, instructional aids and data-processing employees have been added. Occasionally, architects and building inspectors are employed and they too are classified employees unless a provision of local law specifically excludes their being members of the classified service. Then such persons are called "temporary employees" because they are employed for a specific job which terminates when the work is completed.

Certain problems of the certificated staff have their counterparts in the classified service. They include recruitment, selection, assignment, promotion, wage and salary administration, fringe benefits, transfer, seniority rights, retirement, grievances, and evaluation. There are certain differences, too. The classified service is in a different labor market; the employees are

162

more mobile. In some instances, their hours of employment vary with the kind of service offered; some may be employed on an hourly basis and some on a monthly basis. Their lines of supervision may not be as clearly formulated as are those in the certificated service.

This chapter will give the rationale for the classification system, will discuss recruitment and selection as they differ from that in the certificated service, and will identify special problems of the classified service. Two trends in the classified service will be discussed, a trend toward a more sophisticated in-service educational program and a trend toward the use of more instructional aides. The chapter concludes with suggestions for new positions in the classified service to meet new needs and new responsibilities.

RATIONALE FOR CLASSIFICATION

A small school district may have a custodian who is directly responsible for doing all the cleaning, many of the maintenance projects, and even grounds care. Likewise, a small district may have one person serving as receptionist, clerk and bookkeeper. As additional classified persons are added to the staff, it becomes good policy to differentiate between their responsibilities. Normally, the cleaning of a building does not require the skill and knowledge required in an electrician. Neither should the salary of the two positions be equal.

The classification system often groups positions in two ways. First, they are grouped into families of positions. There might be three levels of custodians, for example, designated as Custodian I, Custodian II and Custodian III. Custodian I might be a night sweeper. Such a person would work under the direction of a Custodian II. He would have minimum contact with the public and little contact with pupils. Custodian II would have limited supervisory responsibilities, and he would have some contact with the public and with pupils as he sets up an auditorium arrangement or cleans the cafeteria after a lunch period. Custodian III would supervise several persons. He might establish work schedules for them, and he might evaluate the services of persons serving in his building or under his supervision. He might have many contacts with the public and with pupils.

In addition to custodians there are other families of positions which would include the various levels of bookkeepers, maintenance personnel, transportation employees, clerks and secretaries. The larger the organization, the larger the family of positions, the greater specialization of positions and the more classifications.

Families of positions are also grouped by salary. The determinants of salary usually include the amount of training required for the position, the level of responsibility, the experience needed to qualify for the position and the number of persons to be supervised. A certain level of maintenance man, for example, might be at the same level as a bookkeeper. This decision is subjective and is generally reinforced or justified by comparing similar positions in other districts, government agencies, business and industry.

Positions are also grouped into classes. A class may be defined as a group of positions sufficiently similar in duties and responsibilities that the same descriptive title may be used to designate each position allocated to the class; substantially the same requirements of education, experience, knowledge and ability are demanded; substantially the same fitness tests may be used in selection; the same salary range may be applied with equity. An example of a class would be Clerk I or Cafeteria Helper. Two men filling Clerk I positions might have different jobs to do, but the levels of difficulty would be the same.

JOB DESCRIPTIONS OR CLASS SPECIFICATIONS

A class specification is a formal statement of the duties and responsibilities of a position in a class, illustrated by examples of typical tasks and the qualification requirements for the positions in the class. A class specification should include the following:

1. The official class title.
2. A definition of the class, indicating the type of duties and responsibilities and placement within the organizational scheme.
3. A statement of the typical tasks to be performed by persons holding positions allocated to the class.
4. A statement of the minimum qualifications for service in the class. The minimum qualifications may include education, experience, knowledge, skills, abilities and personal physical traits and characteristics.
5. A statement of distinguishing characteristics which differentiates the class from other related or similar classes.
6. License or other special requirements for employment in the class.
7. Any additional qualifications considered so desirable that any person considered for employment who possesses them may be given additional credit in the evaluation of his qualifications, even though such additional qualifications are not a prerequisite to consideration for employment.

In any classification system, the minimum qualifications should never require a teaching, administrative or other credential, nor should they require work experience that would restrict applicants to teaching-credential holders. Titles should not be assigned if they would restrict competition to holders of teaching credentials.

In writing a job description or in creating a family of positions, consideration should be given to dividing the total duties to be performed within the family of positions in such a way that simple responsibilities are assigned to the entrance-level positions and complex responsibilities to the

164

higher classifications. The overall intent should be to pay the going wage for a particular level of responsibility. Too frequently, the volume rather than the level of work is used as evidence for a request for job reclassification.

RECRUITMENT FOR CLASSIFIED SERVICE

Classified service probably requires more varied skills and backgrounds than certificated service, and the identification of people who have such skills can be more time-consuming than the identification of people who have certificated skills. Certificated people frequently register with college and university placement offices, county school offices, and professional organizations and associations. Anyone seeking a classified position has no single place to register for employment. Classified professional organizations have not yet developed effective placement services, and the civil service type of employment procedures tends to discourage the services of placement offices.

Board policy should direct recruitment activities, and administrative regulations should indicate how board policy is to be carried out. In larger school districts, the school personnel administrator has seen fit to entrust the selection and administration of classified personnel to a specialized person or unit within the personnel department. In some large cities (including New York), responsibilities for noncertificated personnel are shared between the city's civil service commission and the school system's division of personnel.

Board Policy and Administrative Regulation

Here is a sample statement of board policy pertaining to recruitment for the classified service:

BOARD POLICY 4211—Recruitment

1. Persons will be recruited and selected for the classified service on the basis of job descriptions. Job descriptions will accompany notices of vacancies or the description shall be incorporated into the vacancy notices.
2. Vacancy notices shall be distributed to such persons and/or agencies or news media so as to assure a reasonable number of qualified applicants.
3. Persons may be recruited to advanced positions by means of promotion; however, they must meet the qualifications established for the position.
4. When two candidates have equal qualifications, the candidate who is a resident of the district will be given preference.
5. The governing board does not recognize employment in another school district as a basis for transferring to this district any right, privileges or benefits accruing to the employee in his previous school district.
6. The district shall actively seek persons as school employees who show promise of giving superior service.

165

It should be noted that the above Board Policy was numbered 4211. Administrative Regulation 4211 is actually initiated by the school superintendent (probably in cooperation with his cabinet or personnel administrator) and gives directions for the implementation of the policy. Here is the administrative regulation which accompanies Board Policy 4211:

ADMINISTRATIVE REGULATION 4211—Recruitment

Job descriptions will be developed for each classified position maintained by the district, and copies of descriptions will be kept on file in the personnel office. When vacancies occur or when eligibility lists are to be established, job descriptions will accompany or will be incorporated into the announcement of the vacancy.

Vacancy notices shall be distributed to such persons, school and administrative offices and/or agencies and/or news media so as to assure a reasonable number of qualified applicants.

Normally two employees in the same family will not be placed in the same school or department.

When two candidates have equal qualifications, the candidate who is a resident of the district will be given preference.

The governing board does not recognize employment in another school district as a basis for transferring to this district any right, privileges or benefits accruing to the employee in his previous school district.

It is the responsibility of the personnel office working with the department heads to keep job descriptions current.

The Announcement of Vacancies

Following this paragraph are samples of job announcements. It is generally considered good practice to have enough copies of announcements so that one may be available for each applicant. In addition, announcements should be available in each school or building where classified persons work, the central administration office and the local department of employment. A copy of the announcement should be displayed in public buildings. There may be times when giving employees additional copies of the announcement for distribution to their friends will materially assist the recruitment effort. Occasionally, sending the announcement to a newspaper will result in a news story that will attract applicants.

Ads may be placed in newspapers, and certain levels of positions may be advertised in trade journals which have statewide or national circulation. Still another potential source of applicants is found in other school districts; personnel administrators frequently exchange vacancy notices. Local residents who come to the personnel office to apply for employment (drop-in traffic) are by far the largest single source of applicants.

166

PRINCIPAL PERSONNEL ANALYST

A Personal Growth Opportunity
With the Los Angeles City Schools

The Los Angeles City Unified School District, one of the largest school systems in the United States, announces that it will, in the near future, appoint a Principal Personnel Analyst to fill a vacancy on its Personnel Commission (civil service) staff. The appointment will be made on the basis of the results of a competitive examination. Qualified persons from outside the District are invited to apply.

We Offer an Attractive Salary

The top salary, reached on a five-step schedule after three and one-half years, is $17,500. The salary for the first year, the average of the first two steps, is $14,439. The third step, reached after one and one-half years, is $15,673. The fourth step, reached after two and one-half years, is $16,500.

The Basic Responsibilities

There are two Principal Personnel Analysts on the Personnel Commission staff. Each, under the general direction of the Assistant Personnel Director, plans and supervises, with considerable independence, the work of the professional staff of Senior Personnel Analysts and Personnel Analysts.

The Principal Personnel Analyst directs studies which concern the maintenance and development of position classification and compensation plans and the formulation and development of rules and policies, and independently conducts complex personnel research projects. It is anticipated that the person selected for the job will have had extensive experience, both in the technical aspects of merit systems programs and in the supervision and administration of analytical personnel activities. The person selected will also have demonstrated a high degree of competence in interpersonal relations.

Examination Requirements

For admission to the examination the following qualifications are required:

1. Graduation from a recognized college or university. A master's degree in public administration or a related field is desirable.
2. Five years of professional experience in personnel administration including two years of recent responsible supervisory technical experience in position-classification and wage and salary determination.
3. A valid California driver's license must be presented at time of interview. (Out-of-state candidates must present a California license at time of assignment.)
4. Use of an automobile. (Must be available at time of assignment.)

VALLEY UNIFIED SCHOOL DISTRICT PERSONNEL COMMISSION

The Personnel Commission
Announces an Examination for:
CLERK II

Salary $416.00 $437.00 $459.00 $481.00 $506.00

Minimum Requirements:

Must be a U.S. citizen.

One year of general clerical experience including the operation of standard office equipment.

Equivalent to graduation from high school.

Examples of Duties:

Under supervision, assists the public by referring them to sources of information, giving out standard forms, explaining how to complete them, and answering requests for factual information by consulting various available sources; inserts and extracts materials from subject matter

167

files; classifies material by nature of subject matter, and prepares new file folders as needed; maintains informational or operational records; screens reports for completeness and accuracy; lists, abstracts, or summarizes data; answers routine written requests for information by sending materials and form letters; composes routine letters on factual subjects; compiles routine reports from a small number of established sources for review by supervisor; types correspondence, reports, and stencils from various rough draft materials; opens, segregates, stamps, and routes incoming mail; fills envelopes, operates standard office machines and devices; requisitions, receives, and charges out supplies; does machine transcription. Performs specialized tasks characteristic of the specific job assignment at this level of expectancy; if assigned to a school, shall administer first aid in the absence of the school nurse; and to do other related work as required.

Examination:
This is an open competitive examination. All candidates will be given a written examination.

Examination Weights:
Written Examination, 40%
Qualifications Interview, 60%

Final Date for Filing Applications:
Tuesday, November 3, 1970, 5:00 p.m.

Qualified candidates will be notified at a later date for time and place of examination.

VALLEY UNIFIED SCHOOL DISTRICT PERSONNEL COMMISSION

The Personnel Commission
Announces an Examination for:
CAFETERIA HELPER

Salary: $1.83 $1.92 $2.01 $2.12 $2.22

Minimum Requirements:
Must be a U.S. citizen.
Some experience in the large quantity preparation and serving of foodstuffs is desirable.
Equivalent to completion of the eighth grade.
Knowledge of basic kitchen utensils and equipment.

Examples of Duties:
Under supervision, cleans and peels fruits and vegetables, assists in preparing sandwiches, salads, beverages and pastries, serves food to students and faculty, cleans utensils, steam tables, chairs, food containers, serving counters, refrigerators, and other equipment; washes trays, silverware, and serving equipment; operates mixer grinder, dishwashing machine, and other equipment common to large kitchens, may operate a cash register, as required; may supervise student helpers, and to do other related work as required.

Examination:
This is an open competitive examination. All candidates will be given a written examination.

Examination Weights:
Written Examination, 40%
Qualifications Interview, 60%

Final Date for Filing Applications:
Tuesday, November 3, 1970, 5:00 p.m.

Qualified candidates will be notified at a later date for time and place of examination.

168

During the depression years it was not uncommon to find candidates for school boards seeking positions as much to help their friends to find employment as to serve the schools' children. In those years, job descriptions were not yet carefully developed, and impartial standards of employment were not prevalent, if they existed at all. In later years, applicants visited the personnel office and completed an application. Since there might not be an immediate vacancy, the application was filed. Often, the applicant never knew the status of his application. In the meantime other applicants applied and were chosen if openings existed at the time. Because adequate records were not maintained and because jobs were given on the basis of expediency, there was considerable dissatisfaction from applicants, many of whom lived in the community.

The modern solution to this problem is to use a civil-service or merit-system approach. It may be mandated by law, or it may be developed by board policy and implemented by administrative regulation. The sample statement of board policies which follows this paragraph pertains to the selection of classified employees. One should note that promotion and reemployment are factors which also have to be considered in selection.

Selection

School employees shall be selected on the basis of a civil-service type procedure and shall be persons of good character, qualified for the position by training and experience, and shall meet the established standards of the position.

Nondiscrimination

The board shall select employees without respect to race, religious creed, national origin, marital status, or ancestry.

Promotion within the district

All other considerations being equal, promotions will be made from within the ranks of personnel within the system. The overall intent, however, will be to obtain the most suitable candidates wherever they may be found.

Reemployment, Classified

A permanent classified employee who voluntarily resigns from his position and who is reemployed within thirty-nine (39) months after his last day of paid service for a position in his former classification as a permanent or limited term employee, or as a permanent or limited term employee in a related lower class or a lower class in which the employee formerly had permanent status will be reinstated without further competitive examination. His break in service will be disregarded and he will have restored to him all of the rights, benefits and burdens of a permanent employee in the class to which he is reinstated or reemployed.

Again, the administrative regulations which follow spell out the way in which the board policy is to be carried out:

Selection

Classified employees will be selected by a civil-service type of procedure which will typically include a test, an evaluation of training and experience including references from former employers and an oral interview involving two or more employees. Applicants may be disqualified because of their score on tests or on the basis of inadequate training or experience or unsatisfactory references without an interview. Generally speaking no more than two to three times as many persons will be called for a personal interview as positions are available. For example, if an eligibility list of 20 custodians is to be established, no more than 50 persons would be interviewed.

Persons serving on the interview committee shall be:

1. Department head
2. An employee in the department
3. Person designated by the superintendent

The eligibility list shall be used as follows:

1. The principal, department head or other administrator shall select a person from among the top three available persons on the list.
2. When a promotional position is open to only a few employees in the district, an examination may not be required, but an oral interview will be.

Eligibility lists may be declared invalid after four months and shall be declared invalid after one year.

Note: Department heads shall participate in test development and selection. The personnel office will:

1. Order and/or prepare, administer and score tests.
2. Set up interviews; notify applicants and interviewers.
3. Maintain lists of regular employees who are requesting transfer.
4. Advertise vacancies and/or the time when eligibility lists are being established.
5. Advise applicants on the status of their applications.
6. Serve as a consultant to interviewing committees.

Every reasonable effort shall be made to ascertain the applicant's qualifications for employment. Inquiries shall be made to former employers regarding competence for the position, performance, credit rating, character and citizenship.

Reemployment, Classified

A former permanent employee in the classified service who voluntarily resigned his position and seeks reemployment within thirty-nine (39) months of his last day of paid service will be placed on the eligibility list for positions equivalent to, or related to, that in a lower class, without further competitive examination.

If he is selected, he will have restored to him all the rights, benefits and burdens of a permanent employee in the class to which he is reinstated or reemployed. His break in service will be disregarded and shall have no effect on sick leave allowances or seniority benefits.

There are at least two ways of simplifying the paper work associated with applications originating from drop-in traffic. When an applicant applies for a position, he is given one or more announcements of vacancies or descriptions of positions for which he believes he is qualified. He is given a form which describes the selection process. Lastly, he is given one or more insert forms to complete, one for each position for which he is applying. A sample of these forms is given.

VALLEY UNIFIED SCHOOL DISTRICT

Classified Employment Procedure

The Valley Unified School District encourages well qualified applicants to apply for all classified positions.

A civil service type of employment procedure is followed. Job specifications are available for inspection. Persons seeking employment are asked to complete a card indicating the classification of position they are seeking and address the card to themselves.

When an eligibility list is to be established, the cards will be mailed, and the cards will direct applicants to a place where applications will be completed and tests administered. Persons scoring high on the test, possessing the skills and experience for the position will be invited for a personal interview. The interview will involve three persons. On the basis of scores received on tests, evaluations of training and experience and oral interview, applicants will be ranked and placed on an eligibility list or advised that they do not qualify for the position.

Eligibility lists are established for a minimum of four months and may be extended to a maximum of one year.

Persons may be on two or more eligibility lists. When a person accepts a position with the District, his name will be dropped from other eligibility lists unless some unusual circumstance would indicate that the good of the District would be served by other action.

ALL EMPLOYEES MUST BE CITIZENS OF THE UNITED STATES.

VALLEY UNIFIED SCHOOL DISTRICT

PLEASE COMPLETE ONE FORM
FOR EACH POSITION FOR WHICH
YOU ARE QUALIFIED.
Date_____
Telephone Number_____

Name_____
Address_____
City_____ State_____ Zip Code_____

Position _____

An application form and job announcement will be mailed to you when an eligibility list is to be formed for the position. The completed application must be returned to the Classified Personnel Office before the final filing date as stated on the job announcement.

171

These inserts are filed by job classification, not by alphabetical order of applicants. When a vacancy occurs or when an eligibility list is to be established, insert forms are mailed to the applicant. Experience has shown that, by the time the insert forms are sent, many applicants have found other employment. If the applicant has selected other employment, it is up to him to determine whether he still wants to be considered for a position or not. If he wants to be considered, he will notify the personnel office of his continued interest in employment.

An alternative and perhaps superior method is to develop a one-fold, twice-scored application form. Having the application completed at the time of the original contact makes possible a quick determination of eligibility. The form is so designed that it will fit into a window envelope for mailing. The three sections of the second page of the application form are addressed by the applicant, and they provide a report to the applicant on the status of his application.

TESTS AND TESTING PROCEDURES

Tests are an inherent part of the civil-service procedure. A number of companies publish tests for school and business use. Major classifications of tests are intelligence, achievement and aptitude. The test used should relate closely to the knowledge and abilities required in the position. For example, if a major duty is filing, then the written test should include many filing problems. The validity of a test is always a major concern of the personnel administrator, for there are certain built-in hazards in the use of this kind of test. Some people tend to freeze in a testing situation. The typical paper-and-pencil test tends to favor those who have been in school the most recently. Paper-and-pencil tests are perhaps the least valid for those who have language or reading disabilities. In recent years, representatives of minority groups have urged that paper-and-pencil tests not be the exclusive criterion for staff selection, inasmuch as capable individuals with educational handicaps may be denied fair employment opportunities.

Performance tests are useful supplements to paper-and-pencil tests. A typing test is the kind of performance test that can be used in screening a secretary or office typist. It is easy to appraise speed and accuracy in typing. Another advantage is that a performance test in typing can be administered efficiently to a large number of applicants at one time. In other fields, a valid performance test may be more difficult to develop and more time-consuming to administer. Abilities sought in performance tests may include agility, dexterity, organization and speed (as in filing), alphabetizing, and laying out angles with a carpenter's square. Performance tests used to appraise mechanical ability may include diagnosing failures in electrical circuits, including television sets and thermostats.

Test services may be purchased from management services or, in some states, from a state personnel board. The latter, in California, will develop

172

a special test for a unique position, or it will have on file standard tests for standard positions. The personnel board will administer, score, and compare scores with other groups that have taken the test. By no means should the school personnel administrator believe that he must devise his own tests.

Since electronic data processing is becoming more common in public school systems, it is possible that local districts will take more initiative in test development. The computer makes item analysis possible with minimum effort, and that, in turn, greatly facilitates the discarding of items that do not distinguish good applicants from others.

Only brief mention need be made of testing procedures. If a large number of applicants is to be tested, separate answer sheets are recommended. Answer sheets should be designed for machine scoring. When answer sheets are used, it is quite likely that test booklets will be used by the applicants. If test booklets are used a second or third time, they should be monitored to see that former users have not written in them. Another precaution is to make an exact count of the number of booklets given out and to make sure that an equal number is returned after the test. Security of tests between testing periods is important, too. Probably nothing can damage the image of a personnel office faster than rumor to the effect that test information has leaked out before the test was administered.

One personnel administrator, who purchases all of his tests from a state personnel board, does not open the package, which is delivered by U.S. Mail, until he is in front of the group ready to give the test. Unused test forms are either destroyed or returned to the state personnel board.

Administering a test in dictation can pose some serious concerns, including variability in speed of reading passages, mispronouncing words, and the common distractions of clearing one's throat or coughing. A tape recorder is quite effective and more consistent than a person reading a passage to be taken in shorthand. A competent secretary can prepare such a tape. Even test directions may be tape recorded.

For greater test security, additional forms of the same test may be made available. Even mixing the questions by giving them different numbers may be desirable at times. An applicant should not be disqualified from taking a test merely because he has failed it once.

When tests are purchased from the same company and used by districts in a common labor market, applicants who apply in one district may become familiar with the test and then take the same test again in another district. For that reason and for reasons of efficiency in test administration, districts in the same labor market might find it profitable to share responsibilities in testing.

An interview may be construed to be a test. Indeed, some of the higher level positions of classified service are filled by using no test other than an oral interview. The classified interview committee is often composed of three persons. Various factors should be considered in selecting such persons, such as the ability of a committee member to develop rapport with applicants, to interrogate effectively, to listen intently, to make discriminating judgments and then record them in pointed comments. Another factor is the position which a committee member holds. If one member of the committee, say, the personnel administrator, is on each personnel selection committee, the charge may be made that he has too much selecting authority, that one must *know* the personnel administrator in order to obtain employment. Thus, as a general rule, the personnel administrator should rarely serve as a member of an oral committee. A more practical and defensible responsibility for him is to set up oral committees and to be concerned more with the method of selection than with the actual selection. It is appropriate, however, to have an administrator on the interview committee, and because the administrator is usually an articulate person he might even be appointed chairman of the committee. The responsibilities of the chairman differ from the other committee members' only in that he opens the interview, generally sets the stage for it, and sees that it is appropriately conducted and terminated in accordance with the time schedule.

A second member of the interview committee might be a person who is classified at the same level as the applicant or at least in the same family of positions. This person can probably describe the duties and frustrations of the position better than any other person. An incidental advantage is that it involves employees in the selection process, which employees typically respond favorably to. It should be pointed out again that not every person of a particular classification is qualified to serve in a selecting capacity.

The third person may be selected at large. The administrative regulation on selection quoted earlier stated that the third member should be the department head, but that is not always considered good practice because it places too much responsibility for decision making on the department head. In the committee's deliberations, for example, the department head could say that he did not want a certain person to be on the eligibility list, which might affect the decision of the other two committed members far out of proportion to the influence the department head should have as one member of the committee. Criticism might be similar to that directed toward the personnel administrator if he were to participate in each interviewing committee.

When competition is particularly keen for staff positions, it may be advantageous to invite a person from outside of the district to be a member of the committee. When it comes to selecting persons for data processing, accounting and similar specialized positions, people from industry or county offices may well serve on the interview committee.

Under civil service procedures, it is necessary to establish the relative weight of each portion of the examination. Frequently, the selection process consists of three parts: a written test, an evaluation of previous
174

experience and a review of references, and an interview. The written test may account for twenty percent of the total score. The experiences and references may account for thirty percent and the interview for fifty percent. Percentages may vary with the classification of the position. For example, when performance tests are available, their test results might be given a higher value. Whatever weight is assigned to the various parts of the examination, it should appear on the announcement of the vacancy. If weights are assigned after the examination process, the objective value of the selection process is lost.

PREEMPLOYMENT REQUIREMENTS

The application form should identify the major areas of inquiry. That is to say, the applicant should be advised that his former employer will be contacted for reference and that his character will be investigated. Certain families of positions may require a physical examination, which is generally paid for by the district, and the form the physician uses should be provided by the district. Large school districts may have a staff physician. Smaller districts usually have to rely on local doctors. One method used successfully in a medium-sized community was to send a copy of the medical examination form to each physician listed in the community and ask if he would be willing to examine potential employees for a fee specified by the district. Those who responded favorably were placed on a list subsequently given to the applicant, who then selected the doctor of his choice. An applicant could also take the form to his personal physician with the understanding that the physician would receive the same amount as any other physician for the examination.

Still another preemployment requirement should be a chest Xray or other tests to ascertain that the applicant is free from active tuberculosis. In some districts, a tuberculin test is given every two years to all employees who are in contact with children.

SELECTION AND APPOINTMENT

Once a population of applicants has met the description for the job in terms of education, experience, written and/or performance tests, and after references have been checked and physical tests have been passed, a decision must be made about how to identify applicants among the population who should be selected. In some school districts, a department head may select one person from the group. Another method is to rank all applicants according to their combined test scores. The department head who needs an employee must make his selection from among the top three applicants. If a list of fifty eligibles is established, number twelve knows that he may soon have an opportunity for employment and number fifty knows that he might seek another position in the meantime.

The last step in selection is appointment. Normally, the superintendent makes the recommendation to the governing board. Information presented to the board should include the person's name, classification, salary, status (probationary, former employee returning as a permanent employee, substitute or temporary), and beginning date of employment. Boards or superintendents may require more information, but it is not likely to be sought if the board is kept fully aware of the procedures used in selection.

SPECIAL PROBLEMS IN THE CLASSIFIED SERVICE

The problems of recruitment, selection, assignment, transfer, promotion and termination of employment are common to both certificated and classified personnel. However, there are a number of special problems associated with the classified service that do not seem to be prevalent with certificated personnel.

AUDITING POSITIONS AND CLASS SPECIFICATIONS

Auditing as used here means comparing the level of responsibilities assigned to a given position with the level of responsibilities shown on the job description of the position. Auditing thus becomes one of the most complicated responsibilities of the classified-personnel administrator. When a position is created, it is the function of management to specify tasks. Management, including the department head and possibly an assistant superintendent or even the superintendent in a small district, advises the personnel administrator about what duties will be assigned. It then becomes the responsibility of the personnel administrator to combine all recommendations into a job description and to assign the position to a class. It may be his recommendation to use a class already accepted in the district, or the position may be so unrelated to others that it requires a separate class. It should be the responsibility of the personnel administrator to make that determination. In some organizations where there is a separate personnel commission, the commission would make the determination. Even so, recommendation for appointment usually originates with the personnel administrator.

The foregoing paragraph implies that the position has been placed on the salary schedule at the same level as other positions requiring similar skills and responsibilities. In the course of time, however, work loads change, little tasks in offices are changed from one desk to another, and there can come a time when the employee is actually working outside of his classification, which may even become a grievance.

Assume that a clerk and a secretary work in the same office. Because the clerk has some secretarial skills, and perhaps even enjoys using them, she manages to get a certain amount of dictation, perhaps all of it. Ultimately, the clerk leaves her position. The department head has become so accustomed to giving dictation to the clerk that he fails to accept graciously another clerk for a replacement who does not take dictation. The replacement is at a disadvantage. It is for that reason that positions should be audited regularly.

176

The office administrator should not have complete responsibility for making the job classifications in his office or department. He is not aware of comparable duties in other offices, he may not have a sufficiently objective attitude toward his staff, and he may understandably want to obtain the highest possible classification for his staff.

Position classification is the function of the personnel administrator. He presumably has knowledge of the overall administrative requirements. It should be his responsibility to determine whether or not a higher classification is justified—a decision which should be preceded by a thorough discussion with the department head, for ideally both should be in agreement with the final decision. In the final analysis, the decision to reclassify an employee should be based on the level of responsibility within the working period. Decisions based on other rationales are not consistent with the philosophy of employment based on merit. A related problem is differentiating between an increased work load and increased responsibility. Increased work load should result in assigning more labor hours to the position. An increase in responsibility should result in a position reclassification.

Positions and classifications should be reviewed periodically. Some industrial establishments review job descriptions every six months. Such auditing is often demanded by union contract. It is regrettable, indeed, that most school districts have made no provision for auditing positions on a regular basis.

EMPLOYEE MOBILITY

In metropolitan areas, classified employees change positions frequently. Several reasons have been advanced for their mobility, including the following:

1. Opportunities for advancement in classified service are limited. Mobility is far greater at the entrance level than in the higher positions.
2. Some persons find that they do not really like to work around children.
3. Salaries for classified positions are commonly below those of comparable positions in business and industry.
4. Conditions of employment, including interruptions, unrealistic overtime responsibilities and lack of opportunities to meet other adults, may be irritating to an employee.
5. Until recently, the lack of fringe benefits, particularly in terms of insurance programs, was a reason for changing positions.
6. Individuals who perform some of the menial tasks are inclined to change jobs frequently.
7. Girls who take secretarial jobs are of marriageable age.

A district should spend some administrative time in analyzing employee terminations, which can be done through exit interviews. When a person ends his employment in a district, he may make some comments about the conditions of his employment, the quality of leadership, or the condition of the tools with which he had to work—all of which may have implications not only for his termination but also for his successor's satisfaction on the same job.

NEGOTIATIONS WITH REPRESENTATIVES OF CLASSIFIED EMPLOYEES

The principle of negotiations for all employees is well established. While there are many districts which have not yet moved into this arena, it is only a matter of time until they do. Leadership in negotiations has come largely from certificated personnel.

Normally, teachers are affiliated for negotiating purposes either with the American Federation of Teachers or with the National Education Association. Classified employees may be included with either group, but they may also be affiliated with the several trade unions under the AFL-CIO. Complicating the negotiations with classified personnel is the determination of their representative. A large district may have more than a hundred classifications of positions. To have each group represented at the negotiating table would be an almost impossible task. An appropriate procedure may be to have a representative of each of the major classifications participate in the negotiating process. It should be the responsibility of each representative to determine the desires of the people he represents.

In general, the fewer persons the administration has to work with, the more efficient the negotiating process can be. The optimum size of a negotiating group is between five and twelve. A group that size is large enough to fairly represent each class of employee, yet it is small enough to insure good communication.

If the administration has to meet with many groups, a disproportionate amount of time is required in attending meetings. Groups also jockey for more favorable settlements, with the possibility of impairing employee morale. The matter of acceptable representation cannot be settled by administrative fiat, though; it must be settled by working cooperatively with employee groups.

BASIC PRINCIPLES OF SALARY SCHEDULES

Given below are some basic principles of the salary schedule concept for classified employees.

1. Salary schedules should be made public. Normally, the law requires salary publication because it offers protection to both the public and employees.
2. All classified employees should be on the salary schedule; each classification of position maintained by the district should have a place on the schedule.
3. Salary schedules should be equitable. An attempt should be made

178

to pay the prevailing wage rate for each classification of position. Other factors to consider in establishing wage rates include educational requirements, the number of persons supervised, the level of responsibility and the skills necessary for the job.

4. There should be some recognition of length of service. It can be accomplished in part by establishing a five-step schedule, for example. Districts may establish schedules with more or fewer steps, but the intent is to give some recognition to length of service based on the principle that experience on the job makes a person a more valuable employee to the district. Also, there is a discernible trend in some sections of the country to give additional vacation time to employees who have been with the district ten, fifteen, twenty or more years.

5. Salary schedules should be organized in ways to facilitate administration. The establishment of anniversary dates for salary increases is standard practice. If such dates are at times other than at the normal payroll period, both budgeting and payroll preparation are affected. The developing trend of a salary schedule for classified employees with differentials based on preparation may complicate record keeping and salary computations to such an extent that additional help is required. While the addition of help poses no major problem, a legitimate concern is the extent to which the new policy contributes to better service to the district.

6. There should be some rationale for establishing the dollar amounts shown on the schedule. Typically, it is done by making studies of other districts, governmental agencies, and local business and industry.

7. Provision should be made for a regular review. A reasonable requirement has been to review salaries annually, but contract negotiations in recent years have fixed salaries for a two- or three-year period.

Factors to Consider in Establishing Salary Schedules

This section is concerned with the factors involved in establishing a salary schedule. It should be recognized that these are broad guidelines, and in the final analysis there are several exceptions to the weight placed on each point.

1. *Educational requirements.* Typically, persons who have college degrees are paid more than those who have only a high school diploma or an Associate of Arts degree. In making job descriptions it is important to identify the minimum educational requirement suitable for the position. Schools should make provision for the employment of people who have modest educational backgrounds.

179

In our time, there is a need to provide jobs for modestly skilled persons. It is also true that setting unduly high requirements artificially limits the supply of capable employees, is likely to put the wrong person in the job, and results in labor turnover.

2. *Skills required for the position.* The labor market has generally recognized, for example, that an electrician has more skills than a painter. One comes to this conclusion when one compares the typical salaries of the two tradesmen. Granted that it is difficult to compare the skills of an electrician and an accountant, but one can find certain comparisons of the two positions in the labor market generally.

3. *Number of employees to be supervised.*

4. *Responsibility assigned to each position.*

5. *Hours of employment.* It is becoming a frequent practice to pay premium wages for service that goes beyond regular daytime hours.

6. *The hierarchy of positions.* Normally, there are certain benchmark positions, which are defined as positions in other districts or agencies that have similar levels of requirements for entrance and thereafter have similar levels of responsibility. For example, a night sweeper, by whatever title he is called, has a similar responsibility in a school, factory or store; hence the position can be identified as a benchmark position, and salary can be compared with that in several agencies. In schools, this position might be called Custodian I. Custodian II, who among other things supervises Custodian I, might not have a counterpart in other agencies; yet for purposes of salary placement it is appropriate to have a five-percent, eight-percent, or some other fixed increase in schedule. Again, the person who supervises custodians can be identified as holding a benchmark position. All grades of custodian must fall between.

7. A salary schedule should have a format that (a) lists the classes of positions by number, (b) shows the monthly salary of each class, (c) gives the step-one hourly rate and the overtime rate, (d) provides for all steps to be separated by a uniform percentage, and (e) provides for each class to be a uniform distance apart. An example is shown.

MAKING SALARY STUDIES

The advent of negotiations may change traditional ways of making salary studies. Even so, the following suggestions for making salary studies may have some validity in guiding the decision-making process.

1. Employees should be involved in salary studies if they so desire; available communication channels between employees or their representatives and the administration should be made known to

all through school-district and employee publications. Representatives and the administration should make every effort to establish jointly the kinds of information releases to be used. Where differences are recognized, honest statements of the reasons for the differences should be given. Each employee should have an opportunity to express to his representative his feelings and his recommendations for improvements. Representatives should summarize employee recommendations, obtain a consensus from each classification of employee, and formulate each recommendation, first for the group and then for the negotiator or the administration.

2. A calendar of events should be established for anticipated decisions, reports and recommendations.

3. There should be attempts at agreement about which districts, agencies and industries to use in making comparative salary studies.

4. Reports on salary studies should be made available to employees and to the superintendent of schools before any final actions or recommendations are made.

5. Employees should be made aware of the cost of fringe benefits per employee. Fringe benefits may include, but need not be limited to, the costs of district-paid insurance (both health and comprehensive), retirement, leaves of absence, and benefits accruing from longevity of service. Such hidden costs to the district are growing annually, and they distort straight salary comparisons.

6. Recommendations must be presented to the superintendent and to the board for final adoption.

VALLEY UNIFIED SCHOOL DISTRICT

Salary Class and Range for Classified Positions
1968–1969

Class Title	Schedule & Range		Class Title	Schedule & Range	
Office Class			**Office Class** continued		
Account Clerk I	19	437–532	Key Punch Operator	18	425–519
Account Clerk II	21	459–559	Library Clerk I	15	395–481
Account Clerk III	23	481–587	Library Clerk II	17	416–506
Administrative Secretary I	29	559–679	Microfilm Operator	19	437–532
Administrative Secretary II	33	616–748	Multilith Operator	22	470–573
Clerk I	15	395–481	Multilith Technician	26	519–632
Clerk II	17	416–506	PBX Operator Receptionist	17	416–506
Clerk III	19	437–532			
Data Control Clerk	22	470–573	Personnel Clerk	21	459–559
Data Equipment Operator	31	587–713	Principal Account Clerk	25	506–616

Class Title	Schedule & Range		Class Title	Schedule & Range	

Office Class continued

Programmer Analyst	43	787–956
Publications Technician	24	494–602
Purchasing Clerk	25	506–616
School Secretary I	21	459–559
School Secretary II	23	481–587
Secretary	23	481–587
Steno-Clerk I	19	437–532
Steno-Clerk II	21	459–559

Cafeteria Class

Cafeteria Helper	6	318–386
Cafeteria Worker	8	334–405
Cook-Baker	11	358–437
Cafeteria Manager I	16	405–494
Cafeteria Manager II	18	425–519
Cafeteria Manager III	20	447–545

Maintenance and Operations

Custodian I	21	459–559
Custodian II	23	487–587
Custodian III	25	506–616
Custodian IV	27	532–647
Custodial Supervisor	37	679–826
Deliveryman	21	459–559
Equipment Operator	25	506–616
Gardener	22	470–573
Groundsman I	21	459–559
Groundsman II	25	506–616
Grounds Supervisor	37	679–826
Mailman	21	459–559
Maintenance Man I	25	506–616
Maintenance Man II	27	532–647
Maintenance Man III	33	616–748
Carpenter		
Electrician		
Glazier		
Heating and Ventilation		
Locksmith		
Painter		
Plumber		
Refrigeration		
Maintenance Man IV		
AV-Electronics		
Technician		

Maintenance and Operations continued

Maintenance Supervisor	37	679–826
Matron	16	405–494
Plant Manager	35	647–787
Senior Warehouseman	32	602–731
Sprinkler Repairman	25	506–616
Warehouseman	23	481–587

Transportation

Automotive Body Repairman	31	587–713
Bus Driver	25	506–616
Dispatcher	31	587–713
Head Mechanic	35	647–787
Mechanic	31	587–713

Management Class

Assistant Business Manager	60	1194–1454
Director of Accounting	44	806–979
Director of Classified Personnel	48	888–1081
Director of Food Services	36	664–806
Director of Maintenance and Operations	45	826–1004
Director of Transportation	40	731–888
Purchasing Agent	44	806–979
Supervisor of Data Processing	61	1223–1490
Supervisor of Personnel Services	44	806–979

Other Class

Head of Division of Site Acquisition	56	1081–1318
Inspector	44	806–979
Noon Supervisor		Class 15, Step 1, $2.27 hourly
Teachers Aide		Class 15, Step 1, $2.27 hourly
Substitute Clerk		Class 17, Step 1, $2.64 hourly
Substitute Secretary		Class 21, Step

In the illustrations of salary studies which follow, twenty-two districts were chosen because they were more or less the same size and all were unified. In this situation, both the salary committee and the administration agreed in advance that the twenty-two districts were appropriate to study for salary purposes and that the intent was to arrive at a salary recommendation near the average.

Two forms are included to illustrate the way information was gathered. Note that the benchmark position was Administrative Secretary I and that only Administrative Secretary II is based on that benchmark. Clerk I, on the other hand, serves as a benchmark for eight other positions. Data gathered in this form may be plotted as shown. An explanation of it is necessary. (See example on page 185.)

The district that made the study had a salary schedule that had two-and-one-half percent differential between steps and five-percent differential between classes. Since this part of the study was limited to a study of the ranges of the benchmark positions, the dollar amount of the average of the highs and lows for each position was reduced to a percent differential between the average of all districts and the district being studied. Figure 16 most graphically shows the extent to which some positions were out of line.

Data from Figure 16 on page 186 indicate that Clerk I class is approximately three-and-one-half percent below the average of the districts studied and that cafeteria helpers are about four percent above the average. Other classifications are between these two extremes.

A point of view that has been offered in salary settlements is that each benchmark position should be within one step, or two-and-one-half percent, of the average. To raise those classifications that are from two-and-one-half percent to five percent below the average poses no real problem, but to hold those that are two-and-one-half percent to five percent above the average presents a problem. When a general raise is considered, people in such positions may be held at their present salary level. Sometimes referred to as Y-rating the position, it implies that the position will be downgraded, but the employee will be held at his current salary until such time as the schedule catches up to his current placement. However, it is a rare employee who is content to remain at his current salary when a general increase is given. Special consideration is usually given to employees in such situations.

Another dimension of the salary study should include the cost of living, information on which is available from the U.S. Department of Labor. It may be wise for the personnel administrator to explain to the salary committee and perhaps to the whole classified staff the rationale behind the cost-of-living index.

An open procedure has brought on reasonably good feelings between employees and employers in many districts. It has given every employee a chance to participate and it provides for regular communication to employees during the study period. When differences of opinion existed, they were pointed out forthrightly. Lastly, surprises or arbitrary decisions from

Classified Salary Schedule
1968–69

Class	Step I Mo.	Hrly.	Over Time	Step II Mo.	Hrly.	Over Time	Step III Mo.	Hrly.	Over Time	Step IV Mo.	Hrly.	Over Time	Step V Mo.	Hrly.	Over Time
1	280	1.61	2.42	296	1.70	2.55	310	1.78	2.67	325	1.87	2.81	341	1.96	2.94
2	287	1.65	2.48	302	1.74	2.61	318	1.83	2.75	334	1.92	2.88	350	2.01	3.02
3	296	1.70	2.55	310	1.78	2.67	325	1.87	2.81	341	1.96	2.94	358	2.06	3.09
4	302	1.74	2.61	318	1.83	2.75	334	1.92	2.88	350	2.01	3.02	368	2.12	3.18
5	310	1.78	2.67	325	1.87	2.81	341	1.96	2.94	358	2.06	3.09	377	2.16	3.24
6	318	1.83	2.75	334	1.92	2.88	350	2.01	3.02	368	2.12	3.18	386	2.22	3.33
7	325	1.87	2.81	341	1.96	2.94	358	2.06	3.09	377	2.16	3.24	395	2.27	3.41
8	334	1.92	2.88	350	2.01	3.02	368	2.12	3.18	386	2.22	3.33	405	2.33	3.50
9	341	1.96	2.94	358	2.06	3.09	377	2.16	3.24	395	2.27	3.41	416	2.39	3.59
10	350	2.01	3.02	368	2.12	3.18	386	2.22	3.33	405	2.33	3.50	425	2.44	3.66
11	358	2.06	3.09	377	2.16	3.24	395	2.27	3.41	416	2.39	3.59	437	2.51	3.77
12	368	2.12	3.18	386	2.22	3.33	405	2.33	3.50	425	2.44	3.66	447	2.57	3.86
13	377	2.16	3.24	395	2.27	3.41	416	2.39	3.59	437	2.51	3.77	459	2.64	3.91
14	386	2.22	3.33	405	2.33	3.50	425	2.44	3.66	447	2.57	3.86	470	2.70	4.05
15	395	2.27	3.41	416	2.39	3.59	437	2.51	3.77	459	2.64	3.91	481	2.76	4.14
16	405	2.33	3.50	425	2.44	3.66	447	2.57	3.86	470	2.70	4.05	494	2.84	4.26
17	416	2.39	3.59	437	2.51	3.77	459	2.64	3.91	481	2.76	4.14	506	2.91	4.37
18	425	2.44	3.66	447	2.57	3.86	470	2.70	4.05	494	2.84	4.26	519	2.98	4.47
19	437	2.51	3.77	459	2.64	3.91	481	2.76	4.14	506	2.91	4.37	532	3.06	4.59
20	447	2.57	3.86	470	2.70	4.05	494	2.84	4.26	519	2.98	4.47	545	3.13	4.70
21	459	2.64	3.91	481	2.76	4.14	506	2.91	4.37	532	3.06	4.59	559	3.21	4.82
22	470	2.70	4.05	494	2.84	4.26	519	2.98	4.47	545	3.13	4.70	573	3.29	4.94
23	481	2.75	4.14	506	2.91	4.37	532	3.06	4.59	559	3.21	4.82	587	3.37	5.06
24	494	2.84	4.26	519	2.98	4.47	545	3.13	4.70	573	3.29	4.94	602	3.46	5.19
25	506	2.91	4.37	532	3.06	4.59	559	3.21	4.82	587	3.37	5.06	616	3.54	5.31
26	519	2.98	4.47	545	3.13	4.70	573	3.29	4.94	602	3.46	5.19	632	3.63	5.45
27	532	3.06	4.59	559	3.21	4.82	587	3.37	5.06	616	3.54	5.31	647	3.72	5.58
28	545	3.13	4.70	573	3.29	4.94	602	3.46	5.19	632	3.63	5.45	664	3.82	5.73
29	559	3.21	4.82	587	3.37	5.06	616	3.54	5.31	647	3.72	5.58	679	3.90	5.85
30	573	3.29	4.94	602	3.46	5.19	632	3.63	5.45	664	3.82	5.73	696	4.00	6.00
31	587	3.37	5.06	616	3.54	5.31	647	3.72	5.58	679	3.90	5.85	713	4.10	6.15
32	602	3.46	5.19	632	3.63	5.45	664	3.82	5.73	696	4.00	6.00	731	4.20	6.30
33	616	3.54	5.31	647	3.72	5.58	679	3.90	5.85	713	4.10	6.15	748	4.30	6.45
34	632	3.63	5.45	664	3.82	5.73	696	4.00	6.00	731	4.20	6.30	767	4.41	6.62
35	647	3.72	5.58	679	3.90	5.85	713	4.10	6.15	748	4.30	6.45	787	4.52	6.78
36	664	3.82	5.73	696	4.00	6.00	731	4.20	6.30	767	4.41	6.62	806	4.63	6.95
37	679	3.90	5.85	713	4.10	6.15	748	4.30	6.45	787	4.52	6.78	826	4.75	7.13
38	696	4.00	6.00	731	4.20	6.30	767	4.41	6.62	806	4.63	6.95	847	4.87	7.31
39	713	4.10	6.15	748	4.30	6.45	787	4.52	6.78	826	4.75	7.13	866	4.90	7.47
40	731	4.20	6.30	767	4.41	6.62	806	4.63	6.95	847	4.87	7.31	888	5.10	7.65
41	748	4.30	6.45	787	4.52	6.78	826	4.75	7.13	866	4.90	7.47	909	5.22	7.83
42	767	4.41	6.62	806	4.63	6.95	847	4.87	7.31	888	5.10	7.65	933	5.36	8.04
43	787	4.52	6.78	826	4.75	7.13	866	4.90	7.47	909	5.22	7.83	956	5.49	8.24
44	806	4.63	6.95	847	4.87	7.31	888	5.10	7.65	933	5.36	8.04	979	5.63	8.45
45	826	4.75	7.13	866	4.90	7.47	909	5.22	7.83	956	5.49	8.24	1004	5.77	8.66
46	847	4.87	7.31	888	5.10	7.65	933	5.36	8.04	979	5.63	8.45	1027	5.90	8.85
47	866	4.98	7.47	909	5.22	7.83	956	5.49	8.24	1004	5.77	8.66	1054	6.06	9.09
48	888	5.10	7.65	933	5.36	8.04	979	5.63	8.45	1027	5.90	8.85	1081	6.21	9.32

2½% a month raise after ten years of service   (120 working months)
5% a month raise after twenty years of service   (240 working months)

CLERK I

Following is an analysis of the beginning and the top salaries paid to a Clerk I in the various school districts studied:

School District	Salary	School District	Salary	School District	Salary
1	$346–442	8	$354–425	15	$468–503
2	344–415	9	347–418	16	342–416
3		10	391–475	17	334–406
4	356–455	11	352–427	18	369–445
5	340–413	12	350–445	19	409–499
6	351–426	13	361–433	20	386–471
7	366–453	14	389–474	21	342–414
				22	350–426

Average salary range of all districts	$364–441
Simi salary range	$350–$426
Difference	—$14–+$15

The following salaries are derived from the base salary of a Clerk I:

Clerk I	Base Salary
Library Clerk I	Base Salary
Clerk II	Base Salary + 2 Steps
Library Clerk II	Base Salary + 2 Steps
PBX Operator-Receptionist	Base Salary + 2 Steps
Clerk III	Base Salary + 4 Steps
Steno Clerk I	Base Salary + 4 Steps
Steno Clerk II	Base Salary + 6 Steps
Secretary	Base Salary + 8 Steps

ADMINISTRATIVE SECRETARY I

Following is an analysis of the beginning and the top salaries paid to an Administrative Secretary I in the various school districts studied:

School District	Salary	School District	Salary	School District	Salary
1	$455–553	8	$466–561	15	$528–564
2	502–606	9	517–625	16	450–548
3	453–544	10	486–590	17	
4		11	411–499	18	
5	503–610	12	513–655	19	525–639
6	507–616	13	472–567	20	470–571
7	478–593	14	523–636	21	442–514
				22	483–587

Average salary range of all districts	$483–$583
Simi salary range	$483–$587
Difference	+$0–+$4

The following salaries are derived from the base salary of an Administrative Secretary I:

Administrative Secretary I	Base Salary
Administrative Secretary II	Base Salary + 4 Steps

185

	−7½%	−5%	−2½%	Average	+2½%	+5%	+7½%
Clerk I		X					
Maintenance Man I		X					
Offset Operator			X				
Account Clerk I			X				
Director—Certificated			X				
Key Punch Operator				X			
Teachers				X			
Administrative Secretary				X			
Cafeteria Manager I				X			
School Secretary I				X			
Bus Driver					X		
Groundsman I					X		
Custodian I						X	
Cafeteria Helper						X	

either party have been avoided. Salary studies do not replace negotiations on salary matters, but they may be regarded as supplemental to salary discussions by offering some objective data. In many cities, of course, teachers' organizations and personnel divisions make their own surveys. Agreement is facilitated when such studies can be combined into a joint venture.

IN-SERVICE EDUCATION

Problems of providing in-service education may be divided into two general areas. First are small districts that do not have the personnel to develop more than a token training program. Second are larger districts that can draw upon specialized personnel, including members of collegiate communities.

Even small districts can obtain single-shot programs for their classified staff at modest cost, or free. Descriptions of some programs follow.

186

1. The telephone company typically has a speaker available to talk on use of the telephone. One attractive title has been "See Yourself as Others Hear You." The talk may be accompanied by cartoons, which make the event humorous as well as highly informational.
2. Typewriter companies usually have speakers who can demonstrate typewriter care, the production of stencils, and related concerns of secretaries and clerks. Most companies have booklets that can be obtained for in-service education classes. Care should be taken that sales pitches are not worked into presentations by relying on vendors who sell several makes of typewriters and office supplies. Such persons may even help to develop or improve filing systems.
3. Custodial supply salesmen are sometimes available to give talks on cleaning, cleaning materials, and safety. Safety engineers in large plants may be available for talks to school employees.
4. Food-processing companies have persons available to give talks to cafeteria employees.
5. Groundsmen may get the assistance of county farm advisors and of turf and fertilizer salesmen. Manufacturers of insecticides have representatives to tell about insect pests that may threaten school plantings.
6. Schoolbus drivers may have bus rodeos in which drivers compete in driving obstacle courses, in demonstrating safety and in bus inspection.

On occasions, two or more small districts may plan in-service programs together. Having classified personnel visit other districts may develop more pride in their work. Many new ideas may be picked up during the visits. In planning any in-service educational experience, there are two objectives: the increased knowledge to be gained by the employee with the expectation that his knowledge will result in better job performance, and an improvement in the employee's attitude toward his job and his organization.

Some districts are developing growth plans not unlike those that have existed for certificated personnel for some time. The basic purpose is to develop a salary schedule like that for certificated personnel. An abridgement of one is shown below.

LUCIA MAR UNIFIED SCHOOL DISTRICT
Pismo Beach, California

Professional Growth and Incentive Program
Classified Personnel

A. *Professional Growth and Incentive Committee.* (Defines the composition of the committee and outlines its responsibilities.)
B. *Professional Growth Increment.* An increment for professional improvement may be earned each four years. The increment shall be in the amount of $200 per year. (Defines the kind of adult education or

in-service education classes which one may complete to obtain the $200 increment.)

C. *Professional Growth Credit.* (Further defines the kind of work acceptable to apply toward salary increment.)

D. *Credit Application.* (Defines how courses of various length may be equated to semester hour equivalents.)

Rules and Regulations. (Give directions to employees on what they must do to obtain credit, specify the maximum number of credits an employee may take each year, and explain the communication channel an employee must use to gain approval for courses from the Professional Growth and Incentive Committee.)

INSTRUCTIONAL AIDES

As used in this chapter, "instructional aides" is used as a general term which encompasses teachers' aides, auxiliary school personnel, building aides, paraprofessionals, library aides, and noon-yard supervisors. The function of an instructional aide is to relieve a teacher of nonprofessional responsibilities and to assist a teacher so that instruction can be improved.

A noon-yard supervisor is assigned to supervise children during the lunch period. Responsibilities include supervision of pupils in the cafeteria and on the playground, which enables the teacher to have lunch while the children are having theirs so that she can be available for a teaching program when they return from lunch. The cost of providing this service is nominal. As a rule of thumb, it costs about a cent a day per child for noon-aide supervision. Typically, these aides work only an hour or two a day. Because instructional time is not involved, the cost for maintaining this service may come from recreational funds. Recruitment is usually performed by the personnel office, often at the building level.

It is the responsibility of the principal to assign the noon aides to their areas of supervision and to give them special instructions for dealing with accidents, arguments in games, visitors on the playground and other common situations which the aide will encounter

Teacher aides have also been engaged to assist elementary school teachers with housekeeping duties, such as distributing milk and cookies, collecting money for food and supplies, dressing and undressing young children, distributing and taking care of classroom supplies, and aiding during recess time. Aides are frequently assigned to work with teachers of orthopedically handicapped children. Their responsibilities are to assist in moving crippled children, to help them turn pages, to obtain books, and even to help them perform science experiments.

Before 1965, the use of teacher aides and other auxiliary personnel was experimental, supported by foundation grants and state programs. The Elementary and Secondary Act of 1965, however, made available substantial federal aid for the employment of such personnel, and the numbers multiplied. A study made of 382 school districts by the Research

188

Division of the American Federation of Teachers revealed that some 37,500 teacher aides were employed in those districts in the 1968–69 school year, compared to 8,000 four years earlier. Apparently, large school districts are the greatest beneficiaries of such funds, since cities with populations of 50,000 or more employed about 72 percent of all teacher aides. About 60 percent of all aides are used in elementary schools. The following table indicates the distribution of teacher aides among the 382 school districts studied.[1]

TABLE 5

Percent Distribution of Number of Auxiliary Educational Personnel,
By Division and Enrollment, 1968–69

Enrollment	Systems Reporting Number of Aides	Number of Aides		Totals	Percent
		Elementary	Secondary		
6,000–11,999	185	3,340	1,108	4,448	11.8
12,000–24,999	104	2,622	998	3,620	9.7
25,000–49,999	34	1,735	481	2,216	5.9
50,000–99,999	37	4,697	1,578	6,275	16.8
100,000 or More	22	14,149	6,758	20,907	55.8
Totals	382	26,543	10,923	37,466	100%
Percent	64.0%	70.8%	29.2%	100%	

A study of the duties assigned to teacher aides indicated that, among 596 responding school districts, approximately 68 percent assigned teacher aides exclusively to clerical or supervisory responsibilities. About 2.6 percent assigned aides exclusively to instructional activities. The following table reveals the nature of assignments of teacher aides in the 596 school districts studied.[2]

TABLE 6

Percent Distribution of Auxiliary Educational Personnel,
By Enrollment and Duties Performed,
1968–69

Enrollment	Academic		Type of Work Clerical and/or Supervisory		Both		Reporting No Aides	
	No.	%	No.	%	No.	%	No.	%
6,000–11,999	8	4.3	131	70.8	46	24.9	91	28.9
12,000–24,999	1	0.9	71	68.3	32	30.8	28	18.4
25,000–49,999	1	2.9	21	61.7	12	35.3	9	16.1
50,000–99,999			21	67.7	10	32.2	7	14.5
100,000 or More			10	47.6	11	52.4	1	4.0
Totals	10	2.6%	254	67.7%	111	30.0%	136	22.9%

Some teacher aides have been engaged to relieve teachers of patrolling corridors and exits, to supervise bus loading and unloading, to operate visual and audio equipment, and to assist in book and supplies distribution.

The aides described above assist in noninstructional duties. Persons serving in those positions have limited educational background. Some may be high school graduates; others may not have graduated from high school. In large school districts, such persons are recruited directly from minority groups by building principals, with the occasional help of community agencies such as the Anti-Poverty Councils. They not only provide assistance to teachers but also help to establish or strengthen bridges between the school, the teacher, children and parents. Wages, which normally are paid on an hourly basis and are never less than the minimum established by law, typically come from the federal government.

Some aides who have special preparation have been used to assist teachers in instructional programs. They help small groups of children by reading to them, assisting with drill activities, and supervising study. Still another type of aide is one who reads and marks English themes. Such persons are frequently college graduates.

In New York City, an attempt was made to provide a ladder of advancement for aides so that they could become assistant or associate teachers and eventually regular teachers. Associate teachers were required to have two years of college in specific courses. They could assist teachers in instructional activities, and it was hoped that they could ultimately obtain degrees. In 1969, it was estimated that there were about 20,000 teacher aides of various types serving with a staff of about 60,000 teachers and supervisors in the New York City schools. Although the compensation of teacher aides started on an hourly basis with no fringe benefits, movements were started to obtain annual salaries, regular status, pension rights and other fringe benefits. Under New York State law, these groups were entitled to choose an organization to represent them in negotiations. The United Federation of Teachers, in seeking to win the right to represent these groups, published the following advertisement on April 20, 1969, which sets forth organizational goals.[3]

PARAPROFESSIONALS
DON'T BE LEFT OUT!
JOIN THE UFT—THE PROFESSIONAL TEAM!

Many paraprofessionals are choosing the UFT as their collective bargaining representative, but many more must send in their gold designation cards if the UFT is to begin negotiating a September contract for them. Paraprofessionals do not pay dues to the union until it negotiates a contract which they vote as acceptable. But before it even begins to bargain for them, the UFT must receive the designation cards indicating that paraprofessionals have chosen the UFT as their bargaining representative.

190

Those paraprofessionals who are educational assistants, teacher assistants, family workers, family assistants, educational aides, parent program assistants, computer assistants and library aides may obtain the designation cards from the UFT chapter chairmen in their schools.

They should send the gold designation cards immediately to the United Federation of Teachers, 260 Park Avenue South, New York, N.Y. 10010.

The UFT is already proposing a strong contract for the paraprofessionals composed of many items that would increase their job benefits and security. Suggested demands include:

A higher professional yearly salary schedule, based upon training and experience

Job security and tenure rights

A transfer plan based on seniority

Provision for a leave of absence

An effective grievance procedure

Cumulative absence reserve and sick leave

Improved health and welfare benefits

A prompt payment provision

Monthly consultation with the employer

A peak work-load and improved working conditions

A career ladder training provision with release time, and

Pension plan.

In the same New York City publication, the United Federation of Teachers featured the following "career ladder concept" for paraprofessionals.[4]

The future of the teacher-aide concept is bright. The June, 1966, NCTEPS (National Commission on Teacher Education and Professional Standards) *Newsletter* stated that "The use of auxiliary personnel could be one of the most significant advances in education in the past fifty years." Research in modern education is beginning to attract more attention than it has in the past. The result of research will, without doubt, identify some new roles for teachers which will necessitate the termination of others. Many terminated roles will be performed by aides.

A second development in modern education, not yet well accepted by the profession, is the differentiation of teaching responsibilities. From the beginning of the public-school concept until about 1950, a teacher was required to perform all the tasks of classroom instruction and management. No one else was qualified, in the opinion of the public and in the mind of the teacher. Now conditions have begun to change, and they are likely to change rapidly in the future. The teacher daily performs a number of tasks which do not require the amount of training and experience possessed by a teacher. At the same time, the teacher is leaving undone many tasks of a professional nature which would enhance the quality of instruction. A $13,000-a-year teacher should not perform tasks that a $6,000-a-year assistant should be performing. The teacher of the future will learn how

191

THE CAREER LADDER CONCEPT

Title	Qualifications	Training	Job Description
* Apprentice-Intern-Teacher	3 yrs college 2 semesters as Educational Assistant	Auxiliary Personnel	Assists in instruction of assigned class
Educational Associate	2 yrs college (60 Credits) 2 semesters as an Educational Assistant	in all positions on The Career Ladder receive initial	Assumes increasing responsibilities with minimal direction from the teacher
Educational Assistant	60 college credits High School Diploma or Equivalency Diploma	orientation, and on-going in-service	Assists classroom teacher with monitorial, clerical and instructional tasks
Educational Trainee	Minimum-equivalent of 8th grade education	training.	Assists with monitorial and clerical tasks

* Projected titles, not yet approved, and not designed to go into the Civil Service classification, but rather into the Pedagogical classification.

to use an aide just as the physician or the dentist uses a nurse, the engineer his draftsman, and the nurse her aide. The teacher of the future will not be in the classroom from 9 a.m. to 3 p.m. to do the best with what he has; rather, he, as head of a team of professionals and paraprofessionals, will plan and carry out a series of experiences that will influence learning.

This change will not damage the image, status or salary of the teacher. Neither should the teacher become fearful of the qualified aide who presents flash cards or pronounces spelling words for pupils to use in tests, if the aide is working under the guidance of the teacher. The use of aides may make the educational process more complex, but the chances are excellent that education will be more productive. The effective use of instructional aides will involve a fuller assessment of the total educational experience of a child.

SUPERVISION OF CLASSIFIED STAFF

The deployment of classified staff throughout a school system creates some unique supervisory situations. Organizational charts can be established to show lines of authority, yet interesting situations sometimes develop.

In order to maintain district-wide standards, some type of consultant service should be made available. In developing custodial schedules, an agreed amount of time might be provided for noncustodial or noncleaning responsibilities. The role of the custodial consultant, then, would be to attempt to maintain reasonable and equal standards of cleanliness and service throughout the district. Service in this capacity can go a long way in reducing complaints.

Maintenance men are usually assigned to the central office, but they go to a number of schools to work. In schools, their supervision becomes a joint function of the principal and the maintenance supervisor. The principal must have some authority over maintenance men because the safety of pupils may be involved and in order that noise or inconvenience to classes may be held to a minimum.

The supervision of clerks, secretaries and bookkeepers is unique, as there is frequently a close working relationship between them and their immediate supervisor. These persons have occasion to protect their supervisor. They share privileged communication with him. It is known that there are some supervisors who could not survive without the benefit of their secretaries. Many secretaries take initiative in generating routine reports, develop their own procedures, and generally do a fine job. Often, when a secretary leaves, her supervisor realizes that she had been performing much of the daily routine in his office.

Good supervision, then, means that an administrator actually knows what's going on in his office. He should know the filing system and the "when," "why" and "where" of reports. He should have some idea of how long it takes to produce a report, the mechanics of ordering supplies, and a host of related responsibilities. Supervision means that the supervisor is aware of the levels of responsibilities and the specific tasks assigned to each person under his leadership. It is his responsibility to see that people work within their classification. When new responsibilities are added, it is his job to initiate a request for a desk audit.

Supervision typically involves the evaluation of services. The form used is less important than the process of evaluation. The purpose is no less important than the process. The purpose of the evaluation of all employees is the improvement of services. If a conference can lead to improved service, then a paper report is of little consequence. If an employee is not performing well, a written report should describe his behavior patterns or attitudes which need to be changed. If it can be learned that an employee cannot change his ways even after his weaknesses have been indicated and positive suggestions for improvement have been offered to him, then steps may have to be taken to terminate his employment.

PREPARING A SUPERVISOR FOR HIS JOB

For the classified employee, there is still little formal training for supervision, as there is for certificated personnel. But it is emerging. In some cities, it is called Executive Leadership Development. Among the many changes going on in civil service, schools and industry today is a trend toward training for supervision. It is generally agreed that knowledge of the job and skills to do the job are not the only criteria for effective supervision. The supervisor must know how to get people to work as a team and derive satisfaction from their job. In effect, he must be a human engineer, sensitive to people's feelings, respected for his leadership ability, and able to perform under stress. Whether some of these traits are natural attributes or not, they can be developed by training and experience. The training for this level of leadership may well be a coordinated function with the assistance of a community college. School districts and particularly personnel administrators are serving their organization well when they work with a neighborhood college in setting up such a program and in encouraging potential supervisors in the classified service to enroll in the program.

ESTABLISHING NEW POSITIONS IN CLASSIFIED SERVICE TO MEET NEW NEEDS

The school personnel administrator must be continually alert to changes in the administrative and educational needs of his school system if he is to meet the needs of the staff and the community. The appearance of the electronic computer will soon change communication channels, make current reporting forms obsolete, and modify the kinds of work done in several offices, which will result in the need to change job descriptions. For the most part, there has been little systems analysis in school districts. The computer will hasten the study and analysis of administrative record keeping. New positions have already been created in the classified service, and others will be established on the line as well as on the supervisory level.

While supervisors of maintenance men, of custodians, of transportation, and of cafeterias have been standard positions for years, the supervision of clerical services has been slow to develop. It would be perfectly reasonable to create the position of supervisor of clerical services. The person in that position would not only supervise existing clerical activities but would also initiate improvements and new practices to meet new needs.

Yet another possibility for creating new classified positions as the need arises is in the area of business management. As federal and state funds are made available to subdivisions of a district and as decentralization of control over certain activities advances, there may be a need for local business managers to assist district supervisors and even principals.

The school personnel administrator and the supervisor of classified personnel who recognize the dynamic nature of personnel administration must take the initiative in suggesting new types of useful personnel.

In the past, there has been a rather distinct dichotomy between non-certificated or classified employees and certificated employees. The distinction was based primarily on the fact that almost all certificated positions required the basic license to teach. An individual with a degree in education starts out as a teacher; he might then advance to assistant principal or principal, and perhaps later move into an administrative position in the school district. Thus, all certificated administrative positions were filled by individuals who had a license to teach and who came up through the ranks of education. In many instances, state laws required that the individual chosen for an administrative position be eligible for a teaching certificate. This situation has been challenged by those who demand innovations, new approaches and drastic changes in procedures to meet current needs. In addition, there are increasing demands for special educational programs that have an orientation different from traditional ones. As a result, some school districts are turning to professionally prepared, noncertificated employees to fill positions formerly filled by certificated employees coming from the ranks of education. For example, personnel specialists, labor negotiators, facilities planners, budget analysts, and professionally prepared writers are being employed because of the demands now facing school administrators.

The trend toward employing professionally prepared individuals in certificated administrative positions has been illustrated by the Department of Public Instruction of the State of Wisconsin, which recently amended its administrative code to permit the licensing of administrative personnel who have not come from the ranks of education as follows:

195

"PI 3.20 (14) Administrative Assistants. This classification shall apply to central office professional positions not described elsewhere in the certification standards and which positions do not normally involve direct contact with pupils. "(a) To secure a license as an administrative assistant, a person must hold a bachelor's or master's degree with a major appropriate to the professional responsibilities for which employed. The period of licensure shall be three years with renewal contingent upon continued agreement between employment and degree preparation."

This development has led to discussion of whether or not these new certificated positions, traditionally outside of the ranks of civil service, should now be considered civil-service positions. It may be argued that, since they are not directly involved in the instructional process, they should be filled through traditional civil-service procedures, as are other classified positions. On the other hand, one may argue that it is desirable to retain the flexibility inherent in filling these positions without the requirements of civil-service procedures.

Under any circumstances, it would appear that the trend is toward employment of both professionally prepared specialists and traditionally certificated educators in administrative positions in school districts.

9 MAKING PERSONNEL ASSIGNMENTS

GENERAL STATEMENT

One of the most significant and troublesome areas related to the personnel function is that of the assignment of staff personnel. Assignment, as here defined, is the allocation of school personnel to positions in the various operational units within a school system.

Although it seems to be an incontrovertible principle of school personnel administration that the preparation, interest and talents of a teacher should be the major factors in determining her assignment to a position, the fact is that expediency determines her assignment as often as planned design. Individual differences among children are recognized, but too often teachers are regarded as interchangeable cogs in a machine. One has only to ask the educator, the parent, even the child himself, whether teachers are being placed in situations for which they are not really qualified or in which they are not genuinely interested. So widespread is this practice that state and national organizations, such as NCTEPS (National Commisison on Teacher Education and Professional Standards), have protested. The inevitable results of misassignment are low staff morale, inferior teaching and learning, and considerable staff turnover.

Proper staff assignment means, not only that the teacher who has prepared to teach French should not be assigned to teach mathematics, but also that the teacher who has some special talent or interest should be given an opportunity to use that interest, whether it is to conduct a club, a special class, or an interest group.

The problems of staff assignment go beyond fitting the background and preparation of the teacher to the proper position. They include such matters as the induction and orientation of teachers, staffing inner city schools which may be regarded by some as less than desirable assignments, working toward staff integration in what have been all-white districts,

197

arranging for substitute teachers, transferring or reassigning teachers from one school to another, and taking into consideration the wishes of local communities.

Effective staff assignment is one of the surest means by which personnel administrators can aid in accomplishing the goals of education. When those primarily responsible for staff assignment perform in a competent manner, the pupil and the teacher are provided an opportunity to realize, or more nearly approach, that state of balance or adjustment between what they are and what they wish to become. Having assisted in the development of this state of equilibrium, the schools can boast more earnestly that education is taking place.

MATCHING PERSONNEL AND POSITIONS

Several studies have underscored the necessity for placing the right person in the right job. Fawcett maintains that much of the guesswork could be taken out of assignment procedures if careful attention were given to the factor of the compatibility of employees to fellow employees and to the positions for which they are to be employed.[1] Campbell, in writing about differentiated roles, or assignments, reasons that we can no longer view teachers as interchangeable parts.[2] Van Zwoll reports that it may well be that "disregard of individual competencies permits the simple approach to personnel placement of merely having an individual (irrespective of qualification) assigned to each work station."[3] But he says that

> ". . . would be somewhat analogous to using the various figures in a chess game for whatever one wanted to use them at the moment, without regard for the very specialized functions of the respective pieces. The chess player realizes the impossibility of playing the game intelligently under such circumstances. The school administrator must develop appreciation of the impossibility of operating the schools functionally under such circumstances."[4]

Steffensen, as well as others, questions the degree to which personnel administrators can think realistically about the recruitment of individuals for specific positions while taking into serious account such factors as experience, the proper ratio of building staff according to age and sex, and so forth.[5]

Factors Causing Improper Staff Assignment

Of course, every personnel administrator would like to put the right person in the right job. What, then, are the factors which prevent him from doing so? In the first place, he may unfortunately believe that all teachers are interchangeable, or that all teachers certificated in a particular subject are interchangeable. If he does recognize individual differences, he may disregard them in making assignments because additional effort is needed

198

and he may not have the time, staff or equipment to carry out a plan. A second major factor is the inability to locate the needed teacher because of a teacher shortage or because of inadequate recruitment facilities. A third factor is inadequate record keeping. The needs of schools may not be transmitted in specific details; personnel records may not carry sufficient information about staff members or staff needs; sudden needs may develop because of absence or service termination; and records of possible replacements may not be kept up to date. A fourth factor that makes proper assignment difficult arises from changes in curriculum. When new subjects are added and old ones removed, there is the problem not only of finding new specialists but also of assigning excess teachers whose subjects have been removed or deemphasized. A fifth factor that may cause misassignment arises from the personnel administrator's inability to verify adequately the background information, interests and talents claimed by each applicant, as well as his inability to predict the performance of an applicant in a given school situation. For example, an applicant may indicate the ability to develop choral groups. When assigned to this work, he may not succeed, either because his experience was not accurately stated or because he may not be able to meet realistic challenges. A sixth factor leading to misassignment, and probably the most widespread, arises from the actions of principals who, because of the exigencies of programming staff, may assign teachers to classes for which they are not suited. A seventh factor in misassignment occasionally occurs where there is a vacancy and pressures are put on the personnel administrator to appoint a favored individual to the vacancy whether he meets the requirements or not. Many of the factors causing misassignment of teachers are also applicable to the assignment of other staff members, including principals and other school administrators. Nevertheless, from any point of view, one can only conclude that the personnel administrator should, in every case, make a strong effort to match personnel with available positions.

FACTORS TO BE CONSIDERED IN MAKING STAFF ASSIGNMENTS

A formidable list of factors to be considered in making proper staff assignments could be given. Some of the more important ones are cited here.

Grieder, Pierce and Rosenstengel contend that administrators should keep in mind such factors as community mores, the philosophy of education subscribed to by the principal and teachers, the kind of student body with which a teacher will work, and the cultural and socioeconomic background of the teacher.[6]

Paul Lahann and L. H. Diekroeger, reporting on a survey they conducted concerning staff procurement and utilization, found that personnel administrators, for the most part, follow certain basic principles in the assignment of teachers:

"The strength of preparation by the teacher is mentioned by most respondents. The best interest of the system as a whole, and of the specific school, is mentioned in practically every report. In some reports there is definite respect for the preference of the teacher, and the preference and recommendation of school principals. The preference of the teacher and the transportation problem to and from school placement. The compatibility of the culture of the teacher with the culture of the school and the community is another item for consideration. The attitude of the teacher towards minority groups, slow learners, and other . . . problems is a matter for consideration." [7]

Redfern has said that those who staff schools have important responsibilities involving a thorough knowledge of the schools and the ability to judge the potential of an applicant to fill certain positions.[8] He advocates an alertness to applicants who appear to have the qualities for teaching successfully in depressed area schools.

The American Association of School Personnel Administrators has reflected its concern with the problem of teacher assignments in its *Standards for School Personnel Administration*. The organization has proposed an evaluative check list which includes the following: [9]

1. Personnel placement is made with primary concern for the needs of the students as matched by the experience, training, and interests of the teacher.
2. Probationary and beginning teachers are placed in situations where they will have a fair chance to develop into superior teachers and where they will have ready access to skilled supervision and guidance.
3. Other things being equal, each teacher is given a choice of location.
4. A teacher is not given assignments outside the field of his preparation.

In the fall of 1963, the National Commission on Teacher Education and Professional Standards appointed a Special Committee on the Assignment of Teachers. The Committee reported:

"Good placement and assignment are conditioned by (a) adequate information about vacancies, (b) comprehensive employment data gained during recruitment, (c) a careful weighing of the candidate's assets and liabilities during selection, (d) prudent administrative and supervisory judgments when vacancies are being filled, (e) early communication with the teacher when decisions have been completed, and (f) adequate and consistent help during the period of the teacher's induction and orientation to the job." [10]

According to personnel administrators and principals in large cities, the most significant specific behavior of personnel administrators reflecting the difference between success and failure in teacher-assignment activities is knowing the needs of the position to be filled and exhausting all possibilities for finding the candidate whose qualifications and interests best fit the position.[11]

An additional factor that must be considered by the modern school personnel administrator is staff integration, in which members of minority groups are assigned freely to any and all schools in the district in which their talents and abilities can be used.

AIDS TO MAKING PROPER ASSIGNMENTS

One way of becoming familiar with the positions within a school district is to utilize position guides as described by Castetter.[12] A simple, effective position guide is used in the personnel office of the public schools in Kenosha, Wisconsin. There a file is maintained through the cooperation of operational unit heads who supply the personnel office with the following information on individualized cards:

1. Employee's name and marital status.
2. Employee's home address.
3. Employee's home telephone number.
4. School or building assignment.
5. Grade and subject assignment.
6. Comments relative to the assignment, such as those involving extra- and co-curricular responsibilities, the teacher's preparation and experience, achievement levels of pupils in the teacher's class, and special qualifications or specifications of the position.

A Position Guide Data File, when maintained and utilized in an organized and thorough manner, can be of immeasurable assistance to the personnel administrator as he attempts to familiarize himself with positions in his school system. It may also prove helpful in other ways, as in the gathering of information for the publication of an annual personnel directory or roster.

In larger school districts, a folder or record card is maintained on each staff member showing his experience, background, preparation and interests. In some districts, that information has been computerized. Of course, it is essential that these records be kept up to date so that teachers who take special courses while in service may have such training placed on their records.

For each type of position and for each special position, there should be a card or other record setting forth the detailed duties and the qualifications desired of employees. Such information, kept up to date in the personnel office, is helpful in advertising needs and in recruiting.

Application forms should provide information on each applicant's experience, including major and minor areas of preparation, previous ex-

201

perience of an extracurricular as well as a curricular nature, special skills and interests.

A form should be available on which principals and other administrators can report their vacancies and needs to the personnel administrator in specific details that will be helpful to him in seeking replacements. New positions, as they are established, should also be defined in specific terms describing the duties and desired qualifications of personnel.

Many misassignments of teachers could be avoided if the personnel administrator carried out his responsibility for certain fundamental procedures, such as the following:

1. Maintaining up-to-date and accurate lists of vacancies.
2. Investigating applicants before they are employed to verify claimed experience and training.
3. Resisting with tactful yet unyielding perseverance pressures exerted on the personnel office for the employment of favorites, qualified or not.
4. Furnishing specific instructions and guidelines for principals and other administrative staff regarding the effective use of preappointment visits by candidates, when possible, proper assignments of personnel to their staffs, and efficient induction of individuals into various schools and departments.

Changes in curriculum and trends requiring teachers with qualifications and interests unlike those of staff previously employed should be anticipated by the personnel administrator through requests to operational unit heads for forecasts of their prospective staffing needs and by familiarity with such changes through knowledge of available professional literature. Personnel administrators should also assume leadership for the retraining of teachers whose backgrounds are inadequate because of curriculum innovations since the time of the teacher's educational preparation and employment.

COOPERATIVE INVOLVEMENT OF STAFF IN ASSIGNMENTS

Several works already referred to indicate the need for the personnel administrator's involvement in the processes of staff assignments when operational unit heads and assignees are involved. Gibson and Hunt emphasize again "the need for cooperative decision making without the rigidities of undue centralization." [13] And Pittenger has written:

> "Every assignment or reassignment should be a cooperative matter, with the superintendent, supervisor, principal and teacher himself taking part. The principal's desires should be met if possible. . . . The arbitrary placement of teachers by the superintendent or any other central authority is out of line with good personnel management and should seldom, if ever, occur." [14]

Steffensen cites the prevalent practice in small school systems of involving the principal in the selection of staff for his building.

> "The building principal knows best the needs of his particular administrative unit, he knows the composition of his faculty in terms of individual personalities, and he is the best judge of the individual who will fit into that faculty. And, of course, the principal is the administrator who has general responsibility for the total educational program within that building, and that program is a function of the competencies of the staff within the building." [15]

It should be noted, however, that final authority for the assignment of staff rests with the personnel administrator. In discussing this point, Steffensen calls attention to the fact that

> ". . . not only are personnel administrators more proficient than principals because of training and experience in assessing candidates, but they also have a broader perspective of the needs of the entire school system as opposed to the need of any one unit within that system. This does not negate the importance of recognizing placement preference of either the teacher or the principal where possible. Such consultation is assumed. As a basic operational principle it does, however, stress the fact that the personnel needs of the school system must supersede those of any part of it. Final authority would then rest with the personnel department." [16]

Schumacher's study indicates that the second most critical requirement of personnel administrators in the assignment of teachers is to "confer with the principals regarding candidates." [17] Whereas personnel administrators and elementary school principals believe that the single most critical requirement is knowing the needs of the position and continuing to search until a teacher is found whose qualifications and interests fit the position, secondary school principals believe that conferring with the principal regarding candidates is more important.[18]

In most states, certification is intended to insure proper staff assignments. Teaching certificates are endorsed for particular subjects and grade levels. However, that is but a framework to insure minimum competence. Individual differences among teachers properly certificated must be considered. Indeed, there have been suggestions that the teaching profession must play a more important role in enforcing proper staff assignments. T. M. Stinnett expresses this point of view:

> "Among the major reforms needed in teacher certification is the reexamination of currently accepted functions to be served by the process. By any impartial judgment, certification of public school personnel is attempting to serve too many functions. The exercising

203

of this cluster of functions is an impossible task, most of which should be transferred out of laws and regulations to the teaching profession itself." [19]

One can only conclude that, whenever possible, operational unit heads and assignees should be involved in the assignment of instructional staff. That, however, does not preclude the employment of a "pool" of teachers in advance of known vacancies. It simply means that operational unit heads and assignees will be consulted about staff assignments that directly affect them at the time vacancies become known and can be filled.

DECENTRALIZATION AND COMMUNITY INVOLVEMENT IN STAFF ASSIGNMENT

Many of the writings cited earlier in the chapter discuss, either directly or indirectly, the arguments in favor of cooperative decision making in the assignment of instructional staff. A significant study in this area of interest is that of Perry M. Kalick, who reports that ineffective teacher assignments are the result of the growing centralization in large school systems.[20] As the system grows larger, it is likely that:

1. More appointees will be assigned to subjects and grade levels for which they are not fully certified.
2. Final decisions about assignments will be made by central authorities rather than by operational unit heads.
3. Appointees will be given less opportunity to visit the schools to which they will be assigned.
4. Fewer details will be given to teachers about their assignments.
5. Less study will be made of the effectiveness of the initial assignment.
6. Appointees' qualifications for specific assignments will not be determined effectively.
7. The student-teaching experiences of new teachers will not be considered.

It should be noted, however, that district size is not synonymous with quality. While some studies have shown that ineffective assignments are more likely to occur in large school districts, the distinction between superior and inferior quality control lies not in district size but in effective leadership. With such leadership, members of the organization are more highly self-motivated, ego-involved and consistent in their effective behavior and tend to act as if magnetically attracted to the ideals of education and the fulfillment of its goals.

In recent years, decentralization has come to mean more than cooperative decision making among central authorities, operational unit heads and teachers. It has become an attempt to include parents and students in the assignment and evaluation of a staff and in designing an educational program able to solve the problems they view most clearly.

A community should be deeply involved in its school system. It should be given every opportunity to state its wishes through clearly defined channels. This kind of subsystem approach is essential to the solution of problems in large school systems. But that does not mean that a community should control its schools without regard for state laws, the regulations of the board of education, and the expertise of professionally competent educators and school administrators.

Personnel administrators must be responsible professionals who help to provide effective leadership. The responsibilities of leadership in our time include working closely with duly constituted representatives of the community formed as a local board (parents' association). In the matter of staff assignment, the procedural guidelines, the titles and salaries of positions, and the duties and requirements of positions should be developed by the school superintendent, in cooperation with the personnel administrator, and with the approval of the central board of education, which should be responsible for consulting with local representative groups. Guidelines and procedures should indicate the responsibilities of professionals in making staff assignments and the role of the lay board or local group. If overall guidelines have been formulated on reasonable grounds, the position of the personnel administrator in making and defending individual assignments is more tenable. While taking cognizance of the views of leaders of the local community and while consulting such individuals in advance, the personnel administrator nevertheless has the responsibility of making assignments on professional grounds alone. In so doing, he must have the support of the school superintendent, the professional staff, and responsible leaders of the school district.

Personnel administrators must also utilize every opportunity to obstruct the entry of nonprofessional factors into recruitment, selection and assignment practices. Political controls and manipulation by opportunists and extremists, jeopardizing the education of boys and girls, are not new phenomena in personnel administration, nor are they necessary concomitants of community involvement. As in the past, all unprofessional pressures must be opposed strenuously by the personnel administrator, whose efforts must take into consideration the aspirations of the community and of minority groups, and who must be oriented toward new ideas so that he can provide progressive leadership both in the most conservative district and in the most militant district, which may prefer staff assignments of a particular creed or color. The effective leader knows his community and has built up the support of reasonable community spokesmen so that his efforts are supported.

STAFFING INNER CITY SCHOOLS

Inner city schools are generally considered to be those serving segments of a community in which the economically disadvantaged live. Since children who live in such areas have backgrounds that are not within the direct experience of the majority of teachers and since the difficulties of teaching in these areas have been exaggerated, it has not been uncommon for many teachers to avoid teaching assignments in inner city schools.

It seems likely that teachers' objections to inner city school assignments merely represent the expected reaction to beginning a strange experience. As Redfern puts it:

> "There is a matter in 'image' among schools. Despite efforts, on the part of school administrators and teachers, to create a favorable image for all schools, it is not uncommon for the applicant to hold sharply differing perceptions of schools in suburban and depressed areas of the city. Much of the so-called unfavorable image associated with schools in the latter areas often results from lack of familiarity with and mis-information about the school. That this is true is attested by the fact that often, after a teacher who is assigned to a depressed area school becomes acquainted with its pupils, staff and the environmental conditions that prevail, his perceptions and value judgments of the school change. The image of the school becomes different as far as he is concerned." [21]

In New York City several years ago, it was found that the two dozen colleges in the metropolitan area were making little use of inner city schools in their student-teaching programs. The result was that their graduates, in large numbers, were declining appointments to those schools. Conferences were held with college authorities, who agreed to require service in inner city schools as part of student teaching. Shortly, there was a noticeable willingness on the part of graduates to accept appointments to inner city schools. Their fears of the unknown were dispelled by experience.

Among the various solutions to the problem of staffing inner city schools have been (1) a bonus compensation to teachers assigned to these schools (which has been opposed by teachers' groups as "combat pay" and by community groups as stigmatizing their communities), (2) reduced class size and programs, (3) the replacement or remodeling of outmoded facilities and the availability of adequate and convenient parking space, (4) the assurance that such assignments are to be considered temporary, (5) the assignment of more specialized help, such as "buddy" teachers, remedial teachers, social workers, additional assistant principals, etc., (6) compulsory rotation of experienced teachers (which has been opposed on the grounds that teachers assigned by compulsion are not likely to perform at their best), (7) the opportunity to meet parents and community leaders, and (8) the involvement of local teachers' organizations in orienting their members toward the problems of such schools and toward various methods of dealing with them. Whereas these and other expedients are undoubtedly of much value, it is more resourceful to adequately train personnel who are likely to be or who have already been assigned to such schools.

The initial responsibility for such preparation is entrusted to the teacher-training institutions. Much has been done in recent years by schools and departments of education to acquaint their students with the realities of teaching situations in inner city schools. Much more needs to be done. Further emphasis on the behavioral sciences, as well as on methodologies, will effect greater empathy and skill in dealing with the economic, social, cultural and educational problems of the economically disadvantaged. More extensive use of internships, clinical participations, use of appropriate recordings and films, meaningful observations, and student-teaching experiences in inner city schools will help to provide the desired training of teachers who will staff schools serving the economically disadvantaged.

Additional responsibility for the training of inner city teachers rests with our school systems and can be accomplished through well-planned and properly executed in-service projects. For example, courses could include such offerings as Language Development for the Economically Disadvantaged, Development of Perceptual Motor Skills for the Economically Disadvantaged and Experiential Backgrounds in Reading. Such courses are aimed specifically at preparing inner city teachers to deal more effectively with severe limitations in their pupils. Further opportunities for growth in competency should be provided through programs of advanced study, research, institutes, workshops, conferences, committee-participation activities and brainstorming sessions.

Coleman found that children's scholastic achievement is dependent on teachers' expectations for their pupils,[22] which implies that the responsibility for achievement lies with the educational institution, not the child. The quality of teachers is more important to achievement (and to the equality of educational opportunity) than are buildings, books, and the curriculum. The significance of Coleman's findings is obvious to effective personnel administration and its involvement in the in-service training of teachers with respect to their attitudes toward children.

STAFF INTEGRATION

School staff should be so assigned that a proper balance is obtained and maintained in any given operational unit within a school system with respect to such factors as professional preparation, experience, age, sex, etc.

One factor that has received considerable attention in recent years and in many school systems is that of ethnic grouping. The 1954 decision of the United States Supreme Court relative to the desegregation of schools, and more recently the development of civil rights activities, have caused an unparalleled demand for qualified Negro teachers, particularly in large city school districts. The implications for personnel administration may be seen to have two major components: the recruitment of qualified black teachers and the balance of staff integration. School districts in which staff segregation has persisted are required by federal courts to develop and enforce staff integration plans. The order of Federal Judge C. Clyde Atkins in Florida, who ordered a school district to submit a complete faculty integration plan to take effect in February 1970, is an example of required integration.

Teacher recruitment schedules and postings of vacancies through intermittent correspondence are almost certain to include and be directed to colleges and universities that train Negro teachers. The demand for Negro teachers, however, exceeds the supply, and the personnel administrator must be able to tell prospective candidates what his community is doing to provide the incentives that will cause them to seriously consider living and working there.

The personnel administrator also has a responsibility, in the face of demands, to be instrumental in the employment of more teachers of minority ethnic groups in order to work toward a balance in staff integration. He may expect pressures from school line officers as well as from various groups and individuals within the community. Nevertheless, his primary concern should always be to obtain qualified teachers and to maintain the most effective staff in each operational unit, whether the considerations are for teacher preparation, experience, age, sex, or ethnic grouping. To act otherwise is to act contrary to the best interest of schools and children.

In some cities, extremists have demanded black control of schools in predominately Negro districts, black teachers and black principals. Aside from the fact that such demands represent segregation, which is contrary to law, the fact is that there is no evidence that black teachers or black principals are better educators for black children, nor is there evidence that teachers of any other color or nationality are best for children of their own color or nationality. On the other hand, there must be recognition of the aspirations of members of the black minority in our country to reach positions of leadership in our schools. In addition to the recruitment efforts mentioned earlier, some cities, colleges and foundations have set up special seminar programs, internships and scholarships to aid minority group members to advance themselves in the teaching profession and to overcome the handicaps of inadequate earlier education. The problem of staff integration has been difficult and complex for the personnel administrator not only because of community problems but also because of total staff opposition to favoritism for one racial group when it limits the opportunities for others' advancement. Charges of violation of a merit system have been leveled when preference for promotion has been given to black teachers.

If the basic principles of selection and assignment by merit are to be maintained, then the emphasis must be placed upon providing seminars and training facilities to equalize opportunities and to create new positions in which special backgrounds may be utilized.

208

STAFFING FOR LEAVES OF ABSENCE

Leaves of absence, requested by instructional personnel, are granted by school boards for a variety of reasons, including the following:

1. advanced study or research
2. attendance at court proceedings, including jury duty
3. attendance at legal proceedings involving the purchase or sale of the employee's home
4. bereavement
5. convention or conference participation
6. employment-related injury or disease
7. exchange teaching assignments in other school districts
8. full-time service with a teacher's association or union
9. maternity or adoption of a child
10. military obligations
11. observation of instruction in another school building or school system
12. participation in religious exercises
13. personal or family illness
14. personal reasons
15. service in political office
16. summoning by a governmental agency such as the Internal Revenue Service or a draft board
17. rest and restoration of health

Any leave of absence should be viewed as a temporary displacement of personnel, whether or not an individual on leave ultimately returns to a staff assignment. Assuming nothing occurs during the leave for which the teacher would have been dismissed had she remained on duty (e.g., conviction of felony, immorality, physical or mental incapacity to perform her duties), she has a right to return if she desires.

The above does not imply that a returning staff member is always reinstated in her former position. Most school district policies provide for a teacher's reinstatement in her former position if it is vacant, and efforts are made to keep the vacancy through assigning temporary personnel. If, on the other hand, her position has been filled, a teacher is assigned to as similar a position as is available.

Nearly all leaves of absence require staff assignments to replace individuals absent from duty. Such assignments may be for any period of time extending from a few hours to one or more years.

The personnel administrator's responsibility in staffing a vacancy resulting from a leave of absence is, in all instances, to search for a replacement whose qualifications and interests best fit the position. The administrator should inform the replacement as soon as possible of the expected duration of her assignment and the expected condition of her status upon the return of the individual who has been granted a leave of absence. Arrangements should be made for the individual who is on leave to report her intentions to the personnel office before the expiration of her leave, so that proper plans may be made.

REASSIGNMENTS OR TRANSFERS

If the assignment of teachers is effected in the way that has been proposed throughout this chapter, it seems likely that the necessity for and the number of reassignments or transfers can be held to a minimum. However, plans and regulations concerning the movement of staff should be given deliberate consideration. The transfer of staff results from administrative reassignment, voluntary requests for reassignment, reduction in enrollment, and misassignment.

Administrative reassignments, which may be thought of as involuntary reassignments, are generally effected in order to restore teachers returning from leaves of absence, to avoid the apathetic dispositions which sometimes develop when individuals have remained in the same positions for a long period of time, to fill what may be regarded as less desirable positions within a school system, and to provide certain staff members with the opportunity to succeed in situations other than those in which they previously failed.

Most school systems avoid administrative reassignments whenever possible. Many recently negotiated salary and welfare agreements prohibit indiscriminate administrative or involuntary reassignments. It is wise to formulate for review the procedures for such reassignments and to provide affected parties with opportunities for appeal. If possible, such regulations should be adopted after discussion with staff representatives. In the event of a proposed involuntary reassignment, some school districts release teachers from their contracts if they so request.

Forced rotation of staff is not advisable because, as we have maintained throughout this chapter, teachers should not be considered interchangeable parts in an educational mechanism. And forced rotation adversely affects staff morale by reducing their sense of security. Full use of a staff's knowledge of given situations, as learned through experiences acquired in specific positions, is inhibited if reassignments are not made on the basis of objective criteria alone.

Teachers request reassignments for a number of reasons. Voluntary reassignments are generally effected as vacancies become known to the personnel administrator or at specified times during the year. Preference is usually given to personnel having the most seniority within the school system. It is obvious that the practice of reassigning teachers primarily on the basis of seniority may violate certain principles herein suggested as necessary to the production of effective teacher assignment. For example, a school considered "desirable" by the staff would find that all its vacancies would be filled by transfers of upper age teachers. After a while, there would be no young teachers at all on this staff.

In order to meet special needs, some school districts have modified the seniority rule to state that teachers on probation cannot seek reassignments. They have also set up ten-year groupings. Teachers with ten years of experience are in Group A, those with ten to twenty years are in Group B, and those with over twenty years are in Group C. Reassignment preference passes from one group to another instead of following the strict order of seniority established on an individual basis. Following are the procedures and policies regulating reassignments in the schools of Kenosha, Wisconsin.

By agreement between the board of education and the organization representing the teaching staff, all vacancies must be posted in schools and departments, as well as in the office of the teacher organization, as soon after April 15 as possible and as new vacancies occur thereafter. A teacher desiring reassignment obtains a transfer request form from her principal or operational unit head and completes the form, indicating her name, present school and grade or subject assignment and the name of the school or department and the grade or subject to which she desires to be transferred. The teacher then must obtain written approval of the transfer on the form from both the sending and receiving principals and the special area department head, if any. The reassignment is finally subject to approval by the personnel administrator and the assistant superintendent of schools. Only those teachers who have remained in a building for at least two years are eligible for reassignment, and teachers must be fully certified by the state department of public instruction for the position to which they desire to be reassigned.

When reduction in the number of teachers in a building is necessary, the personnel administrator should first consider qualified volunteers. If additional reassignments are necessary, he should regard as the most likely candidates to be moved those teachers most recently appointed to the school system, or he may use an experience grouping system. However, as noted above, every effort should be made to reassign on the basis of what is best for the children of the schools rather than primarily on the basis of seniority.

Regarding the reassignment of instructional staff, several general considerations have been recommended by experienced principals and personnel administrators: [23]

1. Avoid reassigning an already unsuccessful teacher to an area of particularly high expectations.
2. Consider all staff needs of both buildings when reassigning teachers from one to another.
3. Reassign a teacher on the basis of specific knowledge of the teach-

211

er's unhappiness or lack of success, which you obtain from her supervisor and by consultation with the teacher.

4. Honor commitments or explain the reasons for not being able to honor them.
5. Reassign a teacher with the full knowledge and cooperation of the principals and teacher involved.
6. Contact a teacher personally about reassignment.

SUBSTITUTE TEACHER ASSIGNMENTS

Substitute teachers are assigned on a day-to-day, long-term, or permanent basis. A long-term substitute teacher is assigned for less than a year but usually at least a month, while a permament substitute teacher is generally appointed for a school year.

The practice of retaining substitutes to fill long-term vacancies in place of regular certificated teachers has created dissatisfaction in communities—they object to being served by "second-rate" teachers—and in teacher organizations, which regard the use of such substitutes as lowering standards and taking advantage of personnel. In some cities, data indicated that 20 to 30 percent of the staff were substitutes holding substandard certification. Public dissatisfaction caused efforts to alter this situation. First, wherever possible, individuals who met full certification standards were employed to fill temporary vacancies. They were appointed to central or district pools on annual bases and were assigned as needed to fill temporary vacancies. Second, individuals who had served for a specified number of years as substitutes were accorded "regular" status after special arrangements with certification officers or after special legislation which accepted experience in lieu of certain courses, granted time extensions for taking courses, or provided for special certification examinations.

To the extent possible, all substitute teachers should be assigned to temporary vacancies on the basis of the same criteria employed in the assignment of the regular instructional staff. The importance of an adequate supply of qualified substitute teachers, then, is obvious.

The personnel administrator should be continuously aware of the extent of absence among regular instructional staff and the need for substitute teachers. He must have prepared the school system for emergency situations by employing a sufficient number of substitute teachers in advance. Procurement of substitute teachers can be accomplished through a variety of means, including news media advertisements, appeals to community, civic and educational organizations for recruitment assistance, and continuous communication with school staffs regarding their needed help in informing the community about the district's desire to employ more substitute teachers.

It is doubtful that substitute assignments outside of a teacher's preparation can be completely avoided. Substitute teachers should be informed,

212

through orientation and induction sessions, about procedures regarding their employment and service and the expectations of the school district concerning their work. They should be helped to utilize those methods and techniques learned in their areas of preparation, so that the most effective carry-over to other areas of instruction is obtained. Principals must be urged to provide specific guidance with respect to teaching materials and plans for short-term substitute teachers. Some personnel administrators have developed a special pamphlet for substitutes that indicates requirements, salary, benefits, the nature of services and how to seek employment.

Generally, day-to-day substitute teachers are assigned from a central call center. A substitute teacher may be called at any time. Most calls, however, are made in the early morning, after clerks have had the opportunity to transcribe, from automatic answering devices, recorded messages of staff members' intentions to be absent from duty.

Criteria used in making substitute assignments include the quality of past performance as evidenced by evaluations, the principal's preference, geographic location in relation to time factors, the record of a substitute's availability, and academic preparation.

Substitute teachers are paid at rates established by the board of education, usually determined on the basis of degree status, length of experience, and certification standards. Personnel administrators should assume leadership in establishing policies governing fringe benefits and compensation schedules for all substitute teachers.

STAFF ORIENTATION

Typically, orientation programs have been of one day to one week in duration, with new appointees being paid their regular salaries in many school districts, and have included such items as the following: general briefing sessions, inspirational addresses, building and community tours, social get-togethers and meetings with principals and other members of the administrative staff. Teacher evaluations of such programs, although positive in many respects, have generally indicated negative reactions. Criticisms often suggest that sessions and speeches are too long, theory is given too much prominence, insufficient time is spent in the classroom, administrative staff dominates the program and the lack of effective follow-up projects is evident.

Efforts are being made in many school systems, however, to alter orientation programs so that new teachers obtain the help they want and need. For example, as school districts employ their teachers earlier in the year than has been done in the past, they are making assignments earlier, providing teachers with an opportunity to attend summer school classes and institutes in order to prepare themselves better for specific assignments. Earlier notification of appointment also has made it possible for the appointee to visit and establish communication with the school in which he

213

is to serve. Notes of welcome may be sent to him by the principal, the head of the parents' association, or the president of the student government. The appointee may correspond with a designated teacher on the staff.

School systems are also becoming more aware of the advisability and necessity of assigning newcomers to the more manageable or desirable positions, rather than to those requiring the greatest degree of skill, understanding and experience. More time is being spent during orientation periods in familiarizing new teachers with the many clerical details they must master. Such tasks are being presented in shorter and more frequent sessions.

Experimental programs are more in evidence across the country. The National Association of Secondary School Principals, utilizing recommendations made by James Conant, has developed a Project on the Induction of Beginning Teachers. The project is described in four phases by its director, Douglas W. Hunt.[24] Phase I consists of the time before school starts and is designed to help the beginning teacher develop a sense of security and give direction to his planning. During the spring and summer, the new teacher is encouraged to maintain close contact with an experienced cooperating teacher assigned to him.

Phase II is devoted to normal school orientation or special beginning-teacher orientation. Practical assistance and advice from the cooperating teacher is essential in this phase of the program. Items of significance include:

> "Explaining the school schedule, the attendance procedures, the record-keeping system and the location and use of supplies; identifying administrators and supporting personnel (librarian, counselors, nurse, custodian); setting up classrooms; and reviewing opening of school procedures . . ." [25]

During the first semester, Phase III, cooperating and beginning teachers meet to consider the practical arts of teaching. Sessions are concerned with lesson planning, organization of methods and materials, testing, grading, supplementary materials, homework, school policy, discipline, and so forth. In addition to discussions and conferences, activities include the observation of experienced teachers, visits to instructional media centers, training in the use of audiovisual materials, and similar activities.

The final phase of the program, occurring during the second semester, witnesses a gradual movement from practical daily concerns to those of more far-reaching, and sometimes theoretical, considerations, including the important self-analysis of the beginning teacher with respect to his philosophy of education, performance in the classroom, and understanding of children.

Hunt indicates that as far as he knows teaching is the only major profession in which the beginner is given full and immediate responsibility—the same or more difficult assignment than the experienced worker has—

and then he is often criticized because he doesn't perform at the same level as his experienced colleague. The beginning teacher deserves better and so do his students.[26]

That conviction seems to be Hunt's justification for the acceptance of Conant's recommendation:

> "During the initial probationary period, local school boards should take specific steps to provide the new teacher with every possible help in the form of: (a) limited teaching responsibility; (b) aid in gathering instructional materials; (c) advice of experienced teachers whose own load is reduced so that they can work with the new teacher in his own classroom; (d) shifting to more experienced teachers those pupils who create problems beyond the ability of the novice to handle effectively; and (e) specialized instruction concerning the characteristics of the community, the neighborhood, and the students he is likely to encounter." [27]

Because of the budgetary limitations imposed on most school systems, a reduced teaching load may not be possible. The personnel administrator should make every effort to see to it that beginning teachers, if they are assigned five classes, have only teaching duties. Their teaching preparation should be limited to one content area or level, they should not be assigned to extreme groups, and they should be provided with an experienced teacher from whom to get professional help on a confidential and nonevaluative basis. The importance of the proper induction and orientation of new appointees cannot be overestimated. Too many potentially capable teachers, including many who have devoted years of preparation to their careers, resign their positions and give up teaching because of an unnecessarily unpleasant and frustrating initial experience in a school that lacks an effective, comprehensive orientation program. The consequence is unfortunate not only for the young teacher but also for society, which loses the valuable services of a trained teacher.

10 SALARY ADMINISTRATION

GENERAL STATEMENT

Problems centering around staff compensation have become more visible as a result of strikes, sanctions, withheld services, and publicity given to negotiation. The day is long past in which it was regarded as beneath the professional dignity of a teacher to be concerned about his pay or to take action to obtain professional compensation for his services. Salary schedules are an important factor in staff recruitment and retention, and an important element in contract negotiations. If a school district is to attract capable college graduates to its teaching staff, it must meet the competition of the business world in terms of salary schedules and benefits.

In small school districts, the superintendent administers the salary structure of the staff. In large school districts, the function may be placed in the personnel division or in a specialized business-affairs division, or it may be shared between two divisions.

Whether he is directly in charge of the function or not, the school personnel administrator is deeply involved in salary problems, and he must serve as an important resource person in salary matters. The development of salary schedules has become complex in nature, with the need to evaluate proposed differentials of all kinds. As a resource person, the personnel administrator may be involved in providing answers to such questions as the following:

1. What impact does the salary schedule have on staff recruitment and retention? On staff morale?
2. How does the salary schedule compare with that offered in comparable or neighboring school districts?
3. What funds will be needed to meet the salary requirements of next year's negotiated contract?

4. Is the salary schedule fair to all groups—beginning teachers, older teachers, teachers with special preparation, administrators?
5. How have incentives and progress been affected by compensation?
6. How can salary increases be justified to the community?
7. How does the compensation structure promote staff development and optimum service?
8. At what level should the salary of each new entrant be fixed?

EARLY METHODS OF SALARY DETERMINATION

Before the advent of the twentieth century, compensation was generally arrived at by individual bargaining. Rarely did two teachers, even with similar qualifications, receive the same remuneration in a district. Married men frequently received more than single men, single women more than married women, and the number of children that the teacher had could further complicate the structure.

A review of placement files from the last century carries some fascinating reports of early methods of compensation. Teachers were expected to live with certain families. Such board and room obviously became a part of their compensation. Teachers were known to have taken in orphans as part of their responsibility. Teachers were contractually required to supplement their income by tending the furnace of the school, by cleaning the school building and by serving as the town's sexton.

Further discussion of the earlier methods of compensation does not necessarily lead to a better understanding of current problems. Suffice it to say that, in the nineteenth century, schools were generally rural and small; teachers rarely had more than a high school education; and the expectations of the school as a social institution were little more than to make reading, writing and arithmetic available to those who chose to come to school.

ECONOMIC STATUS OF TEACHING

In recent years, newspaper publicity given to salary disputes between teachers and boards of education has created the impression that teachers are being given substantial salary advantages, but that is not in accordance with the facts. Teachers were far behind in salary scales years ago, and the pattern of increase, until recently, was at the rate of between two and three hundred dollars per year. Teachers' salaries are still behind the salaries of other professionals who are of comparable training and responsibility. The reader is referred to Table 6 in Chapter Six.

The difference in starting salary between teachers and people of similar training who enter industry is still substantial, as is indicated in Table 1, which shows the other groups to be from 25 to 50 percent higher.[1]

It is also interesting to note the slow pattern of salary increases given to school personnel over the years, as is revealed in Table 2.[2]

217

TABLE 1
Average Starting Salaries of Classroom Teachers
Compared with Those in Private Industry, 1965–66 through 1968–69

| Position or subject field | Average starting salaries | | | | | |
	1964–65	1965–66	1966–67	1967–68	1968–69	1969–70
1	2	3	4	5	6	7
Beginning teachers with bachelor's degree *	$4,707	$4,925	$5,142	$5,519	$5,941	
Male college graduates with bachelor's degree †						
Engineering	7,356	7,584	8,112	8,772	9,312	$9,816
Accounting	6,444	6,732	7,128	7,776	8,424	8,844
Sales-Marketing	6,072	6,276	6,744	7,044	7,620	8,028
Business Adm.	5,880	6,240	6,576	7,140	7,560	8,016
Liberal Arts	5,712	6,216	6,432	6,780	7,368	7,884
Production Mgt.	6,564	6,816	7,176	7,584	7,980	8,580
Chemistry	6,972	7,032	7,500	8,064	8,520	9,048
Physics	7,200	7,164	7,740	8,448	8,916	9,360
Mathematics-Stat.	6,636	6,672	7,260	7,944	8,412	8,892
Economics-Finance	6,276	6,600	6,732	7,416	7,800	8,304
Other fields	6,360	6,360	7,044	7,644	7,656	8,064
Total—all fields (weighted average)	6,535	6,792	7,248	7,836	8,395	8,929
Women college graduates with bachelor's degree ‡						
Mathematics-Stat.	6,108	6,324	7,104	7,776	8,484	
General Business	4,848	5,520	6,000	6,840	7,104	
Chemistry	6,468	7,056	7,452	8,280	8,532	
Accounting	5,664	6,768	6,984	7,716	8,304	
Home Economics	5,112	5,664	6,276	6,660	7,056	
Engineering-Tech. Res.	7,224	7,260	8,208	8,904	9,672	
Secretary	4,560	4,620	5,088	5,460	5,820	

Index relationship to starting salaries for teachers

Beginning teachers with bachelor's degree *	100.0	100.0	100.0	100.0	100.0	
Male college graduates with bachelor's degree †						
Engineering	156.3	154.0	157.8	158.9	156.7	
Accounting	136.9	136.7	138.6	140.9	141.8	
Sales-Marketing	129.0	127.4	131.2	127.6	128.3	
Business Adm.	124.9	126.7	127.9	129.4	127.3	
Liberal Arts	121.4	126.2	125.1	122.8	124.0	
Production Mgt.	139.5	138.4	139.6	137.4	134.3	
Chemistry	148.1	142.8	145.9	146.1	143.4	
Physics	153.0	145.5	150.5	153.1	150.1	
Mathematics-Stat.	141.0	135.5	141.2	143.9	141.6	
Economics-Finance	133.3	134.0	130.9	134.4	131.3	
Other fields	135.1	129.1	137.0	138.5	128.9	
Total—all fields (weighted average)	138.8	137.9	141.0	142.0	141.3	
Women college graduates with bachelor's degree ‡						
Mathematics-Stat.	129.8	128.4	138.2	140.9	142.8	
General Business	103.0	112.1	116.7	123.9	119.6	
Chemistry	137.4	143.3	144.9	150.0	143.6	
Accounting	120.3	137.4	135.8	139.8	139.8	
Home Economics	108.6	115.0	122.1	120.7	118.8	
Engineering-Tech. Res.	153.5	147.4	159.6	161.3	162.8	
Secretary	96.9	93.8	98.9	98.9	98.0	

(*Table notes on facing page.*)

TABLE 2
Average Salaries Paid Total Instructional Staff,
School Years 1929–30 through 1968–69,
in Current Dollars

School year	Average annual salary	School year	Average annual salary
1	2	1	2
1929–30	$1,420	1949–50	3,010
1930–31	1,440	1950–51	3,126
1931–32	1,417	1951–52	3,450
1932–33	1,316	1952–53	3,554
1933–34	1,227	1953–54	3,825
1934–35	1,244	1954–55	3,950
1935–36	1,283	1955–56	4,156
1936–37	1,327	1956–57	4,350
1937–38	1,374	1957–58	4,702
1938–39	1,408	*1958–59*	*4,939*
1939–40	1,441	1959–60	5,174
1940–41	1,470	1960–61	5,449
1941–42	1,507	1961–62	5,700
1942–43	1,599	1962–63	5,921
1943–44	1,728	1963–64	6,240
1944–45	1,846	1964–65	6,465
1945–46	1,995	1965–66	6,786
1946–47	2,254	1966–67	7,129
1947–48	2,639	1967–68	7,709
1948–49	2,846	1968–69	8,194 [a]

Sources:
Column 2 from U.S. Office of Education and NEA Research Division. Figures for all years ending in even numbers through 1961–62 and for 1940–41, 1942–43, 1944–45, 1946–47, 1948–49, and 1950–51 from the U.S. Office of Education. Figures for other years are estimates by the NEA Research Division.
[a] Preliminary estimates.

There are substantial differences in teachers' salaries in different regions of the United States. The average salary for instructional staff in the Northwest in 1968–69 was $7,008 as compared with a high of $9,462 in the Far West. However, the disparity among the regions has been drastically reduced. In 1939–40, the high region was the Far West, which was 44 percent above the national average, while the lowest was the Southeast, which was 42.9 percent below the national average. In 1968–69, the Far West, which was highest, was 15.4 percent above the national average, while the Northwest, which was lowest, was only 14.5 percent below the national average.[3]

---

[*] Estimated by NEA Research Division for school systems enrolling 6,000 or more pupils.
[†] From annual reports of Frank S. Endicott, Director of Placement, Northwestern University. Salaries are based on offers made to graduates by approximately 200 companies located throughout the United States. 1969–70 salaries are based on offers made in November 1968 to men who graduated in June 1969.
[‡] Computed from data presented in the Endicott reports.

TABLE 3
Mean Salaries Paid Classroom Teachers,
Reporting Systems with Enrollments of 12,000 or More,
by Region, 1962–63, 1964–65, and 1966–67

Region*	Average salary paid			Index: 1962–63 = 100.0		
	1962–63	1964–65	1966–67	1962–63	1964–65	1966–67
1	2	3	4	5	6	7
New England	$6,668	$6,991	$7,672	100.0	104.8	115.1
Mideast	6,988	7,414	8,146	100.0	106.1	116.6
Southeast	5,044	5,463	6,296	100.0	108.3	124.8
Great Lakes	6,663	6,910	7,686	100.0	103.7	115.4
Plains	6,202	6,552	7,004	100.0	105.6	112.9
Southwest	5,653	5,853	6,351	100.0	103.5	112.3
Rocky Mountain	5,720	6,279	6,808	100.0	109.8	119.0
Far West	7,126	7,639	8,481	100.0	107.2	119.0
Total, all regions	6,267	6,669	7,428	100.0	106.4	111.4

* Reporting systems are classified regionally as follows: *New England:* Connecticut, Maine, Massachusetts, New Hampshire, Rhode Island, and Vermont. *Mideast:* Delaware, District of Columbia, Maryland, New Jersey, New York, and Pennsylvania. *Southeast:* Alabama, Arkansas, Florida, Georgia, Kentucky, Louisiana, Mississippi, North Carolina, South Carolina, Tennessee, Virginia, and West Virginia. *Great Lakes:* Illinois, Indiana, Michigan, Ohio, and Wisconsin. *Plains:* Iowa, Kansas, Minnesota, Missouri, Nebraska, North Dakota, and South Dakota. *Southwest:* Arizona, New Mexico, Oklahoma, and Texas. *Rocky Mountain:* Colorado, Idaho, Montana, Utah, and Wyoming. *Far West:* Alaska, California, Hawaii, Nevada, Oregon, and Washington.

Table 3 shows the differences in the average salary of classroom teachers in different regions of the United States.[4]

The trend has continued toward removing the salary differential between elementary and secondary school teachers. In 1955–56, the average differential was 14.5 percent in favor of the secondary school teachers. In 1968–69, the difference was only 6.3 percent.[5]

THE SINGLE SALARY SCHEDULE

By the beginning of the twentieth century, a trend had been established toward uniform salaries based on preparation and years of service. Nevertheless, there was still a class system among teachers; that is, elementary school teachers were paid less than junior high school teachers, and junior high school teachers were paid less than high school teachers, who were paid most.

Later in the twentieth century, the single salary schedule appeared, and it remains the prevalent method for compensating professional educators. It is a graduated scale that provides for years of service, generally referred to as "steps," and for extent of academic preparation, often referred to as "columns" or "classes." Under the single salary schedule, not adopted in New York City until the 1930s, teachers at every teaching level are paid on the same salary schedule, if their preparation and experience are the same in quantity.

At the time of its inception, it was a logical development. Perhaps the easiest way to encourage teachers to obtain increased professional preparation was and is to pay them for advanced preparation. Likewise, teachers who stayed in the profession generally were highly regarded by the community and were thought to be worth more than novices.

Some districts have complicated the single salary schedule by counting only those units beyond the baccalaureate degree, or only upper division and graduate units, or fractional parts of years of service, private school experience or college teaching. A few districts even give credit for military service or work experience. Perhaps the least defensible qualification of the single salary schedule is the limitation of the number of years of rating-in credit. That is, some districts have adopted a schedule that gives credit for only four years of service. Regardless of the number of years of experience of successful teaching experience, the teacher would be rated-in on Step Five, which means that he is given credit for four previous years of experience. Some schedules do not count any experience if it is more than ten years old. Others give partial credit for experience (two years of teaching may count as one step on the schedule).

It appears that all of these factors have been developed rather arbitrarily and with little justification. Again, their virtue must be pointed out: the single salary schedule, with all its limitations and embellishments, has been easy to administer and, to this date, has been accepted by most governing boards and teachers' groups. In fact, there have been moves to set up statewide single salary schedules. These moves have resulted in statewide minimum salary schedules for teachers in thirty-one states.[6] On the national level, we have seen the regional gap in salaries narrowed, although there are still substantial differences in salaries for teachers in different regions of the country. Now that community involvement, accountability and expressions of dissatisfaction have become newsworthy, however, the public and boards of education have begun to look with a more critical point of view at the single salary schedule.

ASSUMPTIONS UNDERLYING THE SINGLE SALARY SCHEDULE

1. Teaching all children in all subjects is of equal importance and, therefore, there should be no difference in the compensation a teacher receives, whether she teaches kindergarten or high school science, provided she meets certification standards.

2. Teachers should be encouraged to teach the subject and level in which they are most interested and avoid seeking change merely because the salary is more attractive for teaching another subject or at another level.

221

3. The more knowledge a teacher has, the more knowledge she is able to transmit to her class. The more professional training she has in courses, the better she becomes as a teacher. Railsback shows the questionable truth of these assumptions.[7] Studies by Watts,[8] and by Washburne and Heil [9] support Railsback's findings. While Clements questions some of the research design in the studies referred to,[10] the findings are so consistent that one must seriously doubt the existence of a uniform relationship between increased academic preparation of teachers and pupil gains.

4. The longer a teacher teaches, the more her salary should be. This assumption varies considerably in practice, inasmuch as some salary schedules provide for ten steps, others fourteen, and still others twenty to thirty. Some variations of schedules provide for a percent increase after a specified number of years, say, twenty. Related to this assumption is the idea that an employee's salary should be greatest when he needs it most; that is, when he has a household to support—a heavy responsibility that usually reaches its peak after ten years of service. Considerations that seldom come to issue include how much pupils profit, comparatively, from experienced teachers and from novices, the usefulness of up-to-date methods and concepts, and how teachers who have considerable experience stand in the eyes of their colleagues, the administration and parents. It is universally granted that there is merit in experience. A professional question that has seldom been raised is, "Does optimum teacher ability reach its maximum at five, ten, twenty or some other number of years for the majority of teachers?"

5. Salary schedules should be formulated so as to minimize frictions and dissatisfaction among teachers which would detract from their professional performance. The certified elementary school teacher does not believe that her work is less important than teaching high school students or that she should be paid less because of her level. Differences in salaries based on sex, need, influence, or other factors irrelevant to the teaching process are equally objectionable to teachers.

6. Salary variations or special incentives are extrinsic, unnecessary and undesirable stimuli for the professional improvement of teachers. As professionals, teachers seek to improve because of their interest in children and their acceptance of professional obligations.

7. From the administrative point of view, single salary is desirable because of the ease with which it can be administered. A clerk who has little training can determine the class and step on the schedule upon which to place a teacher if he knows the number of units completed and the number of years taught. Individual bargaining and arguments are also minimized.

SHORTCOMINGS OF THE SINGLE SALARY SCHEDULE

1. Unfortunately, the single salary schedule frequently rewards "sticking it out" and accumulating pertinent and non-pertinent credits. From the businessman's point of view, it does not reward initiative, creativity,

efficiency, enthusiasm, innovation, cooperation, ability, or improved teaching performance.

2. The beginning step on most salary schedules is adequate for the experience and academic preparation of the novice. But most single salary schedules are inadequate for the "career professional" who continually strives to be a better teacher. All teachers rightfully deserve to be treated and compensated as professionals, which must not be taken to mean that all professionals deserve the same pay or that all even want to assume the rigors and responsibilities inherent in providing a comprehensive program.

3. Many teachers are highly trained and capable specialists who resent the fact that their less capable colleagues are on the same salary schedule.

4. Some men and women enter the profession in the middle years of life. Many have served a successful tenure in another field. How is it possible to justify a starting salary for them at the novice level because of the single salary schedule?

5. The single salary schedule is unresponsive to the law of supply and demand in teaching skills. From time to time a teacher shortage has been acute in one field while another field has had a sizable oversupply. Thus the person who majors in physics with the intention of becoming a physics teacher may well find that he can earn two to three hundred dollars more in industry than he can in education. The same principle holds for those who major in mathematics or industrial arts. With the federal government expanding financial assistance for vocational education programs, there will be an increased need for teachers who have vocational backgrounds. Typically, such teachers will come from industry, where they earn much higher salaries than the typical single salary schedule provides. The single salary schedule thus hampers teacher recruitment that competes with industry.

6. The public finds it difficult to understand and accept the single salary concept in many situations. For example, two third grade teachers may be assigned next door to one another, one a beginning teacher with a $7,000 annual salary, the other an experienced teacher with a $14,000 annual salary. What is the difference in role expectations of these two individuals? Each teacher may have thirty children; each teacher follows the same curriculum; each teacher works the same number of hours; each teacher is expected to produce equally good results in learning. Why is it necessary to pay one teacher so much more than the other?

Salary Variations or Differentials

Various practicalities have caused variations or differentials to be introduced into single salary schedules, usually by the mutual consent of teachers and school administrations. Such differentials have usually been objectively described and available to all staff members who qualify. Usually based on additional academic preparation or professional experience, differentials often come about through negotiations or collective bargaining between teachers' organizations and representatives of boards

223

of education. To present an example, as different steps or levels are set up in a salary schedule, a school administration might seek to achieve a *quid pro quo,* and in many school districts teachers might be required to offer evidence of one or more courses completed in order to qualify for advancement to the next salary step. When experienced teachers who meet minimum state certification requirements seek increases in maximum salaries, the administration might agree to grant increases on the basis of additional preparation or degrees. An advanced salary schedule could therefore be made available to those who have masters' or doctoral degrees.

When personnel administrators recruit teachers of vocational subjects whose industrial salaries are higher than beginning teachers' salaries, they obtain authorization to offer advanced salary credit for industrial experience. Such credit has been on a year-for-year basis or a two- or three-to-one basis. There is often a provision that such advanced credit may not carry an individual beyond the sixth or seventh salary step.

The precedent of offering advanced salary credit for industrial experience has been utilized by school boards to obtain teachers in shortage areas. For example, advanced salary credit may be given to teachers of science or mathematics for business experience related to their subject. Business or technical teachers may receive similar credit.

In other shortage areas, a differential has been paid for special training or courses. For example, a shortage of teachers in special education, home instruction, and speech in New York City led to the payment of a special differential of about $300 to teachers of those subjects for their special preparation beyond the certification requirements of other teachers.

Salary schedules have also been adapted to facilitate the recruitment of experienced teachers from other communities. At one time, teachers who changed districts had to begin at the first level in a new district, or they had to offer two or three years of experience for one year of salary credit. This practice has been changed in most places to year-for-year credit, although an upper limit of from seven to ten years has been maintained in many school districts. Limits exist on the theory that a teacher who has experience in other places must still prove her worth in her new school district and because they make it advantageous for a teacher to enter a school system at the beginning of her career and to remain there.

Experience as a substitute teacher is also creditable for advanced salary standing, although many school districts give greater credit to experience obtained in their own district in order to encourage substitute service. Experience in military service is given salary credit in some school districts on the grounds that the individual is sacrificing his time in the national interest. In some of these school districts, salary credit is given only if military service comes after the individual has begun teaching. Recognizing the desirability of retaining experienced teachers who might be eligible for retirement, and desiring to provide an additional financial incentive for teachers on maximum salary for many years, some school districts have

224

instituted "longevity increments"; that is, salary increments after 20, 25 and 30 years of service.

The idea has occurred to school administrators to pay a bonus or special increment to teachers serving in difficult or inner city schools, which often have high rates of staff turnover and are avoided by new teachers. The idea has not been generally accepted for several reasons. Schools are unwilling to be stigmatized in such a way. It is hard to define "difficult schools" accurately. It is not fair to say that teachers in one school should receive a bonus but that teachers in a neighboring school should not, although many teachers in the latter school may regard their assignments as being just as difficult. Furthermore, teachers in average schools face difficult classes. Should they also receive a bonus? Teachers' organizations have opposed this type of differential as breaking the single salary schedule. They have called it "combat pay" and have proposed massive programs to make "difficult" schools more attractive. In New York City, a bonus of about $500 was paid to the school staff in special schools for seriously disturbed children. Years of experience there showed that staff turnover was frequent and that few teachers sought appointments in those schools, despite the bonus.

The fact that salary schedules are fixed and published has posed some difficulties for teacher recruiters visiting colleges. A recruiter often finds himself interviewing a candidate who seems superior but who has had offers from other school districts. The recruiter would like to be able to offer more than the beginning salary, but he is not empowered to do so, unless the candidate meets some fixed qualifications for higher salary. While the recruiter may be disappointed, he must realize that authority to offer a higher salary to one person on a subjective basis would lead to pressures by influential individuals and abuse of the discretion. Soon all candidates would be offered the higher salary. It is generally accepted now that regulations concerning salaries should be in writing, available for public review, and applied equally to all individuals.

The following salary schedule was adopted in Cleveland after staff negotiations in 1969. It shows the step intervals, the differentials for additional courses and degrees, and "longevity increments." Cleveland also introduced an additional differential of $600 that could be obtained by participating in their in-service program for at least six years.

In New York City, the 1969 contract negotiations, covering a three-year period, reduced the number of salary steps from fourteen to eight. Table 4 on page 227 shows national averages of differentials paid for advanced degrees.[11]

SALARY SCHEDULES FOR SUBSTITUTE TEACHERS

Substitute teachers are used to cover day-to-day vacancies and vacancies that may run from a month to a semester. The qualifications of substi-

Effective August 25, 1969

Step	Schedule A Less than BA	Schedule B BA	Schedule C BA + ½ MA or BA + 30 hrs.	Schedule D MA	Schedule E MA + 15 Grad. Hrs.	Schedule F MA + 30 Grad. Hrs.
1	$5,700	$7,000	$7,300	$7,500	$7,500	$7,500
2	5,900	7,350	7,650	7,850	7,850	7,850
3	6,100	7,600	7,950	8,175	8,175	8,175
4	6,300	8,000	8,350	8,650	8,650	8,650
5	6,600	8,250	8,650	9,000	9,000	9,000
6	6,825	8,500	8,975	9,425	9,625	9,625
7	7,050	8,800	9,300	9,825	10,050	10,050
8	7,275	9,100	9,625	10,275	10,475	10,475
9	7,500	9,400	9,950	10,700	10,900	10,900
10	7,725	9,700	10,275	11,125	11,350	11,350
11	7,950	10,000	10,600	11,550	11,800	12,050
12	8,175	10,300	10,925	11,975	12,250	12,500
13	8,400	10,600	11,250	12,400	12,700	13,000
14	8,650	10,900	11,575			
15	8,900					
16	9,150					
17	9,400					

Longevity Increments — $1,200
    Teaching Service in the Cleveland Public Schools:
        20 Years — $300 effective 9/69
        25 Years — $300
        30 Years — $300
        35 Years — $300

tute teachers vary from partial to full certification; they are paid at a per diem rate in most school districts. The 1969 Cleveland teachers' contract provided that a substitute would be paid $26.00 per day but that, if her assignment continued for more than five days, she would be paid $30.00 per day for the succeeding days of the specific assignment. Substitute teachers who have longer experience may be paid up to $36.00 per day and for some holidays.

In New York City, day-to-day substitutes used to be paid at the daily rate of 1/180th of the annual beginning salary of a teacher. By cumulating days of service, a substitute teacher could advance on the salary schedule up to the seventh step and could qualify for degree differentials, vacation pay and other differentials. In 1968–69, New York City discontinued issuing substitute certificates and required all new temporary teachers to qualify for full certificates. The idea was to provide every class with a fully certified teacher, even for short periods of time. Short-term vacancies were to be filled by the assignment of regulars from district or school pools. Only if the supply of fully certified teachers is adequate can the plan be carried

TABLE 4
Comparison of Mean Scheduled Salaries for Classroom Teachers
1962–63 through 1968–69
(Reporting school systems with enrollments of 6,000 or more)

Preparation level	1962–63	1963–64	1964–65	1965–66	1966–67	1967–68	1968–69	Percent increase, 1968–69 over 1967–68
1	2	3	4	5	6	7	8	9
Number of reporting systems	557	918	1,063	1,071	1,104	1,080	1,999	
Mean scheduled salary for:								
Bachelor's degree								
Minimum	$4,331	$4,564	$4,707	$4,928	$5,144	$ 5,523	$ 5,941	7.6
Maximum	6,426	6,744	6,937	7,278	7,591	8,134	8,690	6.8
Master's degree								
Minimum	4,679	4,946	5,085	5,350	5,600	6,043	6,546	8.3
Maximum	7,053	7,487	7,723	8,167	8,578	9,248	9,981	7.9
Six years (M.A. + 30)								
Minimum	5,310	5,648	5,705	5,900	6,151	6,585	7,154	8.6
Maximum	8,236	8,650	8,975	9,416	9,808	10,399	11,273	8.4
Doctor's degree (or 7 years)								
Minimum	5,417	5,724	5,723	6,057	6,350	6,882	7,471	8.6
Maximum	8,199	8,602	8,917	9,453	9,936	10,751	11,602	7.9

out. It is likely to be more expensive because the pool of teachers must be paid whether they fill absences or not. When there are no absences, the extra teachers can be used for supplementary services.

Whether substitutes teach for a day or for longer periods of time, their pupils are entitled to have qualified personnel. Since one way of attracting qualified personnel is to provide a high salary schedule, school districts must give ample attention to the effects of their salary schedules on the substitute-teacher situation.

SALARY SCHEDULES FOR TRADE TEACHERS

Since trade teachers are not required to have a baccalaureate degree, a special arrangement is necessary if they are to work on a par with other teachers. It has been achieved in many school districts by regarding their minimum required schooling and trade experience (often, seven years of trade experience are required for certification) as the equivalent of a baccalaureate degree. In addition, a trade teacher may offer extra years of experience in order to advance on the baccalaureate schedule. In 1969, Cleveland allowed up to three years of extra credit. Other school districts may allow up to seven years. Trade teachers who complete additional college work are given further credit on salary schedules. It is reasonable,

227

and indeed essential, that trade teachers be given a fair opportunity to reach the maximum step on a salary schedule in terms of the requirements and duties of their position.

SALARY SCHEDULES FOR ADMINISTRATORS

Historically, principals and other school supervisors and administrators had to negotiate individually for their salaries. The same arguments in favor of a general or single salary schedule for teachers, apply equally to school administrators; that is, avoidance of unprofessional influences and low morale. Prior to the adoption of uniform salary schedules for supervisors, such factors as size, location, and level of achievement of the school, and the sex, age, experience and connections of the administrator were considered. Practices in compensating school administrators and supervisors still vary considerably from district to district, but salary schedules are now usually published and are uniformly and fairly applied to all who meet the requirements.

Departmental chairmen and other supervisors may be given a bonus or differential pay above a teacher's salary. The 1969 Cleveland contract provides differentials of from $300 to $800 per year, depending on the size of the department. Many school districts follow the same plan and do not accord tenure to such positions. In some school districts, however, administrative and supervisory positions carry tenure and have salary schedules with step intervals similar to those of the teachers' salary schedule. In some school districts, principals and assistant principals receive a differential. In other school districts, those positions carry tenure and progressive salary schedules.

If a bonus is paid to an administrator, the differential between his salary and that of a teacher is likely to be smaller than what he would receive if he had tenure and a separate salary schedule. His services are thus less expensive to the school district and he can more easily be replaced if he is unsatisfactory. However, school supervision and administration is a profession requiring professional training and know-how. Someone whose services may be temporary and who is not being paid adequately for the arduous work of leadership is less likely to be effective in the position. The temporary bonus approach seems to be poor economy at the leadership level.

Although the idea of a single salary schedule for all teachers has been accepted, principals of secondary schools still have higher salaries than elementary school principals, in most places. A prime reason, of course, is tradition, but most secondary schools are larger and more complex institutions than elementary schools.

Where there are separate salary schedules for school administrators, increases are usually negotiated informally with their associations. In order to avoid the frictions of such negotiations, many school districts have set up a ratio or index relationship between school administrators and teachers. Thus in New York City a high school principal receives 2.0 times the maximum increase given to teachers. A departmental chairman receives 1.5 times the teachers' increase. Following this paragraph, in Table 6, is the index relationship which was set up in state law in New York to govern salary increases of supervisory personnel in the New York City school system. This index does not reflect salary relationship, but merely the increases that are given. School supervisors have urged that total salaries be brought up to the index ratio, but they have not achieved their objective because of the expense. All increases, however, have followed this index since the law was passed in 1964. Table 7 indicates actual salary ratios.

TABLE 6

Ratio of Salary Increases Among
Supervisory Personnel and Teachers
in the New York City School System

Position	Index Number
Teacher	1.00
Chairman	1.45
Assistant Principal	1.45
Elementary Principal	1.70
Junior High Principal	1.85
High School Principal	2.00

TABLE 7

Ratios of Actual Salaries Among
Supervisory Personnel and Teachers
in the New York City School System in 1968 [12]

Position	Index Number
Teacher	1.00
Assistant Principal and Chairman	1.26
Elementary Principal	1.48
Junior High Principal	1.58
High School Principal	1.86

On the national scene, the average maximum salary in 1968–69 for senior high school principals was $17,408 in school systems with enrollments of 25,000 or more; for junior high school principals it was $16,289; for elementary school principals it was $15,428. The average salary for classroom teachers during the same year was about $7,908.[13]

The following table shows the national averages of salaries for administrative personnel.[14] It is interesting to note that administrators' salaries in large school systems (enrollment above 100,000) are not proportionately higher than those in small school districts (above 6,000 in enrollment).

229

TABLE 8
Average and Median Maximum Scheduled Salaries
for Principals and Certain Other Professional Employees
Assigned to School Buildings, 1968–69

			Enrollment Stratum			
Position	1 100,000 or more	2 50,000– 99,999	3 25,000– 49,999	Total 1, 2, and 3	4 12,000– 24,999	5 6,000– 11,999
1	2	3	4	5	6	7
Supervising Principals						
Elementary						
Systems Reporting	25	48	76	149	216	363
Mean	16,867	15,200	15,098	15,428	15,214	15,033
Median	17,247	14,949	15,525	15,561	15,309	15,004
Range—Low	12,431	9,899	9,900	9,899	7,667	6,740
High	24,724	21,825	21,996	24,724	25,040	25,252
Junior High						
Systems Reporting	22	43	68	133	193	301
Mean	17,784	16,079	15,939	16,289	16,303	16,269
Median	17,530	15,789	16,045	16,279	16,250	16,500
Range—Low	13,119	10,339	10,400	10,339	7,667	6,740
High	26,191	22,920	21,990	26,191	23,624	24,540
Senior High						
Systems Reporting	24	48	77	149	204	332
Mean	18,418	17,146	17,258	17,408	17,391	17,024
Median	17,848	17,167	17,260	17,320	17,450	17,162
Range—Low	13,275	11,350	11,140	11,140	8,771	7,040
High	26,191	24,220	22,781	26,191	24,887	26,287
Assistant Principals						
Elementary						
Systems Reporting	23	26	40	89	73	103
Mean	14,450	13,679	13,051	13,596	14,219	13,828
Median	14,235	13,679	13,724	13,748	14,039	13,848
Range—Low	9,926	9,517	8,816	8,816	9,600	6,648
High	19,676	19,045	16,434	19,676	19,794	21,924
Junior High						
Systems Reporting	21	36	59	116	152	214
Mean	14,946	13,876	13,990	14,128	14,703	14,574
Median	15,000	13,833	14,192	14,147	14,635	14,514
Range—Low	9,926	8,799	9,062	8,799	9,110	6,648
High	20,217	19,795	19,338	20,217	21,287	21,924
Senior High						
Systems Reporting	25	42	73	140	173	279
Mean	15,305	14,458	14,759	14,766	15,499	15,316
Median	15,600	14,140	14,935	14,781	15,647	15,316
Range—Low	9,926	9,239	9,309	9,239	8,900	6,648
High	22,055	19,795	20,081	22,055	21,878	21,924

SALARIES FOR PARAPROFESSIONALS AND SCHOOL AIDES

In most school districts, paraprofessionals have been paid an hourly wage with no fringe benefits. The wage has depended on the qualifications and duties of the position and has usually run from $2.00 to $3.75 per hour. As the paraprofessionals become a permanent part of the staff, they will require an annual salary and appropriate fringe benefits. In 1970, the United Federation of Teachers in New York City, representing thousands of paraprofessionals serving in the city's schools, demanded a salary schedule of $6,500 to $9,200 for different levels of responsibility and preparation. There is no doubt that certification requirements and salary schedules for these positions will be developed, and the same principles should be followed in administering schedules as are followed in administering teachers' schedules or those of noncertificated employees.

MERIT PAY PLANS

For nearly a decade there have been rumbles, frequently originating in governing boards, about the single salary schedule. In the 1960s, many boards declared that they did not mind paying high salaries to good teachers, but board members questioned a policy that would permit weak teachers to achieve maximum salaries. It is anticipated that this kind of reasoning will be intensified in the future as a result of expanding school budgets and greater community involvement.

Superficially, merit pay seems to be the obvious answer to the compensation problem: find the best teacher and reward him appropriately. The State of Utah spent about $500,000 on what is perhaps the most comprehensive study of merit pay to date. The results were not encouraging. Who should determine which teachers receive merit pay? By what criteria should "meritorious teachers" be determined? How much pay should be involved? What is the effect on those who fail to receive merit pay? What new problems does merit pay create? Those are questions to which there have been no satisfying answers.

The merit-pay proposal was opposed by teachers' organizations and many school administrators for a number of reasons. (1) It was considered a device to achieve false economies and to keep teachers' salaries down by limiting increases in salaries and acceptable salary scales to a small number of teachers. For example, it might be ordered arbitrarily that only ten percent of a staff would receive merit increases in a given year, with others receiving only a token increase. The ten percent figure might have been set arbitrarily to reduce costs even though 80 percent of the staff deserved the increase. (2) Merit-pay increases have a divisive effect on a staff, creating jealousy and animosity, because some staff members are selected for the special benefit and others are deprived of it. (3) The bases for selection for merit increases have been too subjective and susceptible to favoritism. So many variables enter teaching effectiveness—type of class, type of community, attitude of the principal, goals of the school, intangible changes in the personalities of children—that research has not developed objective bases for evaluating the service of teachers. (4) Objective bases used for selecting "meritorious teachers" have not been regarded as reflecting the true worth of a teacher. For example, in some states merit increases have been given to teachers who could achieve a required score on a standardized test that measured professional background. In practice, this approach discriminates against groups of teachers whose preparation, through no fault of their own, is made at institutions where academic standards and resources are limited. Neither is the correlation between success in the tests and success in teaching regarded as sufficient to warrant their use for salary purposes. In fact, it has even been declared that this approach was used to maintain lower salaries for black teachers.

OTHER PLANS FOR SALARY DIFFERENTIALS

Some authorities believe that the concept of "differentiated staffing" is the most reasonable answer to the criticisms inherent in the single salary schedule and that it can provide for the most equitable compensation for teachers. In its most simple form, differentiated staffing attempts to identify the skills and responsibilities associated with teaching and to reward those qualities appropriately. Much research needs to be done in order to identify them, and wholesale retraining of teachers is required; the public will need to be brought along with the development of the concept. The plan did not evolve as a salary device, but was developed to make effective use of the different skills and abilities of staff members in restructuring staff organization and functions.

The idea originated with the modern personnel practice of describing the task to be done, identifying the training and experience necessary to perform the task, and rewarding the person who performs the task appropriately. That is generally referred to as job description or analysis. Job description for selection in classified service is widely used in school districts, governmental agencies, and industry.

Job analysis makes it possible to differentiate among teaching tasks and to establish different categories in the teaching service, such as "instructional assistant," who performs routine tasks under guidance; "technical aide," who assists with demonstrations and audiovisual work; "coordinating teacher," who coordinates student activities; "diagnostic teacher," who diagnoses learning deficiencies and problems; "lead teacher," who assumes overall responsibility for the learning process of each student and curriculum adaptation for him; and "professional teacher," who is the generalist in teaching. Assuming that such categories could be developed and function properly, the result would be differentiated salary schedules that would depend on the role and performance of each staff member.

Public financial aid to parochial schools and the effects of the federal court ruling on desegregation have caused another line of thought to develop—the "chit system." Much of the subject matter taught in parochial and private schools is of a secular nature, similar to the subject matter presented in public schools. It appears reasonable to many people that

232

a parochial school child should be entitled to a portion of the public money which would be invested in his education if he were to attend public school. Likewise, forcing children to attend integrated schools against their will alienates a large number of voters. It has been suggested that each child should receive, from the school district or the local government, public support in the form of a check which he could use at the school of his choice for a year's education. If he so wished, he could take the next year's check to a different school.

In certain sections of the country, a near balance exists between supporters of private schools and supporters of public schools. In some cities, as many children attend private and parochial schools as attend public schools. In 1969 in New York City, it was estimated that about one million children attended public schools and that about half a million were in private or parochial schools. The passing of tax and bond issues in some communities is becoming increasingly difficult because of this factor.

Competition is almost totally lacking from the public school concept. People reason that the public school is free, a monopoly suffering from the ills of lack of open competition. But suppose that a child or his parents had $500 for a year's education which could be given to Teacher A or Teacher B in a private or parochial school. What difference would it make? Some teachers might like to take 30 children and earn, say, $15,000. Others might settle for a class of 20 for $10,000. Other teachers might have so few students that it wouldn't be worth their while to continue in the profession. It is interesting to speculate on the possibilities of this kind of school organization. To say that it would revolutionize the American public school system is to make a conservative statement.

PAY FOR EXTRA DUTIES

Salary administration has been complicated by current practices of paying staff members additional stipends for extra duties such as coaching, producing a school newspaper, producing school plays, and developing a school orchestra. At one time, these activities were considered to be normal extracurricular programs which teachers had to assume as part of their work. About two decades ago, when teachers' salaries were so low in an expanding economy that most teachers sought to supplement their incomes by taking second jobs, teachers' organizations began to press for compensation for the time required by some extracurricular activities. Pressure for compensation was greatest in athletic team coaching because practice took place for several hours almost every day and a Saturday game required the coach to devote a full day. But coaching teams was also a specialization in itself; coaches were sometimes employed for this purpose alone, without having additional responsibilities for classes. Since hundreds of tickets were sold for games, the activity frequently made thousands of dollars for a school.

In some school districts, attempts were made to avoid initiating a principle of paying for extracurricular service by adjusting teachers' programs so that, for example, a coach would begin the school day at noon and coach the team from two until six in the afternoon. Program adjustments did not work because they complicated class coverage and left coaches dissatisfied with doing two jobs for one salary. In some schools, dramatics or journalism classes were scheduled for the faculty adviser with the understanding that his classes would produce plays or the school newspaper. Such arrangements also had limited success.

It is general practice now to pay personnel for extracurricular activities that require considerable time. Supplementary payments have been worked out after negotiations between staff and administration. They take into consideration tradition (popular sports rate highest), the hours of service required, the number of pupils involved, and special skills required of the faculty member.

The contract or agreement negotiated by the Cleveland Teachers Union in 1969 includes the following stipends for extracurricular work (samples are quoted here from a longer list):

Athletic Coaching		*Senior High*	
Head Football	$1,000.	Dramatics Director	$600.
Head Basketball	1,000.	Newspaper Adviser	700.
Head Baseball	700.	Orchestra Director	300.
Head Tennis	300.	Yearbook Adviser	300.
		Junior High	
		Intramural Director	400.
		Newspaper Adviser	300.

On the national scene, the Research Division of the National Education Association reported for the year 1967–68 that 25 percent of all supplementary payments to teachers for extra duties went for the supervision of competitive sports and that 3.6 percent of all schools provided supplements for nonathletic activities while 71.1 percent paid supplements for both.[15]

Table 9 illustrates the range of payments for extra duties.[16]

FRINGE BENEFITS

Public agencies, including public schools, have been slow to develop fringe benefit packages for their employees. Historically, even the concept of retirement on pension was slow to develop. But there have been rapid gains recently in the number and kinds of fringe benefits available to teachers. After retirement became a common benefit, paid leaves of absence were instituted and major medical group insurance and other types of insurance became available.

The fringe benefit package is a part of the whole compensation plan.

234

No longer is it possible to compare only salaries and to be accurate about the cost of employees. The total cost of fringe benefit options may amount to ten percent of the annual salary of a beginning teacher. Since the same benefits are frequently available to classified personnel, the percentage may be even higher.

The thinking on fringe benefits should not be limited to the dollars immediately paid out on premiums. Certain kinds of leaves of absence are appropriately charged to fringe benefits, including maternity leave, emergency leave, family illness, jury duty and "personal business" leave, to name a few. When substitutes are employed for periods of leave, the results are increased cost to the districts.

The trend is clear. These benefits will increase. More options are likely to become available. Even at this writing, fringe benefits for public service are modest when compared with benefits available in the private sector.

IMPLICATIONS FOR THE SCHOOL PERSONNEL ADMINISTRATOR

The personnel administrator must develop forms on which applicants can submit claims and he must arrange for the prompt processing of such forms. Inefficient administration in this area will result in bitter complaints by individuals who have been working for weeks or months without receiving pay. (See the end of this chapter for a sample form that is used for processing claims for salary credit.) Administrative arrangements concerning salaries in many school districts involve both the personnel division and the finance division, so that plans must be developed cooperatively. The responsibility of each should be made clear.

The personnel administrator must know national and statewide trends in salary matters so that he may serve as a resource person in his school district. He must also make studies of current salary schedules and trends in adjacent and competing areas so that he can render up-to-date and relevant advice during salary negotiations. And he must be able to anticipate salary needs and demands in order to make budgetary provisions for them. In his advisory capacity to the superintendent, he should have reliable information on the adequacy and effects of current salary schedules with respect to staff recruitment, morale, achievement, staff retention and development. Where there are weaknesses, the personnel administrator must prepare proposals to remedy them. In his planning, the personnel administrator must involve representatives of interested parties of the teaching staff, the administration, and the community.

There is no visible evidence that the problems associated with compensation for professional services will diminish in the immediate future. What will probably happen is that the problems will come into better focus so that they may be studied more effectively. The questions below will no

TABLE 9

Mean and Median Maximum Supplements Scheduled Above Regular Salary of Classroom Teachers for Extracurricular Guidance of Selected Pupil-Participating Activities, 1967–68

Scheduled supplements by enrollment grouping of reporting systems

Activity [a]	Strata 1, 2, and 3 (25,000 or more)				Stratum 4 (12,000–24,999)				Stratum 5 (6,000–11,999) systems				Total—all reporting		
	Mean	Median	Range Low	Range High	Mean	Median	Range Low	Range High	Mean	Median	Range Low	Range High	Mean	Range Low	Range High
1	2	3	4	5	6	7	8	9	10	11	12	13	14	15	16
Pupil-participating competitive sports															
Athletic director or faculty manager [b]	$ 963	$ 900	$100	$2,766	$ 813	$740	$275	$2,808	$896	$900	$100	$2,200	$ 896	$100	$2,808
Head coach	1,186	1,000	258	2,682	1,018	898	200	2,631	910	750	150	3,200	1,009	150	3,200
Football	910	830	300	4,000	880	900	240	3,000	995	950	150	3,550	972	150	4,000
Basketball	768	750	300	1,809	880	800	240	2,916	888	825	200	2,650	858	200	2,916
Baseball	560	500	150	1,383	589	600	200	1,290	609	583	200	2,028	593	150	2,028
Track [c]	588	505	150	1,550	629	600	100	1,500	625	580	200	2,100	617	100	2,100
Cross Country	321	278	75	1,135	373	375	100	737	380	350	75	1,100	366	75	1,135
Swimming	448	450	150	1,809	542	550	208	1,012	541	500	100	1,700	527	108	1,809
Wrestling	481	450	150	1,040	579	590	188	1,290	612	600	165	1,254	576	150	1,290
Tennis	333	296	50	1,000	359	350	75	1,000	371	350	75	1,120	359	50	1,120
Golf	299	260	50	958	322	308	85	737	332	300	75	1,000	322	50	1,000
Gymnastics	459	400	100	1,040	476	487	200	1,000	485	434	150	952	476	100	1,040
Rifle	321	350	105	651	336	306	200	500	417	448	100	760	374	100	760
Soccer	402	341	150	1,150	496	500	100	700	533	558	75	1,008	505	75	1,150
Hockey	683	512	178	1,664	548	500	100	900	631	580	25	1,600	622	25	1,664
Bowling	245	200	100	470	310	300	250	412	288	285	75	600	285	75	600
Softball	365	300	50	990	183	182	100	300	271	238	100	595	275	50	990
Volleyball	296	250	25	600	242	225	100	425	193	192	25	325	234	25	600
Water polo	385	361	250	544	409	380	250	669	318	215	200	568	367	200	669
Intramural sports	522	400	100	1,800	463	380	20	1,445	383	350	100	1,200	439	20	1,800
Equipment manager	524	480	250	1,100	531	538	100	800	549	500	150	1,624	541	100	1,624
Cheer leader	291	232	100	958	268	261	25	580	265	250	45	742	268	25	958
Drill team	312	220	140	900	271	253	122	600	224	202	50	473	263	50	900
Trainer	674	645	280	1,600	581	540	100	1,250	608	500	200	1,700	620	100	1,700

Pupil-participating
nonathletic activities

Music															
Director of music [d]	666	600	285	1,400	*	*	*	*	515	400	75	1,860	524	75	1,860
Instrumental music	498	400	100	1,200	399	350	1,300	126	493	449	75	1,600	470	75	1,600
Vocal music	416	350	125	1,277	401	350	1,300	100	440	400	50	1,754	424	50	1,754
School band	654	600	145	1,809	591	500	2,000	100	609	510	75	2,400	614	75	2,400
Dramatics															
Director or coach [e]	391	328	125	1,400	410	358	1,600	100	375	325	50	1,625	387	50	1,625
Production of school play(s)	352	300	130	688	285	260	550	100	317	300	30	1,262	314	30	1,262
Publications [f]															
School newspaper	420	300	150	1,392	332	300	1,000	73	343	300	50	952	353	50	1,392
School magazine	203	150	100	400	178	195	250	100	167	100	55	600	180	55	600
Yearbook	363	300	150	1,040	352	315	826	73	362	314	90	952	359	73	1,040
Debating															
Director or coach	373	300	150	810	392	350	1,008	100	363	336	50	855	373	50	1,008

* Not computed; too few cases.

[a] The activities shown here are found in enough salary schedules to make averages and medians significant. There are occasional references to many other activities but not in sufficient numbers to justify summary data.

[b] Head coach or only coach.

[c] Includes both spring and fall track if they are shown separately in schedule.

[d] Vocal and instrumental combined, or not specified.

[e] May include production of at least one school play.

[f] In a few schedules, supplements are shown for a director of publications; too few cases were found to justify tabulation.

doubt be considered by governing boards and negotiating groups for some time to come.

1. What do we want the teacher to accomplish? Teachers' many routine responsibilities surely represent an inordinate waste of talent and money. Perhaps a quarter to a half of a teacher's time is spent on activities which a person who has less training could do with equal efficiency. If, as some have suggested, teaching becomes the preeminent profession, a master teacher should receive greatly improved compensation and more responsibility, and should be more directly accountable for the results of instruction.

2. Are the skills teachers possess so varied that their placement on salary schedules results in inequity and lack of stimulation? What are the effects of present salary schedules on educational results? Are all teachers really interchangeable in assignments and benefits?

3. Do different levels and subject assignments justify different salary schedules? Inherent in the single salary schedule is the belief that only years of service and academic preparation have meaning for salary placement. A teacher is a teacher regardless of grade level and subject field.

4. It is maintained that the farther a teacher gets from classroom teaching the higher his compensation is likely to be. How can teachers who prefer to teach receive salaries comparable to those given to administrators? Such an arrangement would encourage capable teachers to continue teaching.

5. How many students should a teacher have? Reductions in class size are the most expensive element in a budget. Teachers want small classes but research indicates that class size is not necessarily related to pupil gains. Perhaps a different kind of classroom organization will emerge, one that will permit both small and large group instruction. It is possible that teachers will specialize in both types. The addition of aides and other supporting personnel will affect class size.

These and other questions will be considered by governing boards and teachers' groups. Demands for change come from society as it appraises the products of the public school and because it is concerned with the tax dollar. The demands for change also come from within the profession as it sees professional responsibilities diluted by routine requirements.

Form on which salary credit for prior experience is claimed.

BOARD OF EDUCATION OF THE CITY OF NEW YORK
Office of Personnel—Salary Unit
65 Court Street, Brooklyn, N.Y. 11201

File # _____

Social Security # _____

(Substitute Personnel)

Instructions: Complete Section 1, if you have had prior teaching experience, and Section 2, if you offer other relevant employment experience. All applicants should complete Sections 3 and 4. The application should be mailed, as soon as possible, to the Salary Unit

(Read the reverse side of application for pertinent rules and regulations governing salary credit)

Name (First, Middle, Last) _____ Maiden Name _____

Substitute License—Subject _____ Date of License _____

Current Salary Step _____ Date of Last Increment _____ Home Address _____

1. Teaching Experience: I hereby claim to have had, prior to the issuance of my license as substitute teacher, experience in teaching in schools other than the public schools of the City of New York, for which I desire to claim salary credit.

School and Location	Subject and Grades Taught	Date of Service From To	Days in School Year	Teaching Hours per day	Name of Head of Institution

Do not claim credit for teaching experience for a period
in which you are also claiming business experience

2. Business Experience: I hereby claim to have had, prior to the issuance of my license as substitute teacher, experience in a profession, mechanical or mercantile occupation or in a trade, for which I desire to claim salary credit.

Employer's Name and Address	Nature of Business	Capacity in which Employed	Dates From To	Hours per Week

3. EDUCATION
I have attended the following Educational Institutions:

	Name and Address of Institution Attended	Years of Attendance	Date of Graduation and Degree (if any)
Secondary:			
Trade:			
College or University:			

4. CERTIFICATION
I hereby certify that the statements in this application for Salary Credit are complete and accurate, and that they are true according to my information and belief.

Signature of Applicant _____ Date _____

DO NOT WRITE BELOW THIS LINE

A. Total experience prior to date of issuance of license as substitute teacher credited as equivalent to teaching experience in the New York City public schools: _____ Terms

B. Experience other than teaching _____ Terms

Approved by _____ Salary Unit _____

239

11 PERSONNEL BENEFITS

GENERAL STATEMENT

School systems that have an attractive general welfare and fringe benefit program, appropriate to the school situation, are in a better position to recruit and hold employees. They are also better able to compete for personnel with business, industry and government, which often offer better salaries and more diversified inducements in the form of benefits. A good benefit program also helps to maintain a desirable level of employee morale. In essence, a good program of general welfare and fringe benefits is a distinct asset to a school system.

Nowadays, school system employees and applicants show great concern for the annual salaries they may expect to receive. It has been a common practice for applicants to compare salaries of several school districts and then attempt to "land a position" in the system whose salary schedule appears to be the most attractive. In recent years, the basis for comparison has noticeably broadened to include all general welfare and fringe benefits that are offered by a school system. "What health and hospitalization insurance benefits are available or furnished to your teachers?" "How about life insurance?" These are questions commonly asked of personnel administrators by teacher applicants. The facts seem clear. School systems must recruit their teaching personnel in a "teachers' choice" market. The more desirable applicants, the ones that most school personnel administrators are continually seeking, will continue to be able to choose the school system where they wish to teach. Those systems that are able to include attractive fringe benefits in their employment offer will have a recruiting advantage over those school systems that are unable to include them.

240

GROWTH AND DEVELOPMENT OF WELFARE BENEFITS

General welfare benefits for school employees were limited before 1960. The concept that benefits should be provided and financed by an employer received initial acceptance in the early thirties in governmental agencies, business and industry. With the birth of collective bargaining in the major industrial firms, each new contract expanded welfare benefits. The more these benefits were expanded, the more attractive a position in business or industry became to male, family-oriented teachers who were dissatisfied with their salaries and the accompanying benefits of school systems.

School systems, with their often limited financial resources, were slow to react to this trend because the supply of trained teachers seemed adequate to meet needs. It wasn't until school systems began to experience the frustrations of shortages of fully trained teachers that they considered the added incentives of fringe benefits. Competition among neighboring school districts for teaching talent, for example, led to widespread acceptance of providing sick-leave privileges. It wasn't until the early sixties that health and hospitalization insurance premiums for school employees were paid either in part or fully by a majority of school districts. Group life insurance coverage soon followed.

Expansion of benefits has been most rapid in large metropolitan school systems where teacher organizations, such as the American Federation of Teachers and the National Education Association and their state and local affiliates, negotiate with boards of education for salaries, benefits and working conditions. Smaller school systems that have yet to experience negotiating salary levels with teacher organizations need to know that teachers' major emphasis may be expected to be on expanded fringe benefits.

A research report of the American Federation of Teachers, AFL-CIO, has this to say:

> "Along with the demand for professional salaries, teachers have negotiated for professional levels of fringe benefits and general working conditions. However, the persistent differentials found in salaries are even more pronounced and extreme in the cases of fringe benefits and some specific conditions of work. In these areas, teachers continue to lag considerably behind organized production workers, not to mention noneducational professional workers." [1]

Similarly, a research report of the National Education Association states:

> "Now, with the increasing prevalence of negotiated agreements between school professional staff and boards of education, paid leaves of absence are rapidly becoming items of negotiation." [2]

241

ESSENTIAL ELEMENTS OF A BENEFITS PROGRAM

An appropriate benefits program for school employees should be designed to produce conditions of employment conducive to the continual improvement of the instructional program. To accomplish that objective, benefits programs should:

1. Provide security to the individual employee.
2. Safeguard the mental and physical health of the employee.
3. Foster professional growth and morale.
4. Promote staff stability.

A general welfare program should include provisions for leaves of absence, health protection, life insurance, housing assistance, employee counseling, and social and recreational activities.

LEAVES OF ABSENCE FOR TEACHERS

Leave-of-absence plans should be viewed as one means of maintaining the highest level of quality and efficiency in instructional service. At times it is justifiable, even imperative, for a teacher to be absent from regular teaching duties. An established leave plan assures teachers of increased security, health, peace of mind, or preparation time for professional advancement, and thereby contributes to the improvement of the teaching service.

A National Educational Association Research Study of October 1966 revealed the results of an extensive survey of policies and practices governing teachers' leaves of absence in school districts throughout the United States in 1965.[3] One hundred twenty-nine school systems with enrollments of 25,000 or more were surveyed. The data and conclusions revealed in that survey are highly significant to school personnel in revealing the diversity and extent of current practices. A subsequent study, made in 1969 by the same association for 1967–68, revealed important trends.[4]

Sick Leave

The school system that has not established a specific policy for classroom teachers' sick leave is rare. Nearly all school systems, regardless of size, also grant sick leave with full pay. By 1968, thirty-six states had made statutory provision for sick leave.[5]

The 1965 N.E.A. report indicated that the median number of days of annual sick leave granted was ten.[6] In fact, the policies of 88.4 percent of the 129 responding systems provided ten days or more of sick leave with full pay. Additional sick leave with partial pay was granted in twenty-seven systems. According to a 1969 survey by the AFT-CIO Research Division, 99 percent of the 596 school districts with populations over 6,000 provided annual sick leave with full pay.[7]

Various methods are employed in granting sick-leave benefits. In some school systems, teachers are credited with the entire annual allotment at the opening of the school term, while in others the leave is earned by the month (e.g., one day per month). The annual allotment is usually limited to from eight to fifteen days per year. As reported in 1968, in Pontiac, Michigan, in Kenosha, Wisconsin, and in New York City it was ten days per year; in Newark, New Jersey, and in Boston it was fifteen days per year; in Alaska, it was eighteen days per year.

A frequently used method of providing for unusually long sick leaves is that of accumulating unused sick leave from year to year. According to the 1965 N.E.A. report, cumulative sick leave with full pay was practiced in 27.1 percent of the studied school systems.[8] The median number of days in systems of all sizes was 129.4, and it was over 182 days in those systems with enrollments of 100,000 or more. Only one district reported no cumulative leave with full pay. An N.E.A. research study covering 58 school districts that had negotiated comprehensive agreements for the years 1967–68 revealed that 90 percent of them had short-term, cumulative provisions.[9]

To take care of the prolonged illness of a teacher who has not been in service long enough to accumulate a sufficient bank of sick-leave days, many school districts have a plan for advancing sick leave at full or partial pay, after accumulated leave has been used.

Although there was a time when "proof of illness" was required for all absences, many school districts now permit teachers to be absent for a limited number of days (varying from three to ten) on a self-treated basis. Proof of illness was eliminated for three reasons: teachers objected to the requirement of bringing a doctor's note as an excuse for being absent from work; seeing a doctor was an unnecessary expense in self-treated illnesses; proof of illness became a *pro forma* regulation.

Liberal changes in sick-leave provisions have brought a number of problems to the school personnel administrator. When a stated number of fully paid days of sick leave was allowed each year, some teachers regarded it as a right to be absent, and in some districts teacher absence increased.

Table 1 shows the extent of sick-leave benefits in 556 schools studied by the American Federation of Teachers, AFT-CIO Research Division.[10]

TEMPORARY ABSENCES FOR SPECIAL OCCASIONS

Almost all school districts allow personnel to be absent from duty on occasions of bereavement of a member of the immediate family. The modal length of such absence varies from three to five days, during which teachers are usually paid, although the accounting varies in different districts. In some districts, the absence is charged against the sick leave bank, while in others a "special" leave is granted. Special leaves of absence are given in some districts for attendance at the graduation of a son, daughter, spouse, or the teacher himself. There is little uniformity in dealing with absences for weddings or anniversaries.

TABLE 1
Average Number of Days Sick Leave Granted at Full Pay
in Districts with 6,000 or More Enrollment,
by Enrollment, 1968–69

Enrollment	Systems Reporting Sick Leave	Average Number of Days Leave With Full Pay
6,000—11,999	300	11.8
12,000—24,999	147	11.4
25,000—49,999	49	10.9
50,000—99,999	37	11.2
100,000 or more	23	11.5
Totals	556	11.6

MATERNITY LEAVE

Almost all districts grant maternity leaves. However, in the vast majority of them, only teachers who have acquired tenure are eligible. Such practice has been challenged as being discriminatory without justification. The majority of school systems specify a time when a teacher must report her condition and make a formal request for a maternity leave. In most school systems, a teacher is required to report her condition early in her pregnancy (the third or fourth month). In others, a teacher is required to request a leave as soon as she is aware of pregnancy. In still other systems, there is no deadline for applying for a leave.

Practices regarding the length of time a teacher may continue on duty after she becomes pregnant vary considerably. The most commonly followed practice is to allow the teacher to continue through the fifth or sixth month of pregnancy. In a few systems, the principal is given the prerogative of recommending the appropriate time for the leave to become effective, depending on the health condition of the teacher. If pregnancy causes absenteeism, maternity leave becomes effective as soon as pregnancy is confirmed. Likewise, if a teacher's effectiveness in class is not impaired by pregnancy, she may continue until the eighth month of pregnancy before her leave begins.

Most school systems are specific about the length of time of a maternity leave. In most systems, a leave is originally granted for one year, but a significant number of systems do permit a teacher to return after her child is three months old. A number of systems leave the decision about the date of return from maternity leave to the physician and/or school officials. Most school systems have policies that provide a leave for a teacher who adopts a child. The length of this absence usually corresponds to that permitted after the birth of a child.

ILLNESS IN THE IMMEDIATE FAMILY

The granting of leave for family illness is widely practiced by school systems throughout the country. It is also the general practice of allowing the entire year's allotment of sick leave to be used for family illness. However, some school systems specify that from one to six days of leave at full pay may be used for either illness or death in the immediate family.

RELIGIOUS HOLIDAYS

A leave of absence for religious holidays not observed in the school calendar is granted in most school systems. The most common practice is to allow two to three days with full pay for such leaves. In many systems, days granted for religious holidays are subtracted from a teacher's sick-leave bank or are considered as "personal business" days.

PERSONAL BUSINESS

The practice of granting short-term personal business leaves with full or partial pay is well established in the majority of school systems, especially in large city systems. Although many systems have established a policy that days used as personal business leave are to be deducted from a teacher's sick-leave accumulation, this practice is under fire by teacher-bargaining units. A resolution was adopted at the national convention of the American Federation of Teachers in 1958 urging that five days per year be allowed for this purpose without loss of pay and that these days not be deducted from sick-leave accumulation.

PROFESSIONAL REASONS

Practices for granting leave days for professional reasons were surveyed by the National Education Association in 1965. The summary of their findings appears in the table below.[11]

TABLE 2
Percent of School Systems Granting Leaves of Absence
for Professional Reasons, 1965

		Enrollment		
	100,000 or more	50,000 to 99,999	25,000 to 49,999	Total
Professional study	100.0%	86.8%	85.3%	88.4%
Professional meetings	82.6	92.1	83.8	86.0
Exchange teaching abroad	91.3	81.6	79.4	82.2
Professional organization work	60.9	68.4	69.1	67.4
Visiting other schools	69.6	60.5	66.2	65.1
Paid sabbatical	73.9	63.2	54.5	60.5
Professional organization service (extended leave)	69.6	60.5	57.4	60.5
Department of Defense School	56.5	55.3	63.2	59.7
Research	69.6	50.0	60.3	58.9
Travel	60.9	55.3	60.3	58.9
Exchange teaching in United States	56.5	44.7	57.4	53.5
Work experience	34.8	10.5	14.7	17.7
Number of systems reporting	23	38	68	129

245

Provisions for sabbatical leaves are found in the larger school systems (100,000 or more pupils). An N.E.A. survey of 586 school districts with comprehensive negotiated agreements for the years 1967–68 revealed that 40.5 percent provide for sabbatical leaves.[12] Professional study—formal or independent, or both—is the primary purpose for which sabbatical leave is granted. Many systems also permit a sabbatical for a program of travel and study. A few systems allow such a leave for reasons of health or rest. The minimum sabbatical leave is for one semester and the maximum of consecutive leaves is for two semesters. A few systems do not approve leave for less than two semesters, or one school year.

Seven years of satisfactory teaching is usually one of the requirements for a leave of this type. A few systems require only six years. Although a few systems specify the number of academic credits to be earned during the leave, most systems require only that the application for leave includes a description of the proposed program of study.

In addition to service requirements, most systems list certain other criteria to be considered in approving or rejecting applications for sabbatical leave. Most frequently included is the value of the proposed program to the schools and pupils but also considered in a number of school systems are seniority and the equitable distribution of leaves among grade levels, schools and departments. Age is sometimes a factor. A few systems require a master's degree.

It is rare to find a school system that does not have a fixed policy regarding the number of teachers permitted to take sabbatical leaves during a single semester or a school year. Using a formula of percentage is common practice. The formula used most frequently is one percent of either the total professional staff or the teaching staff only. Some school systems specify a number (rather than a stated percentage) of professoinal employees that may be on sabbatical leave at the same time. In other systems, school size governs the number of sabbatical leaves granted each year. And in other systems, the formula is based on budgeted amounts.

Most systems allow one half of regular salary to teachers on sabbatical leave. Some allow full pay for one semester's leave or half pay for an entire year's leave. A few allow regular salary less the salary of the substitute, or less the minimum for the bachelor's degree. An agreement between the board of education and the organization of school supervisors in New York City in 1969 permitted school supervisors who had accumulated sabbatical leave privileges to take up to one year of sabbatical leave at full pay in lieu of four earned sabbatical leaves at half pay at the time of their retirement. All but a few systems allow full insurance benefits and advancement on the salary schedule as though the teacher had been regularly employed during the sabbatical leave.

Invariably, school systems require a specified period of service immediately following sabbatical leave. Most often, teachers must agree to serve an additional two years. In several systems it is one year. But some require three years of service. Invariably, teachers returning from sabbatical leaves are assured their former, or comparable, positions. It is also common practice to require returning teachers to file reports within a reasonable time following termination of leave.

While some board of education members regard sabbatical leaves as an unnecessary luxury, others who are more farsighted understand the importance of a change in the life of a professional teacher or administrator. It is regrettable that many teachers and administrators never take sabbatical leaves during their professional careers, preferring, often because of inertia, to remain in their usual routine and environment, thereby losing opportunities for professional and personal growth. School personnel administrators might well encourage such individuals to take sabbatical leaves.

A comparatively small percentage of all teachers are able to avail themselves of sabbatical leaves because they cannot live on reduced pay and because they cannot fulfill the service requirements. The following table indicates the distribution of sabbatical leaves according to school size; notice the sharp increase in leaves taken by those who teach in the largest school districts.[13]

TABLE 3
Number of Sabbatical Leaves Granted 1967–68

Enrollment	Number of Teachers	Number of Sabbatical Leaves Granted	Percentage of all Teachers
6,000 to 11,999	121,604	423	.0035
12,000 to 24,999	110,321	367	.0033
25,000 to 49,999	81,128	239	.0029
50,000 to 99,999	141,950	545	.0038
100,000 or more	246,475	4,073	.016
Totals	701,478	5,647	.008

Source: American Federation of Teachers AFT-CIO, *op. cit.*, p. 11.

TERMINAL OR SEVERANCE PAY

Organizations of teachers have sought severance or terminal pay in addition to retirement benefits. This pay is regarded as an aid to the teacher in bridging the gap between full service with full pay and retirement on a pension. It has also been regarded as a sort of bonus for long-term, loyal service with minimum absence from duty. Used to give the teacher an incentive to stay on the job with a minimum of absences, terminal pay is usually based on the unused, accumulated sick-leave bank. The number of school districts granting terminal pay is increasing. In New York City in 1969, the basis for severance pay was unused accumulated sick leave, with

247

TABLE 4
Percent Distribution of Severance or Terminal Pay by Enrollment,
Basis for Qualification, and Method of Payment, 1968–69

	I 100,000 or More		II 50,000– 99,999		III 25,000– 49,999		IV 12,000– 24,999		V 6,000– 11,999		Percent of All Districts Reporting	
Conditions	No.	%	No.	%	No.	%	No.	%	No.	%	No.	%
Granting severance pay	9	37.5	5	12.5	14	29.2	23	15.2	47	15.2	98	17.1
Basis for qualification												(21.9)*
and payment												
1. Years of Service			1	20.0	4	30.7	3	13.0	20	42.4	28	28.4
2. Unused sick leave	7	77.8	1	20.0	5	31.0	14	60.8	21	46.7	48	49.3
3. Both	2	22.2	3	60.0	5	38.5	6	26.1	6	11.5	22	22.4
Method of Payment												
1. Lump sum	9	100.0	5	100.0	13	92.9	21	91.3	43	93.3	91	93.9
2. Other					1	7.1	2	8.7	4	6.7	7	6.1
Not Reporting	1		8		8		1		6		24	4.0

*Weighted average for 1371 systems.

a maximum of one semester at full pay, determined by one day of leave for each two days of unused reserve. The above table indicates the extent of terminal pay plans as reported in a survey of a number of school districts.[14]

PROFESSIONAL ORGANIZATION SERVICE

Long-term leaves of absence for service in a professional organization are permitted by many systems. Since few persons actually have positions that would require such long service, many school systems have never needed a leave policy for this purpose. The usual practice in granting such a leave is to provide no salary at all during the term of leave.

STUDY-AND-TRAVEL LEAVE

It is rare to find a system that does not grant a leave of absence for study, research and travel. Most systems do not pay salaries to teachers on such leaves of absence unless they are taken under sabbatical leave provisions.

EXCHANGE TEACHING

Many teachers prefer to get their travel experiences through exchange teaching. This method insures the teacher of a salary and at the same time provides the home school system with a replacement at little, if any, additional cost. Most systems grant leaves for exchange teaching in foreign countries. Several systems also grant leaves for exchange teaching in the United States. Another method of combining travel with teaching is to become a teacher in an overseas school operated by the Department of Defense. Granting a leave for this purpose is common practice.

248

Court Summons

Most school systems provide a short leave of absence with full pay to answer a court summons. Either court-witness fees are deducted from the teacher's salary or full salary is paid and witness fees are made over to the school system. In many cases, leaves for court appearances are restricted by regulations pertaining to the nature of the summons. Some systems refuse leave with pay if the teacher is the defendant; some refuse leave with pay if the teacher is a litigant or a voluntary witness. A few systems grant leave with pay for a court appearance only if the teacher represents the school board or appears in a case in some way connected with the schools. Leave to answer a court summons is often included in a broad "personal business leave" category. Most systems that grant leaves for court appearances do not indicate the number of days allowed.

Jury Duty

Leave for service on a jury is granted by a large majority of systems. In some states, teachers are exempt by law from this service, but many teachers and other people believe that teachers should not be denied the opportunity to serve on jury duty. Because of the nature of jury duty, most school systems do not stipulate a specific number of days for leave, although a few systems specify from two to ten days. In many systems, jury pay must be given to the school system, and the teacher receives full teaching pay; in other systems, jury pay is deducted from the teacher's regular salary.

Military-Reserve Duty

In most school systems, leave is granted for absence due to military reserve duty. Several systems do not specify the number of days allowed for such leave; however, the number of days granted for such a leave normally ranges from ten to thirty-one.

Emergency Leave

This new type of leave may be given to an employee who has suffered loss of property caused by flood or fire, or loss of dentures or eye glasses or some prosthetic device which would affect the employee's ability to perform his duties.

A summary of prevalent types of short- and long-term leaves of absence for the 1967–68 school year was provided by the National Educational Association's Research Division, which studied 603 comprehensive negotiated agreements, covering some 303,000 professional personnel. Table 5 on page 250 shows the types of leaves most frequently provided in such agreements with full or partial pay.[15]

Statutory Provisions

Most regulations pertaining to leaves of absence for teachers have been adopted by boards of education of local school districts. In many states,

TABLE 5

Comprehensive Agreements Providing
Leaves of Absence with Full or Partial Pay, 1967–68

Reasons for leave	Comprehensive agreements with provision	
	Number	Percent
1	2	3
Short-term leaves		
Sick leave	537*	89.1%
Personal business	412	68.3
Bereavement leave	342	56.7
Jury duty	214	35.5
Family illness	179	29.7
Court summons	168	27.9
School visitations	168	27.9
Educational conferences	143	23.7
Selective service examination	105	17.4
Professional organization meeting	91	15.1
Religious holidays	66	10.9
Graduation exercises	52	8.6
Reserve training	52	8.6
Communicable diseases	46	7.6
General leave, unspecified	24	4.0
Personal legal suit	18	3.0
Weather, flood, etc.	12	2.0
License examination	10	1.7
Medical or dental examination	7	1.2
Long-term leaves		
Sabbatical leave	244	40.5
Extended sick leave	97	16.1
Total comprehensive agreements, 1967–68	603	100.0%

* Five sick-leave provisions were noncumulative: Bloomfield Hills, Mich.; Nankin Mills, Mich.; Anaconda, Mont.; Scituate, Mass.; and Warwick, R.I.

however, legislation sets the specific provisions to which teachers are entitled. In some states, local school systems are free to exceed the benefits guaranteed by statute; in others, the statutes are restrictive.

A survey of statutory provisions dealing with leaves of absence was published by the N.E.A. Research Division in 1966. This compilation is a state-by-state summary of specific statutory provisions for sick leave, maternity leave and sabbatical leave. The information includes all changes through the 1965 legislative year.[16]

EXTRA COMPENSATION FOR SPECIAL ASSIGNMENTS

For many years, teachers voluntarily carried extracurricular activities. When teachers' salaries began to lag behind rises in the cost of living, many teachers sought after-school employment to make up the difference, and volunteers for extracurricular activities were scarce. School districts then

250

TABLE 6
States with Statutory Provisions for
Certain Leaves of Absence for Teachers, 1965

State	Sick leave	Maternity leave	Sabbatical leave	State	Sick leave	Maternity leave	Sabbatical leave
Alabama	X			Michigan	X		X
Alaska	X*		X	Minnesota	X		X
Arizona	X		X	Mississippi	X		X
California	X	X	X	Nebraska	X		X
Connecticut	X			Nevada	X		
Delaware	X	X	X	New Jersey	X		
D. of C.	X	X	X	New York	X		
Florida	X		X	North Carolina	X		
Georgia	X			North Dakota	X		
Hawaii	X		X	Ohio	X		X
Idaho	X			Oklahoma	X		
Illinois	X		X	Oregon	X		
Indiana	X		X	Pennsylvania	X		X
Iowa	X			Tennessee	X	X	X
Kentucky	X	X	X	Vermont	X		
Louisiana	X	X	X	Virginia	X*		
Maine	X		X	Washington	X		X
Maryland	X*			West Virginia	X		
Massachusetts	X		X	Wisconsin	X		

*By state board regulation

went through a period of trying to incorporate extracurricular activities into the regular school day and even hiring teachers to serve during afternoon hours, which of course made team coaching and other after-school assignments compulsory. Such methods have continued but have been supplemented by payments to teachers when normal after-school services cannot be accommodated during the school day.

A study of the American Federation of Teachers Research Division indicated that in the 1968–69 school year 77 percent of reporting districts had a scale of extra compensation for both athletic and nonathletic activities.[17] The most popular nonathletic activities are musical projects, dramatics, school newspaper and yearbook.

GENERAL WORKING CONDITIONS

AUXILIARY STAFF

The teacher shortage revealed the necessity for having differentiated staff assignments. It was recognized that the master teacher should not be used to supervise lunchrooms, hall traffic or yard duty. Auxiliary personnel were engaged to perform those duties, and procedures had to be developed for the use of such personnel during the school day. In recruiting and retaining teachers, an inducement was that there were aides to relieve teachers of nonprofessional duties. The school aides added to the quality of education and increased the professional morale of the teaching staff. The large increase in the number of school aides came after federal funds became available for their use in 1965. Whereas in 1965 there were about 8,000 teacher aides serving in the 382 school districts studied by the Research Division of the A.F.T., there were 37,500 serving in the same districts in 1968–69.[18]

PREPARATION TIME

Teachers' organizations have urged planning or preparation time to be allowed teachers during the school day in order to supplement planning done after school. The goal of A.F.T. units in their bargaining agreements has been to provide a daily planning period for every teacher. If preparation time is given, it more frequently occurs in secondary schools in large school districts. In elementary schools, allowing preparation is more difficult because a teacher generally remains with her class throughout the day. It is of course easier in secondary schools because classes are taught by different teachers each period. On the elementary school level, relief schedules may be developed if special teachers of art, music or health education take complete charge of a class for a while. The following table indicates preparation time in school districts that were studied by the Research Division of the American Federation of Teachers.[19]

TABLE 7

Free Preparation Time, by Grade Division, 1968–69

Number of Hours Per Week	Elementary		Junior High		Senior High		Totals	
	No. of Systems	Average Prep. Time	No. of Systems	Average Prep. Time	No. of Systems	Average Prep. Time	No. of Systems	Average Prep. Time
None	352		174		135		661	
0.1–0.4	30	.34	19	.43	11	.40	60	.38
0.5–2.4	81	1.30	94	1.01	115	1.00	290	1.09
2.5–2.9	43	2.52	11	2.53	9	2.54	63	2.53
3.0–3.4	27	3.10	18	3.25	16	3.20	61	3.17
3.5–3.9	14	3.66	37	3.74	25	3.71	76	3.71
4.0–4.4	10	4.05	55	4.11	59	4.12	124	4.11
4.5–4.9	3	4.50	19	4.56	28	4.55	50	4.55
5.0	28	5.00	150	5.00	175	5.00	353	5.00
Over 5.0	8	6.94	19	7.47	23	7.88	50	7.58
Totals	244	2.49	422	3.63	461	3.73	1,127	3.42

DUTY-FREE LUNCH PERIODS

In many school districts, teachers are required to supervise student lunchrooms or playgrounds during their own lunch periods. The number of teachers in a school thus assigned each day has varied from the total staff to a rotating percentage. Teacher organizations objected that that was detrimental to the health of teachers. By 1969, twelve states legally required school districts to give teachers a duty-free lunch period. Teacher aides can easily assume supervisory service.

Length of School Year and Length of Day

The length of the school year has varied from 175 days to 216 days. Most frequently, 180 days are required, and the average for the 557 school districts studied by the A.F.T. was 189 days.[20] Variations occur in terms of holidays, in teachers' reporting to school several days before the school year begins, and in nonteaching days.

There are also differences in the length of the school day which occur not only among school districts but also within a school district, where elementary school teachers may serve a shorter or longer day than secondary school teachers. Specialists, such as school librarians and social workers, may serve a longer day. In many school districts, teachers are required to go on duty some fifteen minutes before the children arrive and to remain fifteen minutes after school. Teachers' organizations have questioned the need for that and have urged uniformity of hours and service for all teachers.

HEALTH-PROTECTION PROGRAM

Effective teaching demands mental poise, physical stamina and an adequate reserve of energy. Teachers who lack these health qualities are usually unable to carry on a sustained program and are often a serious menace to the health of pupils. Parents and pupils have the right to expect teachers to be in good mental, emotional and physical health, and a school district has the responsibility of providing such conditions and support as will help teachers maintain optimum health.

Administrators of health-protection programs for school employees need to show concern in these specific phases:

1. Preemployment examinations to insure a reasonable level of employee health.
2. Periodic examinations during employment.
3. Examinations upon return to employment after prolonged personal or family illnesses.
4. Free advisory medical service as well as inoculations and emergency treatments.
5. A cooperative program of providing hospital and medical care group-insurance plans.

Preemployment Health Standards

An obligation that every school district owes to its students is to insure that its employees are physically and mentally fit. Many larger school dis-

253

tricts insure that incoming employees are physically and mentally fit by requiring preemployment physical examinations. In some districts, the applicant may have to pay the cost of the physical examination and he may have the right to select his own physician. While many districts assume the cost of the examination, they insist that it be made by the school physician or a physician designated by the district. In some places, the applicant has the option of choosing his own physician and paying for the examination, or he may be examined by the school physician free. In addition, districts require a chest X ray and sight and hearing tests as part of the standard examination. A few districts request that the examining physician recommend any other tests that seem desirable and that he express his opinion concerning how the applicant's health may affect his performance.

In New York City, all new applicants are required to undergo a physical examination given by staff physicians. The Board of Examiners of the New York City school system reported that 17,798 applicants were examined between July 1, 1967, and June 28, 1968. A summary of the unsatisfactory medical cases (about 1.5 percent of those applying) includes rejection for varied reasons. It is interesting to note that the most frequent reason for rejection was unsatisfactory mental health. (See Table 8.)

TABLE 8

Psychoneurosis	110	Epilepsy	1
Obesity	81	Anemia	1
Hypertension	34	Seizure Disorders	1
Defective Vision		Skin Lesions	1
(Eye Disease)	18	Carcinoma	1
Cardiac Disease	13	Inguinal Hernia	1
Defective Hearing	2	Bilateral and	
Diabetes	6	Inguinal Hernia	1
Ulcers	2	Congenital Vascular	
Pilonidal Cyst	2	Intestinal Anomaly	
		with recurrent bleeding	1

Of the above numbers, 49 applicants were found NOT FIT FOR MORE THAN ONE REASON.

PERIODIC EXAMINATIONS

Periodic health examinations are highly recommended in order to maintain personnel health standards and to contribute to good instruction. As Van Zwoll suggests, postemployment examinations every three or four years should be used to detect employees' health problems in their early stages, not to screen employees for dismissal.[21] Castetter suggests that such a systematic health program should be accompanied by prescribed administrative actions for dealing with individuals who are found to need medical attention or who are sources of contagion and for dealing with employees returning after sick leaves.[22]

254

School employees look at health and hospitalization insurance as one of their most important benefits. The practices followed by major businesses and industry once again set the pattern for school systems to follow. Health and hospitalization insurance is expensive, which is why school systems were slow to pay for it. Many systems have three phases of participation.

1. Establishment of a group plan in which the employee pays the full premium at reduced group rates.
2. Joint payment of the premium by the school system and the employee.
3. Full payment of the premium by the employer.

Generally speaking, large urban systems now pay the full premium for family health and hospitalization insurance for their employees. Many systems also provide major medical (extended coverage) benefits.

Collective bargaining has played a major role in providing school employees with greater insurance coverage. Almost without exception, school systems that must negotiate salaries and fringe benefits with teachers' organizations are forced into providing insurance coverage that includes even dental and optical benefits and blood banks. For example, the 1965 agreement negotiated between the United Federation of Teachers and the Board of Education of New York City included a "supplemental benefits" clause under which the Board agreed to pay $140 per teacher per year "for the purpose of making available for each day school teacher supplemental welfare benefits under a plan to be devised and established jointly by representatives of the Union and of the Board." For 50,000 teachers it represented some $7,000,000 annually going into a welfare fund to be managed chiefly by union officials. Their 1969 contract increased the contribution to $205 per teacher. Supplemental benefits included such items as expanded medical and hospital care, prescription drugs, dental care, optical care, death benefits, major medical insurance, disability benefits and college scholarships. While it is true that financing expanded insurance benefits presents strained budgetary problems, offering them has proved to be an essential asset in competing with business and industry for teachers.

LIFE INSURANCE

Various forms of group insurance are increasingly being provided to public school personnel throughout the country. A survey conducted by N.E.A. in 1964 found that over a fourth of all school systems with enrollments of 12,000 or more pupils now pay part or all of the cost of group life insurance for teachers.[23] Since the results of the 1964 survey were published, this practice has become more the rule than the exception.

Group life insurance is intended to provide the individuals in a group with additional low cost insurance during their working years. It is not intended to meet all life insurance needs, but only to supplement the regular life insurance policies of an individual.

Though eligibility requirements differ slightly among companies that write group life policies, Dingman found that policies generally call for the enrollment of between 70 and 75 percent of the full-time certified personnel on active duty.[24] In school districts that offer employees this type of insurance, the amount of coverage differs. A recommended standard is an amount equal to at least one year's salary, to the nearest thousand; that is, an employee earning $6,400 would be entitled to a $6,000 policy; one earning $6,600, to a $7,000 policy.

Dingman also suggests that group life insurance is a powerful morale builder in business, industry and education. Employer and employee benefit because a group life insurance plan:

1. Can provide greater protection for dependents per dollar of cost than any other benefit.
2. Extends coverage to a large number of persons who might not qualify for individual life insurance because they are physically substandard.
3. Provides tax advantages for the beneficiary because death benefits paid under group insurance are not taxable to the beneficiary under existing federal income tax laws.
4. Provides tax advantages to the employee, if the employer (school) pays the premium, because the amount of that premium is not reported as taxable income to either federal or state governments.
5. Buys greater protection for beneficiaries than is possible through a tax-sheltered annuity, which does not provide insurance. In case the school employee dies prematurely, the beneficiary receives only the cash value of a tax-sheltered annuity. Under a group life insurance plan, the beneficiary receives the value of the policy either in a lump sum or in installments.
6. Adds to the feeling of security and stability that a teacher requires if he is to devote all his energy to teaching.

The chief disadvantage of group life insurance is that it is term insurance, providing protection during a contracted period only (usually one-year on a renewal plan). It usually does not have cash, loan or paid-up values, and it may be canceled if an employee retires or terminates his employment, though most group policies may be converted to an individual policy at a higher premium rate.

TENURE FOR TEACHERS

N.E.A.'s 1960 survey of tenure provisions provided by various states for professional staff, revealed that 86 percent of all states have tenure provisions.[25] Since 1909, when the first statewide tenure law was enacted in New Jersey, tenure for teachers has been a controversial issue in public

256

school education. Since its inception, the purpose of tenure legislation has been to protect capable teachers against unfair dismissal. In many states, however, the generally accepted purpose of tenure has been imperfectly translated into statutes and has provided job security for incompetent as well as competent teachers.

The heart of tenure legislation lies in dismissal procedures. Thus far it has been impossible to draft a law that protects competent teachers and also makes it easy to dismiss the incompetent. To believe that a teacher is incompetent is one thing. To prove it to the satisfaction of boards of education, teachers' organizations and state tenure commissions or legal authorities is extremely difficult. Tenure statutes usually include provisions and procedures for dismissal for incompetence, immorality, neglect of duty, unprofessional conduct, insubordination and physical incapacity. Some laws also include "for good and just cause" as a reason for dismissal. In recent years, the matter of tenure has again become a highly controversial issue as leaders of community groups have demanded greater accountability by teachers. In some situations, teachers and principals have been subjected to harassment and forced to resign. It has all led to nonharassment clauses in negotiated agreements that provide special hearings for teachers who complain of being intimidated. Procedures for dismissal are consistently included in tenure legislation, and they normally require that the board of education officially notify the teacher that his or her services are unsatisfactory and that dismissal is imminent. The teacher is then provided with an opportunity for a hearing before the board with benefit of counsel and witnesses. Appeals of the board's decision may be made to the state tenure commission, to a state commissioner of education or another legal authority, and then to the courts.

Tenure legislation also stipulates the procedures to be followed in the dismissal of teachers when a staff must be reduced because of lack of enrollment or finances. Usually, seniority prevails and tenured teachers are dismissed in reverse order of employment. In the event of subsequent reemployment, length of service is the criterion for the order of hiring.

Tenure for administrators is usually tied to tenure for teachers. The universal practice followed in many administrative assignments is to grant tenure only for a teaching capacity, not for administrative responsibility, but many cities grant tenure in administrative assignments such as principalships and assistant principalships.

Because of the difficulties experienced by school personnel administrators and boards of education in dismissing tenured teachers judged to be unfit, increased attention needs to be focused on the service of the teacher during the normal probationary period preceding the granting of tenure. Efforts must be increased to assure a fair teaching program, adequate supervisory and consultative assistance, opportunity to succeed in more than one situation if difficulties arise in the initial assignment, and a fair evaluation.

If evaluators have substantial doubt that a teacher is or can be effective in his or her assignment, dismissal should occur before tenure privileges are granted. What to do about tenured teachers who have served well but who, because of advancing age or other factors, have lost their effectiveness is a constant problem to personnel administrators. Changes of assignment, leaves of absence, and retirement are the most common approaches to this problem. A better approach would be to institute more effective supervision to prevent deterioration.

RETIREMENT

Retirement-benefit plans for teachers exist in all states. It is necessary for the personnel administrator to familiarize himself with the retirement-benefit plan for staff personnel that has been enacted in his state or school system so that he or someone on his staff can counsel all other staff members. The personnel administrator must be cautious about rendering specific advice to individuals because that is more properly the job of officials of the retirement board. To familiarize interested school personnel with eligibility requirements, most state retirement boards have prepared booklets that clearly define requirements and the procedures to be followed. Informative and practical, they include the answers to the most commonly asked questions:

1. Will I receive credit for military service?
2. How do I apply for a retirement allowance?
3. What is the protection for my dependents?
4. If I work after retirement, how will it affect my retirement allowance?

In recent years, the federal government has contemplated entering the teacher-retirement picture. A bill was introduced in 1969 to make it possible for experienced teachers to take positions in different states without loss of retirement money by granting retirement allowances to states.

FINANCING RETIREMENT BENEFITS

With the exception of Delaware, the retirement benefits in all state-wide retirement systems for teachers are financed jointly by teacher and public contributions. The pension plan in Delaware is financed entirely by the State. Of interest is the New York State plan, which required local districts to pay out of local school funds not only the employer's share toward retirement but also the first five percentage points of each member's contribution to the state Teacher's Retirement System. In effect, this system reduces a teacher's retirement contribution, increases his take-home pay, and leaves the retirement allowance unchanged. Although the school district must assume the member's contribution to the extent required, the teacher may elect to forego the bigger pay check and deposit the extra money he would receive with the retirement system for increased allowance

258

at retirement. In recent years, teachers' organizations, particularly in large cities such as New York, have successfully pressed school districts to assume an increased proportion of retirement contributions.

BENEFIT FORMULAS AND AGE REQUIREMENTS

In a study completed in 1964, N.E.A. found that the most commonly used formula in computing retirement allowance is the fixed benefit plan.[26] The allowance is usually computed as a percentage or fraction of the final average salary multiplied by the total number of years of service credit. Two other less commonly used plans provide for an annuity based on the member's contributions. One plan adds a pension derived from public funds; the second plan includes a matching pension from the state. In many school districts, an individual may exercise various options on retirement. He may choose a maximum retirement allowance, if he has no dependents, or he may choose a reduced retirement allowance, making financial provision for dependents who may outlive him. The required length of service before retirement has been decreasing. Whereas 35 years of service were once required in many school districts, it has been reduced to 30 and 25. Seventy was the usual age for retirement, but age, too, has been decreased to require or permit retirement at age 65, 60, 55 or 50. In New York City, staff members who are below retirement age but who have completed a stated length of service are permitted to retire with retirement payments deferred until they have reached authorized retirement age. That has been called a "vesting" right. In some school districts, school staff are permitted to elect a variable annuity retirement allowance instead of a fixed sum. Under the variable annuity plan, they may elect to have all or part of their contributions invested in securities through a mutual fund. When they retire, their retirement allowance is based in part upon the value of the securities after retirement. Since experience has shown that, over the long run, securities tend to increase in value, their retirement income is expected to be greater than it would be under a fixed payment plan.

DISABILITY RETIREMENT

All states except Iowa provide disability retirement in the event that a teacher is unable to carry on regular teaching duties for physical or mental reasons. Ten years of service are usually required, but some states require as many as fifteen years or as few as five.

Generally speaking, teacher-retirement laws have continually improved since 1950. One of the most pressing concerns is to find a way to maintain the purchasing power of the original annuity of the retired teacher, and it is likely to receive increased attention in future years. In some states, supplements to pensions have been voted by state legislatures to aid retired teachers whose pensions are barely at subsistence levels, since they retired in years when salaries were low.

Some districts, with the approval of the United States Internal Revenue Service, have arranged for school personnel to invest part of their salary in annuities that are not taxed as current salary. The annuity, or income from it, is paid to the staff member on his retirement or at a future time. The advantage to him is that he is likely to be taxed less if he receives the money from annuities after retirement or when his income is lower. The disadvantage is that he is deprived of current use of his full salary. Some difficulties are also posed if he leaves the school system or wishes to withdraw and use the money from his sheltered annuity account.

SOCIAL AND RECREATIONAL PROGRAMS

In surveying the practices followed in government and in private enterprise, Van Zwoll found that attention is given to social and recreational programs which have implications for mental health, social adjustment, physical fitness and esprit de corps. School systems also make some provisions along these lines.[27]

There is some question about the need for an elaborate program of social and recreational activities for school personnel. The small school district does not generally need such a program because school employees are usually included in the life of the community. Larger school districts have available such a range of cultural, recreational and social activities and opportunities that it is ordinarily unnecessary for the school system to organize such programs. Besides, teachers' organizations usually do that. Nevertheless, it would seem advisable for the school administration and its personnel division to organize and make available for those who wish to participate in them such programs as can be adequately supported. The personnel office should merely avoid setting up coercive programs that school employees would regard as oppressive and demanding of time that they would prefer to use in other ways.

HOUSING ASSISTANCE

The problem of providing housing assistance for school personnel seems to vary greatly with the times and location of the district. Van Zwoll reminds us that for many years school districts of the one-room-school variety provided a house adjacent to the school for the teacher because of general unavailability of convenient housing, the frequent impassability of roads, low salaries, and the need to provide housing or to suffer the consequence of having a school with no teacher. Van Zwoll also found that for several years following World War II the general housing shortage in the United States was such that even city school districts found it necessary to supplement improved teachers' salaries with apartments or other housing to be able to attract teachers to their systems.[28] For many school systems today, the shortage or soaring rentals of suitable housing often inhibits them from attracting and retaining quality teachers. School systems that accept some of the responsibility for assisting teachers in locating housing will experience less difficulty in attracting and retaining personnel.

THE ROLE OF THE PERSONNEL ADMINISTRATOR

A personnel administrator has two basic responsibilities in administering a benefits program. First, he must be knowledgeable of the benefits programs in surrounding districts so that his district can compete for personnel. Periodic surveys conducted by the American Federation of Teachers and the National Education Association are helpful sources of information on national and state scales. Local trends often are best learned through timely telephone or mail surveys.

Secondly, the personnel administrator has the full responsibility for keeping employees informed about available benefits and retirement programs. Effective informational programs include:

1. Preparation of a benefits brochure that describes each provision. Whenever possible, the brochure should be developed cooperatively by the personnel office and the teachers' organization.
2. Review of the benefits brochure by building administrators and program supervisors or directors, who often are in much closer contact with personnel than is the personnel director and who therefore are in a position to explain the value of benefits to staff members.

Most retirement plans are administered at the state level, but the largest metropolitan systems maintain their own programs. Regardless of the level at which the program is administered, brochures should be available in the personnel office and should be distributed to every employee who is approaching retirement.

12 PERSONNEL IN-SERVICE DEVELOPMENT

GENERAL STATEMENT

In-service education looms large as a personnel function in every school system. It is increasingly being assigned to the personnel administrator, who is expected to plan, develop, initiate, coordinate, supervise and evaluate a systemwide program. Education courses completed by a newly appointed teacher, usually as an undergraduate, are the foundation upon which he builds as he works with children in the classroom. But as he continues in service he encounters new problems or sees old ones from a different viewpoint. He may need assistance in solving new problems or in thinking through developing concepts. It is generally recognized that great growth in teaching ability takes place during the first few years of service. It is for that reason many authorities believe a fifth year of education credits is desirable for teachers, credits to be pursued during the first few years on the job. Then there are teachers of longer experience who have adopted fixed patterns of performance and who would benefit from the stimulation of new ideas, new approaches and experimentation. In-service education for teachers is paralleled in other professions where a professional attends refresher courses, lectures and meetings, and when he reads the professional literature. Not to do so is to fall behind the times and to attenuate the effectiveness of services rendered. Business and industry have realized the values of in-service education and are increasingly making arrangements with colleges and private consultants to provide developmental programs for their staff members.

Probably the most important component of all these programs is the willingness of staff members to participate in in-service programs. Results would be minimal if programs were forced upon individuals, which is why every aspect of an in-service program must be a shared enterprise between the school staff and the personnel administrator. The purpose of this chapter is to provide the school personnel administrator with a framework for making decisions concerning the many facets of in-service education. The chapter is concerned mostly with systematic, planned programs; numerous haphazard, unplanned events can of course promote personnel growth, too.

A DEFINITION OF IN-SERVICE EDUCATION

The term "in-service education" is commonly used to denote planned efforts to promote the professional growth and development of school personnel. "In-service education" and "in-service training" are often used interchangeably, but differences do exist between them, of which Glaser cites two: (1) specificity of the behavioral end products and (2) minimizing vs. maximizing individual differences. Training implies greater specificity (e.g., helping teachers to learn how to demonstrate to pupils in the first grade which materials a magnet attracts) and greater uniformity of behavior (e.g., teaching teachers how to line up pupils in the classroom). Education implies creating end products that are not highly specified (e.g., helping teachers learn to try out alternate ways of teaching about magnets) and maximizing individual differences (e.g., helping teachers to work most effectively by using their own styles of teaching).[1] The concept of in-service education implies greater sharing by the personnel involved in the planning and development of the program than does in-service training. Obviously, many professional growth-and-development programs include aspects of training and of education.

In-service education is, more than anything else, directed toward and concerned with the functioning of the individual—the teacher, principal, supervisor and others—in contrast with concern that is focused upon curriculum, materials or organization. It is based on the assumption that the human being is the key element in the educational process.

NEED FOR IN-SERVICE EDUCATION

A multitude of forces is operating now, requiring increased attention to the in-service education of personnel in the nation's schools.

1. An unduly large number of teachers are poorly or dissimilarly educated. "In June 1965 the NEA Research Division estimated that 15.7 percent of the elementary school teachers had less than four years of college." [2]

2. There has been a rapid increase in and reinterpretation of knowledge, making obsolete much of what teachers and other school personnel learned only a few years ago. Many changes in the physical sciences and mathematics are obvious, but all other disciplines have grown, too.

3. New instructional techniques have been developed of which many

educators are unaware (e.g., computer assisted instruction and use of teacher aides).

4. New and recently developed instructional media, language laboratories, teaching machines, computers and television (open and closed-circuit and videotapes) require new ways of viewing administration, supervision, teaching and learning in the school setting.

5. The failure of new, supposedly "teacher-proof," curricula has reinforced the notion that the best designed and produced curricula founder in the hands of unconvinced, incompetent or shackled teachers, supervisors and administrators.

6. Recently developed organizational patterns such as nongraded programs are being implemented in schools around the nation.

7. New insights into the nature of teaching are being generated as a result of research on teacher behavior in the classroom.[3]

8. The blame for the unsatisfactory achievement of disadvantaged pupils, particularly Negro and Spanish-speaking children, and of other pupils is increasingly being placed upon school personnel who, it is believed, are often ill-equipped in attitude and in skills to help those students; in short, many parents and citizens are rejecting the view that pupils' failures are caused by "deprivation" and poor home life. Rightly or wrongly, they feel the schools are cheating their children.

9. "In view of a mounting, a priori, minority antagonism to white teachers, the problems of teacher training are obvious. We are called upon to prepare teachers to enter classrooms where the students are anti-social, anti-establishment, and anti-whitey," Fantini has stated.[4]

10. The realization by the lay public that approximately three-quarters of current school expenditures are for salaries has caused it to focus its attention on how personnel perform.

11. Pressing cultural forces in our society, increased desire for involvement in decision making, refusal to accept second-class citizenship by large portions of our population, a burgeoning school population, more sophisticated and alert students, and rapidly changing values concerning what life should be like in America, the relationship between the sexes, greater pluralism and diversity are challenging educators to face issues they have seldom encountered with such directness.

12. Increased use of a variety of personnel—teacher aides, auxiliaries, technicians, volunteers—in a move toward differentiated staffing patterns requires new patterns of operations for administrators, supervisors and teachers.

13. The attempt to humanize the school, to view the school as facilitating learning and the emotional and social growth of students.

14. A growing feeling that school systems are obligated to provide for the professional growth of school personnel.

15. A gnawing fear that, if school systems do not provide in-service education, then nonschool and at times even private agencies which may be less qualified, will appropriate the responsibility.

THE TARGET POPULATION

All persons employed by a school system are potential participants in in-service educational programs. Although administrators usually design programs of in-service education for teachers and classified personnel, they must be prepared to involve themselves in growth programs. The American Association of School Administrators noted: "Without easily accessible opportunities for school administrators to engage in vigorous study and discussion of educational problems and issues—to engage in an in-service program through which they can continuously grow and develop—watching rather than doing could very well characterize the leadership of the schools." [5]

The functions of teachers, principals, assistant principals, subject supervisors, consultants, audiovisual and laboratory technicians, auxiliaries, school secretaries, custodians and bus drivers are sufficiently interdependent to affect the operation of the whole school system. Each group should be considered in developing a program of in-service training or education.

PURPOSES OF IN-SERVICE EDUCATION

A National Education Association Research Division study found that, at least for teachers, in-service education is aimed at (1) eliminating deficiencies in teachers' preparation, (2) assisting those who are new in a school and those who are undertaking a new level or field of work, and (3) promoting the continuous improvement of teachers and teaching. [6] The Department of Elementary School Principals proposes that the objectives of in-service education for principals should be continued learning, remedial assistance, keeping pace with change, and increased efficiency. [7]

Jackson argues that in-service education should move away from the "defect" conception of in-service educational goals, that is, the need to repair defects in the functioning of administrators, teachers and others. Referring to teachers, he describes this approach: "It begins with a judgment of weakness, usually diagnosed by an outsider, and proceeds to suggest a remedy for correcting that weakness, usually through a training program designed to change specific aspects of the teacher's behavior in the classroom." [8] He believes instead that striving for greater fulfillment as a practitioner should characterize the professional's desire for growth. "These, then, are the central goals of in-service training from a 'growth' perspective: to help the teacher become progressively more sensitive to what is happening in his classroom and to support his efforts to improve on what he is doing." [9] The same might be applied to other personnel.

Since in-service education implies helping people change, it is with the process of change that those designing growth programs, including personnel administrators, must be concerned. As the first step in stimulating change, the personnel administrator might consider creating in other

265

professionals an awareness of need or a dissatisfaction with present ways of working. The personnel administrator might at least be expected to recognize and take advantage of present discontent. In summary, the principal purpose of in-service education is to encourage a desire to improve, a receptivity to change, a willingness to break inertia, while at the same time assisting the individual to become a more competent, fully functioning teacher and person.

ASCERTAINING NEEDS

In-service educational programs cannot be designed or planned unless one knows what training needs have to be met. Yet systematic, comprehensive programs of collecting, analyzing, interpreting and disseminating information about in-service educational needs are rare.

Clearly, the needs of individuals and groups must be examined from numerous viewpoints. For example, what a specific group of teachers in a local school district needs in the way of in-service education requires collection of data from their administrators and supervisors, parents and pupils, the teachers themselves, local professional groups such as branches of the N.E.A. or the A.F.T., and on-going record keeping (e.g., test results).

A number of techniques are available for determining training needs: performance appraisals, school surveys, personnel statistics, opinion surveys, requests by administrative personnel, examination of personnel changes, and individual and group conferences.

The personnel administrator might avail himself of the services of outsiders to assist him in diagnosing situations. Caldwell suggests that regularly assigned personnel should conduct surveys and assist in determining training needs, although outsiders, usually university consultants, may be used to plan for and train a survey staff, to analyze difficulties, to provide new insight, and to serve as intermediaries in sensitive areas.[10]

There is some question, however, whether or not administrators, who are rating officers, can really analyze the problems that personnel under their supervision encounter. The climate prevalent in individual school systems always influences how accurate that observation is. In every school system, prospective participants in in-service educational programs should try to identify and understand their own needs, which is an almost certain method of securing commitment to an effort to promote change or growth.

Allen's suggestion concerning the determination of teachers' needs is pertinent to all school personnel: "In brief, we need to know what kinds of teachers require what kinds of experiences in what orders and at what times in order to help them meet given performance criteria." [11] The personnel administrator should be aware of his responsibility for planning and designing procedures to accomplish that objective, particularly in the light of incessant demands for accountable personnel.

266

RESPONSIBILITY FOR IN-SERVICE EDUCATION

Designing and implementing in-service education is a shared responsibility of school systems, colleges and universities, professional associations, state departments of education, educational laboratories and centers, and sometimes even private agencies and organizations. Nevertheless, the primary responsibility for in-service education must lie with the school system: "the employing district, because of its direct responsibility for instructional programs for children, must assume the primary role in planning and programming the in-service period of a teacher's growth." [12] Ladd reiterates this view when he notes that

> "despite any claims college people may make, and despite what designers of certification and salary regulations decide, college credit studies will never be able to do the central job of continuing education. The central role is the school system's role as we have outlined. The college's role is to assist the school with noncredit services and to be available with appropriate credit-carrying academic work whenever the teacher . . . is ready for knowledge in chunks." [13]

Colleges have an additional role in that they must prepare beginning teachers to participate effectively in in-service educational programs or else much effort must be expended on developing desirable attitudes toward engaging in such programs. Ideally, every teacher should be concerned about his individual growth, but the organization of facilities and programs must be the responsibility of appropriate officials and organizations.

Within the school system itself, primary responsibility for providing opportunities for professional growth resides with administrators, often personnel administrators. The N.E.A. states it this way: "All staff members may be given the opportunity to participate to a certain degree in many arrangements. Final responsibility, however, rests with the school administrator and, in some cases, with the board of education." [14] Administrators, according to much of the literature, must create a climate in which teachers feel free to admit and discuss professional problems and needs and which allows them to eliminate their deficiencies and strengthen their areas of competence. The administrator, the principal, the superintendent, or the personnel administrator is responsible for facilitating and coordinating in-service education.

Teachers and other school personnel should, of course, share the responsibility for in-service education, at least in the planning and evaluation stages. But there must be clear description of the boundaries of participation and the decision-making powers that teachers, supervisors and others should have. Conflict results when such boundaries become ambiguous.

267

Psychological, social and administrative barriers to good in-service educational programs can be countered by incentives to encourage personnel to participate in growth programs. Two kinds of incentives can be presented for discussion: intrinsic and extrinsic.

Most people, including school personnel, wish to grow in competence, to gain self-esteem and to see constructive purpose and achievement in their work. In-service educational programs, when seen by personnel as relevant to improving their competence, are eagerly sought after. Obviously, programs that meet the needs of people are their own motivation. For example, a workshop for elementary school principals who work in a middle-sized city with a decaying inner city and transient Negro and Spanish-speaking populations would be irrelevant if it were not designed and planned to assist principals to cope with growing parent and community pressures for participation in the school program.

Extrinsic incentives for engaging in in-service education are common in many school systems. These motivating factors can be organized into four categories: (1) professional considerations, (2) administrative and supervisory encouragement, (3) money, and (4) time.

Professional considerations operate when matters such as promotions and tenure arise. Teachers and others are often receptive to professional growth programs when it is made clear that active participation in these programs demonstrates the devotion (extra time and energy) considered essential to rising in the school hierarchy. Of course, it is hoped also that they will become more competent professionals. Certification provisions in many states require some categories of personnel, usually teachers, to participate in in-service educational programs during their first few years of work if they wish to be permanently certified.

Administrative and supervisory encouragement is common and particularly effective when the same administrators and supervisors are in positions to affect the quality of the mental satisfaction of and the tangible rewards for those who are lower in the hierarchy of the school system. The school principal is closest to this criterion, but the personnel administrator is in a key position to develop plans, publicity and recruitment efforts to stimulate participation in professional growth programs. Specifically, he may be able to identify those principals who offer little encouragement for participation in in-service education; he may develop a work conference in order to disseminate information about various programs to principals.

Money is a third and decisive incentive. Monetary rewards or the lack of them can be either direct or indirect.

It is now common to provide stipends for educational personnel who participate in in-service educational programs after normal school hours. Typically, training programs supported by federal funds have followed the pattern indicated in a U.S. Office of Education publication: "Educational personnel attending projects of a short-term duration are eligible to receive, upon application, $75 a week and $15 per dependent or a pro-rata share if the project is part-time in nature, or a lesser sum as determined by the institution or agency." [15]

The rationale for paying personnel to engage in job-related training programs is that teachers and others should not be called upon to take a loss in income because they engage in programs that ultimately benefit the school system. In some communities, a compromise solution has been developed by providing remunerative part-time positions during the summer for personnel while they participate in training programs.

Indirect monetary incentives for participation in in-service education abound. The Research Division of the National Education Association in its survey of salary schedules for classroom teachers noted that nearly a third of all school systems of 25,000 or more enrollment require teachers to show evidence of professional growth at certain intervals in order to earn regular salary increments.[16] That refers, of course, to movement on a vertical scale. Teachers and other personnel often move horizontally to higher salaries through additional training or degrees. As a type of indirect monetary incentive, free tuition at nearby colleges and universities is commonly used in large city school systems (those with over 12,000 enrollment), where personnel administrators are responsible for evaluating professional growth activities 44 percent of the time.[17]

There seems to be so little time that it has become the fourth key factor in pursuing in-service education. Every time slot has been used: immediately after school, in the evening, before school, on weekends and holidays, and during vacation periods. Strangely enough, few school systems (only about 10 percent) give teachers time off during the regular school day to pursue professional growth requirements.[18] The trend, however, with differentiated staffing policies growing in favor, seems to be toward including in-service education as part of the regular school day, perhaps of an extended school day. Some school systems, at this time, devote a number of afternoons from 1:00 to 3:00 p.m. every month to professional growth programs. But they are not numerous.

The personnel administrator should most likely develop a mixture of extrinsic incentives in addition to promoting intrinsic motivation on the part of personnel to grow on the job. He might consider using contract bargaining, or negotiating, to insure that in-service educational programs are financially supported and legally enforceable. An example from the agreement between the New York City Board of Education and the United Federation of Teachers illustrates this concept: "All newly appointed teachers who have not had previous professional employment as teachers will be required to participate in an after-school teacher-training program for a period of 28 weeks during the course of a school year. Such participation is not to exceed two hours per week over a period of not more than fourteen weeks in each of the Fall and Spring terms." [19] Perhaps a long-range, professional growth plan developed by each person in a school system in cooperation with a colleague, usually a supervisor, would provide the intrinsic motivation necessary for real growth.

ORGANIZATION OF AN IN-SERVICE EDUCATIONAL PROGRAM

A study of the organization of in-service educational programs in 145 local school systems in 1957 indicated that over 50 percent of the programs utilized a centrally coordinated approach.[20] It allowed central and local initiative and coordination of systemwide activities. Eighteen percent of the programs were centralized; 26 percent were decentralized. With the nationwide trend to decentralize school districts within larger school districts, it is likely that centrally coordinated and decentralized programs will increase in number. Advantages and limitations of each approach depend upon the resources available in particular school districts and cities and the history of the agencies involved.

The possibility is, however, that what really counts is not the overall organization of in-service education but the internal operation of individual programs, e.g., the leadership developed and the use of problem-solving and other effective techniques. In effect, a fluid organization reflecting the interests and needs of educational personnel is what is called for. For example, short-term, single school workshops may be conducted to help teachers to become adept at diagnosing children's learning needs. A district-wide, task-oriented, laboratory-training program for principals might be conducted just before school opens in September in the field of school-parent-community relations. A school district might use television to conduct a citywide program to help all school secretarial personnel to operate more effectively vis-à-vis teachers, supervisors and parents. In short, a multifaceted program is developed. Provision for some centralization allows for the establishment of expensive, multimedia teacher-training and learning centers for use on a citywide or districtwide basis. On the other hand, only school personnel can really point out the training needs of educational personnel.

The personnel administrator, in developing an organization for in-service education, might well consider the dimensions of organizational health suggested by Miles: (1) goal focus, (2) adequacy of communication, (3) optimum power equalization, (4) resource utilization, (5) cohesion, (6) morale, (7) innovation, (8) autonomy, (9) adaptation and (10) adequacy of problem solving.[21] The success of any efforts to change depend on the health of not only the entire school district but also the in-service organization.

PROGRAMING

An implied aim of in-service education is to reduce the element of chance in staff development. Sporadic, transient, unplanned events may

270

help a person to grow, but they may also lend little or no direction, sequence or relevance to his job performance.

Developing effective curricula for in-service education requires considerable planning. In designing a conceptual framework for in-service teacher education, Edmonds et al. suggest that it might consist of a well-defined curriculum of studies in [22]:

> Understanding of role of school
> Understanding of curriculum
> Understanding of human growth
> Understanding of "self" and "others"
> Understanding of teacher methods
> Understanding of materials
> Skills in communication
> Skills in helping others in problem solving
> Skills in problem solving
> Skills in group process

It would be impractical here to prescribe a program of in-service education for a particular school district. It is possible, though, to suggest characteristics for the curriculum of an effective program. It should be:

1. Individualized
2. Personal
3. Process oriented
4. Performance oriented
5. Relevant
6. Experimental in content and format
7. Developmental and diagnostic
8. Balanced
9. Synchronized and integrated
10. Changing
11. Group- and individual-learning oriented
12. Means oriented

The program must be individualized, for learning is an individual matter and no two persons are the same. The personnel administrator might consider, for example, in what ways individual teachers feel they are being helped to function more competently in their own situations. Specifically, an in-service program might be designed to develop teachers' research skills so that they could experiment with various teaching techniques in their own classrooms. However, each teacher would decide the nature of his own responsibilities. Individualization, of course, implies a variety of programs. The fact is that no one program can meet the needs of all groups.

It should be personal in that it should deal with affective as well as cognitive aspects of learning. If changed behavior is expected as a result of in-service education, the feelings and values of trainees must be of utmost

271

concern to the personnel administrator in his efforts to help people to change.

It should be process oriented, for people learn best about solving problems when they actually engage in their solution. One of the powerful appeals of guided research in in-service educational programs is that it promotes the growth of individuals as they attempt to solve problems important to them. It must assist personnel to develop skills, knowledge and attitudes to help them to continually learn on their own.

It should be performance oriented, emphasizing behavioral objectives. For example, an in-service program designed to improve the quality of administrator-community, organizational relations might be concerned with the specifics of preparing written communications intended for different community organizations. The program would be evaluated on the basis of how few misunderstandings there are between the participating administrators and selected organizations.

The program should be relevant to the needs of trainees. For example, teachers, supervisors and administrators need to have a thorough understanding of the background and the cultural and social life of children and parents with whom they are working. Specifically, in-service education must help teachers and others to develop such an understanding if they are to meet the challenge of parental and community expectations, particularly the changed expectations in disadvantaged communities—Negro, Mexican, Puerto Rican or Appalachian. Yet in-service education programs cannot be limited only to what is relevant to today's teachers' needs, for what is relevant today may be irrelevant tomorrow as schools, pupils and society change. Programs should incorporate a vision and a rationale for operating now and in the future to improve the quality of education.

The program should be both diagnostic and developmental, based upon principles of learning and teaching. It should provide participants with opportunities to analyze their performance (such as by viewing videotapes of teaching a group of children or leading a conference of parents and teachers). Utilizing such analyses, individuals should be helped to solve their own professional problems, to move from one level of performance to a higher level.

The program should be balanced between generalized and specialized learning experiences and between content and method as it applies to teachers. The roles, responsibilities, functions and needs of individual participants influence the direction of the balanced program. For example, auxiliaries, or paraprofessionals, who have been on the job for a year and who have received some general training might be ready for specialized training in the operation and care of audiovisual equipment or in the ways of tutoring a child in one phase of phonics.

The in-service educational program is one part of a concerted effort to improve the quality of education in a specific school or school district. It should be synchronized and integrated with supervisory and curriculum-development processes so that all complement and supplement one another.

272

For example, a program in science newly introduced in a school's primary grades probably will require increased supervisory effort and an in-service educational program in the form of a workshop or short-term institute for teachers. The in-service program must be articulated with the pre-service training that personnel have received, an ideal which has seldom been considered.

In-service education should be continually in a process of change. Society, schools, pupils, school personnel and curriculum are in flux. Change is therefore essential in in-service education if it is to serve changing needs.

It was noted earlier that in-service education should be individualized, both in individual and in group activities. The latter is particularly important if consensus and commitment to change are to be developed within a group of personnel. Furthermore, the possibility of close, interpersonal relationships developing in these situations increases the chances that unfreezing of old attitudes will occur, that real problems will be aired, alternatives studied and solutions tried out. For example, within a school it might be valuable for each teacher to read about or attend lectures on a new program in mathematics, but a mathematics workshop, attended by teachers of various grade levels who publicly commit themselves to try out a particular program, is more likely to effect a permanent change.

IN-SERVICE EDUCATION AND SCHOOL SUPERVISION

Although both supervision and in-service education are concerned with improving the quality of instruction, in-service education is primarily concerned with the development of staff members as practitioners, whereas supervision, broader in concept, includes evaluation of learning, coordination of team programs, curriculum development, public relations, total systems approaches to school learning, and such mundane matters as ordering supplies. Yet school supervision and administration are often interrelated with in-service education. Curriculum development, instructional materials development, and planning or redesigning physical facilities are often handled through in-service education.

Just as in-service education is undergoing radical changes, so supervision as we know it today may be disappearing. For example, Eash notes, "There is indeed reason to question whether the supervisor's role, as it has been defined, can be maintained in the face of the twin emergent forces— the teaching profession's new militancy in negotiating with school boards, and the extensive introduction of the prepared packaged curriculum as the major approach to curriculum development." [23] He recommends that the supervisor become an expert in analyzing the social systems that affect schools and in providing leadership "in designing the curriculum in a comprehensive sense." [24]

The personnel administrator has a double task: (1) to develop an in-service educational program that complements and supports the efforts of school supervisors to effect change in instruction and (2) to incorporate within the in-service educational program components that will assist supervisors to function more efficiently.

STAFFING AN IN-SERVICE EDUCATIONAL PROGRAM

An assumption of this chapter has been that people are the key element in the education of children. It is assumed also that the people who plan, direct and instruct in the in-service educational program are a crucial factor in its success or failure.

Systematic and planned recruitment and selection procedures are necessary to insure the competence and spirit of the persons serving in these capacities. The personnel administrator can be expected to prepare specific job descriptions and qualifications, to publicize available positions, and to arrange for a selection process that includes a combination of objective and subjective measures of evaluation.

The importance of these positions makes it imperative that the best available talent be attracted to the program. To that end, all possible sources of personnel should be tapped: the school system and nearby school systems, colleges and universities, other governmental and government-related agencies. The actual selection of personnel might be a responsibility of a special committee of administrators, university personnel and representatives of the target population to be trained (such as teachers or a representative of the local teachers' association or union).

An essential next step after selection of personnel is their orientation to particular tasks, with follow-up and short-term training sessions that involve evaluating instruction. Strangely enough, this stage is often overlooked or ignored. Yet it is required. Too often, persons selected to lead in-service educational groups have shown expertise in the technical aspects of their jobs, but have had little or no experience working with relatively large groups of adults in a structured program lasting more than a few hours.

The personnel administrator should also make available to all persons associated with the in-service educational program a handbook describing policies, procedures and other details relative to the operation of the program.

In summary, staffing the in-service program must be a planned, cooperatively developed function with leadership exercised primarily by the personnel administrator. Its components include recruitment, selection, orientation, training and evaluation.

ROLES AND RELATIONSHIPS IN THE IN-SERVICE PROGRAM

If in-service education is to be effective, it should involve members of the target population, such as teachers and custodians, university personnel, administrative and supervisory staff, pupils, parents, community leaders, schoolboard members and representatives of state and regional agencies concerned with improving the performance of school personnel.

Hopefully, the principles that characterize an effectively functioning organization also describe the operations of an in-service educational program. It must be made clear, for example, what functions the superintendent of schools delegates to the personnel administrator in relation to in-service education and what roles the latter is expected to play in carrying out his functions. It should be clear which persons or committees have authority to make decisions concerning specific responsibilities.

The quality of the relationships and roles developed among personnel, whether line-staff or collegial on organization charts, depend to a great extent upon the indicators of organizational health described by Miles and noted above. I believe, however, that genuine cooperative effort should characterize each stage in an in-service educational program, including planning, development and evaluation. Within this process, functions and roles are constantly being developed, realized, and redefined.

TECHNIQUES FOR IN-SERVICE EDUCATION

In-service education in American school systems is characterized by its variety of techniques. In a recent study, the National Education Association's Research Division listed nineteen techniques:

1. Classes and Courses
2. Institutes
3. Conferences
4. Workshops
5. Staff Meetings
6. Committee Work
7. Professional Reading
8. Individual Conferences
9. Field Trips
10. Travel
11. Camping
12. Work Experience
13. Teacher Exchanges
14. Research
15. Professional Writing
16. Professional Association Work
17. Cultural Experiences
18. Visits and Demonstrations
19. Community-Organization Work [25]

Others undoubtedly exist. The rationale for school systems utilizing such a variety of techniques was noted earlier; each activity has some potential for inducing change. Furthermore, no one technique is guaranteed to create change in all persons. In effect, different techniques satisfy different needs. Ogletree points out that "methods and techniques are of value only to the degree that they are compatible with the person." [26]

Within each of the group techniques mentioned above, a variety of methods for bringing about change is possible: role playing, brainstorming, critical incidents, case studies, action research, demonstrations, seminars, lectures, sensitivity training, simulation, gaming, microteaching, incident process, and audiovisual instruction, including films, tapes, videotapes, open- and closed-circuit television. Concerning the latter, Esrig outlined in an unpublished study how television in all its varieties could be used to improve teachers' competencies in preactive and interactive teaching-learning situations.[27]

Harris and others explain the relation of selected in-service educational activities to cognitive and emotional objectives. For example, the lecture would probably lend itself to the cognitive objective of knowledge and comprehension, while role playing would lend itself more to developing affective outcomes involving values and attitudes.[28]

The personnel administrator has to consider goals before he can select specific activities. There should be some evidence that the activities do in fact lend themselves to reaching stated objectives.

ADMINISTERING IN-SERVICE EDUCATIONAL PROGRAMS

The personnel administrator is the key person in developing policies and practices to administer and/or coordinate a local in-service educational program for personnel in his school system. Administrative responsibilities might be subsumed under the following headings:

1. Scheduling
2. Facilities and Resources
3. Credit
4. Enrollment
5. Fees
6. Communication, Dissemination and Publicity
7. Recordkeeping

1. SCHEDULING

As Edmonds and others have put it, "learning can best be facilitated when the stimuli to learn are contiguous to the environment where such learning can best occur." [29] There is no one best time for in-service education. It should permeate the whole educational experience according to the nature of needs. Flexibility should be the guide. All attempts should be made by the school personnel administrator not to schedule in-service education on already overloaded school days. It might be possible to integrate in-service educational programs into the school day, building them into the work load of the staff, a policy that would most likely lengthen the school day. Yet a major problem in education is that teachers' days are already so crowded with habitual tasks that they rarely have time to reflect on the consequences of their work.

In actuality, other scheduling is usually practiced. Programs are conducted during summers, on weekends, after school in the afternoons or evenings, and in the morning before school opens. Most common is the course conducted between 3:30 and 6:00 p.m., meeting one or more times a week at the school or in a nearby college or university. Key administrative or supervisory personnel often attend retreats lasting a few days. Only a few school systems allow time off to pursue professional growth requirements on a regular basis. In such cases, administrators must be able to defend the notion that, as a result of teachers' in-service education, children can learn more with fewer hours of direct instruction. What with the trend toward independent learning activities and flexible scheduling, it should not be too difficult a task.

2. FACILITIES AND RESOURCES

The physical environment in which in-service educational activities are provided should facilitate, not hinder, the growth of participants. While that is self-evident, it is still true that untold numbers of training programs have teachers and others in uncomfortably crowded, stuffy rooms, sometimes in the seats of children.

Many alternatives are open to a personnel administrator concerning where he might stage professional growth programs. Although many programs are conducted on nearby university and college campuses, over whose physical facilities the school system has little control, most in-service education takes place on local board-of-education facilities. They should be comfortable and equipped with necessary audiovisual aids and other equipment and materials pertinent to the training program. Specifically, if school secretaries are to be trained, the typical forms, equipment (such as typewriters) and facilities of a school office should be accessible. If teachers are being helped to analyze their own classroom behavior, it may be valuable to use portable television and videotape equipment to televise short segments of lessons for instant replay and analysis.

3. CREDIT

In-service education is often provided with some kind of credit—college credit, graduate or undergraduate; credit applicable to vertical or horizontal salary scales; credit necessary for continued or permanent certification; credit required to obtain or maintain certain positions, such as working with a particular group of children; credit needed to advance to higher positions. Unfortunately, the gathering of credit has become too frequently the only reason that many people participate in in-service education.

The credit feature for programs beyond school hours may be impossible to avoid; however, the goal should be to further the professional growth of school personnel. For example, guidelines for approval by supervisors, principals or the office of the personnel administrator may be established for courses that staff members wish to use for credit on salary schedules or other benefits.

The personnel administrator is often responsible for developing criteria for and evaluating a variety of in-service educational courses and activities

277

for credit purposes. As the size of a school system and the variety and range of in-service educational programs increase, the job grows in complexity. For advice, it might well be desirable for the personnel administrator to consider using a council representing various groups of school personnel or a coordinator to whom responsibilities are delegated.

4. ENROLLMENT

If a formal program of in-service education is developed, rules for enrollment, attendance and other requirements are usually established. For example, the brochure issued by the Newark, New Jersey, Board of Education states: "Credit and a certificate indicating satisfactory completion of a course will be given to those teachers recommended by the instructor provided absences during the course are not in excess of two sessions." [30]

Limits of enrollment in professional growth programs are primarily influenced by two factors: course content and methods used. For example, a two-week concentrated workshop dealing with selected supervisory problems for elementary school principals might involve only the fifteen principals in a district. On the other hand, a program to make elementary school teachers in a school district aware of new instructional materials and equipment might involve a short series of large group presentations and demonstrations. Other requirements might involve final examinations, reports, projects, field trips, visits to local school-board meetings, and the production of instructional or other materials.

5. FEES

The philosophy of in-service education that is adhered to by the personnel administrator determines whether or not costs for training programs conducted beyond normal school hours are partly or wholly met by fees charged to participants. In addition, arrangements made with nearby colleges and universities for college credit influence decisions concerning tuition and registration fees.

If providing in-service educational opportunities is viewed as obligatory for a school system, fees should not be charged; in fact, extra pay or stipends may be offered for engaging in professional growth programs. On the other hand, if in-service education beyond school hours is considered mainly the responsibility of the individual practitioner, then the school system usually provides only the minimum in programs supported by local tax levies.

6. COMMUNICATION, DISSEMINATION AND PUBLICITY

Free and easy communication, both vertical and horizontal, is desirable in any organization. In a program of in-service education so dependent on the interchange of ideas, practices and views, it is essential.

The personnel administrator is responsible in conjunction with others for developing the organization to facilitate open communication and for seeing that rules are established to support free exchange of diverse views.

278

Numerous techniques are available for effecting a free communication network: newsletters, evaluation forms, meetings, instructors' conferences, columns in staff newspapers. Yet the most telling means is the feeling by all concerned that they can freely express their ideas and reactions to a personnel administrator or other person in in-service education.

One particularly useful method for promoting communication is the employment of acceptable peers in training programs. They can often, by alleviating distrust and undue caution, persuade participants of the relevance and feasibility of specific programs.

An essential facet of the communicating process is dissemination of information about the organization and outcomes of in-service educational programs. Too often, well-conceived and planned programs have foundered because of insufficient publicity. In addition, excellently designed and conducted in-service educational programs have gone unnoticed outside the immediate area. In effect, the efforts of educators to improve the quality of instruction through in-service education have often been lonely, isolated affairs. The passage of the Elementary and Secondary Education Act of 1965, the resultant organization of Title III projects, the establishment of educational laboratories and centers, the founding of the Educational Resources Information Center (ERIC) by the U.S. Office of Education and the School Research Information Service (SRIS) by Phi Delta Kappa have enhanced the possibilities for dissemination of educational innovations.

7. RECORDKEEPING

In a continuing program of in-service education, recordkeeping is desirable. It ensures sequence and development in teacher growth. If a school system requires participation in in-service educational programs for salary increases, it is essential. Records such as the names of participants, the results and dates of programs, and any credit assigned are minimum requirements. School systems that utilize long-range professional growth plans should also keep a record of those plans and the extent to which they are realized.

If recordkeeping is essential or desirable, the personnel administrator is responsible for its efficiency. In large school districts, that means centralizing recordkeeping and utilizing computerized data-processing procedures.

An effective record system should enable an administrator to quickly find information regarding such matters as the number of personnel enrolled in programs in selected subject areas, the programs in which individual educational personnel have engaged, and the reasons why people of different ages and at different salary levels do or do not participate in in-service educational programs.

8. SUMMARY

Administering a well-developed program of in-service education requires a staff of competent, alert administrators. They must, as a group, plan, organize and coordinate activities, serve as a clearinghouse for innovative ideas and practices, and communicate clearly among themselves and with all other involved persons.

EVALUATION OF IN-SERVICE EDUCATION

The principal purpose of evaluating a program is to improve future programs. What is to be evaluated must be based upon the objectives of each program. Of course, different persons often assign different aims to the same programs. A teacher participating in a workshop on reading problems may view it differently from the personnel administrator who, with a college's assistance, arranged it. If change in teacher behavior is an important objective, such matters as the presence, amount and direction of change must be considered. Obviously, cause is difficult to determine.

Various phases of in-service educational programs can be evaluated: the planning phase; training sessions; the extent to which what is learned is transferred to the job, on a verbal basis (immediate objective); the effect of the program on the behavior of personnel on the job, whether in the classroom or in the principal's office (intermediate objective); and the effect on pupils (ultimate objective).[31]

Unplanned changes should be evaluated, too, for they could be significant. It is possible, through miscalculation and poor planning, to promote changes in personnel that are the opposite of what was originally intended. This problem may arise in sensitive areas, such as human relations or intergroup education, in which programs aimed at developing better understanding among teachers may instead cause increased intolerance.

It is important to consider that the fact of participating in the program, and not necessarily the content of the program, may be the cause of the effects noted. The tendency is to oversimplify cause-and-effect sequences in human behavior. There is little doubt that all who participate in the program should also participate in evaluating the program, even though this practice is seldom followed.

Available methods for evaluating professional development programs vary in effectiveness, complexity and ease of implementation. Interviews, knowledge tests, performance tests, individual and group personality tests, projective techniques, scales and sociometry are used in product or process evaluation; which are used depends on a number of factors: the depth of investigation, time and resources to evaluate, evaluating criteria, training objectives, and the competence of the investigator himself. A personnel administrator, for example, may decide to use a simple five-by-eight-inch card requesting each participant to evaluate a program at its conclusion, or he may utilize lengthy questionnaires that are sent to a random sampling of teachers in a specific group of programs conducted in his school district.

Finally, much has been said and written about feedback as a key element in evaluation. Careful thought should be given to what data should be fed back to participants and to instructors in in-service educational programs. Feedback should be used to improve the quality of instruction, not to punish people.

SOURCES OF FUNDS FOR IN-SERVICE EDUCATION

In-service education costs money. Where insufficient funds are allotted to it, in-service education often remains haphazard, unplanned and usually ineffectual. While there is no guarantee that the infusion of large sums of money will revolutionize professional growth programs so that they are more relevant to what happens in schools, the provision of money does make it possible, and probably more likely, that it will do just that.

Boards of education are often reluctant to set aside funds, pointing to a lack of evidence for their efficacy. Yet many or most educational appropriations are made on the basis of faith or belief. It is not altogether certain, for example, what effect the introduction of paraprofessionals or of language laboratories will have upon pupils. They have been introduced for a variety of reasons, but highly favorable support from empirical research was not one of them.

The personnel administrator, then, must be informed of the research on in-service education and he must have faith in its value and be able to convey his belief to his superiors as well as to the board of education.

Five major monetary sources are usually available for in-service education: local, city or district funds; county funds; general and special state grants; federal grants; and private or quasi-public funds.

All school districts provide some financial support for in-service education, if only in the form of paying for the salaries of curricular consultants, supervisors and principals who conduct in-service educational programs on occasion. Financial support for continuing programs is another matter, but many local districts are increasingly moving to the view that it is money well spent for the return.

In many states that have strong county educational systems, some funding provision is made to support in-service education either countywide or in individual school districts. More common, perhaps, are the cooperative arrangements made by school districts in one county to foster in-service education.

At a higher level, state support for in-service education is increasing rapidly, particularly since the federal government has decided to aid state departments of education under Title V of the Elementary and Secondary Education Act of 1965. Even before that date, many states were getting involved in statewide programs, particularly via television. Within the next few years, state involvement will grow dramatically as the result of federal legislation. Specifically, Title III of ESEA, providing for innovative programs, is expected to be administered through state departments of education. Part B2 of the Education Professions Development Act of 1968 provided each state, during the 1969–70 school year, with at least $100,000 to spend on projects to recruit, train and retrain educational personnel.[32] The fact is that state departments of education will increasingly provide the stimulus and financial support for local school systems to originate, design and develop their own professional growth programs.

While much money is and will become available from state funds or from federal funds funneled through the states, a great deal is and will become available to local school systems directly from the federal government. Parts C and D of the Education Professions Development Act encouraged local educational agencies to apply for grants to train or retrain almost anyone in the school system, from the superintendent to a teacher's aide. During the 1969–70 school year, approximately $80,000,000 was to be spent for training programs under these parts of the Act. Authorizations for future years will probably increase. The Act holds tremendous potential for a rejuvenation of the entire educational profession.

So far, the discussion has been limited to government funds. Yet much money is provided by numerous, established private associations, foundations and other voluntary organizations that have proliferated in our country. The contributions of the Ford Foundation and the Carnegie Corporation are well known. Local, state and national education associations are also giving assistance in the area of in-service education. The National Education Association and American Federation of Teachers over the years have recognized the importance of professional growth, if one is to judge from their publications.

Although colleges and universities seldom provide funds for the in-service education of personnel in nearby districts, they are often in the position of being able to obtain funds through private and governmental agencies to help such personnel.

The personnel administrator may assume that there has been a multiplication of sources for funding in-service education. It is imperative that he or his associates become familiar with the range and diversity of sources, and adept at designing and coordinating proposals to obtain funds. In fact, the personnel administrator might consider retaining a person solely to coordinate and prepare proposals, or at least contracting proposal writing tasks to local colleges, universities and educational laboratories or centers.

THE ROLE OF THE SCHOOL PERSONNEL ADMINISTRATOR

In-service education has become a major concern in every school system across the country. It is the thesis of this chapter that the personnel administrator has a vital role to play in determining and influencing the extent, quality, direction and impact of the in-service educational program in his school district. The quality of education in today's school systems in large measure reflects their commitment to the in-service education of personnel.

282

13 PUBLIC AND HUMAN RELATIONS

GENERAL STATEMENT

Although public schools continually undergo public scrutiny and criticism, recent years have seen a harshness and turbulence in the intensity of criticism that is most unusual. In this era it has often seemed that any individual with a special grievance or complaint against the so-called educational establishment could be featured in the public press. Much of the dissatisfaction has been justified, inasmuch as changes were long overdue to meet the new needs of times that have encompassed a social revolution. However, it is also true that much of the criticism is based upon a lack of understanding of the objectives, the limitations, and the real achievements of American public schools. Too little time and energy in the past have been devoted by administrators to explaining to the public the goals, organization, procedures, limitations and achievements of the school system. The few efforts made have been sporadic and not very successful. Edward L. Bernays, an authority on public relations, said:

> "to inform public opinion about a given issue, it is necessary to endow that issue with high visibility. Public education has a particularly low visibility, and so requires even greater effort in making the public aware of what is involved and what must be done in the current educational crisis." [1]

Many industrial, organized labor, governmental and educational institutions today realize the importance of public and human relations and have begun to engage specialized personnel to develop and conduct appropriate programs. Yet over a hundred years ago Agraham Lincoln realized the value of public relations when he said:

283

"With public sentiment nothing can fail; without it nothing can succeed. Consequently he who molds public opinion goes deeper than he who enacts statutes or pronounces the decisions. He makes statutes or decisions possible or impossible to execute." [2]

Howard Bonhan, vice-chairman of the American Red Cross, once described public relations as the "art of bringing about better public understanding which breeds better public confidence for any individual or organization."

Closely related to a school district's public relations program, indeed an integral part of it, is human relations. An effective public relations program must be designed to improve relationships between school administrators and the community, between faculty and students, among members of the school staff, and among the various groups and individuals who make up the school district's community.

The school personnel administrator must understand the importance of a public and human relations program; he must understand the essential qualities and procedures of a good program in this field, even in school districts where there is a special public relations staff member. The school personnel administrator has an important participating role in the school's public and human relations program.

OBJECTIVES OF A PUBLIC AND HUMAN RELATIONS PROGRAM

Ten objectives of school public and human relations programs that are widely cited by educators are the following:

1. Inform the public about the work of the schools.
2. Establish confidence in the schools.
3. Obtain support of the educational program.
4. Develop awareness of the importance of education in a democracy.
5. Improve the partnership concept by uniting parents, teachers and community leaders in meeting the education needs of the children.
6. Integrate the home, school and community in improving the educational opportunities for all children.
7. Make known the efforts and achievements of the schools in meeting the needs of the children of the community.
8. Develop an esprit de corps among staff members and a feeling of pride among students and parents.
9. Correct misunderstandings concerning the aims and activities of the schools.
10. Obtain support of the fiscal and material needs of the schools.

Benjamin Fine, for many years education editor of *The New York Times,* described educational publicity as "that instrument that interprets to the public the place of the school, college or educational organization in the community, in accordance with the policy and limitations expressed in the public relations programs of the particular institution." [3]

The school personnel administrator must be involved in achieving many of the general goals of the public and human relations program of the school system. From his specialized position, however, he must be more particularly concerned with the following:

1. Developing in the public an understanding of the goals of his department, its activities, its importance and its achievements.
2. Developing an internal understanding among all members of the school staff, including members of the board of education, of the role and activities of his department.
3. Developing in the public an understanding and appreciation of both the professional and noncertified staff as individuals and as team members of the total educational staff.
4. Developing on the part of the public an understanding of teaching as a profession.
5. Improving human relations between staff and community, between administration and staff, and among staff members.

DEVELOPING A PUBLIC AND HUMAN RELATIONS PROGRAM

To be effective, a public and human relations program must be developed and organized as a total plan. The objectives should be formulated; the responsibilities of individuals must be described; the responsibilities of the director, or the public relations expert, should be set forth; the varied activities should be outlined; and the channels to be used should be indicated.

One important activity in the total program is often overlooked, the activity of getting facts, data and information through research. Edward Bernays gives considerable importance to this element of research as a basic starting point. In proposing a public relations program for education, he declares that research must provide an inventory of what is available, it must provide an accurate picture of public attitudes, it must find what is wrong with the objectives and the activities of an institution, and it must provide an analysis of the different publics to be reached.[4] Indeed, he declares that, in the light of such fundamental research, the objectives of a public relations program may have to be modified. After a statement of objectives and after fundamental research, Bernays advises that a "clear-cut plan of operational organization" be formulated.

CHANNELS TO BE USED IN A
PUBLIC AND HUMAN RELATIONS PROGRAM

NEWSPAPERS

The press has often played a decisive role in developing public attitudes toward the school system. If a school district can afford to employ a professional in public relations, it is probable that a more comprehensive and effective program can be developed. In any case, the public and human relations program should be assigned as the responsibility of one individual, either full-time or part-time, so that coordination of efforts may be achieved. Since the achievements and activities of staff members and children are prime interests of the press, it is important that the school personnel administrator be familiar with essential aspects of dealing with the public press.

Professionals in the field of public relations have given the following advice concerning relationships with the press:

1. One individual should be the coordinator of public information to whom members of the press can apply for information.
2. Members of the press should not be regarded with suspicion or fear but should be treated with courtesy and frankness. If a relationship of trust is to be established, facts and honest statements must be given, rather than one-sided, propagandizing pronouncements.
3. Information should be disseminated on a regular basis, in proper form and with understanding about what constitutes newsworthy stories. Timing is also important in the release of stories. For example, the issuance of a national report on the use of paraprofessionals might be a good occasion for a story about the use of paraprofessionals in the local school district.
4. When situations warrant such action, meetings should be arranged with appropriate members of the local press to obtain their advice, their cooperation and understanding. Leaders of the school staff should get to know appropriate members of the local press on an informal basis as well as in their official capacity.
5. There should be an understanding of the press, both of its mechanical operation and of its professional aspects as carried on by reporters and columnists. Trivial criticism, importunities and unreasonable complaints by school officials do not develop good will with the press.
6. A publicity and human relations conscious staff organization should be developed. The more widespread the interest in obtaining favorable press coverage, the more opportunities will be created for favorable news in the local press.
7. Concealment or attempts at censorship often boomerang into adverse publicity. The press should be given access to staff members who are on the scene of or involved in newsworthy incidents.

Newspaper publishers want to print news that the public wishes to read. Fine has listed the following priorities for publicity: [5]

Pupils' progress and welfare	School staff members and alumni
Instructional program	Voting program
Guidance and health services	Administration and finance
Attendance and discipline	Parent-teachers associations
Enrollment trends	Student activities

The most frequently used method of conveying a story to the press is the "news release." The following qualities have been enumerated for a good release:

1. It answers the most important questions that the reader wants to know about the incident.
2. It highlights the most important aspect of the incident or the story.
3. It is clearly and interestingly written.
4. It follows the rules of good newspaper writing.
5. It cites the authority on which the news is printed.
6. It identifies the persons mentioned.

The following guidance has been given by public relations specialists for the format of a release:

1. The typewritten copy should be mimeographed on white paper, size 8½ x 11 inch.
2. The name of the school or school system should appear at the top left or right of the paper along with the name and telephone number of the individual to be contacted for further information.
3. The release date should appear at the top of the first page.
4. The copy should be double-spaced and one side only of the paper should be used.
5. Pages should be numbered and the word "more" should appear at the bottom of a page to show that more follows.
6. An identifying slug line should be used on the top of all the pages after the first.
7. The finish of the story should be indicated by "end."

Newspaper style should be used in writing a release. It has been described as a reversed pyramid style. The opening paragraph, or lead, contains the most essential elements of the story. The next most important aspect is in the second paragraph and the least important aspect is in the last paragraph. This is done so that, if the article must be cut, the last portion, which is the least significant, will be cut first. The lead paragraph should answer the five Ws: Who? What? Where? Why? When? Occasionally, How is added.

Note how the following leads answer the W questions:

1. All faculty members will be required to participate in a three-session seminar in human relations. The seminar classes will meet in the auditorium in Washington High School from 4 to 6 P.M. on October 3, 10 and 16.
2. All newly appointed teachers will meet the presidents of parent associations at a buffet supper to be held in the gymnasium of Washington High School at 6 P.M., Thursday, September 18.

In judging a publicity release, a check list with the following items may be used.

STYLE AND STRUCTURE
Is the story clear, easy to read?
Is the sentence structure simple, clear and smooth?
Is there variety in sentence structure and length?

TONE AND PURPOSE
Is the tone suited to the subject? Have superlatives been avoided?
Is the story padded?
Will the average reader understand it?

Other advice given by professionals includes the following: do not editorialize in a release, be accurate in presentation, don't exaggerate, don't hide the facts, and don't propagandize.

The following is a sample news release issued by public relations specialists concerning school personnel matters.

For Release: Sunday, February 5, 1967

BOARD OF EDUCATION OF THE CITY OF NEW YORK
110 Livingston Street, Brooklyn, N.Y. 11201

News Bureau, Office of Education Information
Services and Public Relations

The New York City school system is developing a program to determine what qualities are requisite for successful principals, superintendents and other high ranking pedagogical officials.

The project has been initiated by Dr. A, Deputy Superintendent of Schools for Personnel, with the approval of Superintendent of Schools Dr. B and the Board of Education.

It is designed to "give us a practical understanding of our needs in these areas and the direction in which we should be expected to move," said Dr. A.

Dr. C of the Graduate School of Public Administration at New York University, and Dr. D, Associate Professor of Education at Hunter College, are serving as consultants. Both are specialists in the field.

As a first step, interviews of a cross-section of Principals, Assistant Superintendents and others in high-ranking pedagogical positions will be held through February, to enlist their help in developing a questionnaire which will later be sent to all Principals and Superintendents in the City school system. The Personnel Office will use this questionnaire as a basis for developing a long-range plan for career development and executive training.

In a related project, the City school system and the Center for Urban Education of New York City have initiated a pioneering project to determine criteria for successful principals in schools in disadvantaged areas.

"The need for such a study in New York City," Dr. B said, "is emphasized by the fact that 263 of our 603 public elementary schools are located in disadvantaged areas and 65 of our 145 public junior high schools are serving similar sections of the City."

In commenting on the project Dr. A said: "We hope to gain insight into the human qualities, the specialized knowledge, the background influences, the type
288

of schooling, training and supervisory experience which add up to the development of highly qualified principals for schools in disadvantaged areas. The findings should prove invaluable not only to the Board of Examiners for selection purposes and the Office of Personnel for placement and training purposes, but also to the colleges and universities which train our supervisory staff and to urban areas outside of New York City which face similar problems."

Many thousands of pupils in disadvantaged areas should benefit from the results of this study, school officials said.

Various types of stories may be included in press releases. Each serves a different purpose and plays a part in an overall program of public relations. Some of the most frequently used types are the following:

Straight news stories	Feature stories
Running news stories	Human-interest stories
Interview stories	

The straight news story is the most common. It is used to report the appointment of a faculty member, the introduction of a new subject, the winning of a prize. The running news story is a story that continues. It is used when a conference or a series of meetings extends for several days. An interview story is used to highlight an individual's achievements or his views on some special occasion. A feature story may deal with a special subject or a special situation. It can dwell at some length on an achievement in science or health. A concert or a special career conference may be the basis for a feature story. From the viewpoint of a personnel administrator, a feature story might be done on the art or musical backgrounds of selected faculty members. A human-interest story may well focus upon out-of-school factors in the lives of faculty members: their hobbies, trips taken during the summer, or interesting aspects of their family life. The usefulness of such releases is often enhanced by available photographs, which should be clear and interesting.

MAGAZINES AND PERIODICALS

Periodicals represent another source of publicity. National magazines are highly selective in choosing material, and the articles they use must have national interest. However, many newspapers, even in small communities, have magazine supplements on Sunday which may use feature stories about school projects, special reports, special surveys, or significant accomplishments.

Articles for magazines need not all be written by central headquarters staff. All school districts have teachers, principals and others who can write for publication and who may obtain satisfaction from doing so. The personnel office should have a list of individuals who have this ability and interest, and they should be encouraged and assisted, though not necessarily by the personnel office, in writing articles about educational achievements. Suggestions as to articles may be made to them, and recognition of their success in having an article published may be given in a congratulatory note from the personnel director.

RADIO AND TELEVISION

Many of the same types of releases that are sent to the press can be used by radio and television stations during their news broadcasts. However, other types of publicity may be secured through radio and television. Interviews can be arranged with staff members who may, for example, describe their recruitment procedures and experiences or their efforts and achievements in other programs of special interest to the public.

Some school personnel administrators have used radio and television announcements to recruit teachers with special talents that were needed for special classes. In some cities, during a time of teacher shortage, parents who held baccalaureate degrees were informed of special opportunities to obtain certification and a teaching position. Radio and television have been used to cover a special board meeting, a conference such as one on student careers, special events such as Future Teachers Day and Teacher Recognition Day, or an award ceremony for students and staff members.

MOTION PICTURES AND FILM SLIDES

Some school districts have invested in the production of film slides or motion pictures for teacher recruitment or for developing an understanding of the work of the school staff. The films show the school environment, the community environment, teachers in action, school facilities, children in various classroom situations and teachers in working relationships with parents. Special motion pictures and film slides have also been made of such matters as guidance conferences, safety programs, health programs and other special activities. Films that are professionally produced are expensive. However, such films as are shown repeatedly may be worth the investment. Many films that have been useful in public relations programs have been produced by local staff members at moderate expense.

PAMPHLETS, BULLETINS AND BROCHURES

School personnel administrators have used special brochures for recruitment purposes. They depict the school environment, features of the community, teaching requirements, and advantages of teaching in the particular district. Other special pamphlets may be used by a school personnel administrator for internal consumption. For example, there may be pamphlets of orientation for new teachers after they have been appointed. In addition to extending a welcome, such pamphlets may indicate administrative channels in the school system, fringe benefits, salary schedules, courses of study, guidance facilities, and other essential information that teachers

290

should know. Special leaflets produced by the administrator of school personnel might deal with the following topics: maintaining staff health, grievance procedures, rules for transfers, regulations concerning special leaves, opportunities for in-service development within the school district and in neighboring collegiate institutions. Special pamphlets highlighting matters of current interest to the school staff may also be prepared; there might be a special pamphlet to aid teachers in meeting the problems of inner city teaching, a pamphlet on parent-teacher relationships, a pamphlet on the teacher and public relations, or a pamphlet on human relations aspects of school administration and teaching.

HOUSE ORGANS

Most school districts have a newsletter or bulletin used by the superintendent for conveying messages and information to members of the school staff. These publications should be utilized on a regular basis by the school personnel administrator. The members of the school staff should learn to expect to receive personnel information of importance on a regular basis in this bulletin. Such information as the following might appear in a weekly, monthly or special bulletin: opportunities for promotion, arrangements for in-service courses, announcement of faculty professional meetings and conferences, reminders about available staff facilities, reviews of current professional literature, activities of districtwide committees, staff recruitment needs, human-interest stories about staff members, individual or staff achievements. The house organ that appears regularly can be used by the school personnel administrator for conveying important information to the staff (such as dates for chest X rays, dates for filing credentials or requests for leaves), for obtaining information from and assistance by the staff, for winning an understanding on the part of the school staff of personnel problems or activities, for developing an interest in the total school staff as a team, and for enhancing staff morale.

SCHOOL BULLETIN BOARDS

Every school has a bulletin board, usually set up in the general office, on which announcements of various kinds are made available to members of the faculty. These bulletin boards can be utilized by the school personnel administrator in several ways. Fundamentally, of course, the personnel office should give directions and suggestions to the principals of schools on the use and maintenance of faculty bulletin boards. Such directions might properly require the principal to devote one portion of the bulletin board to personnel news from headquarters. In this section, there might be mounted clippings cut from the superintendent's bulletin that are intended for the general information of the staff. Other information of general staff interest can be posted on the personnel section. This information may include the announcement of courses, committee meetings, conference dates and places, vacancies, and other activities arranged or sponsored by the central personnel office.

PERSONAL CONTACTS

The personnel administrator in a school district must be visible and must use his personal talents to develop, on the part of interested citizens in the community, an understanding of personnel operations and achievements. The personnel administrator should therefore be a member of appropriate clubs, appear at appropriate luncheons, participate in committee meetings and conventions, and invite leading members of the community to meet with him in his office or at informal gatherings. He should seek opportunities to be the formal speaker at community meetings, or to be represented by a member of his staff. At other gatherings of informal nature, conversations may lead to a better understanding of the professional problems faced by his division. Of course, there are limits to the time and energy of the personnel director, and he has to schedule such activities in accordance with his and his assistants' available time. However, the development of understanding, loyalty and support on the part of community leaders can be helpful in furthering the personnel activities of the school district.

LETTERS TO THE PUBLIC AND TO STAFF

An important vehicle for public and human relations is the correspondence conducted by the office of the school personnel administrator with applicants for positions, with staff members, and with the public. Each letter conveys some sort of image to the individual who receives it. A letter can be formal, cold and brusk; it can be evasive and unresponsive; it can be effusive and elaborate; or it can be clear, responsive and appropriately cordial. Many letters received by the office of the school personnel administrator seek information or help and guidance of some kind. Responding letters, in addition to providing answers to questions, may express appreciation for the interest and may invite the writer to call at an appropriate time or to follow up in other appropriate ways if the response is not adequate. An enclosure may provide a more detailed answer. In all cases, a reasonably detailed, clear response should be made. If the volume of correspondence is heavy, a form letter may be used, as long as it serves the purpose completely. However, many personnel directors prefer to type the name of the recipient on the form letter or to sign the form letter by hand. A check list response is probably least helpful in developing good public relations. The timing of responses is also important. Excessive delays in responding may either be resented or create the impression of inefficiency and lack of concern.

There are always problems of dealing with letters of complaint. Experienced personnel administrators advise that such letters be answered courteously, that factual data be offered when possible in response to the complaint or criticism, that appreciation of the interest be expressed if appropriate, and that error be admitted with apology if one has occurred. Expressions of outrage, annoyance, resentment or recrimination should be avoided by the personnel director if he wishes to seem professional.

PUBLIC AND HUMAN RELATIONS ACTIVITIES BY STAFF MEMBERS

Ideally, every principal and staff member should be sensitive to the public and human relations aspects of his position, for he is an employee in public service. Principals and school staff members are usually in the front lines of visibility as far as the public is concerned. They should have the guidance of a public relations specialist, if possible. For example, a pamphlet of guidelines in public and human relations, prepared with the assistance of a public relations specialist, should be given to the staff. The personnel administrator has a role to play in the preparation, distribution and utilization of the pamphlets describing such guidelines. Thus, principals and other school officials should receive guidance in the matter of their own correspondence with parents, in their conduct of interviews with parents, and in their relationships with parent and civic organizations, with students, and with the press. Teachers should receive similar guidance.

The school staff should not be in a posture of waiting for public relations opportunities to be pressed upon them in the form of criticism to which responses must be made. Instead, they should take the initiative in seeking opportunities for developing and maintaining good relationships in accordance with guidelines prepared with the collaboration of the school personnel administrator. From the point of view of the school personnel administrator, such guidelines should include conveying to the public an understanding of the efforts, background, training and achievements of the school staff and an awareness of the personnel problems that face the school district. In addition to their personal contacts with individual parents, members of the school staff have opportunities of addressing groups of citizens, contributing to association newspapers, writing letters to the editors of newspapers, writing articles for professional and general magazines, writing books, appearing on radio and television programs, and utilizing all the avenues of public relations that are available to the central headquarters staff. The school personnel administrator is not primarily a public relations specialist, but, since his work concerns people, their activities and achievements, their aspirations, interests and needs, he must not only understand the value, role, and activities of a public relations program, but also exercise considerable leadership in this field.

IN-SERVICE COURSES

In-service courses on the subject of public or human relations may be arranged for teachers and principals through the efforts of the school personnel administrator. Seminars might deal with such topics as techniques of public relations, group dynamics, emerging patterns of community action, building bridges of understanding between the school and the community, and utilizing human and material resources.

In the school district of New York City, the Board of Education established the requirement that all teachers must complete a thirty-hour course in human relations before they could receive a designated salary increment. Guidelines were established for the content and conduct of such a course. The suggested outline included the following topics: orientation, content-factual information, sensitivity training, skills development, community involvement, and survey of materials. Features of the program were the questioning of assumptions, myths and generalizations; appreciation of other cultures; development of techniques of self-awareness; group dynamics, role playing and psychodrama; teaching human relations in demonstration lessons in various curriculum areas; field experiences in the community; discussion of films.

RELATIONSHIPS WITH THE COMMUNITY

In recent years, relationships between school and community have become matters of wide discussion. Such concepts as school decentralization, community control, community involvement, greater community participation, and teacher responsibility to the community reflect the new importance attached to relationships between schools and the community. In some school districts and cities, the questions and problems of these relationships have resulted in tension and misunderstanding between members of the school staff and varied spokesmen for segments of the community. Representatives of the community have sought a more effective role and voice in the program and administration of the school. However, at least part of the dissatisfaction was created by inadequate relationships and understanding, not only between the central administration and the public but also between individual school administrations and staff members and the public.

Parent and community representatives have objected to the passive role they were expected to play in relation to the schools; they have objected to participating in school administration on the level of running tea parties or luncheons to raise funds for phonographs and portable television sets. They have wanted to discuss basic matters of student achievement, school curricula, teachers' attitudes toward students, and their relationships with the school's administrative staff. The school principal who has not been accessible to members of the community, who has pooh-

poohed their objections and complaints, who has talked down to them, who has been patronizing in his attitudes toward them, and who has refused to discuss important problems with their representatives has incurred the animosity of these groups in many communities.

The school personnel administrator must take a leading role in redirecting such relationships between the community and members of the school staff, and he must arrange to meet with appropriate representatives to discuss staff recruitment, staff performance, staff integration and other problems that they deem important. His action should not be to present his views, his plans and his solutions, but to talk with equally interested parties, for the purpose of trying to develop mutually constructive programs.

RELATIONSHIPS WITH STUDENTS

Attention has been focused on the emerging role of students in school administration. The traditional authoritarian relationship has been rejected. The forms of participation and consultation without real substance are being replaced by a genuine sharing in decision making, by frankness in discussing problems, by willingness to discuss all relevant problems and by an atmosphere of mutual respect in discussions between school administrators and students. It is recognized that students, despite lack of maturity in years, have a viewpoint, serious concerns and ideas that are important in decisions made about school programs. That is not to say that all demands of students must be accepted. The role of the personnel administrator must include efforts to guide school principals and other school personnel to adopt the modern view of relationships with students.

EVALUATION OF PUBLIC AND HUMAN RELATIONS

There is no formula for the evaluation of success in this area. There may be objective data, such as the amount of favorable space given in the press, support of budgets by the citizenry, lack of unrest or disturbances in the schools, or the number of parents attending meetings. However, such factors may be influenced by temporary incidents that could cause a reaction and that are beyond anyone's control. Questionnaires on specific elements of relationships, such as activity in a parents' association or satisfaction with a new program, may yield worthwhile information when applied to a representative sample. Informal inquiries may also be useful. One may say that any attempt to evaluate by obtaining reactions is a useful reflection of concern and an ongoing program.

14 STAFF NEGOTIATIONS

GENERAL STATEMENT

Perhaps the most important recent development in the field of school personnel administration has been the insistence of the professional staff to negotiate matters of mutual concern with the school board. The two major teachers' organizations, the American Federation of Teachers and the National Education Association, approached negotiations in a somewhat different fashion, but each had the same basic objectives: to achieve recognition as a partner with the board of education and to be involved in matters of concern in the educational program. These concerns, which initially began with working conditions, have been expanded to cover all aspects of the program, from personnel issues of salaries, hours of work and grievances to curriculum offerings, class size, methods of supervision, supplementary services and other matters related to school policy which boards of education once regarded as their exclusive domain. It must be understood that the teachers' organizations sought more than merely the right to be heard. They sought the right to discuss matters as equals with the board of education on a genuine give-and-take basis.

The more vocal group and the one that initiated the impetus to negotiate was the American Federation of Teachers. Noting the experiences obtained from the great labor organizations in the AFL-CIO, with which the Federation was affiliated, the AFT used the approaches and techniques developed in collective bargaining. The National Education Association, recognizing both the success of the AFT in collective bargaining and the threat to its own organization in national status, developed a competitive program which they called "professional negotiations."

It is the purpose of this chapter to examine some of the events that brought the field of negotiations into such prominence in school personnel administration, some of the procedures developed, some of the essential background information, some of the laws passed, and some of the concerns about the impact and future directions of staff negotiations.

HISTORICAL BACKGROUND OF STAFF NEGOTIATIONS IN EDUCATION

The governmental action that founded collective bargaining in industrial relations was the National Wagner Act, signed into law by President Roosevelt on July 5, 1935. Of this law, Senator Wagner stated: "All collective bargaining is simply a means to an end. That end is not the mere exchange of pleasantries between employer and employee, but rather the making of agreements which will stabilize employment conditions and set fair working standards." In 1947 the duty to negotiate or bargain was defined thus in the amended Wagner Act:

> ". . . to bargain collectively is the performance of the mutual obligation of the employer and the representative of the employees to meet at reasonable times and confer in good faith with respect to wages, hours, and other terms and conditions of employment, *or* the negotiation of an agreement, or any question arising under, and the execution of a written contract incorporating any agreement reached, if requested by either party."

However, the statutes and practices did not encompass public employment. Dealing with groups of employees in government service was slow in developing and, indeed, was forbidden in some localities. In a few cities, a beginning was made in the late 1940s to give public employees the right to organize and thus, presumably, to be heard. Hartford, Connecticut, passed an ordinance in 1945 giving public employees the right to organize. Louisville in 1946 and Cincinnati in 1951 took similar action. During that time, Canadian municipalities were negotiating with their employees on a broad scale involving representatives of some 40,000 persons. In 1946, the Norwalk, Connecticut, Teachers' Association went on strike and obtained a contract, and in 1951 the Connecticut Supreme Court of Errors declared that teachers could organize and negotiate with boards of education. In 1957, the Norwalk Teachers' Association negotiated what is "believed to be the first agreement, under what is now termed professional negotiation, providing appeal provisions." [1] By the end of the 1950s, the stage was set for moving the concept of collective negotiations into the administration of schools.

Two events occurred in the early 1960s which spurred the National Education Association to action in the field of negotiations. In 1962 at the annual convention of the National Education Association in Denver, one of the speakers, James B. Carey, President of the Electrical Workers and a Vice-President of AFL-CIO, stated in strong terms that teachers were not achieving gains because they were not members of a strong organization;

they were being used by boards of education and administrators and were not achieving the recognition they deserved. Possibly his major intent was not to make friends among his audience but rather to obtain converts to the union movement represented by the American Federation of Teachers.[2]

In the 1950s, the union movement suffered a severe setback primarily as a result of two acts of Congress, the Taft-Hartley Law and the Landon-Griffin Law, but also as a result of negative public reaction to many crippling strikes, such as those of the longshoremen and the auto workers, during the decade. These factors, coupled with the advent of automation, caused a significant drop in the growth of blue-collar membership in the union movement and a consequent search by the countrys' workers for other sources of membership. The white-collar workers were an obvious source of membership, and teachers with a common interest were one of the prime sources in this endeavor.

Carey's address succeeded in goading the National Education Association into passing two resolutions at the 1962 convention that paved the way for much of the movement in professional negotiations that occurred after the convention. One resolution endorsed a program to develop a drive for professional recognition and negotiation at the state level as well as at the national level; the other resolution called for the use of professional sanctions when such recognition and negotiation were not obtained.

The other event was the tremendous success of the United Federation of Teachers in achieving exclusive recognition by the Board of Education in New York City as the collective bargaining agent for all teachers in the city's schools. Two teachers' strikes were called, one in 1960 and one in 1962, which paved the way for this recognition on the part of the board of education. On the other hand, it was charged that the National Education Association had done little to assist its membership in New York City. At that time there was a proliferation of organizations within the professional staff of New York City—some 70 in all—representing many special-interest groups. While the United Federation of Teachers in New York started with a relatively small membership—some 4,500 out of approximately 45,000 in the professional staff—it won the support of a majority of the teaching staff by a close margin in the elections held by the board of education to determine the exclusive bargaining agent for the professional staff. The union, an affiliate of the American Federation of Teachers, was so certified.

In the bargaining discussion which followed, the United Federation of Teachers was successful in achieving a really comprehensive contract with the board and significant gains in the bread-and-butter issues of salaries, increments and fringe benefits. Testimony to the success of such recognition in terms of membership is the fact that the United Federation of Teachers' membership increased from 4,500 members in 1962 to approximately 37,000 members in 1966.[3] As a result of its success, the American Federation of Teachers was successful in winning a number of other elections to determine the exclusive bargaining agent, particularly in the large urban areas in the northeastern portion of the United States, among which were Philadelphia, Newark and Detroit.

During the period from 1960 to 1967 the National Education Association increased its membership approximately 50 percent, whereas the American Federation of Teachers, while not as numerous in membership, increased membership approximately 125 percent. Thus, to continue to have an appeal to its membership, the National Education Association had a clear direction to follow, namely to develop a vigorous program of leadership in professional negotiations for its membership.

In 1962 President Kennedy issued Executive Order Number 10988, an action which also contributed to the drive for staff negotiations. Before then, little had been accomplished in the various departments of the federal government to achieve genuine employee recognition. What recognition had been achieved was largely due to the desires of various departmental officials within the structure of the federal government, which varied from limited recognition to almost complete recognition. However, Executive Order Number 10988 outlined the rights of federal employees to negotiate within their departmental structures and delineated the areas in which such recognition could take place. These were in areas of salaries and fringe benefits.

While public education is a function of the state rather than of the federal government as defined by the U.S. Constitution, teachers took a lead from the Executive Order and pressed state legislatures for laws relating to collective negotiations.

Testimony for the success of this drive is illustrated by the developments in one two-year period. Fifteen states passed laws giving teachers the right to promote a program of collective negotiations with local boards of education. These laws, of course, varied from state to state and only a few will be briefly examined here to give examples of the kinds of laws that exist across the land.

CALIFORNIA

Teachers were guaranteed the right to join or not to join employee organizations in California. The law on professional negotiations was known popularly as the Winton Act. Organizations may represent their members in their employment relationships with the local school board. Such relationships are not confined to salaries, fringe benefits, and working conditions, but may include all matters relating to the definition of educational objectives, the determination of the content of courses and curricula, the selection of textbooks, and other aspects of the instructional program.

An interesting part of the California law was provision for proportional representation. A negotiating council was established providing for representation of all professional organizations requesting membership on the council and recognition by the school board. Membership was based on a proportional basis depending upon the number of members the orga-

299

nization represented. The law provided for the number of members of the council to be from five to nine, the members to be determined by the school board. The board must "adopt reasonable rules and regulations for the administration of employer-employee relations." The board must also develop a method such as an audit or affidavit to determine the number of members of each organization requesting recognition.

Originally, the law sponsored by the California Teachers Association, an affiliate of the National Education Association, included the requirement that the board must negotiate in good faith. That was changed in the final law to a requirement that the board must "meet and confer" with the negotiating council. Normally, it has been implemented by the board representative, one of the administrators, acting on behalf of the board. In succeeding legislative sessions, there have been unsuccessful efforts to modify the Winton Act to include "in good faith." The Act in its entirety was strongly opposed by the American Federation of Teachers.

Connecticut

The Connecticut law provided for exclusive recognition of a single organization to form the bargaining unit for all employees. The unit is determined by a vote of the employees. If agreement is not reached, the issue is submitted to an arbitration board. In good faith bargaining was included in this law. The board must bargain on "salaries and other conditions of employment." A provision was included for a written contract to be signed by both parties in the negotiations, if requested. Strikes were outlawed; the solution of any impasse is arbitration.

The law also provided for two units of representation below the superintendent, one for employees with a teaching or special service certificate, and one for employees with a supervisory or special service certificate. The right of an employee or group of employees to present a grievance to the school board was guaranteed.

Michigan

The law providing for collective negotiations in Michigan was not confined to public schools but included most public employees in the state. Provisions guaranteed the right to organize, the right of representative elections conducted by the Michigan Labor Mediation Board, the right of exclusive, representative negotiations conducted in good faith with elected representatives, the right to negotiate the rates of pay, wages, hours of employment or other conditions of employment. The law also defined certain unfair labor practices. While strikes of public employees continued to be prohibited, public employers were no longer required to impose fines and jail terms on public employees who went on strike.

The act further provided that it is the responsibility of the Michigan Labor Mediation Board to determine the appropriate units of representation, to investigate unfair labor practice, to issue cease-and-desist orders, and to provide mediation in event of impasse. Fact finding was provided in the mediation process but was nonbinding. A written contract with a duration of up to three years might be requested by either party in the negotiations.

OREGON

The Oregon law was unique in that it did not contemplate a difference or contest between professional organizations. Over 85 percent of the certificated employees in Oregon are members of local affiliates of the National Education Association.

The act provided for representation of all certificated employees, except the superintendent, by an elected committee. "The right to confer, consult and discuss in good faith" with the board on matters of "salaries and related economic policies affecting professional services" was provided. Negotiations as such were not part of the law. The board established procedures for election and certified the results. The disposition of impasse is by nonbinding recommendations by a three-member committee of consultants. The use of nonemployee assistance, such as consultants, was not contemplated in the law and even the teaching organization was not mentioned as part of the bargaining unit.

WASHINGTON

The Washington act provides that the designated employee organizations and the school board should "meet, confer, and negotiate." The scope of negotiations includes "curriculum, textbook selection, in-service training, student-teaching programs, personnel hiring and assignment practices, leaves of absence, salaries and salary schedules, and noninstructional duties." Advisory impasse procedure was provided by a committee of educators and school-board members appointed by the State Superintendent of Public Instruction. The act provided for exclusive recognition of an employee organization which won an election. Legal recognition of an organization to represent the staff cannot be achieved without an election. The school board must adopt the rules and regulations for the elections.

Administrators and supervisors, except the superintendent, must be permitted representation by the recognized organization and must participate in the elections. Thus, organizations that wish to be considered for the bargaining unit must permit membership of these two groups.

WISCONSIN

Long a leader in the country in the field of employer-employee relations, Wisconsin was the first to provide for collective negotiations between teachers' organizations and school boards. The act included municipal employees beside teachers. Rights to join or not to join labor organizations, rights to be represented by such organizations, and rights to negotiate with the employer on questions of wages, hours, and conditions of employment were included in the act.

The Wisconsin Employment Relations Board was given the responsibility to administer the Wisconsin law. This Board, besides policing prohibited practices such as coercion or intimidation, also determines questions of representation by elections or other means. Orders of the Board are subject to judicial review.

Strikes by municipal employees in Wisconsin were prohibited, but fact-finding mediation by the Wisconsin Employment Relations Board with public recommendations was provided in the act. Provision for negotiations in good faith was also included. Written agreements were to have a duration of not more than one year.

NEW YORK

The New York State Labor Relations Act of 1937 was modeled on the National Wagner Act, which authorized collective negotiations. The New York State Constitution adopted in 1938 states: "Employees shall have the right to organize and to bargain collectively through representatives of their own choosing" (Art. I, Sec. 17).

However, it was not until August 6, 1955, that an application of the spirit of such statutes was made to public employees. On that date, Governor W. Averell Harriman issued an Executive Order "relating to procedures for the submission and settlement of grievances of state employees." The order gave employees the right to organize and designate representatives to adjust grievances. It also required the heads of departments to

> "hold conferences at appropriate times with employee representatives on problems relating to conditions of employment and the continued improvement of the public service . . ."

In 1958, Mayor Robert Wagner of New York City announced that "labor disputes between the City and its employees will be minimized, and that effective operation of the City's affairs in the public interest will be safeguarded, by permitting employees to participate, to the extent allowed by law, through their freely chosen representatives in the determination of the terms and conditions of their employment." Supervisory level employees were included in authorization for collective bargaining.

However, there still existed the question of whether or not teachers were included. The question was whether teachers were employees similar to civil-service workers and therefore eligible or whether they were in a special class to whom collective bargaining did not apply.

In 1961 an entirely new board of education of nine members was appointed in New York City. It officially opened the door to collective bargaining for the school staff with a statement, adopted March 8, 1962, of "Policies and Practices with Respect to Representation of Pedagogical and Civil-Service Employese for Purposes of Collective Bargaining with Board
302

of Education." The seven-page statement authorized employees, including teachers, to select representatives of their own choosing, to form organizations, to obtain exclusive representational rights in collective bargaining concerning grievances, compensation and hours or conditions of employment, and it described the way in which an organization might become the exclusive representative. School supervisors were excluded from these arrangements.

Prior to that declaration of policy, the United Federation of Teachers requested certification as the exclusive bargaining agent for the teachers of New York City's schools. An election was held to determine this and the U.F.T. was so certified by the Board of Education in an agreement entered into July 1, 1962.

In April, 1967, a statewide law was enacted which extended representation and collective bargaining rights to all public employees in the state. Called the Public Employees Fair Employment Act, but commonly known as the Taylor Law, it actually required public employers to negotiate with their employees and to enter into written agreements with them. It also forbade strikes by public employees and set penalties of a fine and imprisonment for up to 30 days for officers who led strikes. A further penalty was elimination of the check-off privilege for collecting dues. The Taylor Law also set up a PERB (Public Employees Relations Board) unit to establish procedures for administration and enforcement. Any identifiable unit in public employment may apply to PERB for certification as the collective bargaining agent of the unit. Under this law, some 3,000 supervisory members of the New York City school staff have claimed recognition. In 1968, for the first time, a collegiate organization of teachers obtained an election to determine if they might represent the college staff in the City University of New York.

NEGOTIATIONS WITH SCHOOL STAFF COMPARED WITH NEGOTIATIONS IN INDUSTRY

It has been apparent that methodology in negotiation as used by industry has influenced the direction of collective negotiations. School boards, administrators and staff, being relatively unsophisticated in the field of negotiation, have turned to the experiences of industry to give direction. The methods of industry in their labor-management relations, certainly to this date, have been more effective in those communities which emphasize collective bargaining rather than professional negotiations. It is suggested by some that, while the former methods have been proved effective in areas such as salaries and fringe benefits, the direction of professional negotiation will be more effective in other areas of public education, such as curriculum. It is also believed by some that the direction of negotiation in industry, where the profit concept exists, is not germane to public education.

The idea of management endeavoring to give as little as possible in

303

order to obtain a better profit for the stockholder, with the employees aware both of the profits of the organization and of their share in contributing to these profits, influences the process of negotiations in industry. Ideally, of course, the concept of the board of education as the employer, the administrator as the representative of management, and the teacher as the employee should not exist, since the public schools are not organized to obtain financial profits. But the relationships and attitudes of employer versus employee nevertheless exist in the school situation.

The board of education is interested in securing the services of staff for as little cost to the taxpayer as possible, and the counter effort of teachers to secure as much as possible from the same taxpayer creates the climate which contributes to the direction industry has assumed in negotiations. Ideally, the administrator is the representative of the board of education, and teachers should negotiate as colleagues with a common purpose in mind, that of developing the best program possible for the education of the children of the community. At this time, though, negotiations have not achieved that goal. Perhaps greater emphasis on issues other than salaries and fringe benefits, such as textbooks, courses of study, educational procedures and other professional topics, would achieve a better climate for negotiations among colleagues.

DIFFERENT VIEWS OF PROFESSIONAL NEGOTIATIONS

The issues and relationships in professional negotiations have been viewed differently. One issue concerns the role that should be played by the representative of the employees. Should his role be that of an equal in the process of genuine bilateral negotiation toward establishing terms and conditions by mutual agreement? Should his role be that of a regularly consulted, interested party whose reactions must be obtained and discussed before a unilateral decision is made by the government representative? Should his role be that of identifying the recipients of early notification of decisions made by the government representative? Should his role be a combination of the above? A second important issue concerns the areas in which the representatives of employees are permitted to make demands or to express wishes. Are salary and hours of work the only acceptable areas? Are curricular problems acceptable areas?

Lieberman and Moskow discuss three basic approaches to the field of professional negotiations.[4] Each is summarized below.

THE MARKETPLACE APPROACH

This is based upon the desire of teachers to sell their services for the best return and school boards to purchase the services for as little as possible. Short-range relationships are the result, with either party free to make a new bargain when the existing one expires. Because of the limited, year-
304

to-year relationship that exists, both parties feel more free to take advantage of each other than if a more permanent relationship were recognized.

THE PROFESSIONAL APPROACH

Here the emphasis is on the fact that teachers are professional employees. In the performance of their professional services, they do not consider it unprofessional to insist upon high fees. Allusion is made to the medical profession. The distinction is drawn between unwillingness and inability to pay for professional services. Negotiations are the solution to unwillingness to pay.

The professional worker, although interested in his client, has an interest in receiving a high fee; the client's interest is service at a low fee. As the physician is interested in equipment and the quality of nursing, so is the teacher interested in curriculum, methods, and textbooks. Negotiations are the way to make such interests known.

THE PROBLEM-SOLVING APPROACH

The emphasis here is on collective negotiations as a problem-solving procedure. The approach is in terms of the best way to get the job done in each situation. The effectiveness of this method must be evaluated in terms of the achievement of goals, both long- and short-range. Both sides must use this approach if it is to be successful. The sacrifice of immediate advantage for a long-range benefit must be material.

PARTICIPANTS IN THE NEGOTIATING PROCESS

There is a difference between the literature and the practice in various communities concerning who should negotiate, both as representative of the board of education and as representative of teachers. Practices vary from the employment of a specialist in the field of labor-management relations to represent the board to the designation of an administrator or administrators for this purpose, and in some communities the board itself assumes the role of the negotiator. The practice of teachers' groups, likewise, varies from utilization of teachers selected by their colleagues to represent them to the employment of specialists, such as labor-relations lawyers. Often the executive secretary of the association or the president is the chief negotiator. The teachers' organization itself determines who shall be its negotiators.

There are advantages and disadvantages of each procedure. Board members often are not qualified for conducting negotiations. Board members are busy individuals who do not normally have the time to devote to the lengthy, time-consuming process of negotiations. Also, it is a troublesome precedent for certain members of the board to assume this responsibility for the total board. The responsibility of the board in most states for making final decisions can make the compromises that are necessary in negotiations unrealistic, difficult, and impossible if one member of the board, as the board's representative, takes a strong stand on an issue. If board members do not personally participate in negotiations, they should be kept in close touch with developments and tentative agreements so that they can understand the total agreement.

The use of a trained specialist in the field of labor-management relations or labor law also presents difficulties. While probably capable in the areas of salaries, fringe benefits, etc., he is often not conversant in the field of education and he may not be aware of the complex factors that can develop in areas beyond the bread-and-butter issues. Teachers are as concerned about curricular problems and working conditions—factors that affect the entire climate of public education—as they are about salary. And a specialized negotiator may not be prepared in those areas.

Opinions vary concerning the use of lawyers in the negotiating process. Some believe that participation by lawyers makes the process too technical and formal. Yet certain legal precedents and requirements should be known. It is generally conceded that the advice of a lawyer should be available and that a lawyer's experience is desirable in drafting written agreements to avoid ambiguity and other technical errors. For example, an agreement may specify that a teacher should have a preparation period each week. Such a statement is ambiguous unless the length of the period is defined and unless there is some recognition of weeks that are fewer than five days long because of holidays. Ambiguities in written agreements may cause so many grievances to be filed and such consequent loss of time and good will that the cost of a legal adviser for agreement-drafting purposes would be more than offset.

Perhaps the best negotiator for the board, in school districts where formal negotiation is practiced, is the superintendent or a member of his staff, supported by appropriate consultants, such as the business manager and a field supervisor. Such individuals, while not trained in the specifics of negotiation, bring a knowledge of the educational program to the bargaining table. Knowing as he does the general policies of the board through long association, having the confidence of the board and the status of his office, the superintendent or his representative is in the best position to negotiate for the board. The head of each negotiating team, moreover, should have power to conclude terms that are likely to be accepted, or else the other side will have little faith in him and will want the key person there. Usually there is one spokesman for each side with his advisers whispering to him. In less formal situations, more than one person on each side may speak.

The role of the personnel officer in the field of collective negotiations varies from one school district to another, depending upon a number of factors. Inasmuch as the vast majority of the problems considered in negotiations are within the realm of the functions of the personnel officer, he is a valuable member of the negotiating team. Often, because of training,

306

background and available time, the personnel officer assumes or is assigned the role of chief negotiator. In districts where the superintendent or a labor-relations specialist is the chief negotiator, the personnel officer is a valuable resource. Many experienced school personnel administrators believe that they should not be designated the principal negotiator for the school board or the superintendent. On the surface, such designation seems to enhance the authority and prestige of the position. In fact, however, it could lead to serious adverse effects. In the first place, a lack of confidence could arise, since it would be recognized that the personnel administrator lacks decision-making power. Because the principal negotiator for the board is usually regarded as an adversary, this role would weaken the future effectiveness of the personnel administrator in his dual capacity as representative of the superintendent and professional liaison person with the staff. A role that many experienced school personnel administrators prefer is that of adviser to the superintendent in the negotiating or collective bargaining process. He might be of additional service in the earlier phases of the process in clarifying points of view, in obtaining data, and in helping others to reach understanding and agreement. In looking to the future of negotiations, one is led to believe that the function of the personnel officer will continue to increase in importance. It should be the obligation of all individuals either aspiring to work in personnel administration or presently in the field to become informed about the processes of negotiations.

THE PROCESS OF STAFF NEGOTIATIONS

Ideally, negotiations should occur over periods of time sufficient for both parties. They should decide upon long-range objectives. Negotiations and decisions agreed upon in a crisis-oriented situation, normally complicated by emotion and pressures, are rarely as satisfactory to either party as those accomplished in a long-range program.

Successful negotiations can best be achieved in an atmosphere of mutual respect. It must be recognized that, while the representatives of the board have power, so do the parties representing the employees. Many weapons are available to the latter, among them the ballot box, the sympathy of the public, sanctions and strikes. The best way to avoid undesirable confrontation and unsatisfactory results is through a continuing program of negotiations before crisis. Willingness to listen, patience, respect for ideas, recognition of the need to compromise, and desire to arrive at a mutually acceptable solution to problems are among the ingredients of a successful program of negotiations. The consequences for public education when these factors fail to become manifest are unrest and low morale among the staff, negative reactions to public education by the public, and futile uses of time and energy by children in school. The grievous loss in instruction to the children of New York City in the strike of autumn 1968, when many weeks of instruction were lost by over one million students, is

307

an example. At the beginning of the 1969–70 school year, teachers were on strike in 53 school districts, according to figures in the September, 1969, issue of the *American Teacher,* a publication of the American Federation of Teachers. Thirteen of them had AFL-CIO representation.

Much has been written about the use of power by the two national teachers' organizations. Each organization has developed a series of increasingly militant power displays culminating in the strike, the ultimate weapon of the American Federation of Teachers, and the use of sanctions, the final weapon of the National Education Association. Each organization has used its device on a number of occasions in the past decade. Teachers' strikes are not new. Teachers called 105 strikes in the United States between 1941 and 1961. The National Education Association has used sanctions in a number of school districts and several times on a statewide basis, as in Utah, Oklahoma and Florida. As a final weapon it would appear that the strike has been more immediately effective. The use of sanctions, which is ultimately a withholding of services, has as its chief objective long-range goals rather than the more immediate results which the strike seeks to accomplish. Neither is desirable, if avoidance is possible; the continuing dialogue that is the essence of a constructive program of negotiations is the positive measure that can be utilized to avoid either sanctions or strikes and can result in a better climate for a successful instructional program.

DEFINITION OF TERMS

Various terms have come into use during the process of negotiations or collective bargaining. Although there may be variations of interpretation in different surroundings, the personnel administrator should have knowledge of their common meaning.

PROFESSIONAL NEGOTIATIONS AND COLLECTIVE BARGAINING

"Collective bargaining" was a term used widely by units of the American Federation of Teachers to describe their dealings and discussions with school boards, which they believed followed patterns of industry in which this term had been used to describe labor-management negotiations. "Professional negotiations" and "collective negotiation" were terms preferred by units of the National Education Association because they believed there were essential differences between their negotiations and those of industry. There are many similarities in the two approaches with respect to procedures, goals and outcomes. Stinnett, Kleinman and Ware list two major differences between the approaches:

> "(1) Professional negotiation procedures can result in the removal of teachers and school boards from the operation of labor laws and labor precedent, whereas collective bargaining procedures, adopted from the private sector, will not. (2) For the purposes of mediation and appeal, procedures will go through educational channels under

professional negotiation and through labor channels under collective bargaining." [5]

It is also true that the process of collective bargaining, which is industry-oriented, may result in strikes, but collective negotiations have resulted in sanctions, which in many respects are similar to strikes. School personnel administrators who have participated in both professional negotiations and collective bargaining have said they could discern only slight difference in the procedures and difficulties of reaching agreements.

SANCTIONS AND STRIKES

Withdrawal of services under professional sanctions may be preceded by such actions as the following: censure through publication of grievances and shortcomings of the school district, notification of the state department of education of the unsatisfactory conditions, advice to members of the association not to accept employment in the school district, and advice to members not to renew their contracts. The support of the state and N.E.A. affiliates may be sought for local organizations. For example, in 1965 the Oklahoma Education Association and the N.E.A. invoked sanctions against the state of Oklahoma to compel educational improvements and the granting of additional funds to school districts. In 1965, the N.E.A. Commission on Professional Rights and Responsibilities published a list of 19 proposed procedures designed to avoid sanctions or strikes by preliminary action.[6] They include petitions to the school board, use of mass media, mass attendance at board meetings, legal action, motorcade, raising defense funds, appeal to higher authority, and issuance of an "urgent advisory" telling members of an unsatisfactory situation in the school district.

IMPASSE

Despite prolonged negotiation, the representatives of the staff and the representative of the school board may be unable to agree on the matter of salary for beginning teachers, or any other matter. Such a situation has been called an "impasse." At some point, they may agree to call upon the services of a mediator, fact finder or arbitrator. A New York State law even requires that when both sides agree that no further progress can be made in settling a particular issue an impasse is to be declared, and the services of a mediating panel must be sought.

FACT FINDING AND MEDIATION

An individual or a panel called in for the purpose of fact finding, sometimes called a board of inquiry, has a task of cutting through the arguments, pro and con, to establish relevant facts that are acceptable to both parties and to the public. For example, if the issue concerned the salaries of beginning teachers, the panel would seek to assemble the data that had been utilized by both sides to set up a factual rationale that might be useful in resolving the dispute. Thus, the panel might make factual com-

309

parisons of the salaries of beginning teachers in one school district with the salaries of beginning teachers in neighboring school districts; the panel might develop data concerning the costs of the salary increases being urged. The function of the fact-finding panel would not be to persuade either side to agree, or to offer a solution of its own, or to reconcile differences, but to obtain, develop and present considerations of fact that should be helpful in resolving a dispute. The duties of the fact finder were described in one agreement that related to grievance procedures: the fact finder should limit his findings strictly to resolving the question of whether or not the employee's complaint is substantiated by the evidence; he should not interpret or apply the provisions of any agreement. A person or panel called on for the purpose of mediation would take a more active role in seeking to resolve the disputed issue. Usually, the mediator or the mediating panel reviews the facts and arguments of both sides with respect to the issue. Each side usually has a separate room that is easily accessible to the mediator, who goes from one group to another carrying specific proposals for reaction. He might suggest compromises, a concession on one side in return for a yielding on the other side, or he might offer advice or a new approach. The successful mediator is a person of great patience, ingenuity, tact and understanding. Often, state or federal agencies offer the services of mediators in public disputes.

ARBITRATION: BINDING AND ADVISORY

Arbitration is different from mediation in that the impartial arbitrator or the arbitrating panel listens to both sides, assesses the situation and the arguments, pro and con, and offers an independent solution. Arbitration may be less satisfactory to disputing parties than mediation because an agreement reached after mediation represents the final consent of both parties, whereas an agreement after arbitration is an agreement that may be imposed without the consent of the disputing parties. Sometimes arbitration is resorted to when mediation fails. It must be remembered that the mediator does not offer a solution of his own, but helps disputing parties to develop their own agreement.

Arbitration may be binding or advisory. Arbitration is binding when both parties, after admitting that they cannot possibly reach an agreement on their own, decide in advance to accept the judgment of an arbitrator or arbitrating panel for solution to the dispute. Under advisory arbitration, the solution recommended by the impartial arbitrator may be accepted or rejected. In some states and in some school districts, binding arbitration is not permitted under law because boards of education are not permitted to delegate their authority to make decisions to any other individual or body. However, advisory arbitration is usually effective because public support is generated for the solution offered by the impartial panel. The American Arbitration Association is a private, nonprofit organization that provides disputing groups with lists of names of professional arbitrators.

310

CHECKOFF

The checkoff refers to the privilege granted to an organization to have its dues deducted from the salary of an employee before he receives it. It is regarded as most important by teachers' organizations, among others, because it facilitates the collection of dues, which otherwise costs time, effort and money. Teachers' organizations that are granted the checkoff privilege by their boards of education usually obtain the written consent of each member to have dues deducted from his or her salary each month or from each salary check.

The value of the checkoff has been recognized to the extent that, in New York State, the Taylor Law required suspension of the checkoff privilege for organizations of public employees that violated the no-strike agreement. The United Federation of Teachers in New York City, upon whom the penalty was placed, was alleged to have regarded it as most severe.

AGENCY SHOP AND UNION SHOP

In labor terms, a "union shop" is a shop in which all workers are required to be dues-paying members of the union. Anyone who is employed in the shop must join and remain in the union as a condition of employment. In an "agency shop," employees are not required to be members of the union, but they are required to share the expenses of the union that are incurred in representing them. That is often not much less than the dues paid by members. The result is that employees in an agency shop often become union members because there is little difference in the cost and there are additional benefits. Thus far, a union shop has not been obtained in public employment on the grounds that individuals employed by the government cannot be required to join any organization as a condition of employment. The agency shop has not been permitted either, on the grounds that it deprives a government employee of part of his salary, which the government has no right to exact as a condition of public employment. In recent years, however, particularly in New York City, organizations representing civil-service employees and the United Federation of Teachers have sought legislation that would give them the privilege of maintaining an agency shop. Their proposed legislation would protect the constitutional rights of individuals who decline to pay by allowing them to waive the agency-shop payments if they waived the benefits obtained directly by the organization. Few would be willing to do that, so most would accept the agency-shop arrangement.

EXCLUSIVE RECOGNITION

Any organization that has the vote of a majority of those it represents is generally recognized by boards of education as the exclusive bargaining and negotiating agent for the entire staff or group. That does not mean that individuals or small organizations may not express their views to the administration or demand the rectification of grievances. It means that in formal negotiations the board of education is bound to listen only to the exclusive negotiating agent in arriving at an agreement. The situation was spelled out in 1961 for employee-management relations in the federal service as follows: [7]

> "Under this system, if an employee organization is chosen by the majority of employees in an appropriate unit it becomes the only formalized representative for the unit. In its dealings with management officials it is considered to speak for all of the employees of the unit, a responsibility which it must, of course, meet.
> "It should be emphasized that exclusive recognition in the form proposed by the Task Force would not prevent any individual employee from bringing matters of personal concern to the attention of management officials, nor, for example, from choosing his own representative in a grievance action."

There are several methods for ascertaining whether or not an organization of employees does in fact represent a majority of the staff. One method is to elect a negotiating or bargaining agent by secret ballot. Another is to present a verified membership list representing a majority of the staff. A third method is to present authorization cards signed by a majority of the staff and designating an organization as the negotiating or bargaining agent. A fourth method is to present signed petitions requesting the board of education to recognize a named organization as the agent. There are several advantages to the employer in dealing with a single bargaining or negotiating agent. The process of bargaining or negotiating is simplified and direct. One is reminded of a newspaper strike that took place in the early 1960s in New York City in which the owners of the newspaper found themselves negotiating with a multitude of unions representing different employee groups. The negotiations were drawn out over a long period of time and were made much more difficult by the varying demands and personalities. Exclusive representation also has a great advantage for a teachers' organization: the one that becomes the negotiating or bargaining agent, even by a slim majority, usually expands its membership greatly and eventually eliminates competition. Teachers develop a more powerful voice because of their unity and their representation by one agent.

PROBLEMS OF SELECTING AN APPROPRIATE NEGOTIATING OR BARGAINING UNIT

Within each school district—where there are administrators from the rank of assistant superintendent to the rank of departmental chairman; teachers of various subjects; school social workers, psychologists, secretaries, custodians, lunchroom workers, paraprofessionals, and so on—one huge organization can represent all, but the varied employee groups may not believe that one organization can adequately represent all of their separate points of view. In some situations, state law decrees that there should be two organizations, one representing administrators and the other representing teachers. Presumably, nonteaching personnel may be represented by an association of their own choosing. In other states, discretion is given to each school district in determining suitable groups, and the wishes of the group of employees are an important factor in determining who represents them, as in New York state under the so-called Taylor Law. Either mediation or lawsuits are used to settle disputes over the appropriate unit.

DETERMINING THE APPROPRIATE UNIT

One method of unit organization is to set up a large negotiating or bargaining unit, such as an organization of teachers, which also negotiates for different groups or subgroups within its organization. For example, the New York City United Federation of Teachers negotiates or bargains for school secretaries, laboratory assistants, psychologists and social workers. In 1969, the United Federation of Teachers in New York City was in a contest with the American Federation of State, County and Municipal Employees to see which organization would win the right to represent groups of paraprofessionals serving in the school system.

Determining the appropriate negotiating or bargaining units for school administrators has posed some problems. Some school boards have been reluctant to enter into formal negotiations with assistant superintendents, headquarters personnel or school principals on the grounds that they represent school management and should be treated differently from the teaching staff. In one school district, the school board objected to having principals in the same organization as the teachers. They charged that a conflict of interest existed since the principals were the board's representatives in dealing with teachers while at the same time joining with them in organizational activities that might be contrary to the wishes of the board of education. However, the notion of conflict of interests largely stems from the private sector, where the plant administrator may determine the salaries, fringe benefits, working conditions and hours of his employees. In a school system, those elements are not determined by school principals but by the board of education. The validity of the conflict-of-interest charge is further weakened by the professional basis of relationships of school supervisors and administrators with teachers. There are, however, other considerations which may make it desirable for school supervisors and administrators to have separate negotiating or bargaining units from teachers. Teachers might believe that their combined unit is dominated by administrative members and that their needs and interests would not receive adequate attention. Teachers might feel inhibited in discussing their claims and demands.

Lieberman and Moskow offer three major criteria for unit determination:

1. Effective staff representation
2. Effective school administration
3. Stability in school board-staff relationship [8]

By effective staff representation, they mean that the unit should be constituted so that it provides a fair and reasonable channel through which the group can receive attention for its legitimate needs. By effective school administration, they mean that the size and number of units should be such that the school district can deal with the representatives. If the number of units is excessive, then unnecessary conflicts may arise as the school board tries to meet the wishes of groups competing with each other. The school board would be able to manage its affairs more effectively if the competing desires could be settled within the teachers' organization before demands were made upon the school board. By stability in school board-staff relationships, they mean that a school district should have a long-range program based on stability of staff representation. Such a situation would not bar changes or improvements but would slow up radical departures from one year to the next as different conditions, methods and types of representation are demanded. Some individuals who have looked far ahead have declared that negotiations on collective bargaining will some day be statewide, with perhaps only one organization representing school staff units in the entire state.

FACILITATING AGREEMENT DURING NEGOTIATIONS OR BARGAINING SESSIONS

The Influence of Attitudes at the Meeting

Negotiating sessions can be hostile confrontations fraught with distrust, ill will, antagonism and animosity, or they can be friendly, businesslike, mutually respectful and cooperative. It is most important that the latter atmosphere prevails, and both sides have a responsibility for seeing that it does. If the representatives of the school board do not believe that teachers have a right to discuss such matters as equals, then a block to constructive discussion begins. If the representatives of the school staff believe that the sole purpose of the school board is to deny all of their reasonable requests, then the solution of problems will be made more difficult. Both sides must take the view that they are not adversaries, not foes trying to take advantage of one another, but meeting as equals to work out reasonable solutions to problems in which their goals are similar.

Time and Place

Negotiating or bargaining should be arranged long before a crisis impends. If a contract is to terminate at the end of a school year, the time to begin negotiations is not two weeks, but four to six months, before that time. In order to provide adequate but limited time for discussion, a tendency has been to reach agreements covering two or three years.

The time of day for negotiating is also important. If staff representatives and representatives of the board of education meet at the end of the school day, the meetings are likely to be less fruitful than if they are held

314

at the beginning of the day, or on weekends or days when the staff representative and the representatives of the school board are excused from their usual activities. At crucial times in the discussions, meetings should be held away from the regular school offices, where school officials may be easily interrupted by routine matters. The place to hold discussions should be one in which the chairs are comfortable, in which there is a large table around which the entire group can sit and face one another in discussion, and in which a small group may remove itself to a corner for quiet discussion. It is also desirable to have available an adjacent room to which one group or the other can retire for private discussion, or caucus.

PREPARATION FOR THE MEETING

Well in advance of the first meeting, the representatives of the school staff should be asked to formulate their requests and demands and to submit them in sufficient copies to be read well in advance by the representative of the school board. If the representative of the school board has counterdemands or requests, they should be made available in writing to the representatives of the staff. These preliminary statements should be studied by both sides and referred to the consulting experts of either side for informed opinions. It is most important that the cost of each item be accurately ascertained by the representative of the school board. For example, reducing average class size by one pupil may require the employment of many new teachers costing tens of thousands of dollars. The total budget must be known, too. The following is a sample of a listing of the demands of the teaching staff in a large city and the counterdemands of the administration.

CITY TEACHERS' ORGANIZATION:
TENTATIVE AGENDA FOR NEGOTIATIONS

1. New Salary Schedule—Including 20 year longevity
2. Hospitalization—Total Family
3. Reduced Class Size
4. Increased supplies
5. Hot Lunch Program—Protection of teacher rights
6. Night and summer school sick leave and increased pay
7. Increased substitute rate
8. Special substitute
   A. Increased rate
   B. Clarification of Appendix, Section 7, Page 41
9. Equal sessions for kindergarten teachers
10. Establishment of the More Effective Schools Program
11. Additional Life Insurance, effective September 1, 1969
12. Substitutes for special subject teachers in elementary schools
13. Student trainees—Compensation for training teacher
14. Student teachers—Minimum of $100 for critic teacher
15. Coaches and Athletic Directors (includes junior high school)
16. Equalization of rates between community center instructors and adult education teachers

17. Head Librarians—Department chairman differential
    A. Librarians to provide unassigned period for classroom teacher
18. Attendance workers mileage allowance increase
19. Miscellaneous Salary Adjustments
    A. Juvenile Court
    B. Psychologists
20. Primary Unassigned Period
21. Differential System Expanded
    A. Junior high music teacher
    B. Senior high girl cheer leaders
    C. Elementary safety council
22. Guidance Counselors increased differential
23. Teacher Assistants—salaries and working conditions
24. Nurses salary schedule and working conditions
25. Liability coverage of those who must transport pupils
26. Automobile Insurance—dues deduction
27. In-Service Program—amount listed on contract
28. Continuation of Department Head Status once appointed
29. Severance pay
30. Recognition of law degree on Schedule E
31. M.A. + 30 hours—Schedule F
32. Problems and disposition of Grievance Procedures
33. Establishment of Committee to re-study promotion policy

INTENTIONS OR DEMANDS OF THE BOARD OF EDUCATION

Mr. Joseph Smith, President
City Teachers' Organization
Dear Mr. Smith:

Listed below are policy changes that the Administration of the City Public Schools plans to implement effective January 1, or at the time the revised agreement becomes effective. These changes are submitted to you at this time in order that you may make the necessary accommodations.

1. The number of professional days will be increased from the present four (plus 180 days when pupils are present) to eight (plus 180 days when pupils are present).
2. Teachers are to remain in their respective building 30 minutes beyond the regular school closing time for parent and/or pupil conferences, lesson preparation, faculty meetings, in-service meetings.
3. As a part of the equitable distribution of extra duties (as indicated in Section 14 of the agreement) teachers will be expected to be available for at least four evening assignments.
4. New teachers will be given 39 week contracts and the additional week will be the week immediately preceding the first week of regular teacher assignments and that time will be used for in-service education.
5. All differentials will be certified to the Clerk-Treasurer as of January 31 and June 15 of each school year for work performed during the semester preceding above dates, and one half of the differential will be paid on each date.

6. Unassigned periods are to be used for pupil and/or parent conferences, lesson preparation or other relative instructional effort in the building.
7. Continuing contract teachers will be evaluated, using normal evaluation procedures, every third year.
8. Teachers are to accept special substitute assignments, for special substitute rate of pay, when volunteer plan is insufficient to cover classes because of lack of substitutes.
9. All employees will be required to submit a doctor's certificate verifying illness when sick leave extends to five or more consecutive school days, including paid or declared holidays.
10. A procedure is to be developed between the Cleveland Teachers' Union and the Administration for due process removal of teachers serving in differential positions.
11. Beginning September, teachers will be paid on a 20 pay basis (September through June).

Sincerely yours,
WILLIAM H. JONES
Assistant Superintendent for Personnel

Once the demands of both sides are reviewed, a total agenda is developed and no new items may be added except by mutual consent. This is to put some limit on the scope of the negotiations, which might otherwise keep growing. The personnel administrator should know that, once an item is agreed upon, it is unlikely to be withdrawn. He should therefore not advise acceptance of the item unless he believes that it is permanently acceptable.

FACILITATING THE NEGOTIATING PROCESS

In advance of the meetings, statistics and data should be obtained on topics or issues that are most likely to come up. On request of the school staff, relevant data should be made available by the administration. Such studies should include data on salaries of school staff in surrounding communities and in other parts of the state, data concerning class size in the school district and in surrounding districts, and data concerning staff turnover. It is most important that data provided by the administration be accurate and honest.

PROCEDURES DURING THE NEGOTIATING SESSION

In small school systems where the staff is stable and satisfied, negotiating sessions may be completely informal—relaxed meetings between the school personnel administrator or superintendent and one or two staff representatives. In most situations, though, formal meetings are called for. There, the requests or demands of the staff and the administration, prepared and studied in advance, can be discussed one by one. Notes of the discussion, together with elements of agreement and disagreement, should be maintained by each side. A tape recording is not considered desirable

317

since it may result in making participants feel obliged to make statements for the record rather than to engage in free discussion. If both sides agree, it is possible to designate one individual, perhaps an impartial stenographer, to take essential notes. In the early sessions, items on which agreement is readily achieved should be completed. It is desirable, at the end of each session, to prepare a memorandum of understandings and agreements. Unless that is done, both sides will have different recollections of what was agreed on and what was rejected.

All sorts of possibilities develop at negotiating sessions. On some items, additional information is requested by one or both sides. They may be laid over for future sessions. There may be an indication by one side that it is willing to yield a given point if the other side similarly yields. One side may request that time be taken out for a caucus, after which the group may return with a counterproposal or a variation of its initial request. It has been found that, other things being equal, publicity hinders the chances for agreement. Once the opposing views have reached the public, each side may tend to harden in its position because of its fear of public reaction or the reaction of the members of the association. Since agreements, concessions and compromises are contingent upon other concessions and agremeents, it is considered wise to postpone any announcement until the entire written agreement has been approved by both negotiating teams. All agreements, therefore, are considered tentative. Of great importance during the discussions is the creation of a spirit of bargaining in "good faith." It is achieved by considering proposals seriously, showing a willingness to compromise, and avoiding frivolous proposals. As the negotiations reach the most difficult issues, both groups may find it desirable to engage in around-the-clock negotiations. Although they are wearisome, experience has indicated that sustained sessions often result in agreements.

MATTERS THAT MAY BE NEGOTIATED

The process of negotiation or collective bargaining differ from school district to school district, but the matters that are negotiated differ as well. In most school districts, procedural agreements are reached after informal discussion. They contain such items as recognition of the negotiating agent, description of the negotiating procedures, and a procedure for resolving deadlocks. According to an N.E.A. Research Bulletin, in 1966-67 there were 1,540 known agreements on file, of which 1,142 were such procedural agreements. The remaining 398 agreements (about 26 percent) were comprehensive agreements containing specific items of all kinds.[10] The N.E.A. Research Bulletin covering the year 1967-68 showed 2,212 negotiated agreements on file, of which 603 (about 27 percent) were comprehensive agreements.[11]

The following table indicates the range of topics covered in written agreements between boards of education and organizations of teachers.[12]

318

TABLE 1

Frequency of Occurrence of Provisions Among 1,540 Agreements
on File with the N.E.A. Research Division
for the 1966–67 School Year

Negotiation Procedure

Procedure for recognition of employee organization	374
Provision for specific items included or excluded from negotiation	456
Provisions for negotiation sessions	1,061
Procedure for impasse in negotiation	524

Scope of Agreement

General statement of parties to agreement	629
General statement of recognition	903
Classification of persons covered or excluded under agreement	421
Effect on prior rules and policies	256
Information pertinent to negotiation, e.g., financial and budgetary reports made available to the representative organization	543
Nondiscrimination clause against membership in employee organization	528
Use of school communication system, bulletin boards, and mail boxes	458
Use of building facilities, e.g., assembly hall	371
Check-off or dues deduction	335
Organizational representatives allowed time off without loss of salary for negotiation sessions or grievance hearings	172

Teacher Activity

Individual or minority representation to the administration	187
Teacher's rights under law not abridged	115

Board Rights

General statement of responsibility	227

Instructional Program

School calendar or year	253
Pupil ratio and class size	222
Instructional aids which are available for the teacher's use in the development, planning, and teaching in the classroom	169
Selection and distribution of textbooks	140
Student extracurricular activities supervision	131
Integration of education for textbooks, pupils, and staff	116

Parent-teacher conferences	94
Curriculum review	85
Teacher aides to relieve the teacher of extraneous duties	73
Teacher qualifications	66

Personnel Policies and Practices

Grievance procedure	369
Method of selection of arbitrator, mediator, or review panel for grievance procedure	324
Transfers	265
Promotion to higher classification, supervisor, or administrator	243
Teaching assignment in subject areas	242
Procedure for teacher evaluation	241
Lunch period for elementary teachers	237
Lunch period for secondary teachers	222
Assault cases and pupil discipline	234
Teacher facilities, e.g., lounge, parking space, desk, storage room	214
Duty-free periods for planning, etc.	213
Teaching hours or day	203

Salary Policy

Salary credits for prior growth and experience	267
Salary schedule	366
Salary increments for professional preparation	361
Extra-duty pay for special activities	277

Fringe Benefits

Terminal leave or severance pay	110
Tuition reimbursement	97
Travel allowance for transportation, food, or lodging	95

*Part or full premium payments
by board or other agency*

Health insurance	226
Life insurance	94
Income protection or disability insurance	34
Liability insurance	32

*Available through board
cooperation only*

Tax-sheltered annuity	41
Life insurance	20
Income protection or disability insurance	18

Absences with full or part pay

Sick leave	106
Personal business leave	163
	319

TABLE 1 (*continued*)

Absences with full or part pay (cont.)		*Absences without pay*	
Educational conference	152	Maternity leave	233
Bereavement leave	142	Military leave	193
Jury duty	130	Sick leave	138
Sabbatical leave	126	Public office or political campaigns	99
Court summons or other legal ac-		General (not specified)	98
tion	108	Peace Corps	92
General (not specified) leave	106	Professional business leave	88
Other school visitations	104	Sabbatical leave	66
Selective service examination	88	Foreign exchange teaching	30
Family illness leave	34		

The status of a board of education under law is such that, according to some legal authorities, it cannot fix conditions of employment in the public service on a contractual basis because this is a legislative prerogative. However, the board of education may voluntarily decide to adhere to certain practices and conditions of employment set forth in a "memorandum of understanding," "a statement of policy," or "an agreement," until it uses its authority to change the practices or conditions. It is believed by some legal authorities that legislative action by the state is required before a board of education can voluntarily negotiate and enter into an agreement with representatives of its staff, and by 1969 eight states had passed such enabling legislation. Notwithstanding legal precedents and requirements, the trend is toward written agreements between boards of education and organizations representing their school staffs. It should be pointed out that there are legal opinions that boards of education can make voluntary agreements with teachers' organizations without state legislative action. The form of such written agreements usually follows a uniform pattern, with which school personnel administrators should be familiar.

PREAMBLE

The written agreement usually begins with a general statement of cooperation and accepted goals, such as the following:

> "Meeting the educational needs of the children of ————— city demands the maximum cooperation of all concerned. The Board of Education and the Organization of Teachers therefore pledge that their joint efforts will be dedicated to the achievement of the standard of educational excellence that all pupils deserve and that the community has a right to expect."

RECOGNITION

A written agreement also usually includes a clause stating that the school board recognizes the organization as "the exclusive bargaining representative" of the group or groups for whom the agreement is being written. Here is an example.

ARTICLE I
Union Recognition

The Board recognizes the Union as the exclusive bargaining representative of all those assigned as classroom teachers in the regular day school instructional program and all those employed as per session teachers (except supervisors and per diem substitutes).

The term "classroom teachers in the regular day school instructional program" (herein referred to as "day school teachers") comprises the following teacher categories:

Teachers of kindergarten classes; teachers of grades 1A through 6B; teachers of grades above 6B; teachers of early childhood classes; teachers of music, fine arts, health education, sewing, industrial arts, home economics, classes for children with retarded mental development, classes for the blind, sight conservation classes, classes for crippled children, health conservation classes, classes for tuberculous children, hospital classes, speech improvement, and schools for the deaf; teachers in day academic and day vocational high schools; teachers of library in junior high. . . .

Nothing contained herein shall be construed to prevent any Board official from meeting with any employee organization representing classroom teachers for the purpose of hearing the views and proposals of its members, except that, as to matters presented by such organizations which are proper subjects of collective bargaining, the Union shall be informed of the meeting and, as to those matters, any changes or modifications shall be made only through negotiation with the Union.

Nothing contained herein shall be construed to prevent any individual employee from (1) informally discussing a complaint with his immediate superior or (2) processing a grievance in his own behalf in accordance with the grievance procedure hereinafter set forth in Article VII.

Nothing contained herein shall be construed to deny to any employee his rights under Section 15 of the New York Civil Rights Law or under the State Education Law or under applicable civil service laws and regulations.

FAIR PRACTICE

Fair practice clauses are frequently included in a written agreement. They indicate that the organization pledges it will not discriminate against individuals. An example follows.

ARTICLE II
Fair Practices

The Union agrees to maintain its eligibilty to represent all teachers by continuing to admit persons to membership without discrimination on the basis of race, creed, color, national origin, sex or marital status and to represent equally all employees without regard to membership or participation in, or association with the activities of, any employee organization.

The board agrees to continue its policy of not discriminating against any employee on the basis of race, creed, color, national origin, sex, marital status or membership or participation in, or association with the activities of, any employee ogranization.

PROVISIONS FOR MEETINGS

Contracts usually provide for monthly meetings between representatives of the school staff and the superintendent; other meetings provided for include an annual school board meeting and periodic organizational activities.

NO-STRIKE PLEDGE

The concluding portion of an agreement may have a no-strike pledge, such as the following:

> "The Organization and the Board recognize that strikes and other forms of work stoppages by teachers are contrary to law and public policy. The Organization and the Board subscribe to this principle that differences shall be resolved by appropriate and peaceful means without interruption of the school program. The Organization therefore agrees that there shall be no strikes, work stoppages or other concerted refusal to perform work by the employees covered by this agreement nor any instigation thereof."

DURATION OF WRITTEN AGREEMENT

The concluding portion of the agreement generally specifies its duration, which usually varies from one to three years. It sometimes specifies when negotiations for a new agreement may begin. Many written agreements terminate on June 30. School boards may prefer that terminal date because additional time is provided during the summer months, when a new agreement can be developed if one has not been agreed to by the end of June. Some organizations of teachers prefer the agreement to run until September 1 in order to avoid the possible lapse of time between July 1 and September 1 when no agreement may be in effect.

CONDITIONS OF EMPLOYMENT

The great variety in the conditions of employment may become the basis for an agreement between the board of education and the organization representing the staff. Salary, length of school day, transfers, grievance procedures and fringe benefits are included most widely. However, there has been a tendency to include matters of class size, curriculum, teacher qualifications, teacher evaluation, teacher programs, etc.

THE FUTURE OF STAFF NEGOTIATIONS

In attempting to look into the future it would appear that negotiations or collective bargaining will continue to grow as a force on the educational scene. A continuing and understandable desire on the part of the staff to be considered as colleagues and partners in the educational program will not diminish. There is a probability that the two rival teacher organizations will unite to form a stronger united front in bringing greater pressures for partnership recognition on boards of education. Indeed, *The Wall Street Journal* on Oct. 13, 1969, headlined a news article: "First Tie Between the A.F.T., N.E.A. Forged As Flint, Mich., Affiliates Form a New Unit." The article went on to describe how an agreement was reached between the 1,500 N.E.A. members and the 270 A.F.T. members to merge and affiliate with both parent organizations. The current rivalry can only weaken the effectiveness of both organizations. There will be increasing emphasis on more definitive and explicit contract provisions. These are likely to show greater and greater concern for issues beyond salaries and working conditions as the staff displays an increasing desire to participate in policy making in all areas of the educational program. Teacher militancy will continue in the foreseeable future and will not be ignored. Boards of education and the public have the same basic objectives as the staff and that is to improve education. It will be the responsibility of boards and administration to channel this militancy through positive negotiations in the direction of achieving the best possible instructional program for the children of the district they serve. Once teacher organizations cease to have to fight for members by showing how much they are doing against the foe, they will be able to turn toward what some board members would call more constructive approaches. At the same time boards of education must show a greater willingness to regard their school staff as professionals who are partners in the school enterprise rather than hired mercenaries.

Stinnett, Kleinman and Ware have this to say of the future:

> "A basic premise of professional negotiation is that these groups (*teachers, administrators and school board members*) can solve together the problems they face. State legislation is proposed as the most satisfactory means of doing this, but the absence of state legislation should not prevent the cooperative development and adoption of professional negotiations on a district-by-district basis throughout the nation.

There are some who see beyond this to a time when statewide agreements will be the pattern. Since staff negotiations represent a new relationship and a new activity, there are many problems that are to be solved in the future. The achievements of the negotiating process will have to be evaluated. The process is costly in money, time and energy, and it is fair to try to ascertain whether the process has resulted in better education. How has the process affected the attitude of society toward education? As a result of negotiations, is society more keenly interested in education, more willing to support education to higher financial limits? How have the negotiations affected the attitudes of youth toward education? The attitudes of the teaching staff itself? One thing seems certain: if the negotiating process is to have long-range meaning and benefit for education, school boards, representing the public, and the teaching profession must come to agreement on the fundamental objectives of education and the best ways of achieving these objectives.

15 GRIEVANCE PROCEDURES

GENERAL STATEMENT

The phenomenon of grievance procedures in public education is not new. Many school systems, particularly the large ones, have had some process by which teachers and other members of the staff could make their grievances known. However, it should be recognized that grievance procedures were slow to be formalized in teaching when compared to industry, which was most likely caused by the type of relationship that generally existed between teachers, administrators and school boards. It is only within the past four or five years that both major teachers' organizations, the National Education Association and the American Federation of Teachers, really started working for grievance procedures in the agreements and contracts they developed through collective negotiations. Many teachers didn't feel that they had the right to have a grievance procedure. Some felt it was "unprofessional." Others did not believe they needed one. Many school systems are still without any kind of grievance procedure and many will undoubtedly continue to operate without one in the foreseeable future.

There are many definitions of grievances, but generally an employee feels he has been aggrieved when he is under the impression that he has been dealt with unfairly by whatever criteria are set up by his employer.

Grievance procedures of long standing were set up by administrations. They usually gave the employee a route up the administrative ladder, culminating with the superintendent of schools or someone delegated by him to handle the responsibility. There was usually no appeal from the decision of the superintendent.

Most of the written grievance procedures described in the preceding paragraph were brief. Some school systems had grievance procedures, but they were not committed to writing. This usually was the situation in smaller school systems where most school policies were unwritten. Obviously, having an unwritten grievance procedure is better than not having one at all, until misunderstanding develops with regard to procedural details. A National Education study of 603 comprehensive negotiated agreements between boards of education and teachers' organizations in school systems of 1,000 or more pupils revealed that, for the school year 1967-68, over 98 percent included written grievance procedures.[1]

The failure to formalize grievance procedures by committing them to writing and making them available causes misunderstandings to occur. Personalities may well enter into various phases of the procedure. Not only may teachers be affected by a failure to have a written grievance procedure, but personnel in supervisory and administrative positions may feel that their rights have been disregarded, too.[2] Another advantage of written procedures is that they frequently come about as a result of collective thinking. The organized and written grievance procedure originated in the private sector of labor-management relationships as a by-product of collective bargaining. Collective bargaining in the private sector produced written contracts.

Once the contracts became operative, the charge that management was not following the provisions of the contract, as employees interpreted them, became common. These charges became known as grievances. As grievances increased in quantity and became more sophisticated, the private sector began the practice of detailing grievance procedures in the collective bargaining process. The primary purpose of the grievance procedure in the private sector is to resolve differences of opinion with regard to the interpretation of the provisions in the contract as they affect the rights and privileges of employees.[3]

In 1964, New York State passed legislation governing grievance procedures prior to the time it had any legislation related to negotiations for teachers. The state law on grievance procedures covered all public employees and teachers, according to the interpretation of the state education department attorneys. The legislation in part read as follows:

> "Grievance shall mean any claimed violation, misinterpretation or inequable application of the existing law, rules, procedures, regulations, administrative orders, or work rules of a government or department or agency thereof, which relates to or involves employee health or safety, physical facilities, materials or equipment furnished to employees or supervision of employees; provided, however, that such terms shall not include any matter involving an employee's rate of compensation, retirement benefits, disciplinary proceedings, or any matter which is otherwise reviewable pursuant to law or any rule or regulation having the force and effect of law."

This New York legislation falls far short of how we currently view grievance procedures, but it did serve a real purpose. It compelled many districts that did not have any type of written procedure either to adopt one or to

326

operate under the broad framework of the law. Conspicuously restricted from the grievance procedure are matters involving employees' rates of compensation. It is an exclusion that would be difficult for teachers and administrators to accept today.

STRUCTURING THE GRIEVANCE PROCEDURE

The first section of an effective grievance procedure is usually devoted to defining terms used in the procedure. The first definition, and one that should be written with extreme care, is for "grievance." It should be defined as a claim by one of more teachers based upon an alleged violation of a policy, rule, regulation or any item in the agreement.

The definition of a grievance which follows is from the Taylor Township, Michigan, agreement:

> "(1) that there has been to him [the employee] a violation, misinterpretation or inequitable application of any of the provisions of this agreement, or (2) that he has been treated unfairly or inequitably by reason of any act or condition which is contrary to established policy governing or affecting employees, except that the term 'grievance' shall not apply to any matter in which (1) a method of review is prescribed by law, or (2) the Board of Education is without authority to act."

Many school personnel administrators believe it should not include a complaint. A complaint is generally viewed as friction arising at the local level and involves a difference of opinion between two persons. Teachers and administrators are the parties most frequently involved. In most cases, the problem is resolved at the level where the complaint was initiated and does not fall into the category of a grievance.[4]

A complaint occurs, for instance, when a teacher states that he is not receiving his mail promptly or never gets it. The principal, or someone delegated by the principal, should look into the situation to see that his mail, as well as the mail of other teachers, is delivered or being placed in the designated locations within a reasonable time. The immediate resolution of this type of complaint should do much to improve teacher morale. Such complaints are not uncommon in the normal operation of a school. They should be easily resolved in normal, positive teacher-administrator relationships. If they are not resolved, they could lead to a lowering of teacher morale and a general deterioration of teacher-administrator relationships. They also might become items for the next round of negotiations.

Many definitions still contain the exclusions that were included in the original New York State governing procedures. They exclude from the grievance procedure any action relative to disciplinary proceedings or any other matters that are otherwise reviewable pursuant to law, or any rule

327

or regulation having the force and effect of law. Not uncommon is the phrase that the denial of tenure is in no way to be construed as a grievance.

DEFINITIONS

The word "days," as it is applied to any period of time noted in the agreement, should be defined. A common definition provides that "school days" means teacher-duty days. During the summer, days usually means all weekdays except holidays. Unless days is specified as "school days," it usually means "running calendar days," including weekends and holidays. The Gary, Indiana, Grievance Procedure defines days as follows:

> "Days, unless otherwise specified, shall mean all days other than Saturdays, Sundays, and legal holidays. Saturdays, Sundays and legal holidays shall be excluded in computing the number of days within which action must be taken or notice be given."

The important element here is to agree on the definition and to define days clearly so that there can be no misunderstanding or misinterpretation.

Administrative positions, such as supervisor, department head, principal and superintendent, need definition. Phrases like "the principal or his designee" and "the superintendent or his designee" are needed if the administration reserves the right to delegate responsibilities.

LEVEL ONE

Level one of most grievance procedures permits a grievance to be resolved in the simplest way. Some grievance procedures provide two steps at this level. On occasion, these two steps are referred to as a step and a half. The oral grievance may be considered as a separate step or as a half step at level one.

Decisions about differences of opinion and complaints are part of the continuing give-and-take between teachers and their immediate supervisors. This should not be discouraged by a grievance procedure which makes either party feel that, if any difference of opinion takes place, the wheels are being set in motion for a complicated process.

A procedure which has merit is to make the first step of the grievance procedure an oral step wherein the teacher informs the principal that he has a grievance and is attempting to resolve the matter informally before committing it to writing.

An example of a grievance that might be resolved in the oral step of a grievance procedure is when a teacher informs her principal that she feels her room is damp and that it is affecting her health. The principal should attempt to determine the validity of the grievance. If the room is damp, the maintenance department might be able to correct the situation. The teacher should be kept informed about what can be and is being done. If the condition cannot be corrected, then steps should be taken to avoid using the room or, if that is not possible, the teacher assigned to the room should be rotated. In most cases, the grievance can be resolved at this point.

328

If the aggrieved person is not satisfied with the disposition of his grievance at the oral step, or if no decision has been reached within a specified period of time, he may then file the grievance in writing with his principal or immediate supervisor.

An example of a written grievance is as follows:

> Thirty-two children have been assigned to my first grade class. The policy governing class size, which was adopted by the Board of Education, effective September 1, 1968, states that . . . class size in grades one through six shall be no longer than thirty.
>
> I am herewith filing a grievance declaring that the policy governing class size for elementary grades has been violated. Immediate compliance is requested by adjusting my class size to be in conformity with school policy.

Once the grievance has been committed to writing, the principal or immediate supervisor has the responsibility for making his decision within a specified period of time and communicating it in writing to the employee presenting the grievance. It is at this point that it becomes crystal clear that we are witnessing a departure from the days of unilateral decision making by the administration of the school or unit. Decisions made by the administrator must be weighed in terms of the agreement and what is educationally sound. The realization that his decision might be taken for review to a higher authority, such as the superintendent of schools, the board of education, or even an outside arbitrator, causes the administrator to think through each decision he makes.

Level Two

Level two of the grievance procedure usually provides the aggrieved person, if he is not satisfied with the disposition of his grievance or if no decision has been rendered within a specified period of time, with the option of filing his grievance with the superintendent of schools. In large school districts, there may be an intermediate source before the grievance is presented to the superintendent or his designee. It might well be the personnel administrator, an assistant, associate, deputy or area superintendent. It would depend upon the size and administrative organization of the school system.

At this point, there is usually some variance with regard to the course of action to be followed. In some cases, the procedure makes provision for the superintendent to review all of the written material presented by the parties involved, upon which he makes his decision.

If the grievance is not resolved by the superintendent's decision based on his review of the written material, the teacher usually has the option of requesting a meeting with the superintendent. Decision making by the superintendent based on his review of the written material is not common, but has some merit. However, this review should not take from the teacher the right to meet with the superintendent. This meeting is usually a formal one

329

following whatever format has been outlined in the grievance procedure or by mutual consent. It should be remembered that at this level the goal is to attempt to arrive at a mutually satisfactory resolution of the grievance. Within a predetermined period of time, the superintendent should be required to make his decision and communicate it in writing to the employee presenting the grievance.

BOARD LEVEL

It is at this point that the greatest variance occurs in grievance procedures. If the aggrieved is dissatisfied with the decision of the superintendent, then the grievance may follow one of several paths. Most common is the third and usually terminal step for the aggrieved; that is, to take his grievance to the board of education, whose decision usually is final. The board will usually meet with the aggrieved or provide him with the opportunity for a hearing. Within a specified period of time, the board should make a determination and communicate it in writing to the employee presenting the grievance.

Grievances, as noted in the definition given earlier, usually apply only to matters relative to the application and interpretation of the agreement and board policy and do not relate to matters that are reviewable by law.

ADVISORY ARBITRATION

A fairly common route in public education grievance procedures after the first or second level is that of taking the grievance to arbitration, but the decision made by the arbitrator is often advisory because it has been held in some states that a government agency cannot delegate its decision-making authority to another party. The board still has the option of hearing the grievance and rendering its own decision. Obviously, the arbitrator's decision is given serious consideration by the board of education, and in most cases the decision of the board follows the recommendations of the arbitrator. A survey made by the National Education Association of 603 comprehensive agreements negotiated between teachers' organizations and boards of education in districts with 1,000 or more pupils showed that 83 percent of the grievance procedures go outside the school system for final appeal. Of these, 47 percent are for advisory decision and 53 percent are for binding decision.[5]

BINDING ARBITRATION

The aggrieved individual who is not satisfied with the decision rendered by the superintendent of schools can also file a written request to submit the grievance to arbitration, the decision of the arbitrator to be final and binding on the aggrieved person and the board of education. He must file within a specified time limit. The procedures followed by the arbitrator can vary, of course. He usually confers with the superintendent and
330

the aggrieved person and issues his decision within a specified period of time from the date of the close of the hearings, or, if all hearings have been waived, then from the date the final statements and proofs are submitted to him. The format of the hearing before the arbitrator may also be outlined in the grievance procedure, arrived at by mutual consent, or determined by the arbitrator. The arbitrator's decisions should be in writing, setting forth his findings of fact, his reasoning and his conclusions on the issues submmitted.

The following table indicates the extent to which grievance procedures studied by the National Education Association for the year 1967-68 utilize sources outside the school system for final appeals.[6]

TABLE 1

Number and Percent of Grievance Procedures with Final Appeal
Inside and Outside the School System, 1967–68

State	Grievance procedures	Inside appeal		Outside appeal	
		Number	Percent*	Number	Percent*
1	2	3	4	5	6
Colorado	1			1	100.0
Connecticut	49	8	16.3	41	83.7
District of Columbia	1			1	100.0
Illinois	19	6	31.6	13	68.4
Indiana	2			2	100.0
Maryland	1			1	100.0
Massachusetts	105	6	5.7	99	94.3
Michigan	295	41	13.9	254	86.1
Montana	1			1	100.0
New Jersey	4	2	50.0	2	50.0
New York	22	6	27.3	16	72.7
Ohio	2	2	100.0		
Pennsylvania	3	2	66.7	1	33.3
Rhode Island	17	3	17.6	14	82.4
Virginia	1			1	100.0
Wisconsin	27	13	48.1	14	51.9
Total	550	89	16.2	461	83.8

*Computation of percents based on number of grievance procedures in each state.

ARBITRATION COST AND SELECTION OF AN ARBITRATOR

An arbitrator is usually selected according to the system prescribed by the grievance procedure. The American Arbitration Association is most frequently used as the source of arbitrators acceptable to both the school system and the teachers' organization. It is not uncommon for large industries to employ permanent arbitrators who are acceptable to both sides.

Arbitration costs, whether advisory or binding, are usually shared equally by the board and the teacher filing the grievance, although a board may accept the full cost if the appellant is judged to be in the right. The teacher's portion of the arbitration costs is usually assumed by the teachers' organization representing the teacher. A study by the National Education Association for the school year 1967-68 indicated that the average cost for the arbitrator was $513 and the legal fees averaged two and half times the arbitrator's cost.[7]

The first grievance arbitration case in the public schools occurred in 1966 in Warren, Michigan. The Michigan Education Association reported that the cost for arbitration in the case was $3,500, 80 percent for legal fees and 20 percent for the arbitrator.[8]

The six sources of third party assistance are usually the following:

1. Parties specifically named in the agreement.
2. Parties selected jointly by the parties to the agreement.
3. State education department official.
4. State labor board official.
5. United States Mediation and Conciliation Service.
6. American Arbitration Association.

REPRISALS

Most grievance procedures make some statement relating to reprisals. It offers assurance that no reprisals of any kind will be taken by the board of education or by any member of the administrative or supervisory staff against any teacher, any representative of a teacher, any member of a teachers' organization supporting the teacher, or any other participants in the procedure when a grievance is filed.

REPRESENTATION

It is generally accepted that any teacher filing a grievance may be represented at any level of the grievance procedure by himself or, at his option and expense, by a representative selected by him. Teachers' organizations may represent teachers filing grievances.

WAIVER OF GRIEVANCE

An important item to have in the grievance procedure is a time limit for filing a grievance. It eliminates the possibility of continued threats being made to the effect that, if certain conditions are not met, a grievance will be filed. The provision should clearly state that the grievance should be considered waived if a teacher does not file the grievance within whatever time limit is agreed upon in advance after the teacher knew or should have known of the act or condition that created the grievance.

A time limit for the filing of a grievance also contributes to having grievances filed according to an orderly process. It places the resolution of the grievance closer to the time the grievance occurred. It increases the probability that those who were involved will remember what happened in greater detail and what the conditions and other circumstances were. As time passes, the people who were close to the situation are more likely to forget or are no longer available.

EXTENDING TIME LIMITS

All time limits set forth in a grievance procedure should have the flexibility to be extended by mutual consent in writing. If they are extended, it should be for a specific time. Should there fail to be written mutual agreement to extend the time, then the original time limits must be in effect. If the person filing the grievance fails to pursue any steps within the time limits provided, he usually has no further right to press the grievance. If the school system fails to meet any of its time limits, it then subjects itself to additional grievances, and in some cases penalties.

FORMS

It is important that appropriate forms for filing grievances and notices and for making reports and recommendations be prepared in advance. The task of preparing such material might well be submitted to a subcommittee with teacher and administrative representation. These forms and materials should be given appropriate distribution so as to facilitate the operation of the grievance procedure.

FILING OF MATERIALS

No uniformity exists with regard to how documents, communications and records dealing with the processing of grievances should be filed. Many teachers and teacher groups prefer that such records should be filed separately from the personnel files of participants.

The use of these files also varies. Their greatest use is to insure proper follow-up of the result of the grievance, but they are also used in determining precedents to guide decisions on other grievances. In New York City, for example, the Director of Staff Relations sent the following memo:

"To: District Superintendents, Unit Administrators, Elementary School Principals and to Principals of Junior High Schools with Elementary classes

Re: Programs of Teacher of Library in the Elementary Schools

Attached is a copy of the decision of the arbitrator in a case involving Article IV A, 3 e of the Agreement which deals *solely* with the program of a *teacher of library* in the elementary schools.

You will note that the arbitrator construed the contract language in question to mean only that the number of *full* teaching periods in the program of the teacher of library must be limited to 20 per week."

Grievance Report Form

Building	Assignment	Name	Date Filed

Type of Grievance (check one)   _____A non-economic

_____B economic

Level I

Date Cause of Grievance Occurred _____

Statement of Grievance _____

Relief Sought _____

Signature_____ Date_____

Disposition by Principal _____

Signature of Principal_____ Date_____

Position of Grievant _____

Signature_____ Date_____

Level II

Date Received by Superintendent or Designee _____

Disposition of Superintendent or Designee _____

Signature_____ Date_____

Position of Grievant _____

Signature_____ Date_____

Level III

Date Received by Board of Education _____

Disposition by Teachers' Council _____

Signature_____ Date_____

Disposition by Board _____

Signature_____ Date_____

Position of Grievant _____

Signature_____ Date_____

Level IV

(Applicable to Type B Grievances Only)

Date Submitted to Arbitration _____

Disposition by Teachers' Council _____

Signature_____ Date_____

Disposition and Award of Arbitrator _____

Signature of Arbitrator_____ Date of Decision_____

(If additional space is needed in reporting items, attach additional sheet(s))

The award of the arbitrator and the complete text of the arbitrator's opinion were attached to the memo. The main purpose of the memo and its attachments was to summarize the essential elements of the arbitrator's award.

The Minneapolis grievance procedure requires that all grievance documents be treated as confidential material and should not be released beyond the superintendency and personnel department, except as released by joint action of the teacher filing the grievance or his authorized representative and the superintendent.

FREQUENCY OF USE OF THE GRIEVANCE PROCEDURE

There do not seem to be any general conditions which govern the rate of grievances filed per year in a given school system. Many factors may contribute to the number and types of grievances filed:

1. Competition between rival teachers' organizations.
2. Systemwide low teacher morale.
3. Individual faculty-administrator relations.
4. The direction of the final decisions in grievances filed.
5. The desire on the part of a teachers' organization to have grievances submitted.
6. General administrative and supervisory attitudes toward observing agreement items.

There needs to be a willingness on the part of the teaching staff and the administration to work cooperatively in providing the best education possible for boys and girls of each school system. On one hand, the administration should not seek to provoke grievances. On the other hand, teachers should not use the grievance procedure as a weapon for obtaining unjustified demands or for the harassment of an administrator. Both should attempt to follow the letter and spirit reached in negotiations or discussions.

Castetter gives important advice concerning the frequency and nature of grievances.

> ". . . the psychological effect resulting from mere availability of grievance machinery to organization personnel is far more important than the manner in which it is to be utilized. When sincere administrative efforts are made to deal with personnel problems, the number of cases which run the full line of appeal are likely to be minimal." [9]

The grievance procedure should be considered as carefully structured machinery designed for the purpose of settling legitimate grievances. Submitting a flood of frivolous or unwarranted grievances would clog the machinery and cause a backlog of unresolved legitimate grievances. This would actually defeat the purpose of the grievance procedure and deny due process to teachers who have valid grievances.

Caution should be exercised in evaluating the service of an adminis-

335

trator solely on the basis of the frequency or lack of frequency of grievances. Democratic administrators may have more grievances filed against them than autocratic ones. Circumstances and external factors may be beyond the control of any single administrator. Administrators should not regard grievances as personal affronts. They should be recognized as an accepted step in modern personnel practices, even though that may be difficult for many administrators.

USE OF ARBITRATION

The use of arbitration in the grievance procedure is in a state of change. *Negotiations Management* reports that in a recent study the impartial third parties for adjudication of grievance disputes were seldom used:

> "In about 85% of the cases the final decision was made by the school board. In about 10% of the cases it was the superintendent and in about 5% of the cases it was by advisory or binding arbitration. However, in industry about 150,000 agreements have been written employing binding arbitration as the final step in resolving grievances.
>
> "Due to changes in state statutes, grievance procedures are changing rapidly. Culminating grievance arbitration is being incorporated into agreements in Michigan, Massachusetts, and Rhode Island. Several hundred now exist in these states alone." [10]

Board Responsibility and Arbitration The real problem school boards are faced with in dealing with binding arbitration of grievances is whether they can, or should, delegate the authority with which they are charged. Boards of education may not be fearful of giving up their authority, but they are concerned with their legal responsibility. They are also reluctant to abdicate the moral responsibility they feel has been placed upon them.

Teachers' Viewpoint of Arbitration Teachers, on the other hand, believe that it is extremely difficult for the board of education to be impartial in making decisions relative to teacher grievances. They seem to feel that boards have an obligation to back their administrators, which, they believe, places teachers at a distinct disadvantage in going to boards of education for a final decision.

Role of the Arbitrator There seems to be considerable movement in the direction of making more use of arbitrators in the final steps of the grievance procedure, either in an advisory capacity or with decisions binding both parties. The arbitrator is usually not asked to set policy but to rule on whether existing policy was followed. An arbitrator can be viewed as an umpire in a ball game, being completely impartial.

Qualifications of Arbitrators Arbitrators must be well trained and suited for their work. They should know the field of education and its unique features. They may need to become familiar with broad sections of a total agreement before making a recommendation on a single dispute. They

336

should have the ability to sort out the key facts from all the material presented, those pertinent to the issues being discussed. Arbitrators must be impartial and should not be impressed by pressure or emotionalism.

CHARACTERISTICS AND OBJECTIVES OF GRIEVANCE PROBLEMS

No one grievance procedure can, or should, be used as a model for all school systems. The grievance procedure should be developed cooperatively within a school district. One side should not dictate all of the conditions. The procedure should be written in language that all who are involved can understand. It should not be written by and for attorneys. The grievance procedure should be published in enough copies to be readily available to the school staff.

Although grievance procedures vary from system to system, some characteristics and objectives are found in most accepted grievance procedures. They are as follows:

1. Definition of what problems constitute grievances.
2. Definition of terms used.
3. Clear time limits for various phases.
4. Opportunity to resolve the grievance at the point of origin.
5. Opportunity to resolve the grievance on an informal basis.
6. Basic agreement on the establishment of the grievance procedure.
7. Language which can be comprehended by all involved.
8. Ready availability of the written grievance procedures.
9. Opportunity for those filing grievances to be represented.
10. Assurance that there will be no reprisals for filing grievances.
11. Availability of related, previous grievance decisions in order to establish precedents.
12. Waiver of grievances submitted beyond specified time limits for filing.
13. Opportunity for involvement of competent, impartial arbitrators.
14. Cost of arbitrator to be borne equally by teacher and board.
15. Availability of necessary forms and materials.
16. Requirement that all decisions and requests for appeal beyond the informal first stage be committed to writing.
17. Clear statement of the various steps in the grievance procedure.
18. Clear statement of who will make the final decision.

THE ROLE OF SCHOOL PERSONNEL ADMINISTRATORS IN GRIEVANCE PROCEDURES

Personnel administrators, working with other members of the staff, should periodically evaluate the grievance procedure used in their school districts. They should be familiar with the changes taking place in other districts. They should have up-to-date information on the nature, frequency and disposition of grievances filed. Where there is no separate office responsible for grievance procedures, it would be proper for the personnel administrator to keep records and files of grievances and to see to it that decisions are carried out fairly and promptly. Several key questions need to be asked: Is the grievance procedure improving teacher-administrator relationships? What educative steps should the personnel administrator take to see that this tool of personnel management is properly used? The answers to these and other pertinent questions will give personnel administrators direction in terms of effectively implementing the existing grievance procedure or making proposals for desired changes at the appropriate time. Of major importance is the administrator's development of a personnel program that will create high morale, a program that will eliminate the causes of grievances. Creation of such a program should involve the cooperative efforts of field supervisors (such as school principals) and teachers. The school personnel administrator who concentrates only on streamlining the grievance machinery is neglecting a primary factor, that of studying grievances to see how conditions can be changed to avoid future grievances.

SAMPLE GRIEVANCE PROCEDURES IN TWO CITIES

CRANSTON, RHODE ISLAND

GRIEVANCE PROCEDURE FROM THE MASTER AGREEMENT BETWEEN
THE CRANSTON SCHOOL COMMITTEE, CRANSTON, RHODE ISLAND,
AND THE CRANSTON TEACHERS' ASSOCIATION
FOR THE PERIOD SEPTEMBER 1, 1968, TO AUGUST 31, 1969

Grievance Procedure

I. Definitions

1. A "grievance" shall mean a complaint by a teacher or the Association (1) that there has been as to him or it a violation or inequitable of any of the provisions of this contract or (2) that he or it has been treated inequitably by reason of any act or condition which is contrary to established School Committee policy or practice governing or affecting employees, except that the term "grievance" shall not apply to any matter as to which the School Committee is without authority to act.

2. An "aggrieved person" is the person or persons making the complaint.

3. A "party in interest" is the person or persons making the complaint and any person who might be required to take action or against whom action might be taken in order to resolve the complaint.

4. The term "days" when used in this article shall, except where otherwise indicated, mean working school days; thus weekend or vacation days are excluded.

II. Purpose

The purpose of this procedure is to secure, at the lowest possible administrative level, equitable solutions to the problems which may from time to time arise, affecting the welfare or working conditions of teachers. Both parties agree that grievance proceedings will be kept as informal and confidential as may be appropriate at any level of the procedure.

III. General Procedures

1. Since it is important that grievances be processed as rapidly as possible, the number of days indicated at each level should be considered a maximum, and every effort should be made to expedite the process.

2. In the event a grievance is filed on or after June 1, which if left unresolved until the beginning of the following school year, could result in irreparable harm to a party in interest, the parties agree to make a good faith effort to reduce the time limits set forth herein so that the grievance procedure may be exhausted prior to the end of the school term or as soon thereafter as is practicable.

3. In the event a grievance is filed so that sufficient time as stipulated under all levels of the procedure cannot be provided before the last day of the school year, should it be necessary to pursue the grievance to all levels of the appeals, then said grievance shall be resolved in the new school term in September under the terms of this agreement and this article, and not under the succeeding agreement.

4. The Association shall appoint one representative for each building who shall act in all grievance cases within his school. The Association agrees to furnish the Committee with the complete list of such representatives at least ten days before the effective date of this agreement. The Association shall have the right to designate the same individual as its representative in one or more schools, or to substitute a different representative for the one originally designated as its representative for a particular school, provided such substitution is made in writing to all parties in interest.

5. At all levels of a grievance after it has been formally presented, at least one member of the Association's Grievance Committee shall attend any meetings, hearings, appeals, or other proceedings required to process the grievance.

6. Nothing herein contained will be construed as limiting the right of any teacher having a grievance to discuss the matter informally with any appropriate member of the administration, and having the grievance adjusted without intervention of the Association provided the adjustment is not inconsistent with the terms of this agreement.

7. A grievance shall not be submitted for decision to any administrative personnel who are themselves members of the negotiating unit. Where administrative personnel are named in the grievance procedure to receive grievances and they are members of the negotiating unit, the grievance shall be submitted to the next highest authority who is not a member of the negotiating unit.

IV. Initiation and Processing

1. *Level One.*

A teacher with a grievance will first discuss it with his principal or immediate superior, either individually or through the Association's school representative, or accompanied by the Association's representative or by a representative of his own choosing with the objective of resolving the matter informally.

2. *Level Two.*

A. Any teacher may present a grievance in writing within five (5) days following the act or condition which is the basis of his complaint, to the superior (for example, department chairman, unit chairman, supervisor or director) of the employee against whom the grievance exists and who has jurisdiction of the act or condition involved. Information copies of the grievance shall be sent by the teacher to the principal of the school in which the teacher is serving, to the representative of the Association, and to the Superintendent. The hearing on such grievance shall be held by the teacher's superior within fifteen (15) days of receipt of such written communication.

Within five (5) days after hearing of the grievance at the level specified above, the person hearing the grievance shall make his decision in writing and mail it to the grievant and to all persons officially present at the hearing as well as the building principal and the Superintendent.

B. If the aggrieved employee has instituted his grievance with a person other than a principal, he may appeal the decision on such grievance to his building principal. Such appeal shall be made in writing within ten (10) days from the date of receipt of the written decision rendered by the administrator to whom it was initially submitted. The appeal shall include a copy of the decision being appealed and the grounds for regarding the decision as incorrect. It shall also state the names of all persons officially present at the prior hearing, and such persons shall receive a copy of the appeal. A hearing on the appeal shall be held within fifteen (15) days of receipt of the appeal, and the building principal shall render his decision within ten (10) days therafter. At least five (5) days prior to the hearing on the appeal, the principal shall notify persons present at the prior hearing of the time and place of the appeal.

C. In any situation in which a teacher does not serve under the administrators listed above in (A) above, or if the teacher's grievance is based upon an act or condition for which his building principal is responsible, the teacher shall submit his grievance to the principal of the building in which the act or condition occurred. Such grievance shall be presented in writing five (5) days following the act or condition which is the basis of the complaint. The hearing on such grievance shall be held by the principal within fifteen (15) days of receipt of such written communication.

Within five (5) days after hearing of the grievance by the principal, he shall make his decision in writing and mail it to the grievant, all persons officially present at the hearing, and the Superintendent.

3. *Level Three.*

A. Within ten (10) days of receipt of the decision rendered by the principal pursuant to Section 2 above, the decision of the principal in regard to such appeal may be further appealed to the Superintendent.

B. Appeals to the Superintendent shall be heard by the Superintendent within twenty (20) days of his receipt of the appeal. Written notice of the time and place of hearing shall be given five (5) days prior thereto to the aggrieved employee, his representative if any, the Association grievance representative, the Chairman of the Grievance Committee, and any administrator who has theretofore been involved in the grievance.

C. Within fifteen (15) days of hearing the appeal, the Superintendent of Schools shall communicate to the aggrieved employee and all other parties officially present at the hearing his written decision, which shall include supporting reasons therefor. A copy of the decision shall be sent to the Chairman of the Grievance Committee.

4. *Special Procedures for Salary or Leave Related Grievances.*

A. Any grievance based on a complaint that the employee has been placed in the wrong salary schedule or step, or that he has been improperly denied an increment, or that his salary has been miscalculated, shall be filed directly with the appropriate administrator under the Superintendent of Schools. Any grievance based upon a complaint by an employee as to an absence refund, sabbatical leave, or leave of absence without pay, shall be filed directly with the administrative officer handling such matters for the Superintendent of Schools. Any such grievances shall be filed within ten (10) days after the grievance arises. The appropriate administrative officer shall conduct a hearing on such grievance within twenty (20) days and shall render his decision in writing within five (5) days after concluding the hearing.

B. The decision of any business or administrative officer to whom a grievance is presented, as hereinabove set forth, may be appealed to the Superintendent in writing within fifteen (15) days of the date of the decision appealed. The Superintendent shall conduct a hearing on said appeal (see Section 5C below) within twenty (20) days of receipt of such appeal and shall render his decision in writing within ten (10) days after concluding such hearing.

5. *Initiation of Special Types of Grievances.*

A. Where twenty-five or more members of the negotiating unit in more than one school, or a group of special teachers from several buildings, have a grievance arising from the action of authority higher than a principal, the Chairman of the Grievance Committee, in the name of the Association on their request, may initiate a group grievance in their behalf. In such case a written grievance may be filed originally with the administrator having jurisdiction over the act or condition and information copies of the grievance shall be sent simultaneously to the principal or principals of the employees involved.

B. The Association shall have the right to initiate or appeal a grievance growing out of an alleged violation of Association rights under this contract. Any such grievance shall be initiated by filing the written grievance in the first instance with the appropriate administrator having jurisdiction of the subject matter or the unit member or members affected. A hearing on such a grievance shall be held within twenty (20) days of its filing.

In the event such grievance is originally filed with an administrator other than a principal, an information copy of such grievance shall be sent simultaneously to the principal or principals of the employees involved. Any appeal from the decision of such administrator shall be made directly to the Superintendent of Schools in writing within fifteen (15) days of the date of the decision appealed from.

C. Appeals to the Superintendent or grievances filed originally with him under this article shall be heard by the Superintendent within twenty (20) days of the receipt by him of the appeal or grievance. Written notice of time and place of hearing shall be given five (5) days prior thereto to the Chairman of the Grievance Committee and any administrator involved in the grievance. The Superintendent shall render his decision in writing within ten (10) days after concluding the hearing.

D. If a grievance is based upon a specific act by the School Committee, and (1) the school administration has no discretion in the administration or application of the act of the Committee; and (2) the Committee act is of such a nature that no further action or implementation by the administration is relevant to whether there has been an actual violation of the grievant's rights under this agreement, the grievance may be initiated at the level of the Superintendent in accordance with the procedure set forth in Section 5C above.

6. *Arbitration.*

A. A grievance dispute which is not resolved at the level of the Superintendent under the grievance procedures herein may be submitted by the aggrieved employee or by the Association as specified herein to an arbitrator for decision if it involves the application or interpretation of this agreement, except that a grievance concerning any term of this agreement involving School Committee discretion or Committee policy may be submitted to an arbitrator for decision only if it is based on a complaint that such discretion or policy was applied discriminatorily, i.e., that it was applied in a manner unreasonably inconsistent with the general practice followed throughout the school system in similar circumstances.

B. A grievance may not be submitted to an arbitrator unless a decision has been rendered by the Superintendent of Schools under the grievance procedure, except in cases where, upon expiration of the time limit for decision, the aggrieved employee or the Association filed notice with the Superintendent of intention to submit the grievance to arbitration and no decision was issued by the Superintendent within fifteen (15) days after receipt of such notice.

C. The proceedings shall be initiated by filing with the Superintendent and the American Arbitration Association a notice of arbitration. The notice shall be filed within ten (10) days after receipt of the decision of the Superintendent of Schools under the Grievance Procedure, or, where no decision has been issued in the circumstances described above, three (3) days following the expiration of the fifteen (15) day period provided above. The notice shall include a statement setting forth precisely the issue to be decided by the arbitrator and the specific provision of the agreement involved.

D. Within ten (10) days after such written notice of submission to arbitration, the Superintendent and the Association will agree upon a mutually acceptable arbitrator and will obtain a commitment from said arbitrator to serve. If the parties are unable to agree upon an arbitrator or to obtain such a commitment within the specified period, a request for a list of arbitrators may be made to the American Arbitration Association by either party.

E. The parties will be bound by the Voluntary Labor Arbitration Rules of the American Arbitration Association regardless of how the arbitrator is selected; except that neither the Committee nor the Association nor any grievant shall be permitted to assert any ground in arbitration if such ground was not disclosed to the other parties in interest prior to the decision being appealed to the arbitrator, or to assert any evidence known to the decision being appealed.

F. The arbitrator shall limit his decision strictly to the application and interpretation of the provisions of his agreement and it shall be binding upon all parties involved. However, he shall be without power and authority to make any decisions:

  (i) Contrary to, or inconsistent with, or modifying or varying in any way, the terms of this agreement or of applicable law or rules or regulations having the force and effect of law;

 (ii) Involving Committee discretion or Committee policy under the provisions of this agreement, except that he may decide in a particular case, involving Committee discretion or Committee policy, whether or not the Committee applied such discretion or policy discriminatorily, i.e., in a manner unreasonably inconsistent with the general practice followed throughout the school system in similar circumstances;

(iii) Limiting or interfering in any way with the powers, duties and responsibilities of the Committee, applicable law, and rules and regulations having the force and effect of law.

G. The costs for the services of the arbitrator will be borne equally by the Committee and the Association.

7. *General Provisions as to Grievance and Arbitration.*

A. No reprisals of any kind will be taken by the School Committee or by any member of the administration against any party in interest, any School Representative, any member of the Grievance Committee or any other participant in the grievance procedure by reason of such participation.

B. The filing or pendency of any grievance under the provisions of this article shall in no way operate to impede, delay or interfere with the right of the Committee to take the action complained of, subject, however, to the final decision on the grievance.

C. Nothing contained in this article or elsewhere in this agreement shall be construed to prevent any individual employee from presenting and processing a grievance and having it adjusted without intervention or representation by the Association if the adjustment is not inconsistent with the terms of this agreement; except that no grievance may be submitted to arbitration without the consent of, and representation by, the Association.

343

D. Any party in interest may be represented at all stages of the grievance procedure except arbitration by a person of his own choosing, except that he may not be represented by a representative or an officer of any competing teacher organization. When a teacher is not represented by the Association, the Association shall have the right to be present and to state its views at all stages except Level 1 of the grievance procedure.

E. The sole remedy available to any teacher for any alleged breach of this agreement or any alleged violation of his rights hereunder will be pursuant to the grievance procedure; provided, however, that if a teacher elects to pursue any legal or statutory remedy for any alleged breach of this agreement or any alleged violation of his rights thereunder, such election will bar any further or subsequent proceedings for relief under the provisions of this article. Recourse by a teacher to the grievance procedure shall constitute a waiver of any legal or statutory rights to relief for the act or condition which is the subject of the grievance.

F. Failure at any step of this procedure except Level 1 to communicate the decision in writing on a grievance within the specified time limits shall permit the grievant to proceed to the next step. Failure at any step of this procedure to appeal a grievance to the next step within the specified time limits shall be deemed to be acceptance of the decision rendered at that step.

The time limits specified in any step of this procedure may be changed in any specific instance by mutual agreement.

G. All documents, communications and records dealing with the processing of a grievance will be filed separately from the personnel files of the participants.

H. Forms for processing grievances will be jointly prepared by the Superintendent and the Association. The forms will be printed by the Committee and given appropriate distribution by the parties so as to facilitate operation of the grievance procedure.

I. The Association agrees that it will not bring or continue, and that it will not represent any employee in, any grievance which is substantially similar to a grievance denied by the decision of an arbitrator; and the Committee agrees that it will apply to all substantially similar situations the decision of an arbitrator sustaining a grievance.

J. In the course of investigation of any grievance, representatives of the Association will report to the principal of the building being visited and will state the purpose of the visit immediately upon arrival.

K. Every effort will be made by all parties to avoid interruption of classroom activities and to avoid the involvement of students in all phases of the grievance procedure.

L. Each grievance shall have to be initiated within five (5) days of the occurrence of the cause for complaint, or, if neither the aggrieved nor the Association had knowledge of said occurrence at the time of its happening, then within five (5) days of the first such knowledge by either the aggrieved or the Association. Appropriately posted and dated School Committee notices relating to rules and regulations, also sent by registered mail to the President of the Association, shall be considered as binding the Association and all members of the negotiating unit with knowledge of the subject matter related in such notices.

M. If any member of the Association's Grievance Committee is a party in interest to any grievance, he shall not serve as the Association's grievance representative in the processing of such grievance.

N. It will be practice of all parties in interest to process grievances after the regular work day or at other times which do not interfere with assigned duties; provided, however, that upon mutual agreement by the aggrieved person, the Association, and the Committee to hold proceedings during regular working hours, the grievant and the appropriate Association representative will be released from assigned duties without loss of salary. The Association shall have the right to designate one teacher as its Grievance Chairman, and the Committee shall not preempt more than ten (10) unassigned periods a year from the teaching schedule of the chairman.

DISTRICT OF COLUMBIA

GRIEVANCE PROCEDURE FROM THE MASTER AGREEMENT
BETWEEN THE BOARD OF EDUCATION OF
THE DISTRICT OF COLUMBIA AND
THE WASHINGTON TEACHERS' UNION, LOCAL 6

Grievance and Arbitration

A. Definition

A grievance shall mean a complaint by a party that (1) there has been a violation, misinterpretation or misapplication of the provisions of this Agreement or of established policy or practice thereunder, or (2) an employee's health or safety is jeopardized by conditions which can be corrected by the Board, or (3) there has been misapplication or unfair practice under existing laws, rules or regulations.

B. Procedure

1. Either the employer or an employee or the Union may raise a grievance, and if raised by the employee, the Union may associate itself therewith at any time except as hereinafter otherwise provided. If raised by the Union, the employee may not thereafter raise the grievance himself, and if raised by the employee, he may not thereafter cause the Union to raise the same grievance independently.

2. Grievances shall be settled as follows:

a. Where grievance is raised by an employee

Step 1.

A discussion between the employee and his immediate superior to the end that the dispute may be resolved expeditiously and informally. At the employee's option, there may be present at such discussion representatives of the Union or any other school employee selected by the aggrieved employee who is not an officer, agent, or representative of another teacher organization. At the immediate superior's option, there may be present at such discussion additional persons selected by such immediate superior. The employee shall indentify the discussion as Step 1 of this grievance procedure.

Step 2.

If the dispute is not settled at Step 1 within 2 school days, then within

5 school days thereafter, the matter shall be reduced to writing and again considered by the same persons as referred to in Step 1. The decision made at this Step shall be communicated in writing to the teacher. The specific written grievance presented at Step 2 shall be used solely and exclusively as the basis for Steps 3, 4, and 5.

Step 3.

If the dispute is not settled at Step 2 within 5 school days after reduction to writing, then the dispute shall be submitted in writing within another 5 school days to the Superintendent of Schools. The Superintendent, or his designee, and those he may further name shall meet with the persons referred to in Step 1 within 10 school days of such submission and the Superintendent, or his designee, shall render a decision thereon in writing within 10 school days of such meeting.

Step 4.

If the employee or Union is dissatisfied with such decision, then within 10 school days after its rendition, he or the Union may appeal same in writing to the President, Board of Education, who shall schedule a hearing thereon within 10 school days after the said appeal is filed and the Board shall render a decision in writing at the next regular meeting of the Board after the conclusion of such hearing. The Board at this step may act through a duly constituted committee of the Board.

Step 5.

If the Union is dissatisfied with such decision, it may request arbitration of the dispute as follows, provided that no provision of this Agreement which is stated to be a matter of policy shall be subject to arbitration:

(a) The request for arbitration must be in writing, addressed to the President, Board of Education, and must be made within 10 school days after the rendition of the decision in Step 4.

(b) The question in dispute shall then be referred to an arbitrator selected by the parties from a panel or panels submitted by the American Arbitration Association, provided that the parties may mutually agree on a different method of selecting an arbitrator than that herein set forth.

(c) The arbitrator shall hear and decide only one grievance in each case. He shall not be bound by formal rules of evidence. He shall be bound by and must comply with all of the terms of this Agreement. He shall have no power to delete or modify in any way any of the provisions of this Agreement. He shall have the power to make appropriate awards. The arbitrator shall render his decision in writing within 30 days after the conclusion of the hearing. The decision of the arbitrator shall be binding upon both parties and all employees during the life of this Agreement. Fees and expenses of the arbitrator shall be borne equally by both parties.

No individual employee himself may invoke this Step 5.

b. Where grievance is raised by the Union or Employer

If the dispute involves an individual employee, the steps shall be the same as those outlined in 2a above, except that the participants shall be the Union, the employee, the latter's immediate superior, and also the additional persons, if any, selected by the immediate superior in Step 1.

If the dispute involves a matter of general application, the initial step shall be Step 3 as outlined in 2a above. The initial step shall also be Step 3 in any case where the grievance has arisen from the action of an official other than the immediate superior. In all cases under 2b, the initiating party, if any, as outlined in Steps 4 and 5, shall be the Union.

C. General

1. No matter shall be entertained as a grievance hereunder unless it is raised with the other party within 10 school days after the occurrence of the event giving rise to the alleged grievance.

2. All time limits set forth in this Article may be extended by mutual consent, but if not so extended they must be strictly observed. If the matter in dispute is not resolved within the period provided for any step, the next step may then be invoked, provided that if a party fails to pursue any step within the time limits provided, he shall have no further right to press the grievance.

3. If the Union is not a party to a proceeding under this Article, then the disposition of the dispute shall not be a precedent with respect to it.

4. No hearing as provided in Step 4 or 5 above shall be open to the public or persons not immediately involved unless all parties to the same agree.

5. The fact that a grievance is raised by an employee, regardless of its ultimate disposition, shall not be recorded in the employee's personnel file or in any file or record utilized in the promotion process; nor shall such fact be used in any recommendations for job placement; nor shall an employee be placed in jeopardy or be subject to reprisal for having followed this grievance procedure.

6. Any hearing provided for in this Article shall be conducted at a time and place which will afford a fair and reasonable opportunity for all persons, including witnesses, entitled to be present to attend. When such hearings are held during school hours, all employees who are entitled to be present at the hearing shall be excused with pay for that purpose.

7. All parties shall have the right at their own expense to legal and/or stenographic assistance at Steps 4 and 5.

8. The employees in the unit, the Union, and the Board shall follow the procedures set forth in this Article with respect to any grievance they may have and shall not follow any other course of action to resolve their grievances. If either side breaches this provision, it shall thereby forfeit the right to invoke the provisions of this Article as to the incident involved.

9. No recording device shall be utilized at Steps 1, 2, or 3 of this procedure. No person shall be present at any of these steps for the purpose of recording the discussion.

10. At Step 3 there shall be a single chief spokesman on each side, provided that this shall not preclude any participant at Step 3 from speaking thereat.

16 PERSONNEL ADMINISTRATION AND LEGAL PROCESSES

GENERAL STATEMENT

Education law is a complex field—entire volumes have been published on it—and there are many legal concerns of public personnel administration. A school personnel administrator is not expected to be a legal expert. The board of education's attorney should always be consulted whenever a legal problem arises or is likely to arise. The purpose of this chapter is to familiarize the administrator with some of the basic concepts of the law as they appear in personnel administration. It is not intended to serve as a legal rulebook for personnel administrators. Laws fluctuate from state to state and from locality to locality. What may be generally recognized as a rule of law in one state may not be recognized at all in another state. California may require that all teachers' employment contracts must be in writing, but Texas may recognize oral contracts as valid. The personnel administrator would therefore be wise to have some knowledge of the relevant laws in his state. An awareness of basic concepts of legal processes in personnel administration may aid the administrator in carrying out his duties in an equitable manner, in avoiding problems, and in knowing when to seek the advice of an attorney.

Despite the diversification in the field of law, many similarities deserve specific attention. Four significant topics will be discussed in this chapter: (1) certification, (2) school personnel and contracts, (3) tenure, and (4) constitutional and other rights of teachers. Legal provisions regarding negotiations are discussed in the chapter on staff negotiations.

DEVELOPMENT OF THE LEGAL STRUCTURE OF EDUCATION

Education in the early days of our country was a local, voluntary, and usually religious oriented activity. The Constitution of the United States makes no specific reference to education. Cubberley states:

"It is not surprising, however, when we consider the time, the men, and the existing conditions, that the founders of our Republic did not deem the subject of public education important enough to warrant consideration in the Constitution or inclusion in the document." [1]

Although some of our early presidents, including Thomas Jefferson in 1806 and James Madison in 1817, proposed constitutional amendments that would have given the federal government power over education, the amendments never developed. Many state constitutions up to 1818 made no mention of education, either.

State concern and involvement in education came about in the mid-eighteenth century as a result of many factors, among them: recognition of educational inequalities in various parts of the state, a philosophy of government that urged state involvement in social progress, and the efforts of social and educational leaders. The state took jurisdiction over education under provisions of the Tenth Amendment to the Constitution, which states that "the powers not delegated to the United States by the Constitution, nor prohibited by it to the States, are reserved to the States respectively, or to the people." However, the states decided to exercise regulatory control while leaving the administration of schools in local communities and cities where it had been. At the present time, each of the fifty states has provisions for education in its constitution that vary from brief to extended statements. Alaska has the following provision: "The legislature shall by general law establish and maintain a system of public schools, open to all children of the state . . ." (Art. VII,1,11). In Maine, the provision reads as follows: "The Legislatures are authorized, and it shall be their duty to require the several towns to make suitable provision, at their own expense, for the support and maintenance of public schools . . ." (Art. VIII). Pursuant to the constitutional provisions, many state laws have been enacted governing all aspects of school administration.

The federal government in the past few decades has become increasingly involved in public education through its executive arm and the United States Office of Education, through legislation which has granted funds and set up regulations under which national guidelines have been promulgated, and through judicial decisions involving constitutional provisions and federal laws. Constitutional authority for involvement of the federal government in education has come largely from the general welfare clause in Article I, Section 8: "The Congress shall have power to lay and collect taxes, duties, imposts and excises, to pay the debts and provide for the common defense and general welfare of the United States."

CERTIFICATION

Before a teacher in any state may enter into a contract of employment, he must be certified by that state. Because state certification laws vary from state to state, it is necessary to consider the specific laws of each state in order to determine the prerequisites for certification.

In many states, the certification-issuing agency is vested with discretionary authority. State certification statutes should be analyzed to discover whether or not such discretionary authority exists. If the standards for certification are unreasonable and the agency exercises its powers in an arbitrary and capricious manner, its determination denying the teacher state certification will not be final and can be appealed either to the next highest administrative agency or to a court within the jurisdiction. In most instances, though, the issuing agency prescribes higher standards than those required by specific legislative statutes.[2] Some states permit the employment of a teacher before he has been certified but do not permit him to perform teaching services prior to state certification. Besides fulfilling state certification requirements, many teachers may also be required to meet local certification standards in order to teach in certain school districts.[3] Local administrative regulations and codes should therefore always be consulted to ascertain local requirements. Legally, a certificate is twofold in purpose: it serves as a prerequisite for the employment of teachers and it is a necessary qualification for state aid. If state statutes explicitly require certification and a school district disregards such qualifications, the state may deny the school district financial aid. The personnel administrator should keep in mind that teachers who teach without certificates are mere "volunteers" and are not entitled to compensation for their services.[4] State laws usually provide that it is unlawful to pay a teacher who is not certificated. For example, a North Carolina statute states:

> "The county or city superintendent, or other official, is forbidden to approve any vouchers for salary for any personnel employed in violation of the provisions of this section and the treasurer of the county or of the city schools is hereby forbidden to pay out of school funds the salary of such person." [5]

CONTRACTS

The law of contracts is the body of rules governing the interpretation and enforcement of bargain promises. The principal objective of these rules is to give effect to the reasonable expectations of the parties arising from the bargain. A contract is an agreement between two or more persons consisting of a promise or mutual promises that the law will enforce, or the performance of which the law in some way recognizes as a duty.[6] The essential requirements of a contract are: (1) mutual assent, (2) consideration, (3) the agreement must not be one declared void by statute or by rule of the common law, (4) the parties must have complete legal capacity, (5) the agreement must be in the form required by law, and (6) the object of the contract must be a lawful one.[7]

350

The term "agreement" is a much broader concept than "contract." An agreement includes promises that may or may not be enforced. If the agreement is invalid, it cannot be the basis for a contract. All contracts are agreements, but not all agreements are contracts. An agreement generally consists of an offer and an acceptance, whereas a contract always requires more than mere mutual consent.

Regarding contracts, the personnel administrator's first concern should be where the authority to contract lies. Under the law a school district is a legal entity. It is a corporate body possessing the power to sue and be sued, to purchase and sell real and personal property, and to make contracts and be contracted with. Generally, a superintendent does not have the authority to enter into teachers employment contracts on behalf of the school board.[8] With few exceptions, the superintendent may legally only recommend teacher appointments. The cases are in conflict concerning whether or not a school board has the power to extend the contract of employment beyond the school board's period of office.[9] If a statutory regulation limits the board's contractual powers to its current term of office, however, such extended contracts will be invalidated. The contract of employment is a contract for personal services. If it is entered into for a definite term, it will be considered an entire contract for the period covered. If all legal requisites have been fulfilled and a teacher attempts to rescind his contract, he may be liable for breach of contract and subject to a lawsuit. An invalid contract between a district and a teacher may be ratified and made valid by permitting the teacher to enter upon his duties. In such cases, the ratified contract is as legal as if it had been valid in the first instance.[10]

An employment contract should be specific and contain all the essential terms of the agreement. A promise to employ a teacher that does not state either the character of the employment or the compensation for it is so indefinite that the law cannot enforce it, even if consideration is given for it.[11] A teacher's employment is subject to reasonable rules and regulations of the board of education.[12] This applies whether the rules existed prior to signing the contract or after the effective date of the contract.[13] Even if a teacher does not know about the rules or regulations, if it appears that he should have known of their existence prior to the agreement they will be given effect as part of the contract. It is a well-established rule of law that in order for a contract to be enforceable it must be in the form required by law. Most states require that teacher-employment contracts be in writing, but legal authority exists to the effect that, if the contract is not in writing and the teacher is qualified and renders services with the board's knowledge, the courts will recognize the services rendered by the teacher and allow him to recover compensation for the services rendered.[14]

Local boards of education have considerable latitude in the matter of the salaries of personnel within the budget, provided that they comply with pertinent statutes (e.g., minimum-salary levels) and provided that their salary schedules are reasonable and applied impartially to individuals and groups of individuals.

The Supreme Court of California stated the guiding principle succinctly in 1941:

> ". . . within the limits fixed by the School Code, the Board has discretionary control over the salaries of the teachers. However, . . . the legislature has enjoined on such Boards, within reasonable limits, the principle of uniformity of treatment as to salary for those performing like services with like experience." [15]

Since public funds are involved, a board of education cannot arbitrarily decide that a favored teacher with certain experience and duties is to be paid more than another teacher with similar experience and duties. Proposals for merit-pay increases have been limited by legal requirements of objectivity in determining who shall receive increases. Salary differentials can be set on the basis of preparation, experience, or duties, but they must be applied fairly to all who meet the objective standards. This principle also affects recruitment, since the recruiter cannot offer a higher salary to one prospective teacher just because he is impressed with the applicant's personality, or even his recommendations. Many states have "equal pay" laws prohibiting salary differentials based on sex.

With respect to activities outside the classroom, a teacher may be required to perform tasks incidental to classroom activities irrespective of whether or not the contract specifically calls for the performance of such incidental duties. Such services must come within the implied duties of a teacher's contract.[16] Ticket selling, field excursions, lunch and bus duties, although incidental, have been found to come within the implied duties of a teacher's contract.[17] However, calling upon a teacher to drive a school bus, to perform tasks which are janitorial in nature, or to sit beside a school gate and collect tickets at a football game have been found not to be obligations of a teacher under his employment contract.

Many texts refer to the removal of a teacher for cause as a termination of the contract. In reality, the contract is being terminated by the board, but only because the teacher has breached one or more of its provisions. The breach is the decisive factor because it effectuates the termination of the rights under the contract. Generally, a teacher may breach a contract in any of the following ways: incompetency, immorality, misconduct, neglect of duty, insubordination. All of these elements may serve as legitimate grounds for dismissal under the concept of "just cause" and effectively terminate the contract. The most compelling reason for the above grounds serving as a basis for dismissal is that every teacher is charged with the responsibility of setting a good example. A 1939 Pennsylvania decision put it this way: "It has always been the recognized duty of the teacher to conduct himself in such a way as to command the respect and good will of the community." [18] Although marriage, child bearing,[19] insubordination, immorality and politi-

352

cal activities have been cited as causes for dismissal, judicial decisions have not been uniform in always allowing dismissal for such reasons. The facts and circumstances of each case determine the question of whether or not the contract has been breached and therefore constitute sufficient grounds for removal. Admissions of improper conduct are not always sustained by the courts as reasons for dismissal. In some cases, the courts ordered reinstatement when a staff member convinced the court that his admission had been forced by threats of giving him an unsatisfactory reference if he did not resign. Thus it is illegal as well as improper for a personnel administrator to coerce a staff member into resigning under threats of punitive action.

Bolmeier lists these legal guidelines for school boards concerning dismissals:

1. The power to dismiss a staff member for proper cause may not be set aside by the contract.
2. Procedures in dismissal proceedings must follow existing statutes.
3. In the absence of such statutes, the staff member must be given notices of charges and a fair hearing before an impartial body.
4. The burden of proof of incompetency or other proper cause rests upon the school board.
5. The board can demand only average performance and qualifications, not superior performance.
6. Teachers have the right of appeal to courts or higher state authorities.
7. Objective testimony by school administrators carries considerable weight with courts.
8. Impact on the welfare of children is a most important factor in the court's reaching a judicial opinion.[20]

Hamilton and Reutter list four elements that are generally required by statute in dismissal proceedings against tenured teachers:

1. Notice must be given to employees that dismissal is being contemplated in sufficient time for them to prepare a response.
2. A specific statement of charges must be presented in reasonably objective form and of such nature as to constitute legal grounds for dismissal.
3. A fair and impartial hearing must be provided either before the school board or its properly designated representative, and the results must be considered by the board, for only the board in corporate action has the power to dismiss the teacher.
4. An appeal procedure should be provided to the staff member.[21] Although formal hearings are not required for teachers on probation and other staff members who do not have tenure, and although the regulations may state that such teachers may be dismissed with-

out any statement of reasons, the trend has been to provide such individuals with reasons and with an opportunity to be heard under the "due process" concept.[21]

Since the contract of employment is a legally binding document, it should be drawn up by the school district's attorney and should be reviewed periodically by an attorney. In large school districts, the contract of employment may be a brief notice of appointment mailed by the personnel office with an acceptance form to be signed and returned by the applicant. The rules and regulations governing appointments and acceptances are set forth in bylaws of the board of education and in circulars of handbooks made available to applicants. An example of such a notification of appointment can be seen in the first contract. The teacher applicant in New York City who receives such a notice of appointment is required to confirm appointment by filling out another form, seen in the second contract, which needs the signature of the principal of the school, and returning it to the division of personnel. The third contract was prepared by a state department of education (West Virginia) and is used by school districts within the state. Some school districts have a form for probationary teachers that differs slightly from the form used for a "continuing contract." (See following three samples.)

TENURE

Teachers' tenure laws attach specific rights to teaching positions, including the right to be retained in employment indefinitely, subject only to removal for certain enumerated causes and in a prescribed manner.[22] A statute prescribes the causes for removal of a teacher who has acquired tenure. A tenure statute may provide for dismissal of a teacher for other good and just causes. Such statutes are merely intended to regulate dismissal for causes personal to a teacher, not for causes outside a teacher's control.[23] A school board may not add causes for removal to those enumerated by statute. That would constitute an *ultra vires* action—going beyond its legal authority—on the part of the school board. If the school board acts in an *ultra vires* manner, a teacher may justifiably appeal its decision.

Despite the attainment of tenure by a teacher, his position remains basically one of employment.[24] Therefore, terms different from those previously imposed upon him may be imposed upon him as a tenured teacher. While new terms must be calculated to meet the current needs of the school and the school system, they cannot be arbitrary. Changes and new terms rest solely upon the school administrator's reasonable discretion.[25] A major reduction in a teacher's responsibilities may be accompanied by a corresponding reduction in salary.[26] Tenure is not an assurance against the reduction of a teacher's salary. While reasonable reductions in a teacher's

354

BOARD OF EDUCATION OF THE CITY OF NEW YORK
Office of Personnel—Bureau of Appointment
65 Court Street, Brooklyn, N.Y.-11201

Teacher

Notice of Appointment

You are hereby appointed as teacher of_____
(Subject and License)   (Rating)

to_____

(District)   (School)   (Borough)

effective on_____, for a probationary period of service of three years.

Any inquiry relative to this appointment should be addressed to the Bureau of Appointment, 6th Floor, at the above address.

Social Security No._____   File Number_____

To:

For the Chancellor
Very truly yours,
JOHN DOE
Deputy Superintendent of Schools

Enclosures: (Please read each one with care.)

NOTE: The enclosed certificate of commencement of service and the oath of allegiance **must** be mailed on the afternoon of the first day of service in order to consummate this appointment. **This certificate must also be mailed by those in military service and by those who will accept appointment in absentia because of maternity & child care leave.** If it is not your intention to accept the appointment, a written declination must be forwarded to the Bureau of Appointment and the District Superintendent by return mail. The principal should also be informed.

Social Security No._____

File No._____
(To be filled in by appointee—
obtain from license, substitute
or regular)

BOARD OF EDUCATION OF THE CITY OF NEW YORK
Office of Personnel, Bureau of Appointment
65 Court Street, Brooklyn, N.Y. 11201

Certificate of Commencement of Service

To consummate appointment, this certificate and application, properly filled out must be mailed by the teacher to the Bureau of Appointment at the address shown above, **on the afternoon of the first day of Service.** The Adjustment of the Appointee's Salary Depends upon the prompt return of this form. Failure to return this form and oath of allegiance will result in the withholding of salary.

An appointee on leave of absence for purposes of maternity and child care or for military service may accept an appointment in absentia by filing this blank with application for leave (signature of principal not necessary).

If the appointee does not desire to accept the appointment offered, a written declination must be filed immediately with the Bureau of Appointment at the above address.

APPOINTED FROM _____

(Eligible List)   (Date of List)

I, _____, hereby certify that I began actual and personal

(Maiden Name)

service under appointment as _____ in _____

School   Borough

_____ on _____ day of _____, 19 _____.

District

I hereby certify that the above statement is correct, and that the appointee has been assigned to a class in grade _____

(Signature of Principal) _____

Were you a regular appointed employee (not reg. substitute) of the N.Y.C. Board of Education immediately

prior to this appointment?   (Yes)_____ (No)_____

If so, indicate _____

District   School   Borough   Rank and Subject

If not, were you a **former** regular appointed employee of the N.Y.C. Board of Education (Not substitute)

(Yes)_____ (No)_____

Appointees who desire to claim salary credit for prior outside experience should fill out the reverse side of this page. FAILURE TO CLAIM SUCH CREDIT AT THIS TIME WILL PRECLUDE ANY FUTURE CLAIM FOR SUCH CREDIT.

Immediately preceding this appointment I was a substitute teacher compensated

1—Without Differential   C1 ☐
2—With First Differential   C2 ☐
at_____   3—With Second Differential   C6 ☐
(Salary Step)   4—With Promotional Differential   ☐

356

Teachers, psychologists, school social workers, attendance teachers, school secretaries and laboratory specialists may be eligible for one or more of three salary differentials which may be granted for thirty semester hours of approved study beyond the baccalaureate degree or for further study taken under certain conditions. Each differential must be applied for individually. The circular "Salary Information for the New Teacher," previously mailed to you, describes these in general. Detailed information is available at the school.

Have you been granted any such differential?   Yes ☐   No ☐

If you believe yourself eligible for any differential not yet granted to you, you should make application without delay. (There are penalties for late application)

I hereby certify that I have read the above and that my statements are correct.

(Signature of Appointee)_____

Oath of Allegiance

I do solemnly swear (or affirm) that I will support the Constitution of the United States of America and the Constitution of the State of New York and that I will faithfully discharge, according to the best of my ability, the duties of the position of

For Office Use Only

_____

(Title of Position)

_____

(School, Borough of)

Sworn to before me this

_____

_____day of_____

(Signature of teacher)

19_____

_____

(Address)

_____

(Notary Public or Comm. of Deeds)

Teacher's Probationary Contract of Employment

THIS CONTRACT OF EMPLOYMENT, made and entered into the _____ day of _____,

19____, by and between THE BOARD OF EDUCATION OF THE COUNTY OF _____, State

of West Virginia (hereinafter called Board), party of the first part, and _____

_____

(Name of Teacher)

of _____, a teacher holding a _____

    (Post Office)   (County)   (State)   (Kind of Certificate or Permit)

teacher's certificate or permit issued under the laws of the State of West Virginia, and now in force (hereinafter called Teacher), party of the second part:

WHEREAS, at a lawful meeting of the Board of Education of the said County of _____

held at _____, on the _____day of _____, 19____,

the Teacher was duly appointed for employment as_____in the

public schools of said_____County, at a salary for the school employment

term beginning on or after the first day of July, 19____, of_____

($_____) per month for the 19____-19____school term. This contract shall be for (_____),

                                                                                  one

(_____), or (_____) school terms, and

  two   three

WHEREAS, Section 2, Article 2, Chapter 18A of the Code of West Virginia, as last amended, provides, among other things, that before entering upon their duties all teachers shall execute a contract with their boards of education, in the form prescribed by the state superintendent of schools, and that every such contract shall be signed by the teacher and by the president and secretary of the board of education; and

WHEREAS, this contract is in the form prescribed by the state superintendent of schools:

NOW, THEREFORE, THIS CONTRACT WITNESSETH:

That pursuant to said appointment and in consideration of the said monthly salary to be fixed and paid by the BOARD for the said school term in the manner and at the times prescribed by law, the Teacher agrees faithfully to perform all the duties of said position and employment, and agrees faithfully to observe and enforce the rules and regulations lawfully prescribed by legally constituted school authorities insofar as such rules and regulations may be applicable to said county.

THE PARTIES HERETO MUTUALLY AGREE:

(a) The services to be performed hereunder by the Teacher are to commence with the teacher's employment term beginning on or after the first day of July, 19____, and are to be performed in such school or schools, and at such place or places as may be designated by the Superintendent, with the approval of the Board.

(b) The length of the school term is to be fixed by the Board pursuant to law.

(c) This contract is made subject to the authority of the board of school finance to require a county board of education not to contract for the employment of a teacher at a monthly salary in excess of the monthly salary fixed by Section 2, Article 4, Chapter 18A, and in compliance with Section 7, Article 9B, Chapter 18 of the Code of West Virginia as last amended.

(d) The services to be performed by the Teacher shall be such services as are required by law, by the lawful rules and regulations of the state board of education and by the lawful rules and regulations of the Board.

358

(e) The services to be performed under this contract shall commence on the date herein specified, and should the school in which the Teacher is employed be closed temporarily for necessary repairs, or because of the destruction of the building in which such school is conducted, school shall be suspended accordingly until necessary quarters are provided, but any such suspension shall not in any manner affect the employment term of such school, and quarters shall be provided without unnecessary delay, and, in any event, in time to complete the employment as provided by law.

(f) In event an elementary school is closed during the school term pursuant to Code 18A-2-2 if the teachers are not transferred or reassigned, they shall be placed upon a preferred list as provided by law.

(g) The school in which the Teacher is employed may be recessed for such times and for such periods as may be mutually agreed upon from time to time.

(h) The salary for the last month's services rendered in any school year shall not be paid until the Teacher shall have made all reports and performed all duties lawfully required of the Teacher within the period of the school year.

(i) This contract may be terminated at any time by mutual consent of the Board and the Teacher.

(j) The power of the Board to suspend or dismiss the Teacher for immorality, incompetency, cruelty, insubordination, intemperance, or wilful neglect of duty, in pursuance of the provisions of Section 8, Article 2, Chapter 18A, Code of West Virginia, is in no manner impaired or affected.

(k) In the event the Teacher should fail to fulfill this contract, unless prevented from so doing by personal illness or other just cause, or unless released from this contract by the Board, or if the Teacher shall violate any lawful provision hereof, the Teacher shall be disqualified to teach in any other public school in the state for the period of the school year next ensuing and his credentials may be held for that period of time, according to law.

(l) The marriage of the Teacher shall not be considered a failure to fulfill this contract, or to be a violation thereof.

(m) In the construction and operation of this contract of employment, it shall at all times be subject to any and all laws now existing or that may hereafter be lawfully enacted relating to the fixing of the salaries of teachers, the increase or decrease of such salaries and the length of the school term.

(n) This contract shall terminate if at the beginning of any school term the Teacher does not hold a valid teacher's certificate covering the period of such term; provided that if a teacher is employed on good faith on the anticipation that he is eligible for a certificate and it is later determined after he has actually begun teaching that he was not eligible, the State superintendent of schools may authorize payment by the county board to the teacher for the time taught not to exceed three months.

(o) The operation of this contract shall be suspended for such period or periods of time as the Teacher, by reason of prolonged personal illness, may be unable to perform the duties herein required of the Teacher.

(p) In the construction and operation of this contract of employment, if the contract as indicated on page one is for a period of one, two, or three years, the Teacher may, from year to year, or from time to time, be assigned to other and different positions in the same school, or to other and different positions in other and different schools and that, in any such event, the salary of the Teacher may be increased or decreased, in accordance with changes in the kind of position or changes in the kind of duties but must be notified on or before the first Monday in May.

(q) This contract is not a continuing contract and shall be applicable only to a person not presently holding a continuing contract with this Board.

(r) If this contract, as indicated on page one, is for a period of one, two or three years, the salary for the second and third years shall be in conformance with Section 2, Article 4, Chapter 18A of the Code of West Virginia, as last amended; plus any local salary schedule in excess of minimum salaries that may be adopted by the county board of education.

WITNESS the following signatures as of the day, month and year first above written.

_____

President County Board of Education

_____

Secretary County Board of Education

_____

Teacher

The foregoing form is prescribed in pursuance of one of the provisions of Section 2, Article 2, Chapter 18A of the Code of West Virginia, as last amended.

STATE SUPERINTENDENT OF SCHOOLS

salary may be exercised by a school board,[27] it can never reduce a salary after a school year has begun. Any salary reduction will most likely be fought in the courts by the teacher as an arbitrary decision of the school board.

Tenure virtually guarantees the right of a teacher to continued employment in a position of the same rank or grade as that to which the teacher was elected under a tenure law. Subject only to the requirement of reasonableness, a school district may assign teachers to any functions they are certified for, according to the needs of the district. Tenure does not bestow on the school teacher a vested right to a specific school or to a specific class level of students within a school.[28] An arbitrary assignment of a tenured teacher will not be tolerated by the courts, especially if the transfer is to harass or punish a teacher for a presumptively legal act. In the case of *Finot v. Pasadena City Board of Education, 58* Cal. Rptr. 520 (1967), the California court held that the transfer of a high school teacher of tenure status from his assignment by the school board because he insisted on wearing a beard, in violation of an administrative policy of the school principal, constituted a violation of the teacher's constitutional rights, under the first amendment. Another frequent cause for removal of teachers who have attained permanent tenure status has been immorality.[29] An act of immorality does not necessarily have to be an act involving moral turpitude.[30]

Not all state legislatures have enacted effective tenure laws. Some state laws merely require that a teacher be given advance notice of the nonrenewal of his employment contract. This is classified as a continuing contract law of the spring-notification type. A continuing contract law is legally distinct from a tenure law because it contains no provisions for notice, statement of charges, or right of hearing before a teacher is discharged. Other states have laws containing provisions for annual or long-term contracts. Long-term contract laws include only the period for which a contract may be entered into between the school board and the teacher. Therefore, the personnel administrator is urged to check his state's statutes in order to determine what type of law has been enacted.

Tenure laws are effective for a staff member as long as the position exists. If the position is abolished, the staff member does not have the right to a nonexistent position. In some jurisdictions, the abolition of a position has been used unjustly to eliminate an unwanted staff member. To prevent abuses, laws have been passed to give necessary protection to incumbents. For example, the abolition of a job title, and the immediate creation of a new job title with substantially the same duties, in order to get rid of an incumbent serving under the first job title, has been ruled illegal. The nature of the duties is the determining factor, not the job title. Moreover, laws have been passed to compel the transfer of a tenured teacher to an equivalent position if his position is abolished.

The burden is placed on the school district to show that no position

360

exists which the displaced, tenured teacher is qualified to teach. If an individual or several individuals must be displaced because one or more positions are abolished, seniority generally determines who is to be displaced. One court put the decision this way:

> "Seniority is a matter not to be treated lightly. . . . Where a reduction in teaching staff is called for, the Board's first consideration should be how to retain those teachers with the longest years of service by realigning the staff so that the remaining teachers, after the reduction has been effected, can teach the subjects of those who, because of lesser seniority rights, have been suspended." [31]

The Supreme Court of Louisiana made the following decision in 1955:

> "An honest discontinuance of his office does not automatically remove a permanent teacher from the school system. He remains therein and should forthwith be placed in a position of standing equal to that formerly held, if it be possible. In any event, he is nonetheless entitled to the salary attributable to the status he has attained even though he be reemployed in a position of lesser rank." [32]

When there is no similar position to which an incumbent can be assigned, statutes may provide that he should be given preference for employment if a similar position becomes available.

RIGHTS OF TEACHERS

Because of the influence exercised by teachers, the courts have been inclined to scrutinize their conduct. It has at times caused teachers to be relegated to the status of second-class citizens, and the custom in many communities has often been to compel teachers to exercise their rights with a restricted descretion. The controversial areas of teachers' rights concern freedom of speech, loyalty oaths, and the right to a fair hearing.

The first amendment to the constitution guarantees to every citizen the freedoms of speech, press, assembly and petition. A personnel administrator will generally be concerned with this area. The problem arises most frequently where a teacher criticizes a school board or school official publicly. In many instances, teachers have felt compelled to criticize school officials or policies by addressing public meetings, by circulating petitions in a community, or by publishing articles in a newspaper. In each of the above examples, the first amendment rights become the paramount issue if a teacher has been dismissed for criticizing school personnel or policies. More recently, the courts have applied the first amendment in cases that have concerned loyalty oaths, the right of a teacher to form and join a union, and the right to teach the theory of evolution in a public school.

Regarding the right of a teacher to criticize school policies and offi-

361

cials, the Supreme Court of the United States held in *Pickering v. the Board of Education* that, without proof of false statements knowingly and recklessly made by the teacher, the exercise of his right to speak on issues of public importance may not be the basis for his dismissal from public employment. In that case, a teacher had been dismissed after a local newspaper published a letter in which he criticized the school board and the district superintendent of schools for statements made about teachers' opposition to the board's revenue referendum.[33] In another Supreme Court decision, the Court reversed a decision of the Supreme Court of Alaska that had sustained a dismissal of two teachers by a local board of education.[34] The teachers had been dismissed on the grounds of immorality for distributing in violation of a statutory regulation a letter containing false statements disparaging the superintendent. The board also had found that the "immorality" of one teacher had consisted of private conversations with various teachers in which he solicited their support to oust the school superintendent. The "immorality" of the other teacher was that he had made a speech to a labor union about disbanding the school board. After many appeals and hearings, the Supreme Court finally reversed and remanded the case to the state court of Alaska for further consideration in light of its decision in the Pickering Case, which had conclusively extended the first amendment rights of teachers to speak out on issues of public concern.

One of the most interesting decisions rendered by the Supreme Court in recent years was the case of *Epperson v. State of Arkansas*,[35] involving teaching the Darwinian theory of evolution. Arkansas had a statute that prohibited teaching the theory of evolution in a state-supported school. The statute also provided that a violation of the statute would constitute a misdemeanor and subject the violator to dismissal from his position. In a suit brought by a high school biology teacher challenging the constitutionality of the statute, the Supreme Court of Arkansas sustained the statute as an exercise of the state's power to specify the curriculum in the public schools. The Supreme Court of the United States reversed the decision on the grounds that it violated the first and fourteenth amendments. The *ratio decidendi* was that, while a state has a right to prescribe the curriculum for its public schools, it may not prohibit on pain of criminal penalty the teaching of a scientific theory if that prohibition is based upon reasons that violate the first amendment. Likewise, in *Meyer v. Nebraska*, 43 S.Ct. 625, the Supreme Court struck down state legislation prohibiting the teaching of German to nonpublic or public school pupils because the legislation was an arbitrary interference with the liberty of teachers to pursue their calling.

With regard to the right of a teacher to join or form a union, it has become apparent that so prohibiting a teacher violates his constitutional rights as set forth in the first amendment. Teachers cannot be dismissed from their positions for asserting their right.[36] Also involved is the constitutional question of whether or not the teacher's right of free speech is impinged upon.[37]

362

With reference to the first amendment, the U.S. District Court for Eastern Texas has summarized this field of law by stating that teachers are not made second-class citizens in regard to their constitutional rights simply because they are on a public payroll. Even though governmental purposes may be legitimate and substantial, they cannot be pursued by means that broadly stifle fundamental personal liberties when the ends sought can be more narrowly achieved. Laws and official regulations that restrict the liberties guaranteed by the first amendment should be narrowly drawn to meet the specific evil aimed at.[38]

Loyalty oaths have become a frequent area of constitutional litigation. Not every loyalty oath is declared unconstitutional. Whether or not a teacher is required to take a loyalty oath depends upon the language of the particular state statute and the requirements of the oath. If the oath is vague, it is sure to be declared unconstitutional. Loyalty oaths are a proper subject for legislative enactments, but laws must be sufficiently definitive to eliminate controllable activities without deterring legitimate expression.[39] If a statute requires a teacher to execute an oath stating that he will support the federal and state constitutions and faithfully discharge the duties of his position according to the best of his ability, the courts will uphold such an oath on the grounds that the statute imposes no restrictions upon political or philosophical expressions by teachers. A state does not interfere with teachers by requiring them to support the governmental systems that shelter and nourish the institutions in which they teach, nor does it restrict teachers by encouraging them to uphold the highest standards of their chosen profession.[40]

A loyalty oath will be declared unconstitutional if the signing or executing of the oath reflects guilt by association with an organization. Such an oath generally attempts to equate membership in an organization (e.g., the Communist Party) as a reflection of guilt. The courts have repeatedly held that an individual is entitled to be judged by his own conduct, not by that of his associates.[41] For such an oath to be valid, it must contain a clause requiring that the member of the organization has the specific intent to further the illegal aims of the organization. This intent must be proved by actions or by other evidence related to him in particular.

One of the most perplexing legal problems in the field of administrative law is the question concerning the right of a teacher to a fair hearing. Generally, only in a constitutional field where a quasi-judicial power is being exercised are adequate notice and a fair hearing requirements. If the administrative agency is in a nonconstitutional field, if it is a nonjudicial agency, and if no specific statute exists granting the requirements of a fair hearing, then the decision of the agency is generally final and there will be no appellate recourse to the courts as long as there is procedural conformity with the statutory regulations.[42] Agencies, therefore, whether or not of the independent regulatory type and even though delegated or exercising only legislative or executive powers, may, nevertheless, be judi-

363

cially reviewed because of a full hearing requirement imposed by statute.[43] If an administrative hearing is statutorily or constitutionally required, it must be preceded by notice and an opportunity to be fully prepared for and heard by the agency. Such hearings are analogous to judicial hearings in courts of law, so statutory or "due process" requirements are necessitated.

If a substantial constitutional right is involved and no prescribed statute exists, a teacher is entitled to a fair hearing. For example, if a teacher is dismissed for less than adequate cause, even though no method of procedure has been established the teacher is entitled to notices of charges against him and to a hearing before an impartial board. If those rights are denied, the teacher has an immediate recourse to the courts without exhausting the administrative agency. It is the general rule of law that one must exhaust the appellate roadways of the administrative agency before he can turn to the courts for relief,[44] but that is not applicable if a teacher has been deprived of a substantial constitutional right. Likewise, if a school board's determination is arbitrary, it can be appealed. If a teacher is given adequate notice and the opportunity for a fair hearing, he may not complain that his rights have been violated if he does not attend the hearing.[45]

The finding of an agency must be supported by the weight of evidence. If a school board conducts a hearing on a teacher's dismissal and subsequently dismisses the teacher, but the finding for dismissal is not supported by the weight of the evidence, the courts will overrule the finding of the school board.[46]

School-segregation decisions have had an impact upon teachers and other school personnel as well as upon pupils. School-segregation cases that affect teachers have come from charges that the assignment of teaching personnel was made on a racially segregated basis and charges that there was discrimination when only Negro teachers were discharged as a result of the consolidation of schools in the implementation of desegregation plans.

In reinstating two Negro teachers who were improperly discharged, the United States Court of Appeals ruled that the board of education must establish "objective standards of employment and retention of teachers consistent with the Fourteenth Amendment." [47]

School personnel administrators have been troubled by the possibility of libel suits brought against them or other school administrators by staff members who have received adverse or unsatisfactory reports on their service. Judicial decisions thus far have regarded personnel reports of principals and other supervisors to the school superintendent or personnel administrator, copies of which were given to the staff member, as privileged communications in the performance of public duty. However, the fact that such communications may be scrutinized by legal authorities underscores

364

the desirability of having guidelines for personnel and school administrators in making evaluations of personnel.

1. Evaluations of personnel should never be based upon personal animosity or resentment and should never be made in a desire to harm or retaliate against a staff member.
2. Evaluations should be couched in judicious, temperate, objective language and should be supportable by evidence in memoranda, recollection, notes and calendar references.
3. Evaluations of staff members should be discussed only in official capacity, through official channels and with individuals entitled to be informed—never in social situations. If there is any doubt about the propriety of the discussion, it should be avoided.
4. Statements evaluating individuals adversely should never be made to public media without specific advice of counsel.
5. Reference forms requested by duly constituted official bodies should be filled out fairly and objectively with statements that can be objectively supported.

Laws change and judicial decisions also change as the climate of public opinion changes and as social progress continues. For example, the Supreme Court of the United States in 1952 upheld the New York State Fineberg Anti Subversive Law, which made membership in a subversive organization *prima facie* evidence for disqualification from appointment or retention in the public schools of the state.[48] However, in 1967, the United States Supreme Court in *Keyishian v. Board of Regents of the University of the State of New York* reversed that decision by a 5 to 4 vote, declaring that the statutes that made membership in the Communist Party *prima facie* evidence for disqualification from teaching were impermissibly broad.[49]

The trend in many legal decisions and statutes in recent years has been to place limitations upon the broad and vague powers of public administrators, including those in school personnel administration. Two such related tendencies have been expressed as the "due process" concept and "open disclosure." In the past, school boards had broad and sweeping power to take action against or to issue orders to staff members if such orders were not expressly limited or prohibited by statute. But the principle of due process has been invoked to require that such orders or actions be taken with valid explanations and supporting reasons.

It has therefore been ruled in some jurisdictions, for example, that teachers may not be summoned for medical or psychiatric examinations without good and specific reasons, that teachers may not be transferred to another school in the district without due process, and that teachers may be suspended only for a limited time without a hearing. Under the principle of open disclosure, decisions have been made in some jurisdictions that require copies of reference documents used in determining an individual's hiring or promotion to be made available to him. The New York State School Decentralization Law of 1969 required that all interview tests for teaching and supervisory licenses in the New York City school system be recorded and that a copy thereof be furnished on request to each applicant.

Another example of social progress affecting statutes and public employment has been the tendency to aid handicapped persons in obtaining employment. Thus, the New York State Legislature in 1967 passed a law declaring that blindness can not be a reason for denying employment or certification to a teacher. Decisions by educational certification authorities have also eased other physical-medical restrictions placed upon entering teachers with respect to hearing deficiencies, orthopedic deficiencies and other medical and physical limitations.

In another area, namely, the employment of school aides and auxiliary personnel, statutes and state regulations concerning certification of school personnel, which previously were rigorously applied, have been relaxed, chiefly by a social change, to allow maximum local flexibility in employing teachers' aides. There is no doubt that this situation will change in the future as clarification of the duties, relationships and preparation of auxiliary personnel occurs.

17 PERSONNEL EVALUATION

GENERAL STATEMENT

Although this chapter refers chiefly to the evaluation of teachers, the principles and procedures used in evaluation may be applied, after adaptation, to other employees in the organization, both certificated and classified, and to administrative personnel as well.

The traditional context of the meaning of staff evaluation is that an individual is employed to perform a certain function within a total organization; the evaluation is a report on the degree of success or the quality of service offered. In an industrial organization, an employee's performance in his function may be appraised more readily. Has he increased sales? Is he producing more units? Is he producing better units? The performance of a teacher or other professional staff member is not so easily appraised, for there are intangible elements in his achievements as well as objective elements, and more variables must be considered. Objective elements could include the performance of a teacher's class on standardized achievement tests, but intangible elements might include the influence of the teacher on the attitudes and personalities of his students. Among the variables to be considered are the preparation and background of pupils, the goals and philosophy of the school and community, the cooperation and attitude of the parents, the plant and facilities of the school, the support of the school's administration, and the experiential background of the teacher. Other variables lie in the backgrounds and beliefs of the individuals performing the evaluative function. Moreover, the purposes of the school organization may change as a result of the demands of society. Examples of these changes would include, but not be limited to, forced integration, changing board policies, the discovery of new knowledge, the availability of new instructional materials, and new methodology. These changes may mean that the teacher's role will change. It must be recognized, therefore, that

367

staff evaluation involves subjective judgments and is a complex professional undertaking that must be approached with understanding and caution. In an article in the *New York Post* of September 6, 1969, columnist Bernard Bard quotes educational consultant Fred C. Manasse as pointing up the following differences between industry and education:

> "In industry, the output is defined—this is one of the first principles of good management. A worker in industry knows exactly what the outcome of his work is supposed to be. In education objectives are usually vague. Teachers seldom know what, specifically, their students should know or be able to do at the end of a lesson."

Evaluation includes the process of communication by which the employing agency advises its employees of the effectiveness of their service toward the ongoing purpose of the agency. The process of evaluation has changed through the years from an authoritarian appraisal by a school official to a cooperative effort in which the teacher's rights must be protected. Indeed, there are teachers who maintain that staff evaluations are an anachronism, an affront to the professional integrity of a teacher, and that the only proper evaluation of a teacher is self-evaluation for self-improvement.

The purposes of evaluation have been expanded from mere retention to improvement of service. Forms and procedures have changed. In recent years, demands by community leaders for greater "accountability" by teachers have raised questions about who should perform the evaluation. What voice should parents or the community have? Should students have a voice? What is the role of the personnel administrator in the process of evaluation?

PURPOSES OF EVALUATION

If it is assumed that staff evaluations will continue to be required by school districts in the foreseeable future, consideration must be given to the purposes of evaluation and to the best methods and procedures for achieving those purposes.

The principal purpose of evaluation is to improve instruction in the broadest sense. It has become such a cliché that thoughtful understanding of its meaning has been impeded. Evaluation does not mean that improved instruction will take place merely by telling employees that they are doing a good job, a mediocre job or a poor job. It does not mean that detailing or listing a teacher's strengths and weaknesses will automatically bring about an improvement in his teaching. Evaluation must occur in a framework of relationships and other efforts, perhaps more significant than evaluation itself, that contribute to improved instruction. The success of evaluation depends on the teacher's motivation to seek better ways of presenting subject matter, to analyze students' needs and abilities more carefully, to stimulate student initiative and creativity, to gain new insights

368

into growth and behavior, and to assess his own impact on students. Improvement in instruction does not necessarily mean working harder, giving more assignments, correcting more papers or demanding more homework. It is more likely to mean a creative effort at making instruction more meaningful, increasing motivation, and presenting material in a more exciting way. Also implied in the improvement of instruction should be a willingness on the part of the teacher to try promising methods and procedures rather than to continue in a comfortable routine.

There are ways other than evaluation to improve instruction. Some teachers profit considerably by visiting other classrooms, others by attending conferences. Appropriate reading may inspire others. In-service courses, institutes and lectures, as well as departmental or grade-level meetings, may all contribute to the improvement of instruction.

Perhaps no task on the labor market today demands as many skills as teaching. Not only are there variables in each teaching situation, but a teacher also has an individual value system, personal abilities and disabilities, a special background of training and understanding of human relationships, a certain degree of commitment to the job, and an individual perception of the role of teacher. Developing and applying such variables to a specific situation is the task of the employee, with the aid of his supervisors. Since evaluation is a continuous process of observation and communication for the purpose of achieving the goals of the organization, those performing the evaluation should always be ready to give assistance to the staff member. The evaluator's job is to share in developing a better staff, to create a climate in which employees can perform efficiently, and to work toward making the objectives of the employee parallel the purposes of the organization.

The second purpose of evaluation is to identify and encourage the retention of effective personnel. Although intended to be positive and non-threatening, this purpose carries the implication that ineffective personnel should not be retained. This is the area that presents problem situations which ultimately come to the attention of the personnel administrator, although it may be the responsibility of the instruction department, the building administrator and others to take the initial action in the identification of those who should not be retained. However, the recommendation to retain or to officially terminate the employment of a teacher must be made by the personnel administrator, usually on the basis of written and oral reports made by supervisory personnel.

A third purpose of evaluation is promotion. In essence, it is using past performance as a basis for predicting future success.

A fourth purpose of evaluation is to meet the legal requirements of the state or the governing board. Such requirements have public relations value, although their authors were probably concerned with the improvement of service.

A fifth purpose of evaluation concerns the granting of tenure. Almost all school districts require a special evaluation before tenure is granted. Since tenure usually means that a teacher may be retained for his professional lifetime, school boards want to be certain that he meets required standards before they grant tenure.

Evaluation is occasionally used for salary placement. Research has not yet validated this method of compensation, as logical as it appears to be. More problems than benefits seem to be associated with merit pay and the fair selection of those who are to receive it.

HISTORICAL DEVELOPMENT AND DISCERNIBLE TRENDS

It is clear from the early records of public school service that the moral and spiritual values held by the teacher were of utmost concern to those responsible for employing him and for evaluating his service. The teacher was to be no ordinary mortal; he was to have no vices and was also to be responsible for such menial maintenance tasks as stoking furnaces and doing the cleaning. Next to exemplary moral and spiritual quality was the requirement of ability to discipline a class. Discipline was teacher control of the class and the tighter the control the better.

The next development came from the introduction of professional school administrators in large school systems. Those at the top would tell those at the bottom what to do and how and when to do it. The stress in evaluation was on conformity rather than on creativity. This type of evaluation even went as far as to direct the way in which seats were to be lined up and bulletin boards displayed. The most successful teacher was the one who most punctiliously carried out the instructions of the school administrator. Indeed, the child seemed to fit in at the second level of concern rather than at the top.

At the third stage, educators began to show greater consideration of the nature of the learning situation. Pupil-teacher relationships became important. There was recognition of children's individual differences, for which the teacher should provide. There was provision for interest centers; child-made bulletin boards were acceptable, and variations in the pace of classroom activities were encouraged. There was understanding that all teachers could not proceed in the same way with all children. Administrators became aware of individual differences among teachers and applied this awareness when evaluating competence.

A fourth stage in the progress of evaluation came with the growth of strong teachers' organizations, which insisted upon the treatment of teachers as professionals. No longer were evaluations to be imposed by administrators. The teacher was to share in the evaluative process by discussing the nature, standards and substance of evaluation, which was no longer to be regarded as an end in itself but as one step in a program of improvement

370

in instruction. Teachers gained the right to challenge evaluations, to request hearings on the fairness of evaluations, to obtain counsel, and to file grievances.

Some new dimensions are about to be added to evaluation, including the skill to diagnose difficulties in learning and the ability to lead or work in a teaching team. A child's retardation has specific causes. Effective education for him requires understanding of those specific causes and a program to help him as an individual. Teachers are recognizing that they may be more skillful in some aspects of teaching than others. The result is team teaching, planning and working with one's peers, which requires new skills and creates a new area to evaluate.

Another new dimension may be the extent to which a teacher individualizes instruction. As was indicated earlier, historically the teacher was concerned with the class and groups within the class. Now the emphasis is moving toward individualization of instruction. The new instructional technology will encourage the further individualization of instruction, which will require teachers to become more perceptive of each child's progress.

It is strange, indeed, that the teacher's ability to diagnose learning difficulties and to accommodate individual differences has not previously been given adequate weight in evaluation. In most other professions, the proper diagnosis of the problem is the gateway to success. The teacher was undoubtedly prevented from performing individual diagnosis by class size and the lack of proper equipment and facilities. Further, if he suggested that additional equipment, teaching materials, field trips or additional professional services were desirable, he would be charged with building up educational costs, which would, in effect, rock the boat.

If any single pattern can be identified in the field of school personnel evaluation, it is that of a less rigid and more constructive rating. Instead of a multipage form bristling with percentage points and numberless subcategories, the rating device of the future promises to be a comparatively brief instrument that reduces key elements of good teaching into a few major headings. It will be administered informally in an atmosphere of mutual understanding and desire to improve the instruction of children. Contributing to the general pattern will be the following trends:

Toward more comprehensive and selective evaluation by teacher-training institutions.

Toward the use of cooperatively developed rating instruments.

Toward coevaluation of personnel directly concerned.

Toward the use of evaluation as a valuable in-service improvement device instead of an excuse for dismissal.

Toward cooperative evaluation of classified employees as well as teachers.[1]

Evaluation in the future, then, may center more on the teacher's ability to diagnose and treat learning difficulties. It requires high professional skill, and it may be one factor that will encourage differential staffing, for not all teachers will immediately master the skill of diagnosis. To accomplish such a level of teaching, that is diagnosing learning difficulties and providing individualized instruction, the teacher should have additional authority. That may mean, among other things, that the teacher should have the right to transfer students to other situations, to request various types of examinations, to suggest follow-up activities with paraprofessionals, to suggest cooperative efforts with parents and to change curricular requirements to fit the needs of the child. This does not suggest that the teacher will have additional unilateral authority. Rather, the teacher's recommendations will be sought and decisions will be made by all who have instructional, guidance, supervisory and/or administrative responsibility for the educational experiences of the child.

WHO EVALUATES?

The prevailing practice is for the teacher's immediate supervisor to evaluate him. Under the present system of delegating responsibility, it is appropriate. There are some visible signs, however, that the responsibility will soon be shared in some manner with others, who will include members of the teaching team, students and even representatives of the community. Even one's peers may be involved.

Just how peer groups, students and the community will participate in the evaluation of teachers isn't clear at this time. It may be that they will have a more active role in the development of standards for evaluation. It appears that the judgment about granting tenure or dismissing unsatisfactory teachers will continue to be a function of professional administration. It is just as certain, however, that others have a stake in the evaluation process. This change probably means that the process of evaluation will vary. Evaluation forms may give way to description of teaching performance.

Logic requires that evaluation become a shared responsibility: since society pays for or supports the schools, it demands accountability and a participating role in the process of evaluation. The purpose of the educational organization is to help students, so they should have some voice, too. Students can probably best contribute to the evaluation of teachers through informal or indirect communication channels and through their designated representatives. There are, of course, many dangers in having students evaluate individual teachers. Teachers themselves must share in developing standards for judging competence since they are the ones directly affected by any evaluative procedure. Charles Frankel in his book *Education and the Barricades* makes the following statement, according to a citation in the *New York Post* of September 6, 1969:

372

"A wise faculty and administration will do well to try to find out what student opinions about teachers are. But they had better conduct the canvass informally and discreetly. Teaching is a professional relationship, not a popularity contest."

Teachers have charged that other professionals are not evaluated as closely. That is probably true, but schoolboard members argue that practitioners of other professions are evaluated by their clients, who decide whether or not to continue to patronize them. Students do not have such a choice.

It is proper that teachers should have a developing responsibility in the evaluative process. Most likely it will result in better instruction. It will improve the status and dignity of the teacher and will create better relationships between the administration and the teaching staff. In addition to sharing in the development of objectives, standards, procedures and forms for evaluation, it has been suggested that teachers should evaluate the performance of their peers. The evaluation of teachers by other teachers carries with it a number of problems. Teachers are understandably reluctant to criticize or mention the inadequacies of their colleagues, and analysis of teaching ability requires special training that all teachers do not have. In some situations, there has been experimentation with elected departmental chairmen. This procedure has not been accepted widely because elected chairmen are understandably reluctant to evaluate their colleagues. The values of peer interaction seem to lie more in the process of discussion of observed teaching or intervisitation than in formal evaluations. Great value can also be obtained from self-evaluation by teachers, but it must be pointed out that training is necessary for fruitful self-evaluation.

Some may say that evaluation really isn't necessary. The teacher is a professionally trained person and, as such, should be permitted to practice and to grow on the job.This hypothesis has not yet been accepted by board members. Some may concede that, with an enthusiastic staff, well trained, working in complete harmony in a supportive community and under good leadership, a formal evaluation of professional services by the principal may be unnecessary from the point of view of the improvement of instruction. In effect, evaluation is inherent in their daily operations through joint planning and self-directed conferences. However, board members point out that there are staff members with certain degrees of apathy, obsolete methodology, conflicting philosophies, or poor interpersonal relations. Some type of evaluation must be made to determine if the staff is making optimum contribution to the purpose of the organization. The purpose of evaluation in whatever form and method used is to bring about a change in the behavior and attitude of the staff that will be consistent with the purpose of the organization.

At the outset of this section it was stated that the prevailing practice is for the principal to evaluate the teachers on his staff, which immediately puts the principal in a dual role. He must give the teacher support and encouragement, positive suggestions for improvement, and opportunities to gain insights by visiting other classes; he must also suggest reading material and develop rapport and the desire for free interchange of ideas; however, he may also be called upon to document the inadequacies of a teacher, to rate a teacher as satisfactory or unsatisfactory. When it comes to the dismissal of unsatisfactory teachers, the principal must demonstrate that he has offered positive suggestions, and that even with such help the teacher has not responded positively. The principal's duty in evaluating or rating teachers can impair the freedom of exchange between him and his staff by developing distrust or caution on their part. Thus in large school districts the assistant principals or visiting consultants who are removed from a rating role carry the major supervisory role, while the principal becomes the rating officer. In other school districts, principals have carried out their supervisory and rating responsibilities while maintaining the good will of their faculty by the fairness and sympathetic understanding of their approach.

Frequently, a teacher who is about to end a probationary period is visited and evaluated by an assistant superintendent. While the staff of the school personnel administrator does not visit teachers for evaluative purposes, it usually carries the responsibility of developing standards and procedures of administering the evaluative process.

Evaluation of teacher effectiveness is a complex undertaking for a number of reasons. In the first place, appraising any human behavior is difficult, especially attempts to measure the effects of individuals (teachers) upon other individuals (students). Secondly, there is the difficulty of establishing agreed upon criteria for any evaluation. Harold Mitzel, summarizing research on teacher education, states:

> "More than a half century of research effort has not yielded meaningful, measurable criteria around which the majority of the nation's educators can rally." [2]

Thirdly, there is the difficulty of deciding upon the evaluative procedures. Should the academic achievements of students be used? Should their skills, appreciations, or attitudes be appraised? Should the work and behavior of the teacher be observed and appraised aside from any measurement of student changes? Despite these complex problems, school districts are compelled to evaluate teachers in recruiting, promoting, and granting tenure, and in other respects.

It is well, however, for the school personnel administrator, who must make such decisions, to understand the complexities and uncertainties of evaluation. Mitzel offers some guidance in his summary. He declares:

> "Upon the assumption that the most appropriate criteria of teacher effectiveness are those which have relevance to significant educational outcomes, it is critical which outcomes are selected." [3]

374

Thus a school district is in a position to decide which criteria it wishes to stress, which it considers most relevant to its needs. Should development of students' intellectual powers be the major criterion? Should the development of social attitudes be the major criterion? In other words, the evaluative process of the school personnel administrator should be based upon criteria developed by responsible representatives of the community and the profession, including the school superintendent and the board of education, and should be carried out with due regard for the complexity and uncertainties of evaluation so that there may be provisions for appeals or reviews of evaluation.

STANDARDS AND PROCEDURES FOR THE
EVALUATION OF TEACHERS

A number of principles are involved in evaluating teacher performance. The most basic principle is that evaluation standards and procedures should be developed in consultation with teachers or their representatives. A second principle is that praise should be given as freely as criticism. Some school principals are hesitant to express praise for fear that their commendations will haunt them if the teacher turns out to be unsatisfactory. A principal should develop a feel for praising when it is due and for criticizing when it is due so that these are not regarded as undiscriminating gestures. A third principle is that standards should be applied to all staff members equally and fairly. Unjust evaluations are resented by individuals and by the staff generally, and they impair the validity of the evaluator in the future.

In general, teachers should be given the following information about the school district's practices and standards of evaluation:

1. They should know at the beginning of their contractual obligation the procedures and the criteria by which they are to be evaluated. Good personnel practice is to distribute a teachers' handbook containing rules and regulations governing teachers' rights and responsibilities. It should include a standard evaluation form. The usual practice is to perform a formal evaluation of all new teachers once or twice a year. Orientation sessions prior to the opening of the school term should provide time to discuss the purpose and nature of the evaluative process, the time that evaluations are due, and the supervisory philosophy of the school. It is during the orientation sessions that the proper climate for the evaluative process should be established. Effort should be made during orientation sessions, and in subsequent meetings, to ease the teacher's mind of fear or tension concerning evaluation, for the purpose of evaluation is essentially positive, and it is designed to be helpful.
2. Teachers should be informed of how evidence is gathered for eval-

uation. They should be advised that evidence for formal evaluation comes through classroom visits; a review of lesson plans and of methods of handling pupil problems; observations of relations with students, with other school personnel, and with parents and community; and observation of the physical condition of the classroom, the handling of extracurricular activities, and fulfillment of administrative routines. Teachers should also be advised that performance is assessed in reasonable perspective, that hearsay evidence does not influence decisions, and that data are not recorded in closed files for the purpose of punitive action. Good practice is to immediately share with the teacher, in written memoranda and consultation, any specific criticism that could eventually become a factor in retaining his or her services.

3. Teachers should be informed of the major purpose of evaluation, namely to improve instruction. The purpose of evaluation is to encourage discussion, to establish communication, to resolve little problems before they become large, to set goals cooperatively in order that the goals of the individual and of the organization will parallel each other.

4. Teachers should be able to discuss the evaluation with the evaluator. This concept is related to role perception. Teachers are well trained and specialized in their procedures and methodology. The evaluator needs to listen to the problems the teacher faces and the recommendation the teacher has to offer. The time has passed when the administrator makes unilateral decisions regarding the quality of services. There must be honest dialogue between teacher and evaluator. When there are differences of opinion, others should be brought in for role clarification, to establish fact, to assess the situation. The purpose of the discussion is to arrive at a consensus after agreeing on the facts of the situation and at the same time to preserve the integrity of the individuals involved.

5. Teachers should also be given an opportunity for self-appraisal. Stoops and Rafferty comment on self-evaluation:

> "It is probably true, however, that maximum results in the field of self-evaluation are to be received from the construction by teachers themselves of their own evaluation instrument. A teaching group that has sufficient initiative to embark upon the devising of such an instrument, and sufficient knowledge of measurements and statistics to produce a valid rating method, will be repaid richly in increased knowledge of its own faults and virtues. Self-evaluation is usually not the complete answer to the rating problem in any school system, however, if only because there will always be some teachers who will refuse to go along with the announced pur-

poses of the program. Human nature being what it is, many of the personnel who need to take stock of themselves most thoroughly will be the very ones who will decline to do so." [4]

Concerning self-evaluation, Hagen and Thorndike say:

"The trend toward self-evaluation may produce desirable educational outcomes in terms of sensitizing school personnel to deficiencies in their present procedures and encouraging them to make innovations and improvements.[5]

Given below is a list of questions that may be useful to teachers in self-evaluation:

1. In what ways do you show that you are really interested in your students?
2. Do you try new approaches?
3. Do you praise good work?
4. Do you know your students as individuals?
5. Do you work hard? Is your instruction planned carefully?
6. Are your decisions fair? Do you keep your word?
7. Can your students talk to you?
8. Do you motivate your students?
9. Do your students respect you? Do you respect them?
10. Can you inspire your students to have enthusiasm?
11. Do you set an example?
12. How do the community, the administration and your fellow staff members see your contribution to the whole educational enterprise?

There are published self-evaluation scales for teachers. If these are to be most useful, the teacher should be free to use them without revealing his own ratings to his principal. A principal who asks his teachers to evaluate themselves on such a scale and to turn in their self-evaluations to him will lose the value of the rating scale because teachers may be unwilling to reveal their own weakness to their rating officer.

Another way of making a self-appraisal, or even a classroom observation, is to think of the framework within which the evaluation must be made. The framework consists of at least five areas:

Communicative. Is good communication established between pupil and teacher, teacher and principal, teacher and teacher, teacher and parent?

Sociological. Is leadership being demonstrated, and are power, authority and influence all emanating from

377

the proper sources? Is a cooperative, socialized attitude being developed?

Aesthetic. Is there enough rhythm, balance, harmony, "comic relief" to release tension? Are appreciational aspects being developed?

Psychological. Is there an acceptance rather than a rejection of students, peers and administrators? Are there efforts to understand people, to develop sympathetic impulses, to analyze behavior? Are experiences paced, well timed for work, relaxation and fun, competitive at times, cooperative at other times?

Cognitive. Is there evidence of real thinking? Is there a growing respect for knowledge and rational approaches to problems?

6. The teacher should be able to respond to the evaluation in writing. Rules and regulations should be reviewed carefully to determine that a grievance procedure is available for staff members when they believe they have been unfairly evaluated. Grievances are more likely to come when the administrator has not established good and consistent communication. Grievances generally come when a poor evaluation comes as a surprise. There should be no surprises in the evaluative process.

7. The teacher should sign the evaluation form and be given a copy of it. A statement should be on the form to the effect that the signature does not necessarily mean agreement with the statements appearing on the form. The signature means that the individual has seen the form and that it has been discussed with him. The signature on the form is in compliance with the concept that nothing should be in the employee's file without his full knowledge.

Stoops and Rafferty summarize the principles of evaluation as follows:

Evaluation should be based on established principles. The following principles are suggested for adoption and use by superintendents:

1. Genuinely democratic procedures should be applied.
   a. The evaluation should demonstrate fairness to the employees.
   b. The employee should know what is expected of him, and he should be fully acquainted with the appraisal technique.
   c. The employee should know the exact nature and degree of dissatisfaction with his service and be given time and aid for correction of these deficiencies.

d. Employees desiring a review of their evaluations should feel free to contact the principal or superintendent.

e. Age, sex, marital status and religion and other personal matters which do not affect the employees' performance should not be considered in the evaluation.

f. Ratings though necessarily subjective, should be based upon as many positive evidences as possible.

2. The first step in setting up an evaluation program should be development of a set of performance standards.

3. The community and the school system should be informed about the evaluation program and given a chance to improve it.

4. An evaluation program should be studied critically and always subject to revision.

5. Evaluation should be a professional improvement and guidance device.

6. Evaluation is of little value unless there is an attempt to correct weaknesses discovered.

7. Appraisal should be a continuous process.

8. Each employee should be given a copy of evaluation policies when first hired; evaluation policies should be set forth in detail in the district handbook or similar publication.

9. The evaluation should demonstrate impartiality to all employees.

10. Self-appraisal by teachers and others should be encouraged.

11. The primary factor in the success of an evaluation program is the quality of human relations governing use of the evaluation instruments rather than the quality of the instruments themselves.

12. The evaluator should rate only those aspects with which he is most familiar and omit comment on other items.

13. Evaluation programs should discourage comparisons of one employee with another.

14. The latest rating of an employee should be the major one to be considered rather than an average of all ratings.

15. The evaluator should be alert for symptoms of beginning mental, social and physical maladjustments and prescribe preventive activities.

16. Follow-up conferences should accompany the written evaluation.

17. Purposes of the evaluating program should be both administrative and supervisory in nature, the emphasis being placed on the improvement of instruction.

FREQUENCY AND TIMING OF EVALUATION

Ideally, evaluation is a continuous process in which a teacher may evaluate his own performance each day or engage in frequent discussions with his colleagues or with consultants. However, formal visits by a supervisor or rating officer will vary in their frequency. They may be made on invitation of the teacher or in accordance with a schedule for different groups of personnel that have been set up by the school superintendent.

Generally, an evaluation for probationary teachers is prepared once or twice a year. When problems are present, additional evaluations may be required. Early December and early March are months used for these two evaluation periods.

In recent times, there has been a growing resistance of tenured teachers to formal evaluations. With this attitude, the evaluative process is not likely to be productive. There are several points to be considered in the evaluation of tenured teachers:

1. The negative attitude of some tenured teachers toward evaluation may stem from unilateral decisions of autocratic administrators of former years.
2. The negative attitude of tenured teachers may be more closely associated with job security than with the improvement of instruction.
3. Tenured teachers, particularly those with long years of service, may be reluctant to accept new methodology, new technology and new subject-matter content. They may resist evaluation because of their feeling of insecurity about being pressured to apply new methods of which they may not approve.
4. Some teachers, after gaining tenure, lose interest in growth and are concerned merely about maintaining the status quo.
5. There are many teachers of long experience and professional pride who object to evaluations because they have had reason to question the professional competence of the evaluator.
6. On one hand, it is true that all teachers and all elements of the educational enterprise including supporting services and all facilities should be evaluated regularly to determine whether they are making the appropriate contribution to the purpose of the whole educational enterprise. On the other hand, little will be gained by the process of evaluation if it is resented or resisted by large groups of teachers who have tenure. When teachers themselves become more involved in the evaluative process so that there is less fear and suspicion, it is likely that there will be a more agreeable

acceptance of evaluation. Meanwhile, compromises have been adopted in different school districts. In some school districts, tenured teachers are not given a detailed evaluation, but merely an end-of-year statement of "satisfactory" or "unsatisfactory." In other districts, tenured teachers are given formal evaluations once in two or three years. In some school districts, formal evaluations are discontinued when a teacher has reached maximum salary. School district regulations, however, must make provision for situations in which a teacher's services have deteriorated to a point of questionable satisfaction. Teachers being considered for promotion may need to be evaluated more frequently or in a special procedure.

A GUIDE FOR EVALUATING
PROFESSIONAL PERFORMANCE

Formal evaluations of service must be based on specific criteria. Frequently, the criteria have been vague. It is understandable that both teachers and the community have begun to react negatively to vague or arbitrary evaluation. Another rather common tendency is for evaluators to rate high those individuals who contribute most to the evaluator's security. Such evaluation has also been resented by teachers as being based on improper criteria.

To overcome these criticisms, a formal guide should be developed that will give both direction and uniformity to formal evaluation. Hagen and Thorndike, in reviewing research on "evaluation," state:

"The first step in a complete evaluation program is to select and define the attributes or qualities that are important in providing the picture from which an evaluative judgment is to be made." [7]

The process of evaluating, they point out,

". . . involves three distinct aspects: (a) selecting the attributes that are important for judging the worth of the specimen to be evaluated, (b) developing and applying procedures that will describe these attributes truly and accurately, and (c) synthesizing the evidence yielded by these procedures into a final judgment of worth." [8]

The development of such a guide can very well be a process involving several groups of people, all representing different interests. These groups should include administrators, who should probably be charged with conducting the evaluation conference and preparing the evaluation form or narrative report, teachers, students and representatives of the community. It is most important that all participants know the purpose of evaluation. This is the point on which much controversy currently exists. Because of poor practices in former years, the absence of criteria against which the

381

evaluation is often made, the lack of skill in conducting the evaluation conference and the uncertain objectives of the evaluation, there exists an actual fear of evaluation that causes many teachers to resist even participating in the development of criteria.

The following guide was proposed in a city for use in appraising the services of teachers. It is not intended that each teacher be given as comprehensive a report as is indicated. This is intended more as a study guide for supervisors and teachers interested in self-development.

A PROPOSED GUIDE FOR EVALUATING PROFESSIONAL PROFICIENCY

The supervision and evaluation program for professional staff members in the Unified School District is aimed at implementing the following four purposes:

1. To improve instruction.
2. To identify and render assistance as soon as possible to professional staff members in need of help.
3. To identify and encourage the retention of effective personnel.
4. To assist each person to realize his highest potential as a teacher.

Definition of the Satisfactory Teacher

1. The effective teacher in this district is characterized by a high degree of success with students in the classroom. He is a stimulating and effective teacher with excellent preparation. He has the ability and the willingness to use that background to influence learning.
2. As a professional person this teacher shows evidence of keeping abreast of current trends in education and improving as a teacher.
3. As a person he shows a conscientious responsibility to all of his assignments.
4. As a professional colleague he is interested in working with his fellows for the improvement of the school and its policies. His attitude is constructive as the ethics of the profession require.

The following form has been prepared as a guide to the district standards for professional proficiency.

Instructional Skill

A. Classroom Control
   1. Secures voluntary cooperation.
   2. Has a minimum of behavior problems.
   3. Handles behavior problems individually when possible.
   4. Practices principles of democratic leadership with students.
   5. Helps students acquire good study and work habits.
   6. Has developed a guidance approach to discipline.
B. Planning and Organization
   1. Plans each day carefully.
   2. Allows for flexibility in utilizing immediate educational opportunities (field trips, audiovisual aids, community resources, library, etc.).
   3. Uses out-of-class time in preparation and organization of classroom activities.

4. Divides his time satisfactorily among his various responsibilities.
5. Maintains well-organized classroom records.
C. Methods and Techniques
   1. Varies method and content to suit individual differences and goals.
   2. Directs interesting, varied, and stimulating classes.
   3. Helps students achieve satisfactorily in fundamental skills.
   4. Encourages growth in democratic participation and sharing of responsibilities.
   5. Motivates and inspires students to reach their maximum potential.
   6. Is willing to experiment with new ideas.
D. Room Environment
   1. Maintains an attractive and healthful classroom.
   2. Cares for all equipment and books under his charge.
   3. Has work areas arranged for maximum student stimulation and accomplishment.
   4. Displays concern for care and use of school property.
   5. Provides effective housekeeping procedures.
   6. Provides good working environment as evidenced by attention to light, heat, and ventilation.
E. Pupil Evaluation
   1. Helps each student appropriate goals for himself.
   2. Plans, executes and evaluates with pupils.
   3. Helps students evaluate themselves and their growth.
   4. Uses various acceptable techniques to evaluate learning (tests, grading practices, etc.).
   5. Practices guidance functions as evidenced by provisions for individual differences.
   6. Makes use of special services and facilities for those children whose needs cannot be adequately met in the classroom.
F. Judgment
   1. Uses unbiased judgment in the selection of instructional materials and presenting differing points of view.
   2. Uses considered judgment in carrying out classroom and out-of-classroom responsibilities.
   3. Tries to understand both sides of a question.
   4. Exercises good judgment in discussing school problems.

Professional Qualities

A. Use of Professional Services
   1. Seeks appropriate help when needed.
   2. Uses staff resources to enhance and improve program.
   3. Uses available consultants and helping personnel when appropriate.
B. Acceptance and Support of Decisions
   1. Accepts group decisions without necessarily agreeing.
   2. Accepts personal responsibility for attention to administrative requests.
   3. Adheres to and supports school and district policies.
   4. Does not abuse privileges.

C. Knowledge of Subject Matter
1. Possesses adequate subject matter background.
2. Acquires adequate depth and breadth of subject matter preparation (knowledge of fact, concepts in field, etc.).
D. Professional Growth
1. Is critical of, and constantly trying to improve, his own work.
2. Is continuously growing professionally through study and experimentation.
3. Participates in professional activities.
4. Participates fully in activities designed to meet the needs of his particular school.
5. Is proud of his profession and attempts to promote respect for it.
6. Contributes through activities toward the further improvement of teaching as a profession.

Personal Attributes

A. Personal Appearance
1. Dresses appropriately.
2. Is well groomed and poised.
3. Displays careful posture.
4. Maintains good general appearance.
5. Exemplifies personal neatness.
B. Voice and Speech
1. Speaks clearly and distinctly.
2. Uses good English.
3. Speaks in a well modulated voice.
4. Attempts to correct personal speech habits and mannerisms which detract from effective teaching.
C. Promptness and Accuracy
1. Makes reports accurately and turns them in on time.
2. Displays promptness in keeping both appointments and work assignments.
D. Dependability
1. Carries out assignments and duties as assigned.
2. Operates effectively in the absence of direct supervision.
3. Complies with school routines and rules.
4. Shows mature control in handling emergencies.
E. Health and Vitality
1. Is physically able to perform his duties.
2. Is not handicapped by too frequent absence or illness.
3. Has good attendance record.
4. Is sufficiently energetic in performance of duties.
F. Emotional Stability
1. Accepts criticism or recognition gracefully.
2. Maintains sound emotional adjustment.
3. Is calm and mature in his reactions.
4. Displays the refinement, character, and objectivity expected of the professional person.
5. Possesses a good sense of humor.
6. Is constructive in outlook.

Relationship With Others

A. Teacher-Pupil Relationship
   1. Shows genuine respect, concern and warmth for children.
   2. Recognizes each student's emotional and social needs.
   3. Has genuine concern for all his students.
   4. Maintains an atmosphere of mutual respect.
   5. Recognizes pupil interest as a way of enhancing learning.
   6. Seeks to understand pupil behavior before making evaluative judgments.
B. Teacher-Staff Relationship
   1. Success in working cooperatively with colleagues.
   2. Cooperates willingly with immediate administrators.
   3. Uses discretion and consideration in speaking of his colleagues.
   4. Carries a fair share of out-of-class responsibilities.
   5. Displays sensitivity and concern for others and recognizes another's beliefs, attitudes and values.
   6. Contributes thinking to the professional planning of the staff.
C. Relationship with Parents
   1. Works understandingly and cooperatively with parents.
   2. Supports and participates in parent-teacher groups.
   3. Effectively interprets the school program to the public as occasion permits.
   4. Uses contacts with parents to build strong working relationships.
   5. Makes effective use of teacher-parent conferences.

Even with the cooperative development of the evaluation instrument including the criteria against which the evaluation is to be made, there needs to be built into the guide a procedure for review. It is just as important that the reviewing procedure be cooperatively developed as it is for the evaluation instrument to be cooperatively developed.

PROCEDURE FOR REVIEW OF EVALUATION

When position security of a professional staff member is questioned, or when he feels that an injustice has been done in the evaluation matters, he should have a recognized means of review and hearing by a group on which his peers are represented. To accomplish this aim the following procedures have been developed in one school district:

1. If after the evaluation has been completed and the evaluation report has been received by the professional staff member, he believes that the evaluation was not adequate or not accurate, or that proper procedures were not followed, he or a member of the central administrative staff may request within ten (10) school days of the receipt of the report a hearing before the Professional Relations Committee. [This may be called a Review Committee established for this purpose. Such a Review Committee may be established at the building level, the district level, or both.] The membership of the Committee should be spelled out in detail as should their method of selection, their tenure on the Committee and who will be the presiding officer.
2. The Review Committee shall have privileged communication with the staff,

the administration and the teacher requesting the review. The Committee shall have the rights of classroom visitation and access to evaluations, reports or other data. The report of the Committee shall be forwarded to the superintendent if such action is deemed necessary by the Committee. The Committee shall have the right to majority and minority reports, if necessary, in its recommendations.

3. If the staff member so desires, he has the right of appeal directly to the superintendent. If, after appeal to the superintendent, he feels the necessity or desire to appeal to the board, this shall be granted and a hearing placed on the agenda of a regular or special meeting of the board.

METHODS AND FORMS USED

As used in this section, "method" refers to the time, place, procedures and person(s) involved in completing the formal evaluation form, which is usually required at the end of a probationary period, at stated intervals during the probationary period, at year's end for other teachers, or whenever stipulated in a school district's regulations. The assumption is that there have been informal conversations between the evaluator and the person being evaluated which relate to the evaluation concept as well as classroom visitations and even memoranda exchanged prior to the formal report.

An evaluative conference involving two persons, the evaluator and the person being evaluated, is recommended before each formal evaluation. Each person should be aware of the form which is to be completed. Some evaluators prefer to complete the form in tentative fashion prior to holding the evaluative conference. This procedure can save considerable time. In such cases, the persons being evaluated are performing at a satisfactory level and no major problems exist. An alternative is to complete the form during the conference, which is a more appropriate method when minor problems exist. It is more time-consuming, but it provides for greater depth of understanding.

Still another method is to have the person being evaluated bring to the conference a completed form, as does the evaluator. The differences in ratings are then discussed. If the rating form is of the checklist type, this is a reasonable method to use. Its chief value is to help the person being evaluated to view himself as others may view him. The differences in the ratings become obvious topics of discussion. Each party to the evaluation must give examples of behavior or situations that prompted the rating. As a result of such discussions, it is expected that there will be more agreement on objectives, and situations will be viewed from a similar perspective.

In many school districts, the evaluation form is mailed to the staff member with no prior discussion. There is provision for discussion only if the staff member objects to an item. This procedure may be followed because an administrator wishes to save time or to avoid what may be an

386

embarrassing discussion. Omission of discussion eliminates an opportunity for professional exchange of views that may help improve instruction.

When it appears that continued employment may be one of the reasons for the evaluation, it is appropriate to involve others in the evaluative conference. This could involve department heads, assistant principals or other teachers as the individual case might dictate. Such a conference might result in a narrative summary rather than a completed check list.

Following is a form that has been made for the formal evaluation of teachers. Again it is emphasized that it is not the form that is of paramount importance, but the effect of the evaluative conference as it contributes to the improvement of instruction. The form itself is little more than a way to start the conference. When cases of dismissal are involved, the form is relatively ineffective, for a large amount of documentary evidence supporting unsatisfactory performance must be available.

Perm. Appt. Due_____   File No._____
              Date

BOARD OF EDUCATION OF THE CITY OF NEW YORK
Office of Personnel—Bureau of Teachers Records

Report on Teacher Under Probationary Appointment for Continued Service

Name_____ School_____ District_____
    (Last Name) (First Name) (Initial)

License_____ Appointment to present rank_____19_____

(Read instructions on reverse side of blank)

PRINCIPAL'S REPORT

	1st Year	2nd Year
Number of times late (Not present twenty or ten minutes before morning or afternoon sessions respectively)	_____	_____
Time lost through lateness	_____	_____
Number of times absent	_____	_____
Time lost through absence (number of days)	_____	_____

A. Personal and Professional Qualities

1. Personal appearance _____
2. Voice, speech, and use of English _____
3. Professional attitude _____
4. Sympathetic understanding of children _____
5. Resourcefulness and initiative _____
6. Evidence of professional growth _____

B. Pupil Guidance and Instruction

1. Effect on character and personality growth of pupils _____
2. Control of class _____
3. Maintenance of a wholesome classroom atmosphere _____
4. Planning and preparation of work _____
5. Skill in adapting instruction to individual needs and capacities _____
6. Effective use of appropriate methods and techniques _____
7. Skill in making the class program attractive and interesting to pupils _____
8. Extent of pupil participation in the class and school program _____
9. Evidence of pupil growth in knowledge, skills, appreciations, and attitude _____
10. Attention to pupil health, safety, and general welfare _____

C. Classroom or Shop Management

1. Attention to physical conditions _____
2. Housekeeping and appearance of room _____
3. Care of equipment by teacher and children _____
4. Attention to records and reports _____
5. Attention to routine matters _____

D. Participation in School and Community Activities

1. Maintenance of good relations with other teachers and with supervisors _____
2. Effort to establish and maintain good relationships with parents _____
3. Willingness to accept special assignments in connection with the school program _____

E. Additional Remarks: _____
_____
_____
_____
_____

Principal's estimate of general fitness _____

Is continued service recommended? _____

_____ 19 _____   Signed _____

I have read the foregoing report   Principal _____

_____
        Signature of Teacher

DIRECTOR'S REPORT
(To be filled out for teachers of special subjects or supervisory teachers)

_____

_____ 19 _____   _____
                                                    Director

DISTRICT SUPERINTENDENT'S RECOMMENDATION

_____

_____ 19 _____   _____
                                              District Superintendent

INSTRUCTIONS

1. The principal, upon completing the report after the teacher shall have signed it, will forward it to the Director, if any, or to the District Superintendent, who, after entering his estimate and recommendations, will transmit it to the Bureau of Teachers Records.
2. The following terms shall be used by Principals in rating teachers on this blank: Satisfactory, Unsatisfactory or Doubtful. The terms Excellent, Good and Needs Improvement may be added in parenthesis.
3. In recording absence and lateness, do not include non-attendance.
4. **Penalty for excessive absence**
   Permanent appointment shall be postdated if a teacher is absent in excess of:
   (a) 10 days for a one year probationary period;
   (b) 20 days for a two year probationary period;
   (c) 30 days for a three year probationary period.

TENURE OF APPOINTMENTS AND OF LICENSES (See)

Section 100—Subdivisions 3-7-8—By-Laws of the Board of Education.

EVALUATION OF SUPERVISORY AND
ADMINISTRATIVE PERSONNEL

PURPOSES OF EVALUATION

The basic purpose of evaluating administrative and supervisory personnel, including central-office and building personnel, is to improve the instructional services provided by the school unit or school district. Although individual administrators and supervisors may have different specific duties, their goal nevertheless must be the improvement of the educational enterprise. For example, an administrator of school transportation, a head of a supply division and a building principal may have different responsibilities, but their success or lack of success must be measured in terms of the extent to which their efforts improve instruction in the school or school district. Thus the purpose of evaluating teaching personnel and supervisory and administrative personnel is the same. However, administrative and supervisory personnel must provide leadership, set conditions, provide materials and contribute to a climate in which optimum instruction can take place. Inherent in providing this climate is the development and maintenance of good communication channels, the establishment and enforcement of policies and regulations that will make positive contributions to this climate, the involvement of the groups affected, and gaining support for those ideas and activities that will promote the educational enterprise.

GUIDING PRINCIPLES IN THE EVALUATION OF
SUPERVISORY AND ADMINISTRATIVE PERSONNEL

1. The purposes of the evaluation should be discussed with and made clear to the individual being evaluated so that he not only accepts the purposes but also shares in formulating them. There should be no punitive purpose in the evaluation. It should represent an earnest, fair and sincere effort to appraise supervisory or administrative performance in order to bring about improvement. The administrator should be encouraged to believe that a constructive approach will be used, that equal effort will be expended to ascertain his strengths and his weaknesses, and that the evaluation will be a professional, cooperative one.

2. The evaluation should be planned, not haphazard. It should be expected if not invited by the administrator, not thrust upon him. It should follow an orderly timetable, a copy of which should be given to the individual who is being evaluated so that he and those under his supervision can properly participate in the evaluative process.

3. The individual who is being evaluated should not only participate in a discussion of the purposes of the evaluation but also share in the planning of the evaluation and the establishment of its standards, objectives, and procedures.

4. The evaluation should be comprehensive and should utilize specific criteria for appraisal. For example, if a building principal is being evaluated,

390

all aspects of his responsibilities should be reviewed: his relationships with the community, relationships with staff, relationships with pupils, care of building, progressivism, supplies, supervision of instruction, curricular activities. Instead of vague criteria, such as "leadership" or "efficiency," criteria should be more specifically defined; for example, innovations in curriculum, extent to which he encourages staff initiative, extent to which he involves students in worthwhile activities.

5. The evaluation should be tempered to the particular job or school situation in which the administrator is functioning. For example, a building principal who is functioning in a neighborhood that has exhibited hostility towards school administrators must be evaluated in a different light from a building principal who has been serving in a neighborhood that has been fully cooperative with school administrators.

6. The specific objectives of the evaluation should be in harmony with the objectives of the total school district as enunciated by the school superintendent and the board of education. These objectives should have been made known to school administrators within the district, and efforts should have been made to have the administrators accept and implement the objectives of the school district. Moreover, assistance should have been given over a period of time to administrators to enable them to achieve objectives. An evaluation might thus be limited to the particular objectives set by the school district; for example, improvement of pupils' reading ability, improvement of community understanding of the role of the school, or improvement of student government.

7. The evaluation should be free from bias. It should be conducted by an individual or individuals whose judgment is respected and whose impartiality and sympathetic understanding are recognized by the administrator being evaluated.

8. Objective evidence should be sought. It is recognized that subjective judgments may be unavoidable in an evaluation, but they should be based upon objective data and evidence.

9. Sufficient time should be allowed for the evaluation so that there is no appearance of undue haste or rush.

10. Individuals whose qualifications are respected should perform the evaluation. Too often an evaluation has been vitiated by the fact that the individual being evaluated has questioned the background or capability of those performing the evaluation. Another reason for the unpopularity of evaluations with school administrators is that often there is a belief that the judgments rendered were predetermined, that there was an ax to grind, or that the evaluation was conceived of as a punitive measure.

11. The professional reputation and integrity of the administrator being evaluated should be respected. Since it is likely that the administrator will continue to carry on his responsibilities, no actions, comments or remarks should be made which would impair his usefulness or his relationships with faculty, parents or students.

12. An opportunity should be provided for the administrator to see a tentative copy of an evaluation before it becomes official so that factual errors may be corrected. He might thus also have an opportunity to respond to critical judgments so that his reactions could be considered by the official for whom the evaluation was being done.

PROBLEMS IN THE EVALUATION OF SUPERVISORY AND ADMINISTRATIVE PERSONNEL

1. The first problem is to determine the purpose, scope, criteria, procedures, standards and instruments to be used in the evaluation. If the purpose is an end-of-year evaluation of a probationary principal or other administrator in order to determine whether the individual should be rated satisfactory for continued service, then the procedures and techniques should be geared to that particular purpose. If the purpose is to evaluate the extent to which a more limited objective has been achieved, such as improvement in reading skills, or the facilitation of supply ordering, or building cleanliness, the evaluation might be more narrowly conceived.

2. Another problem is to determine the frequency of evaluation of such personnel. Satisfactoriness of probationary service is frequently evaluated or rated at the end of each year, and again more extensively at the end of the probationary period. In a great many school districts, evaluation of administrative personnel is rarely undertaken unless a crisis occurs. It must be pointed out, however, that a crisis can sometimes be averted by periodic evaluations, whether formal or informal, which call to the attention of the school superintendent weaknesses which require remedy before they flare into crises. Evaluations which occur too frequently are regarded as nuisances by the personnel involved and lose their effectiveness because of resentment. There have been instances in which school districts or specific school activities were evaluated several times during one year by different committees. If resentment is incurred, it is doubtful that an evaluation will achieve a constructive and lasting result. A formal evaluation every five or six years would seem to have value. In a great many districts, however, an informal evaluation, conducted more frequently, might be more productive in allowing the school superintendent to keep in close touch with the progress of the educational enterprise and in allowing supervisors and administrators to review their own progress.

3. A third problem is to obtain the participation and candid cooperation of the administrative and supervisory personnel being evaluated. Since such personnel are quite busy, they must be convinced that the investment of time in the evaluation is worthwhile. If they have an attitude of fear or distrust, their participation is likely to be of a defensive nature, and the evaluation is not likely to be very useful. It is not easy to allay suspicion and distrust merely by expressed assurances. The total record of relationships among the school superintendent, the board of education and administrative and supervisory personnel is likely to govern the attitude of the

392

individuals being evaluated. If prior evaluations of administrative personnel in the school district have resulted in punitive action or embarrassment of the administrative personnel, subsequent evaluations are sure to be regarded with distaste by other individuals. On the other hand, if prior evaluations have been used as cooperative, professional instruments for improvement, without penalty and on a proper level of confidentiality, there will be little objection to subsequent evaluations.

4. A fourth problem is to enlist qualified individuals to perform the evaluation. The superintendent or his assistant might perform the evaluation if he had time. The evaluation of probationary personnel is often done by assistant superintendents who may review the record of the probationer as indicated in his responses to a detailed questionnaire and who may visit such an individual for a brief period of time. Assistant superintendents may make informal evaluations of school buildings or the performance of supervisory and administrative personnel by periodic short visits. However, a more formal and extended evaluation would require consultants with appropriate background to perform the required duties. Thus, reading consultants might be brought into a district to make an evaluation of the effectiveness of the program of reading instruction in the school district or in selected school units. Consultants of more general background might be brought in for an evaluation of the work of an administrator with more comprehensive responsibilities.

5. A fifth problem is obtaining data that will give the evaluation validity. Whenever possible, objective data should be obtained; for example, reading scores, arithmetic scores, achievement test scores, samples of correspondence, attendance records, staff turnover records, staff notices, and so on. When expressions of opinion are sought, efforts must be made to secure opinions that represent a proper cross section of the group being surveyed. A derogatory or strongly negative statement by one parent, one teacher, or one student should not be given much weight unless it is representative of the attitude of the group. There are also problems of interpreting data. If achievement scores are considered, they should be viewed in terms of the potential of the group. A low ranking in achievement scores by pupils in any given school may not be the fault of the principal of the school. There may be factors beyond his control which cause the achievement test scores to be low.

6. Another problem is the proper use and follow-up of an evaluation. The utilization factor is clear where an evaluation is conducted to determine which principal or other administrator should be promoted to a higher position, or where the evaluation is conducted to determine if a probationary administrator should be rated satisfactory. The problem arises in situations in which an evaluation of more comprehensive nature was designed to improve supervision or administrative governance. Granted that the supervisor or administrator has shared and cooperated in the evaluation, granted that the contents and recommendations were discussed frankly and

sympathetically, a frequent weakness in utilization of the evaluation, nevertheless, is that, after discussions and agreement on those areas in which improvement is to be sought, the evaluation is filed and forgotten. Rarely is there a persistent follow-up of the evaluation to see that genuine efforts are made to effectuate the improvement and to carry out the agreements that were arrived at in discussion.

PROCEDURES AND TECHNIQUES USED IN EVALUATING SUPERVISORY AND ADMINISTRATIVE PERSONNEL

The procedures and techniques that are used in any evaluation depend upon the purposes of the evaluation. If the purpose is to appraise performance in a single area, such as student growth in social studies or in reading, evaluative procedures are likely to be based upon standardized achievement tests. If a broader type of evaluation is desired, then other techniques must be employed. The following are some of the major procedures and techniques that may be employed in the evaluation of supervisory and administrative personnel.

1. *Informal or indirect evaluation.* In this type of evaluation, the superintendent or another school official may form a judgment through informal discussions with individuals who know about the work of the administrator being evaluated. The superintendent gets to know the reputation of the administrator as reported by individuals who have worked with him, who have worked under his supervision or who have supervised him. This is probably the type of evaluation most frequently used for school administrators. It is not the most reliable type, though, because a person's reputation is often formed by the image he portrays through his behavior and words, rather than through his accomplishments. The superintendent may not be able to select a cross section of those who are in the best position to render reliable reports. This type of evaluation is the easiest to make.

2. *Observational visits.* This evaluation involves seeing how the administrator performs on the job. It ideally provides objective information on which to base judgments. During an observational visit a discerning superintendent or his representative can often learn much about school and staff morale, plant maintenance, utilization of supplies, care of equipment, personal relationships and other elements. During such a visit, the individual being evaluated also has an opportunity to present his views to the visitor. To be most useful, an observational evaluation should be planned in some detail, notes should be made of what is observed, definite criteria should be set down for inquiry, and ample time should be allowed for the visit. Observational visits are least satisfactory when they are unplanned and when they are so brief that an unfair sampling is obtained.

3. *Documentary analysis.* In this type of evaluation, the administrator is asked to submit a report on his problems, efforts and achievements. Documentary evidence is required to support his statements. The report is reviewed by the superintendent or his representative and judgments are

394

made on the administrator's performance. The advantages of such an evaluation are that objective evidence is furnished, the individual being evaluated has an opportunity to present appropriate responses, and the evaluator can study the documents at his leisure. The disadvantages are that the individual being evaluated may resent the paper work involved in preparing a lengthy report, the report may not be as accurate or revealing as an on-site visit and discussion, and the personalities of the school, staff, student body, and community leaders cannot be adequately conveyed.

4. *Student achievement.* Frequently, evaluations are made on the basis of student achievement on standardized tests. A principal or departmental chairman whose students perform well on various achievement tests or whose students show substantial increases in achievement, as measured by standardized tests, is often evaluated as a superior administrator or supervisor. Such judgments are often made by inexperienced members of the community and sometimes by newspaper reporters. They may tend to oversimplify problems. The truth is that many factors outside the control of the building principal or the departmental chairman help to determine pupils' success or failure in achievement tests.

5. *The survey.* The survey is the most comprehensive type of evaluation. It may be conducted by personnel chosen for the task from within the school district, by outside consultants, or by a combination of these. A survey may utilize many techniques and procedures in developing an evaluative report. For example, questionnaires may be used to obtain information from the administrator being evaluated, from his staff members, his peers, students, parents and others. Similarly, interviews may be used to obtain information from those who are qualified to provide it. There may be an examination of relevant records, such as records of meetings that the administrator arranged, records of reports that he has prepared, minutes of meetings he has conducted, correspondence he has written, and so forth. There may be on-the-scene observations of his conduct of meetings, of his relationships with staff members and students, of staff and student morale in the school, and of activities taking place under his supervision. Standardized tests may be administered to appraise student achievement.

6. *Self-evaluation.* There is much to be gained from self-evaluation by administrators. The administrator who sincerely and voluntarily makes an evaluation of his own performance reveals an interest in and a desire for improvement. This desire is fundamental to making advances. The best survey and the best evaluation are often not worth the trouble because they are not accepted by the administrator. If there is no acceptance and no follow-up to an evaluation, no improvement is likely to take place. The weakness of self-evaluation is that the administrator who performs it may not be aware of important deficiencies existing in his performance and relationships. If self-evaluation is used, a comprehensive recording form prepared by an outside agency should be used because it encourages the administrator to rate himself in categories that might not otherwise occur to

395

him. The process of self-evaluation also includes the possibility of the administrator asking his peers, those he supervises and others to rate him, even anonymously, for his own benefit. A copy of a rather detailed evaluative form used by one administrator who was interested in learning how others regarded his efforts follows.

Related to self-evaluation is a more formal evaluation by consultants who can be called in by the administrator himself, with or without the knowledge of his superintendent, for advice. These consultants would not be sent in for a formal or informal evaluation by the administrator's superintendent, but would be called in by the administrator himself for an evaluation to be prepared for him and for his use, without a copy being sent to the superintendent. The value of such an evaluation by consultants is that the administrator might be less defensive and more ready to accept their judgments and to act upon them in an effort to improve himself. When evaluators are sent in by a higher-up, there is often fear, suspicion, resistance and concealment on the part of the administrator being evaluated. Few school districts have been willing to engage consultants to report only to the administrator who seeks their services. This procedure might well be explored to see if it is more productive than the traditional evaluation imposed from above.

MONTEBELLO UNIFIED SCHOOL DISTRICT
Montebello, California

Personal Appraisal Report for _____

You are asked to give an appraisal of the educational, professional, and leadership services of the person named above in order to help him recognize those areas needing improvement and to help him develop understanding and security in performing his administrative and supervisory responsibilities. Although many areas of concern could be identified as being important to successful service as an educational leader, the emphasis in this appraisal report is on *ability, training, performance,* and *attitudes.*

There are several statements under each of the four areas listed. Please indicate in the evaluation column the response that best describes your judgment of this person's "*operational level*" in regard to each descriptive statement. The three operational levels used in this appraisal represent broad bands rather than specific points on a fixed scale. The lowest level should indicate areas that are in need of attention. The second evaluation band should be used to indicate areas that seem satisfactory and perhaps adequate when viewed against an "average" operational measurement. The third level of appraisal should indicate that this person is superior or well above average in regard to the described item.

Please feel free to give your candid appraisal on each item, knowing that no identification of individual responses will be made and that only the compiled data will be used in the analysis of the appraisal. Space is provided on each page of the report to allow for comments or statements that clarify your evaluation of that area of the appraisal. A report of the study will be given to you and will become the basis for staff implementation for improvements. Those items receiving the lowest average scores will be given special attention during the next year.

Thank you sincerely,

Date:_____

397

I. GENERAL ABILITIES	"Operational Level"		
	Needs Atten.	Ave.	Sup.
1. Displays **intellectual ability** and capacity.			
2. Shows **depth of thinking** that is critical yet creative.			
3. Manages his assignment with **alertness and foresight**.			
4. The way he works shows **initiative and resourcefulness**.			
5. Shows **competence and maturity** in his leadership.			
6. Has wide **interests** and makes a contribution to them.			
7. **Supports and participates** in professional organizations.			
8. Seems to be in good **physical health.**			
9. Has sufficient **energy and vitality** for his position.			
10. Displays **enthusiasm** for the leadership role.			

COMMENT:

II. PROFESSIONAL TRAINING

1. Shows **preparation and skill** for his position.			
2. Has a clear-cut and usable **philosophy of education.**			
3. Demonstrates understanding of the **educational program.**			
4. Understands and uses good **administrative techniques.**			
5. Has adequate knowledge of child **growth and development.**			
6. Approaches his leadership role in a **scholarly manner.**			
7. Shows **thoroughness** in the way he works.			
8. **Manages his time** to be most helpful to all.			
9. Displays **dignity** in his position.			
10. He **gets things done**—on time and well.			

COMMENT:

III. PERFORMANCE (Actions and Decisions)

1. His practices are **consistent** with his stated beliefs.			
2. He tests and **evaluates** his administrative practices.			
3. The **responsibilities** of his position are **performed well.**			
4. His actions develop a sense of **trust and integrity.**			
5. Problems are **dealt with directly** and without rancor.			
6. His actions indicate that he values **teamwork.**			
7. He **works well with** individuals and the staff as a whole.			
8. He lets people **know how he stands** on issues.			
9. He **doesn't pretend** everything is always perfect.			
10. He has a desirable **sense of self-reliance.**			
11. He includes in **policy making** those affected by the policy.			
12. In **dealing with problems,** he includes the parties affected.			
13. He makes good **personal growth** and self-improvement.			
14. His decisions are **fair.**			
15. He is **firm** in carrying out decisions.			
16. He is **accurate** and discriminating in his work.			
17. He **utilizes** community **resources** and personnel.			
18. **Decisions** by the staff **are implemented.**			
19. He gives **major attention** to planning and improvement.			
20. His decisions tend to **strengthen** the staff.			

COMMENT:

III. PERFORMANCE (Reactions)

	Needs Atten.	Ave.	Sup.
1. He is **thoughtful** of the feelings of others.			
2. He is **receptive** to the suggestions and ideas of others.			
3. He **gives credit** where credit is due.			
4. He is **willing to work** for the betterment of all.			
5. He is a **good listener.**			
6. He is **willing to help** on little as well as big things.			
7. He **admits** his own **mistakes** and tries to remedy the errors.			
8. The way he works **promotes good will.**			
9. He **gives** ample **support** to his colleagues.			
10. He **inspires** and helps you to greater accomplishment.			
11. He tries to look on the **"bright side"** and be encouraging.			
12. He **receives good** staff and community **support.**			
13. He knows and **practices** good **democratic techniques.**			
14. He helps you feel your own **sense of worth.**			
15. His **leadership** is recognized and **accepted** by the staff.			
16. He tries to be **sympathetic, kind and patient—yet firm.**			
17. He presents ideas in an **affirmative** manner.			
18. He **handles** problems adequately.			
19. He **administers** district **policies** acceptably.			
20. His **record of accomplishment** is satisfactory.			

COMMENT:

IV. ATTITUDES (Personal and Social Values)

	Needs Atten.	Ave.	Sup.
1. Has a high sense of **moral responsibility.**			
2. Is **adjustable** to changes in plans or conditions.			
3. **Displays patience** even under trying conditions.			
4. He carries his responsibilities **willingly and cheerfully.**			
5. Displays good **mental health** by his actions.			
6. Carries out his executive duties without **tension.**			
7. Is able to maintain a **sense of personal balance.**			
8. He works in ways that show his **trust in others.**			
9. Is **attentive to good grooming,** posture and dress.			
10. Has a **sense of humor.**			
11. Has a well-adjusted and **balanced personality.**			
12. Is **courteous** and considerate to others.			
13. Is **friendly** and approachable.			
14. It is **pleasing** to be in his company or to talk to him.			
15. He has a high degree of **respect for others.**			
16. **Appreciates** the efforts of others.			
17. Doesn't grant **special privileges** to some and not others.			
18. Shows by his actions that he **likes you.**			
19. When there is a **will of the group,** he tries to find a way.			
20. Practices acceptable **social behavior** for his position.			

COMMENT:

STANDARDS AND PROCEDURE FOR EVALUATING CLASSIFIED PERSONNEL

Objectivity of evaluation of classified personnel may be easier to achieve than with certified personnel. The kind of objectivity varies with the classification. For custodians, it may be standards of cleanliness related to area to be cleaned. For clerical personnel, it may be accuracy of typing, speed of filing, alertness to specific details.

Since classified personnel generally work with people, their relationships with people must be included in the evaluation process. This area tends to be more subjective than objective. The concern for success in interpersonal relations should be mentioned in the job description.

The principles governing the evaluation of classified personnel are essentially the same as those governing the evaluation of certificated personnel. They include:

1. Knowing the criteria against which the employee will be evaluated.
2. Knowing the purposes of evaluation, namely, to improve service, discover problems or annoyances and suggest ways of overcoming them.
3. Encouraging dialogue pertaining to promotional aspirations, job satisfaction and loyalty to the organization.
4. Participation by employees in developing the evaluative procedures and forms.

One special purpose of evaluation of classified personnel is to determine whether or not the employee is working within the proper job classification. There is a common tendency to request a higher job classification with additional work load rather than to request additional hours of service. An honest evaluation may frequently mean that additional hours of time should be assigned to the position rather than increasing the level of job classification.

There are two kinds of evaluation instruments in use. The first, a rather uncommon method, is to have a separate evaluation form for each classification of employee. Large districts are more likely to use different forms than are small districts. The advantage of this form is that specific traits associated with the classification of position may be identified, so an evaluation conference can be more specific. The disadvantage is that it requires a significant amount of time to develop a sufficient number of forms for each of the positions. The second form is a kind of universal form that may be applied to all classified personnel. See the example of this kind of form.

Whether such forms should require two, three, or more quality-of-performance standards may be debated. There are those who prefer just two columns: "Meets District Standards" and "Need Improvement." Others prefer "Above Average," "Average" and "Improvement Needed as Indicated." This kind of rating becomes highly subjective unless there are well-defined criteria for "Average" and "Above Average."

400

Performance Report for Classified Employees

Last Name	First Name	Probationary Rating: First_____ Second_____
Classification	Job. No.	Permanent Rating Annual Rating_____ Period_____to_____
Division/Department	Supervisor	Due in Personnel Office_____

1. Above average   2. Average   3. Improvement needed as indicated.

THIS IS YOUR RATING IN:	1	2	3	Supervisor's Comments (Required for ratings of 3)
1. QUALITY OF WORK Accuracy, thoroughness, neatness, knowledge, skill.				
2. QUANTITY OF WORK Volume, application, time and equipment utilization.				
3. WORK HABITS Initiative, resourcefulness, punctuality, safety considerations, assuming fair share of work load.				
4. PERSONAL RELATIONS Cooperation, relationships with fellow employees and public, willingness, cheerfulness, patience, teamwork.				
5. PERSONAL FITNESS: Integrity, sobriety, stability, loyalty, dependability, judgment, appearance, physical condition.				
6. SUPERVISORY ABILITY (if applicable)				

REMARKS (Optional—Supervisor or Employee may make additional comments here)

_____ I recommend this employee for continued employment.

_____ There is some doubt as to whether this employee will become or remain a permanent classified employee.

_____ Definite improvement as noted above must be shown if this employee is to become or remain a permanent classified employee.

Signature of Rater

Date

Signature of Employee

Date

Signature of employee does not mean he agrees with rating.
It simply means he has seen the report of his Supervisor.

If a three-column rating form is used, it is proper to make the assumption that the employee being rated is "Average." During the course of the evaluative conference, it would be appropriate to point out what the employee does that is better than average and below average.

A separate form, "Notice of Unsatisfactory Service," is often used when an employee's work becomes or continues to be unsatisfactory between evaluations. The unsatisfactory written statement confirms that the employee has been told of his unsatisfactory service, and the form becomes a basis for further disciplinary action, such as demotion, suspension or dismissal.

A separate evaluation form, more commonly a letter, commending outstanding performance is encouraged. Such evaluation is particularly useful for considering employees for promotion as well as for improving morale.

Again it should be pointed out that the purpose of evaluation is positive—to be helpful in improving understanding, to improve skills and to encourage confidence on the job. It is not intended to debase or to threaten. At the other extreme, it is necessary to dismiss unsatisfactory employees, and this must be accomplished by advising them of their inadequacies, giving them positive suggestions for improvement, and giving them time to develop acceptable standards of performance.

EVALUATION OF THE PERSONNEL OFFICE AND STAFF

It is of paramount importance that the personnel office should have its responsibilities clearly delineated by administrative regulation. If functions overlap or if responsibilities are shared with other offices, the naming of the ultimate decision maker should be slated in the appropriate part of the regulation. Any subsequent evaluation of the office or of its personnel should begin with a study of the performance of the office within the scope of the administrative regulations.

A personnel office may have a single administrator or it may be divided into a supervising administrator with several secondary level administrators, or even classified personnel in charge of a given section. Regardless of the number of subdivisions in the personnel office, each subdivision should have its responsibilities specified in the administrative regulations. Each person serving in a subdivision should know the kinds of decisions he is expected to make and the kinds of decisions he should refer to his supervisor, to colleagues or to other offices.

Once the responsibilities have been properly placed in accordance with the administrative regulations, it is desirable, from time to time, to appraise the adequacy of such tangibles as forms in use and office equipment and arrangement. If a computer becomes a district's information center, the updating of forms and their purposes becomes a necessity, for the information on the forms becomes a part of the total data bank which may become the basis of reports, research or projections. Forms must be evaluated and updated even if no computer is in use.

Certain industries—General Dynamics Corporation, for illustration—have found that an appraisal of forms results in significant dollar savings to their organization. It was found that money could be saved by combining forms, eliminating forms no longer of use, converting to data-processing forms, shortening forms, and revising filing systems. It is suggested here that school districts might study the adequacy of all forms they use with a view of determining the value of each form, the length of time it should be kept, and the most practical means of filing it.

One simple example of the personnel function will illustrate the point Suppose a woman teacher becomes married after employment. Her name, of course, must be officially changed. What offices need this new information? The office in the building in which she works, the personnel office, the payroll office, the instruction office, the county office, the state credential office, the state and/or local retirement office, and the Social Security office. What is the most efficient method of sending the information to those offices? How many original forms are initiated along the way as opposed to carbon or Xerox copies?

Also to be evaluated in the personnel office is the office equipment. Here are some points to consider:

1. Are all typewriters equipped with the same type so that portions of long documents may be typed by several persons?
2. Is a typewriter available for special purposes, as making titles and name tags?
3. Is some type of duplication equipment readily available—ditto, mimeograph, Xerox, photo-copy or other kind?
4. Is substitute calling set up for dial-a-card, tape, or some other rapid and accurate system?
5. Is a telephone recorder or electronic secretary available for employees to leave messages?
6. Are filing systems adequate—visible files, vertical files, drawer files, card files?
7. Are telephone installations rigged for efficient transfer of calls and intercommunication connections?
8. Are the storage facilities for forms and supplies available and conveniently located?
9. Is the reception room complete with adequate chairs for waiting in comfort and with writing desks? Is the waiting room located so that those talking in interview rooms will not be heard in the reception area?

Another point to consider in evaluating the personnel office includes the competencies and characteristics of the employees assigned to the office.

In addition to the skills required for each position level, workers in personnel offices must have a number of personal traits. These employees must:

1. Understand the significance of privileged communication.
2. Recognize that the office is a service office, not just a production office.
3. Have accurate information readily available, information applicable to the responsibility of the desk.
4. Understand the rules, regulations and procedures associated with the responsibility of the desk.
5. Be willing and able to assist other persons in the office during periods of illness or peak loads.
6. Be capable of remembering detail.
7. Be productive on the job in spite of numerous interruptions.
8. Have patience with those who grasp ideas slowly, are remiss in following through with their responsibilities, and have problems of which the employee may not be informed.
9. Be capable of making decisions appropriate to their responsibility and of referring other decisions to the proper persons.
10. Admit freely any mistake they have made in order that the proper correction may be made and apologies offered.
11. Advise their superior in advance when it is likely that problems will come to his attention, and fill him in on the background of the problem.
12. Assist in anticipating problems, ordering forms and supplies, and having equipment serviced.
13. Be alert to the image of the office and be able to make positive contributions to that image.
14. Have a capacity to be loyal to the office personnel and the organization.
15. Show enthusiasm for their job.

Such competencies are the real traits one needs to evaluate in the personnel office staff. It is assumed that selection tests would screen out those who do not have reasonable proficiency in typing, spelling, shorthand, filing, and so on.

Other traits in the list above are more properly discussed with the employee at the time of an incident rather than at a formal evaluation conference. The important concept, however, is to advise employees of the traits required for the position as they accept employment in the department and to review them periodically thereafter. Only when persons are unsuited to personnel work and are subject to dismissal should documentary evidence be obtained.

Most important is the evaluation of the performance of the personnel office. Do recruited teachers meet the requirements of their positions? Have effective school administrators been chosen by the personnel office? Has

404

the personnel office set up an effective in-service developmental program for the staff? Is staff morale high? Is staff turnover low? Those are some of the basic questions which the personnel administrator should consider in a periodic evaluation of the performance of his office. The evaluation may be formal or informal. Questionnaires to staff members, community leaders, officers of parent associations and representatives of students can reveal elements of strength and weakness. Interviews with a sampling of new teachers, experienced teachers, school administrators, community leaders and others may yield evaluative comments. There may even be occasional formal studies of the effectiveness of the personnel office by paid consultants. Comparisons of performance by students on standardized achievement tests may also shed light on staff performance if all factors relevant to student achievement are taken into consideration.

SPECIAL EVALUATIVE CONFERENCES

At one time or another, the personnel administrator finds himself in a counseling role with respect to evaluations. One of the most common types of these situations is in the area of professional advancement. Employees want to know what promotional opportunities may be available, what licenses will be required, where to get them and whether they might be considered for the position. As a counselor, the personnel administrator endeavors to help the individual make a personal assessment of his abilities, talents, long-range goals and any obstacles he may have to overcome.

Related to this kind of question is counseling with individuals who have not been accepted for a promotion. Often such individuals need encouragement to greater preparation and continued effort. Other individuals may be unsuited for the position and really should be counseled to pursue other paths of self-fulfillment. When persons continue to take tests for a given position and are never selected, morale problems are apt to develop. Perhaps it is more kind to say that the opportunities for promotion in a given organization are unlikely. If a person still wants to be considered, he may be advised to try in another district. This is a difficult conference in which to be engaged and this advice should rarely be given since one can rarely predict the future with certainty.

The personnel administrator also has a role in resolving problems or reducing tensions between teacher and school administrator. This may involve being a mediator between the two. In a sense, this is a kind of an informal evaluation session, and it may be an appropriate time to consider a transfer. A personality conflict may be resolved by a transfer, although it may not solve a problem based on incompetence.

When a teacher believes that a dismissal proceeding is getting under way, he may want to discuss with the personnel administrator possible courses of action. It is most desirable for the personnel administrator to be straightforward and honest. His function at this point is not to support the point of view of the principal or the teacher. His responsibility is to see that proper procedures are followed, that communication channels are open and that both parties understand the school district's regulations and the legal and ethical consequences of each course of action that may be taken.

There are occasions when matters involving evaluation of personal behavior and appearance require counseling sessions. Typically, this is done at the building level, but some complicated cases will come to the attention of the personnel administrator, including difficulties with other teachers, alcoholism, excessive absenteeism, health problems, difficulties with individuals in the community, and marital problems.

There are times when a staff member's performance continues to be unsatisfactory over a period of time despite many efforts to bring about a change. In such situations or when illness and absenteeism become continual problems and the instructional program suffers over an extended period of time, retirement may be an alternative to dismissal. In fact, one of the reasons for the generous provisions of some retirement plans is to provide for such a situation. A conference at which this suggestion is made is not a pleasant task, but it remains the responsibility of the personnel administrator.

Some large districts are now maintaining a special counseling service for school employees whose evaluations have revealed serious problems. Industry has provided for such a service for many years. Good counseling service will be worth the cost.

TENURE PROBLEMS AND HEARINGS

The tenure law protects teachers from unreasonable dismissal without due process. Before tenure laws became common, teachers were dismissed for a variety of reasons only superficially related to an evaluation of the quality of their performance. Believing this to be unfair, teachers' organizations and sympathetic citizens were able to have tenure laws passed. Teachers now enjoy considerable security on the job.

It is recognized, however, that there are situations in which dismissal from teaching service may be necessary. It was never the purpose of tenure to make the schools a haven for incompetent employees, but some citizens complained that strict tenure laws have made this almost a reality.

The following are frequently listed grounds for dismissal:

1. Incompetence.
2. Being convicted of a felony.
3. Being convicted of deviate sexual behavior.
4. Unprofessional conduct.
5. Refusal to abide by reasonable rules and regulations.
6. Having a physical or mental condition unfitting the teacher to instruct or associate with children.

7. Dishonesty or lack of integrity.
8. Engaging in any act detrimental to the welfare of the school and the pupils.

In the majority of the cases involving dismissal, it is incumbent upon school employees, usually administrators, to make the charges, collect the evidence, provide the testimony, and at the same time advise the employee of his rights and be able to demonstrate that reasonable effort has been made to help the defendant overcome the problem with which he is being charged. The difference in the rights of probationary and tenured employees, as far as dismissal is concerned, is becoming less clear-cut. Historically, teachers had almost no job security. With the advent of tenure laws, a probationary period was established during which the teacher could be dismissed almost at will, but the tenured teacher was protected by law. The current thought is that probationary teachers should also be protected from capricious termination. Therefore, there is the requirement of almost the same documentation of charges and behavior in practice. Assuming that a charge of unsatisfactory service has been made, the following factors and types of evidence should be considered minimum for evidence and documentation:

1. *Persistent nature of the difficulty.* Except under unusual circumstances, the unsatisfactory conduct on the part of the employee has been persistent and sustained.
2. *Repeated warnings.* The employee has been warned repeatedly of the unsatisfactory nature of his work or his conduct.
3. *Frequent assistance.* There must be written reports showing that real efforts have been made to help the employee overcome his difficulties, but that the efforts have not been successful. Transferal is sometimes used, but with caution. Unless there is some reasonable expectation that the transfer will result in a different attitude or improved behavior on the part of the accused, it may be expedient to continue the documentation which will ultimately lead to dismissal.
4. *Close supervision.* Since the discovery of his difficulties, his work has been closely supervised, and the principal has personal knowledge of the employee's failure to improve.

In preparing acceptable evidence, all of the preceding types of data must be:

1. *Specific in nature.* General charges carry little weight. Factual evidence of deficiencies in specific professional competencies and personal qualities must be presented.
2. *Extensive in scope.* An isolated case does not constitute sufficient evidence except under unusual circumstances. A number of instances of any incompetence or defection must be submitted.

407

3. *Recorded.* All specific charges must be backed up by written memoranda made by the observer immediately after the various times when the deficiencies were actually observed. Likewise, all occasions in which assistance is given and all advisory conferences should be made matters of official record immediately thereafter.
4. *Dated and timed.* It is of great importance that, at the time records of unsatisfactory performance and notes on visits and advisory conferences are made, they include dates, the actual clock minutes involved, the type of class and the period of the day. Visits lasting a considerable part or all of the period are more likely to provide good evidence than is a brief visit.
5. *In original drafts.* Written evidence at dismissal hearings must be in the original drafts made at the time of or immediately following the observation or the conference. Materials that have been reorganized or copied at a later date in preparation for a hearing are usually not considered acceptable as evidence.

Fortunately, dismissals are rare. Obtaining the amount and kind of documentation referred to above is time-consuming. It is difficult to give helpful and supporting suggestions for improvement and at the same time to be gathering evidence for dismissal; nevertheless, this is one of the skills expected of the school administrator.

Given below is a sample of an accusation against a probationary teacher, followed by a portion of a statement of the charges which would be presented to the governing board. The supporting evidence is presented in sufficient length to demonstrate the extent of the documentation necessary. It should also be noted that the statement of charges must be supported by original documents made by the principal and others at the time of the observations and conferences. The original records must be available if the employee requests a hearing.

To the Honorable, the Board of Education
Ladies and Gentlemen:

IN THE MATTER OF THE DISMISSAL

OF JOHN DOE   ACCUSATION

A PROBATIONARY CERTIFICATED EMPLOYEE

The undersigned herewith files the following charges against JOHN DOE, a probationary certificated employee of the _____ District of the _____ County assigned to Central High School as a teacher of Business Education, and asks for his dismissal from his position with said school district, effective June 16, 1971, under the provisions of Section 13444 of the Education Code for the following cause which relates solely to the welfare of the schools and pupils thereof:

Unsatisfactory performance as a teacher as evidenced by professional evaluations made by experienced school personnel whose duties include the supervision and evaluation of classroom teachers.

Mr. John Doe was first employed as a substitute teacher of Business Education on September 16, 1967. He began his probationary service on April 28, 1968 at Central High School and has continued in that assignment to the present time. He has been generally considered to be satisfactory until, during the period of October 1, 1969 to April 15, 1970, his performance became unsatisfactory to the point that a rating of Weak was given on his evaluation by his principal. At that time the principal recommended that Mr. Doe be retained in service but that his work be evaluated with extreme care. The Assistant Superintendent, Division of Secondary Education, conferred with Mr. Doe and advised him that it would be necessary for him to show considerable improvement in his work before he could be recommended for permanent status. On many occasions supervisors, consultants, and school administrators have conferred with Mr. Doe on methods of improving his teaching techniques. Mr. Doe has either been unwilling or unable to accept and implement these recommendations. He was rated Unsatisfactory on December 13, 1970 by his principal with the recommendation that he be discontinued from service. Detailed charges which set forth the specific acts or omissions of the employee complained of in the foregoing cause and in this Accusation, are contained in the Statement of Charges which is at this time before the Board of Education as a separate document, is on file in the Office of the Board Secretaries, and is hereby referred to and made a part hereof as fully as if it were set out at length herein.

WHEREFORE, the undersigned respectfully requests that:

The Board notify said employee of its intention to dismiss him upon the sixteenth day of June 1971, unless within five (5) days after the date of service of said notice the said employee filed with the Board of Education a Notice of Defense as provided in Section 11505 and 11506 of the Government Code, copies of which shall be attached to said notice.

The Notice be served upon the employee by personal delivery; that a copy of this Accusation and the Statement of Charges be attached to the Notice, and that a Notice of Defense as provided for in Government Code Sections 11505 and 11506 be included in the letter.

If within the time specified the employee files the Notice of Defense to these charges and requests a hearing, the Board of Education will hold a hearing in accordance with Chapter 5 of Part 1 of Division 3 of Title 2 of the Government Code.

STATE OF CALIFORNIA
}
SS.
COUNTY

Robert E. Smith, being first duly sworn, deposes and says:

That he has read the foregoing instrument and knows the contents thereof and that the same is true to the best of his knowledge, information and belief.

_____

Robert E. Smith
Associate Superintendent of Schools

Subscribed and sworn to before me

this _____ day of _____

1970

Notary Public in and for said

County and State.

My commission expires _____.

To the Honorable, the Board of Education
Ladies and Gentlemen:

IN THE MATTER OF THE DISMISSAL

OF JOHN DOE

A PROBATIONARY CERTIFICATED EMPLOYEE

The undersigned herewith files the following charges against JOHN DOE and hereby refers to and incorporates by reference the ACCUSATION presented to the Board of Education on this same date. The following cause for the dismissal of Mr. Doe relates solely to the welfare of the schools and the pupils thereof.

Unsatisfactory performance as a teacher as evidenced by professional evaluations made by experienced school personnel whose duties include the supervision and evaluation of classroom teachers.

CHARGES

The cause of unsatisfactory performance as a teacher exists by reason of the following:

410

A. Lacks sufficient detailed knowledge of the subject matter to be presented to each class each day, as illustrated by the following examples.
   1. On November 9, 1968, a consultant in Business Education asked Mr. Doe the topic he was to teach to his class that day and he replied that he did not know.
   2. On October 6, 1969, the Supervisor of Business Education observed that Mr. Doe made errors in explaining the process of posting to his bookkeeping class.
   3. On November 10, 1969, the principal of Center High School observed in the General Business class that Mr. Doe did not know which problems he had assigned for homework.
   4. On November 16, 1969, the Business Education Supervisor observed an instance in which Mr. Doe made errors in explaining the posting process. On the same date, in another Bookkeeping class, she observed that he had not previously read the instruction sheet for use in a practice set. That same day in a class in General Business she noted that the lesson plan called for homework to be placed on the chalkboard but the pupils stated they had no assignment.
   5. On March 1, 1970, another consultant in Business Education observed Mr. Doe become confused in explaining the trial balance to his bookkeeping class; and in another class on the same date, she observed that he was unfamiliar with several aspects of unemployment compensation to the extent necessary to explain to the class the bookkeeping tax entries.
B. Does not have the ability to make clear and understandable explanations, as illustrated by the following examples:
   1. On October 6, 1969, the Supervisor of Business Education observed an explanation by Mr. Doe to a Bookkeeping class regarding the source of the balances in financial statements which explanation was not understandable to the pupils.
   2. On October 25, 1969, the principal listened to Mr. Doe give an inadequate and incomplete explanation of General and Miscellaneous Accounts to his Bookkeeping class.

TERMINATIONS OF SERVICE

Whether terminations of service are voluntary or involuntary, a number of principles are involved in the personnel function:

1. *Reasonable notice should be given.* This is true for either kind of termination, resignation or dismissal. It is recognized that a variety of situations resulting in termination may develop, and in some cases giving reasonable notice is not possible. However, two weeks should be considered the minimum. When involuntary terminations are involved, it is only fair to give the individual as much time as possible to find other employment. Also, in some states specific dates of notification of failure to reemploy are specified in the law or in negotiated contracts. The notice of termination of service should be either delivered to the individual by hand or sent by registered mail.

2. *Specific charges should accompany a notice of dismissal.* Notices of dismissal should never come as a complete surprise. If the evaluation process has been carried out in accordance with the suggestions in this chapter, the individual will know and already have in his possession evidence of all of the specific shortcomings that would be presented in a hearing.

3. *The employee should be advised of his rights.* The law and the school district's regulations usually specify the rights of the individual. The administration should make every effort to make the individual completely aware of his rights. These rights usually include a right to a hearing before either the governing board or a hearing officer, the right to have counsel, and the right to challenge the procedures of the administration if the letter of the law has not been followed.

4. *Persons who resign.* Persons who resign, as well as those whose services are terminated, should be advised of their retirement options, their major medical plan option, their responsibility for maintaining their credentials in force, and their responsibility for maintaining their placement file.

5. *Provision should be made for an exit interview.* Helpful information may be obtained through an exit interview. It is recommended that a staff rather than a line administrator conduct this interview. Normally when persons are leaving a district they are more willing to discuss the adequacy of the instructional supplies and facilities, the openness of communication channels, and their reaction to the leadership under which they worked. The intent of the exit interview is to gain information upon which better policies and procedures may be developed and improved interpersonal relations may result. These interviews are time-consuming and, unless they are performed by a person skilled in the art of interviewing, they may not be worth the time and effort. Teachers may resent having to go through an exit interview; principals may fear the result of the exit interview. The right person must be selected for this delicate responsibility.

THE ROLE OF THE PERSONNEL ADMINISTRATOR IN EVALUATION

The personnel administrator has a number of major responsibilities in evaluation.

1. He should develop, with committee participation, a handbook for teachers and one for administrators which will give the necessary guidance for both concerning the purposes, procedures and time for formal evaluations. The handbook should clarify the roles and the

responsibilities of all those who participate in the evaluative procedure. The book should foster a cooperative and professional spirit and should contain guidelines for all types of informal evaluations.

2. He should establish a procedure for conferences which would provide for consultants, peers, or others to participate in making helpful suggestions to those not meeting accepted standards of performance.
3. He should assist principals and others in improving their documentation. He should make certain that accurate records of observations and conferences are being kept, and he should be available to offer assistance in techniques to those who conduct evaluation sessions.
4. He should prepare the necessary charges and documentation for the board and/or the hearing officer when dismissal proceedings are required, and he should be sure that the staff member is justly treated.
5. He should arrange periodic conferences or seminars for administrative personnel to consider their evaluative responsibilities, not only toward individual staff members but also toward their staff as a whole. Case histories and research findings may be presented at these sessions.
6. He should periodically arrange for an evaluation of his own department and achievements in the recruitment, selection, and development of personnel.

Experience has shown that, in carrying out these tasks, the personnel administrator should:

1. Be aware of the nature of privileged communication and safeguard the rights of others to confidentiality.
2. Be certain of the accuracy of the information used for decision making.
3. Seek professional assistance from his colleagues, the county counsel, the professional associations. A hearing may become a sticky situation. Others may have had some experience which will help the personnel administrator.
4. Avoid making decisions in haste or under duress.
5. Follow established procedures; take no short cuts. Individuals may say they will resign, then never get around to completing the document. Short cuts may deprive a person of his rights or they may get his school district into unnecessary technical difficulties.
6. Avoid obtaining a resignation under duress. A person may be released for cause. Regulations or state laws outline the procedures to be followed in any dismissal proceeding. It is suggested that these be followed to the letter. It is proper to maintain a helpful

413

and supporting role to the individual as long as he is a member of the staff.

7. Provide reasonable protection for the parties involved. School districts, their employees and the students should avoid adverse publicity. It is not necessary, it is not good personnel administration, and it is not proper to hurt individuals because of any act of commission or omission on their part. The objective should be to settle all personnel problems as fairly and quietly as possible.

8. Make no improper promises or threats. Evaluators have been known to say, "I'll give you a good recommendation if you will resign." Such a statement is unethical, morally wrong and not in the best interest of the teaching profession.

9. Be reasonably certain that he can win a dismissal case; otherwise, he should not press it. Probably more damage can be done by losing a case than by permitting a marginal teacher to remain in the classroom.

10. Discuss letters of reference. A letter of reference should be factual. Even though a person has been dismissed, some of his behavior patterns probably have been satisfactory, even commendable, and this positive report should be mentioned with minimum comment, unless the individual is totally unsuited for teaching. The intent of a reference is not to deny an individual employment. Many a person has failed in one situation and achieved success in another.

11. Involve the right people in the evaluative process. The right people may include department heads, assistant principals, members of the central staff, representatives of the county office. If the person has graduated from a nearby college, it may be appropriate to invite a former professor. The developing role of professional organizations may result in a team of local teachers to assist in the appraisal.

NOTES

CHAPTER 1

1. Harold E. Moore, *The Administration of Public School Personnel* (New York, 1966), p. 6.
2. William B. Castetter, *Administering the School Personnel Program* (New York, 1962), p. 26.
3. Castetter, p. 33.
4. Moore, p. 8.

CHAPTER 2

1. Ordway Tead, "Personnel Administration," in *Encyclopedia of the Social Sciences,* eds. Edwin B. A. Seligman and Alvin Johnson (New York, 1934), p. 88.
2. R. Oliver Gibson and George F. Roberts, eds., *Working Papers Related to the Specialized Preparation of School Personnel Administrators* (Buffalo, 1967), p. 74.
3. Howard S. Bretsch, "Staff Personnel Administrators," in Donald J. Leu and Herbert C. Rudman, eds., *Preparation Programs for School Administrators: Common and Specialized Learnings* (East Lansing, Mich., 1963), pp. 182–195.
4. Gibson and Roberts, p. 9.
5. Gibson and Roberts, pp. 10–22.

CHAPTER 3

1. Department of Health, Education and Welfare, Office of Education, *Statistics of State School Systems.*
2. Department of Health, Education and Welfare, Office of Education, *Biennial Survey of Education in the United States.*
3. S. J. Coleman, "Concept of Equality of Educational Opportunity," *Harvard Educational Review,* 38: 7–22, Winter 1968.
4. Joseph Monserrat, "Integrating the Urban Schools," in *School Integration: A Puerto Rican View* (New York, Columbia University Bureau of Publications, 1963), p. 2.
5. Harry N. Rivlin, "New Teachers for New Immigrants," *Teachers College Record,* 66: 8, 1965.

6. Edmund W. Gordon, "Relevance and Pluralism in Curriculum Development," *IRCD Bulletin,* V, iii: 3, Summer 1969.
7. Gordon, p. 3.
8. Gordon, p. 4.
9. Task Force on Economic Growth and Opportunity, Chamber of Commerce of the United States, *The Disadvantaged Poor: Education and Employment* (1966), p. 7.
10. Richard G. Hatcher, "The Age of a New Humanity," *Freedomways,* Spring 1969, reprinted in *IRCD Bulletin,* Summer 1969, pp. 11–19.
11. Robert Bendiner, *The Politics of Schools— A Crisis in Self-Government* (New York, 1969).
12. Department of Health, Education and Welfare, Office of Education, annual survey, *Federal Funds for Education and Related Activities.*
13. Department of Commerce, Office of Business Economics (includes Hawaii and Alaska beginning 1960); Bureau of the Census.
14. William Van Till, "In a Climate of Change," *Role of Supervisor and Curriculum Director in a Climate of Change* in the ASCD Yearbook (Washington, 1965), pp. 7–29.
15. National Education Association, *Education in a Changing Society* (Washington, 1963), pp. 122–130.
16. Van Till, p. 28.
17. Ole Sand, "Bases for Decision," *Role of the Supervisor and Curriculum Director in a Climate of Change,* the ASCD Yearbook (Washington, 1965), pp. 50–64.
18. American Association of School Administrators and Association for Supervision and Curriculum Development, *Organizing for Improved Instruction* (Washington, 1965), p. 8.

CHAPTER 4

1. I.B.M. Technical Publications Department, "System 360 Data Processing in the City of Memphis School System," in *Data Processing Application* (White Plains, 1969), pp. 33–40.

CHAPTER 5

1. Edgar W. Knight, *Education in the United States* (Boston, 1951), p. 329.
2. Knight, p. 335.
3. G. K. Hodenfield and T. M. Stinnett, *The Education of Teachers* (Englewood Cliffs, 1961), p. 155.
4. New York State Education Association, *New York State Education,* January 1970, p. 11; Peter Rossi, "Social Characteristics of 1961 College Graduates Entering the Field of Education," *American Education Research Journal,* VI, iiii:649, November 1969; Psychological Corporation, *Miller Analogies Test Manual,* revised (New York, 1970); pp. 6–9.
5. Hodenfield and Stinnett, pp. 9–10.
6. Hodenfield and Stinnett, p. 11.
7. James B. Conant, *The Education of American Teachers* (New York, 1963), p. 154.
8. Conant, p. 155.
9. Conant, p. 172.
10. Elmer R. Smith, ed., *Teacher Education— A Reappraisal* (New York, 1962), p. 9.
11. Smith, pp. 12–13.
12. National Commission on Teacher Education and Professional Standards, *New Horizons of the Teaching Profession* (Washington, 1961), p. 72.
13. National Commission on Teacher Education and Professional Standards, *Changes in Teacher Education—An Appraisal* (Washington, 1964) pp. 63–507.
14. National Education Association, *Schools of the Urban Crisis* (Washington, 1969), pp. 36 and 37.
15. National Education Association, *Urban Crisis,* p. 57.
16. Conant, p. 10.
17. Conant, p. 11.
18. Conant, p. 11.
19. The Commission, pp. 141–145.
20. National Council for Accreditation of Teacher Education, *Annual List, Number Fifteen* (Washington, 1969), p. 3.
21. National Council for Accreditation of Teacher Education, *Standards for Accreditation of Teacher Education* (Washington, 1968), pp. 1–11.
22. National Education Association, *A Manual on Certification Requirements for School Personnel in the United States* (Washington, 1967), p. 1.
23. The Association, pp. 53–54.
24. The Association, pp. 55–56.
25. The Association, p. 19.
26. The Association, p. 27.
27. Myron Lieberman, *Education as a Profession* (Englewood Cliffs, 1956), p. 6.

CHAPTER 6

1. National Education Association, *Schools of the Urban Crisis* (Washington, 1969), p. 34.
2. National Education Association, *Teacher Supply and Demand in Public Schools* (Washington, 1968), p. 45.
3. The Association, p. 48.
4. The Association, p. 19.
5. H. B. Gilbert, I. Bogen, G. Lang and P. M. Kalick, *Teacher Selection Policies and Procedures in Large Public School Systems in the United States,* final report on cooperative research project S-334 (New York, Board of Examiners of the Board of Education, 1966), p. 17.

6. National School Public Relations Association, *The Big Talent Hunt* (Washington, 1969), pp. 29–30.
7. See the unpublished report (New York Board of Examiners, 1966) by H. B. Gilbert, I Bogen, G. Lang and P. M. Kalick, *Teacher Selection Policies and Procedures in Sixty-Two School Systems Affiliated with the Metropolitan School Study Council Compared with Those of Large Public School Systems in the United States,* p. 16.
8. Gilbert et al., *Teacher Selection,* for research project S-334, p. 16.
9. National Education Association, *Economic Status of the Teaching Profession* (Washington, 1968–69), p. 14.
10. The Association, p. 29.
11. *The Big Talent Hunt,* p. 31.

CHAPTER 7

1. H. F. Otto, "Principalship Preparation at the Crossroads," *Educational Leadership,* 13: 28–32, 1952.
2. K. E. McIntyre, "The Selection of Elementary Principals," *The National Elementary Principal,* 44:42–47, 1965.
3. R. M. Hall and A. M. Vincent, "Staff Selection and Appointment," in *Encyclopedia of Educational Research,* ed. C. W. Harris (New York, 1960), p. 1377.
4. Arthur L. Benson, "Testing Procedures in the Administration of Educational Personnel," *Education,* p. 246, December 1954.
5. See the unpublished report (New York Board of Examiners, 1966) by H. B. Gilbert, I. Bogen, G. Lang and P. M. Kalick, *Teacher Selection Policies and Procedures in Sixty-Two School Systems Affiliated with the Metropolitan School Study Council Compared with Those of Large Public School Systems in the United States,* p. 15.
6. American Association of School Personnel Administrators, *Principles and Procedures of Teacher Selection* (Kansas City, Mo., 1951), pp. 58–59.
7. Gilbert et al., pp. 11–12.
8. Gilbert et al., p. 16.
9. Fink v. Finegan, 270 New York 356.
10. E. J. Barnes and S. L. Pressey, "Reliability and Validity of All Examinations," *School and Society,* 30:719–732, 1929.
11. R. Morse and J. W. Hawthorne, "Some Notes on Oral Examinations," *Public Personnel Review,* 7: 15–18, 1946.
12. S. M. Corey, "The Interview in Teacher Selection," *Journal of Educational Research,* 26: 525–531, 1932.
13. O. C. Trimble, "The Oral Examination: Its Validity and Reliability," *School and Society,* 39: 550–552, 1934.
14. David G. Ryans, "The Interview in Teacher Selection Can Be Improved and Used Effectively," *Nation's Schools,* 43: 45–46.
15. American Association of Examiners and Administrators of Educational Personnel, *Principles and Procedures of Teacher Selection* (1951), p. 91.
16. McIntyre, p. 16.
17. Richard A. Siggelkow, "Meaningful Interviews with Beginning Teachers," *Nation's Schools,* 53: 43–46, June 1954.
18. McIntyre, p. 15.
19. Gilbert et al., p. 15.
20. K. E. McIntyre, *Selection and On-the-Job Training of School Principals* (Austin, Tex., 1960), p. 9.

21. Conrad Briner, "The Superintendent and the Selection of Subordinate Administrators," *Administrator's Notebook,* VIII, No. 6 (Chicago, February 1960).
22. William B. Castetter, *Administering the School Personnel Program* (New York, 1962), p. 214.
23. National Education Association, *Estimates of School Statistics,* research report 1968-R16 (Washington, 1968), p. 13.
24. McIntyre, *On-the-Job,* p. 9.
25. J. K. Hemphill, D. C. Griffiths and N. Frederiksen, *Administrative Performance and Personality* (New York, Columbia, 1962).
26. J. Lloyd Trump and Lois S. Karasik, *The First Fifty-Five* (Washington, National Association of Secondary School Principals, 1967).
27. McIntyre, *On-the-Job,* p. 4.
28. National Education Association, *Schools of the Urban Crisis* (Washington, 1969), pp. 34–35.

CHAPTER 8

1. American Federation of Teachers, *Survey of Teachers' Fringe Benefits and General Working Conditions in School Systems with 6,000 or More Pupils* (Washington, 1968–1969), p. 18.
2. American Federation of Teachers, p. 19.
3. *The United Teacher,* April 20, 1969, p. 6.
4. *The United Teacher,* April 20, 1969, p. 8.

CHAPTER 9

1. Claude W. Fawcett, *School Personnel Administration* (New York, 1964), p. 16.
2. Roald F. Campbell, "Implications for the Practice of Administration," *Behavioral Science and Educational Administration,* National Society for the Study of Education (Chicago, 1964), p. 297.
3. James A. Van Zwoll, *School Personnel Administration* (New York, 1964), p. 129.
4. Van Zwoll, p. 130.
5. James P. Steffensen, *Staff Personnel Administration,* Department of Health, Education and Welfare, OE-23027, Bulletin 1963, Number 6 (Washington, 1963), pp. 15–16.
6. Calvin Grieder, Truman M. Pierce and William Everett Rosenstengel, *Public School Administration* (New York, 1961), p. 230.
7. See the unpublished report (Kansas City, Mo., 1963) by American Association of School Personnel Administrators, *Proceedings of Twenty-Fifth Annual Conference.*
8. George B. Redfern, "The Personnel Director Views the Problem," read at symposium on the role of the teacher in the urban depressed area school (Washington, December 4, 1964).
9. American Association of School Personnel Administrators, *Standards for School Personnel Administration* (Kansas City, Mo., 1960), pp. 36–37.
10. National Education Association, *The Assignment and Misassignment of American Teachers* (Washington, 1965), p. 53.
11. See the unpublished dissertation (Marquette) by Alvin J. Schumacher, "Critical Requirements of Personnel Administrators in the Assignment of Teachers," p. 32.
12. William B. Castetter, *Administering the School Personnel Program* (New York, 1962), pp. 181–182.
13. R. Oliver Gibson and Herold C. Hunt, *The School Personnel Administrator* (Boston, 1965), p. 410.

14. Benjamin Floyd Pittenger, *Local Public School Administration* (New York, 1951), p. 144.
15. Steffensen, pp. 18–19.
16. Steffensen, p. 19.
17. Schumacher, p. 32.
18. Schumacher, pp. 26-32.
19. National Education Association, *A Manual on Certification Requirements for School Personnel in the United States* (Washington, 1967), p. 7.
20. P. M. Kalick, *Teacher Assignment in Large Public School Systems, A Comparison with a Reference Group of School Systems* (New York, Columbia, 1963).
21. Redfern, p. 1.
22. James S. Coleman, "Equality of Educational Opportunity" (Cambridge, Harvard Colloquium Board Conference, Fall 1967).
23. Schumacher, pp. 25–26.
24. Douglas W. Hunt, "Teacher Induction: An Opportunity and a Responsibility," *Bulletin of the National Association of Secondary School Principals,* Vol. 52, No. 330: 132–135, October 1968.
25. Hunt, p. 134.
26. Hunt, p. 135.
27. James B. Conant, *The Education of American Teachers* (New York, 1963), pp. 70–71.

CHAPTER 10

1. National Education Association, *Economic Status of the Teaching Profession* (Washington, 1968–69), p. 51
2. The Association, p. 9.
3. The Association, p. 7.
4. The Association, p. 12.
5. The Association, p. 7.
6. National Education Association, *State Minimum-Salary Laws for Teachers* (Washington, 1968), p. 5.
7. See the unpublished dissertation (Iowa, 1965) by Charles E. Railsback, *A Comparison of the Reliability and Validity of Two Types of Criterion Measures for the Evaluation of Instruction.*
8. See the unpublished dissertation (Ohio, 1964) by Gary D. Watts, *A Correlation Analysis between "Level of Achievement" and Certain Teacher Characteristics in Selected School Systems.*
9. Carleton Washburne and Louise M. Heil, "What Characteristics of Teachers Affect Children's Growth?," *School Review,* pp. 420–428, Winter 1960.
10. Millard Clements, "Research and Incantation: A Comment," *Phi Delta Kappan,* p. 107, October 1968.
11. The Association, *Minimum-Salary Laws,* p. 19.
12. National Education Association *Maximum Salaries Scheduled for Administrators, 1968–69* (Washington, 1969), pp. 62–63.
13. The Association, *Economic Status,* p. 5.
14. The Association, *Maximum Salaries,* p. 9.
15. National Education Association, *Extra Pay for Extra Duties* (Washington, 1968), p. 5.
16. The Association, *Extra Pay,* p. 9.

CHAPTER 11

1. American Federation of Teachers, *Survey of Teachers' Fringe Benefits and General Working Conditions in School Systems with 6,000 or More Pupils* (Washington, 1969), p. vi.

417

2. National Education Association, *Paid Leave Provisions for Teachers in Negotiation Agreements* (Washington, 1969), foreword.
3. National Education Association, *Leaves of Absence for Teachers* (Washington, 1966), pp. 72–79.
4. The Association, *Paid Leave Provisions*, foreword.
5. The Association, *Paid Leaves*, p. 6.
6. The Association, *Leaves of Absence*, p. 72.
7. The Association, *Paid Leaves*, p. 8.
8. The Association, *Leaves of Absence*, p. 72.
9. The Association, *Paid Leaves*, p. 5.
10. American Federation of Teachers, p. 8.
11. The Association, *Leaves of Absence*, p. 47.
12. The Association, *Paid Leaves*, p. 5.
13. American Federation of Teachers, p. 12.
14. American Federation of Teachers, p. 13.
15. The Association, *Paid Leaves*, p. 10.
16. The Association, *Leaves of Absence*, p. 78.
17. American Federation of Teachers, pp. 12–13.
18. American Federation of Teachers, p. 18.
19. American Federation of Teachers, p. 21.
20. American Federation of Teachers, p. 25.
21. James A. Van Zwoll, *School Personnel Administration* (New York, 1964), p. 318.
22. William B. Castetter, *Administering the School Personnel Program* (New York, 1962), p. 321.
23. National Education Association, *Group Insurance Coverage Increasing* (Washington, 1965), pp. 84–85.
24. Erwin Dingman, "Using Fringe Benefits Profitably," in *School Executive's Guide* (Englewood Cliffs, 1964), p. 181.
25. National Education Association, *Teacher Tenure Laws* (Washington, 1960), pp. 81–85.
26. National Education Association, *Retirement Statistics, 1964* (Washington, 1964), pp. 99–107.
27. Van Zwoll, p. 322.
28. Van Zwoll, p. 346.

CHAPTER 12

1. Robert Glaser, "Psychology and Instructional Technology," in *Training Research and Education* (Pittsburgh, 1962), pp. 3–5.
2. National Education Association, *Teacher Supply and Demand in Public Schools* (Washington, 1966), p. 80.
3. Association for Supervision and Curriculum Development and the Center for the Study of Education, *The Way Teaching Is* (Washington, 1966).
4. Mario Fantini, "Teacher Training and Educational Reform," read at the Santa Barbara Conference on the Reform of Teacher Education (Santa Barbara, Calif., May 1968). Quotation taken from mimeograph copy, p. 10.
5. American Association of School Administrators, *In-Service Education for School Administrators* (Washington, 1963), p. 41.
6. National Education Association, *NEA Research Memo* (Washington, 1960), p. 1.
7. William L. Pharis, *In-Service Education of Elementary School Principals* (Washington, National Education Association, 1966), pp. 9–10.
8. Philip Jackson, "Old Dogs and New Tricks: Observations on the Continuing Education of Teachers," read at the Santa Barbara Conference on the Reform of Teacher Education (Santa Barbara, Calif., May 1968). Quotation taken from mimeograph copy, p. 10.
9. Jackson, p. 14.

10. Lynton K. Caldwell, "Determining Training Needs for Organizational Effectiveness," *Personnel Administration,* 26: 13, March-April 1963.
11. Dwight W. Allen, "In-Service Teacher Training—A Modest Proposal," read at the Santa Barbara Conference on the Reform of Teacher Education (Santa Barbara, Calif., May 1968). Quotation taken from mimeograph copy, p. 23.
12. Fred Edmonds, James R. Ogletree and Pat W. Wear, *In-Service Teacher Education: Crucial Process in Educational Change,* Vol. 39, Sept. 1966, No. 1 (Lexington, Ky.), p. 20.
13. Edward T. Ladd, "Address at Miami Beach Conference," in *The Development of the Career Teacher: Professional Responsibility for Continuing Education,* ed. Roy A. Edelfelt (Washington, 1964), p. 36.
14. National Education Association, *In-Service Education of Teachers* (Washington, 1966), p. 5.
15. Department of Health, Education and Welfare, Office of Education, *Guidelines: The Preparation of Proposals for Educational Personnel Development Grants* (Washington, 1969), p. 31.
16. National Education Association, *Salary Schedules for Classroom Teachers, 1965–66* (Washington, 1965), p. 25.
17. National Education Association, *Professional Growth Requirements* (Washington, 1966), p. 9.
18. National Education Association, *Professional Growth,* p. 9.
19. "Agreement between the Board of Education of the City of New York and the United Federation of Teachers," *New York Daily Column,* June 27, 1969, p. 19.
20. Marvin L. Berge, Harris E. Russell and Charles B. Walden, "In-Service Education Programs of Local School Systems, National Society for the Study of Education, *In-Service Education for Teachers, Supervisors, and Administrators,* 56th Yearbook, Part 2, ed. Nelson B. Henry (Chicago, 1957), p. 212.
21. Matthew B. Miles, "Planned Change and Organizational Health: Figure and Ground," Center for the Advanced Study of Educational Administration, *Change Processes in the Public Schools* (Eugene, Oregon, 1965), p. 13.
22. Fred Edmonds, James R. Ogletree and Pat W. Wear, *In-Service Teacher Education: Crucial Process in Educational Change,* Bulletin of the Bureau of School Service, Vol. 39, No. 1, Lexington, 1966, p. 31.
23. Maurice J. Eash, "Supervisors: A Vanishing Breed?" *Educational Leadership,* 26:73, October 1968.
24. Eash, p. 77.
25. National Education Association, *In-Service Education of Teachers,* (Washington, 1966), pp. 7–10.
26. James R. Ogletree, *Person-Centered In-Service Education: Why Not?* Vol. XXX, No. 1, September 1957, Bulletin of the Bureau of School Service, p. 25.
27. Bernard Esrig, "In-Service Education of Elementary School Teachers Via Television with Special Reference to New York City" Ed.D. Dissertation, New York, Teachers College, Columbia U. 1968, pp. 229–239.
28. Ben M. Harris et al., *In-Service Education: A Guide to Better Practice* (Englewood Cliffs 1969), pp. 36–41.

29. Fred Edmonds et al., *In-Service Teacher Education: A Conceptual Framework,* Vol. XXXVI, No. 2, Bulletin of the Bureau of School Service, 1966, p. 25.
30. Board of Education, Newark, New Jersey, Department of Personnel, *In-Service Education Courses for Teachers: 1969 Spring Semester,* 1968, p. iii.
31. Basic Systems Incorporated, Systems Division, *Program Development for In-Service Teacher Education in the New York State Education Department* (New York, 1966), pp. 100–110.
32. The Croft Federal Aid Service, "Project Planning Advisory," February 15, 1969, No. 185.

CHAPTER 13

1. Edward L. Bernays, *Public Relations* (Norman, Okla., 1952), p. 278.
2. Bernays, p. 183.
3. Benjamin Fine, *Educational Publicity* (New York, 1951), p. 3.
4. Bernays, pp. 280–281.
5. Fine, p. 365.

CHAPTER 14

1. T. M. Stinnett, J. H. Kleinman, Martha L. Ware, *Professional Negotiation in Public Education* (New York, 1966), p. 7.
2. T. M. Stinnett, *Turmoil in Teaching* (New York, 1968), pp. 4–5.
3. Stinnett, p. 48.
4. Myron Lieberman and Michael H. Moskow, *Collective Negotiations for Teachers* (Chicago, 1966), pp. 7–10.
5. Stinnett, p. 16.
6. National Education Association, *Action Programs When There Is a Local Crisis* (Washington, 1965).
7. National Education Association, "A Policy for Employee-Management Cooperation in the Federal Service," in *Report of the President's Task Force on Employee-Management Relations in the Federal Service* (Washington, 1961), p. 25.
8. Lieberman and Moskow, pp. 129–131.
9. National Education Association, *What's Negotiable?* (Washington, 1968), p. 42.
10. National Education Association, *Grievance Procedures for Teachers in Negotiation Agreements* (Washington, 1969), p. 5.
11. National Education Association, *Research Bulletin* Vol. 46, No. 2, p. 43.
12. Stinnett et al, p. 206.

CHAPTER 15

1. National Education Association, *Grievance Procedures for Teachers in Negotiated Agreements* (Washington, 1969), p. 5.
2. "Local Associations Ask about Grievance Procedures," *NEA Journal,* Vol. 56, No. 8, p. 63.
3. Eric F. Rhodes and Richard P. Long, *The Principal's Role in Collective Negotiations* (Washington, 1967), p. 39.
4. American Association of School Administrators, "Grievance Procedures," in *The School Administrator and Negotiations* (Washington, 1968), p. 66.
5. The Association, p. 12.
6. The Association, p. 13.
7. The Association, p. 15.
8. The Association, p. 15.

9. William B. Castetter, *Administering the School Personnel Program* (New York, 1962), p. 325.
10. "Grievance Procedures and Collective Negotiations," *Negotiations Management.* Educational Service Bureau, Washington, Vol. II, No. 5, p. 5, 1968.

CHAPTER 16

1. Ellwood P. Cubberley, *Public Education in the United States* (Chicago, 1934), p. 84.
2. K. Alexander, R. Corns, W. McCann, *Public School Law: Cases and Materials* (Minn., West Publishing Co., 1969), p. 381.
3. E. Bolmeier, *School in the Legal Structure* (Ohio: W. H. Anderson Co., 1968), pp. 156–157.
4. Bolmeier, p. 155.
5. *Public School Laws of North Carolina,* 1965, Chap. 115, sec. 155.
6. L. Simpson, *Handbook of the Law of Contracts* (Minn., West Publishing Co.), 1965, p. 1.
7. Simpson, p. 7.
8. *Big Sandy School Dist. No. 100-J Elbert County v. Carrol,* 433 p. 2d 325 (1967).
9. *Tate v. School Dist. No. 11,* 324 Mo. 477, 23 SW 2d 1013 (1929).
10. R. Hamilton, *Legal Rights and Liabilities of Teachers* (Wyoming, School Law Publications), 1956, p. 6.
11. 47 Am. Jur., Schools, Sect. 115.
12. *Special School Dist. of Fort Smith v. Lynch,* 413 SW 2d 880 (1967).
13. *School City of East Chicago v. Sigler,* 219 Ind. 9, 36NE 2d 760 (1941).
14. *Burns v. Thompson,* 64 Ark. 489.
15. *Fry v. Board of Education,* 17 Cal. 2 d 753, 112 P. 2 d 229 (1941).
16. *McGrath v. Burkhard,* 131 Cal. App. 2d 367, 280 P. 2d 864 (1955).
17. *Parrish v. Moss,* 200 Misc. 375, 106 NYS 2d 577 (1951).
18. *Horasko v. Mount Pleasant Township School Dist.,* 335 Pa 369, 6A (2d).
19. *Campbell v. Wishek Public School Dist.,* 150 N.W. 2d 840 (1967).
20. Bolmeier, p. 159.
21. Robert R. Hamilton and E. Edmund Reutter, Jr., *Legal Aspects of School Board Operation* (New York City, Columbia, 1958), pp. 65–66.
22. 47 Am. Jur. Sect. 127.
23. 47 Am. Jur. Sect. 136.
24. *Eastman v. Williams,* 124 Vt. 445, 207 A 2d 146 (1965).
25. *People ex rel. Cinquino v. Board of Education of City of Chicago,* 230 NE 2d 85 (1967).
26. *Appeal of Ritzie,* 372 Pa. 588,94A2d729(1953). Contra see, *Dugas v. Ascension Parish School Board,* 81 So 2d 817 (1955).
27. *Brown v. Hanford Elem. School Bd.,* 69 Cal Rptr 154 (1968).
28. *Adelt v. Richmond School Dist.,* 58 Cal. Rptr. 151 (1967).
29. *Board of Trustees of Mt. San Antonio Jr. College Dist. of Los Angeles v. Hartman,* 55 Cal. Rptr. 144 (1967).
30. *Watts v. Seward School Bd.,* 421 P2d 586, certiorari granted, 88 S.Ct. 34, (1967).
31. *Welsko v. Foster Township School District,* 383 Pa. 390,119 A.2d 43 (1956).
32. *Dugas v. Ascension Parish School Board,* 81 So. 2d 817 (La 1955).
33. *Pickering v. Board of Education of Town-*

ship *H.S. District 205,* 225 NE 2d1, certiorari granted 88 S. Ct. 1731 (1968).

34. *Watts v. Seward,* supra.
35. *Epperson v. State of Arkansas,* 89 S.Ct. 266 (1968).
36. *McLaughlin v. Tilendis,* 398 F 2d 287 (1968).
37. *Albaum v. Carey,* 283 F.Supp. 3 (1968).
38. This decision was rendered in December 1969, in the U.S. District Court for the Eastern District of Texas. The action was instituted by a teacher named Billy Don Montgomery against the Tatum School District Board. No citation is available at this time.
39. *Keyishian v. Board of Regents of the University of the State of New York,* 88S. Ct. 675 (1967).
40. *Knight v. Board of Regents of the Univ. of the State of New York.* 269 F. Supp. 339. (1967) affirmed 88S. Ct. 816 (1968).
41. *Gilmore v. James* 274 F. Supp. 75 (1967); also see *Vogel v. County of Los Angeles.,* 434 P 2d 961 (1967).
42. *Riddle v Bd of Education of the State of N. Mexico,* 435 P 2d 1013 (1968).
43. Forkosch, M. *A Treatise on Administrative Law* (Bobbs Merrill Co., Inc. Minn.) c. 1956, p. 246.
44. Forkosch, p. 247.
45. *Snider v. Kit Carson School Dist. R-1 in the County of Cheyenne,* 442 P 2d 429 (1968).
46. *Hale v. Bd. of Ed., City of Lancaster.* 234 NE 2d 583 (1968).
47. *Rolfe v. County Board of Education of Lincoln County, Tennessee,* 391 F. 2d 77, United States Court of Appeals, Sixth Circuit, February 19, 1968.
48. *Adler v. Board of Education of the City of New York,* 342 U. S. 485, 72, S.Ct. 380 (1952).
49. *Keyishian v. Board of Regents of the Univ. of the State of New York,* 87 S. Ct. 675, 1967.

CHAPTER 17

1. Emery Stoops and M. L. Rafferty, Jr., *Practices and Trends in School Administration* (Boston, 1961), p. 441.
2. Harold E. Mitzel, "Teacher Effectiveness," in *Encyclopedia of Educational Research* (New York, 1960), p. 1481.
3. Mitzel, p. 1485.
4. Mitzel, p. 428.
5. Elizabeth P. Hagen and Robert L. Thorndike, "Evaluation," in *Encyclopedia of Educational Research* (New York, 1960), p. 485.
6. Stoops and Rafferty, pp. 424–425.
7. Hagen and Thorndike, p. 483.
8. Hagen and Thorndike, p. 482.